Starving to Death in a Sea of Objects

Starving to Death in a Sea of Objects

The Anorexia Nervosa Syndrome

John A. Sours, M.D.

JASON ARONSON INC.

Northvale, New Jersey • London

ISBN: 0-87668-426-6 (hardcover)
ISBN: 0-87668-435-5 (softcover)

Library of Congress Catalog Number: 80-68043

Manufactured in the United States of America. Jason Aronson Inc. offers books and cassettes.
For information and catalog write to Jason Aronson Inc., 230 Livingston Street, Northvale,
New Jersey 07647.

to Dinah and our children:
Christopher, Caroline and Jane

Contents

FOREWORD *by Otto F. Kernberg, M.D.*   ix

PREFACE   xiii

1. INTRODUCTION   1

2. STARVING TO DEATH IN A SEA OF OBJECTS:
   A NOVEL   9
   I. After the Summer   13
   II. On the Way   89
   III. Brief Return   141

3. THE HISTORY OF THE ANOREXIA NERVOSA
   SYNDROME   203

4. THE ANOREXIA NERVOSA SYNDROME   219

5. PHENOMENOLOGICAL ASPECTS OF
   ANOREXIA NERVOSA   267

6. FAMILIES OF ANOREXIA NERVOSA PATIENTS   317

7. DEVELOPMENTAL PATTERNS IN
   THE ANOREXIA NERVOSA SYNDROME   331

8. THEORY AND TECHNIQUE IN
   THE TREATMENT OF ANOREXIA NERVOSA   357

MEDICAL GLOSSARY   379

BIBLIOGRAPHY   383

ACKNOWLEDGMENTS   433

INDEX   435

Foreword

by Otto F. Kernberg, M.D.

Anorexia nervosa has long been considered one of the most dramatic of psychiatric syndromes. Its symptoms are idiosyncratic and its outcome potentialy fatal. Because the assumed causes of this illness span the broad spectrum from neurophysiological predisposition through unconscious intrapsychic conflict to familial and cultural factors, anorexia nervosa raises fundamental theoretical questions regarding the interaction of biological and psychosocial determinants of illness.

Dr. Sours has undertaken the challenging task of presenting a survey and study of this syndrome in a book that can be read with profit by psychiatrists as well as other mental health professionals and the educated layman. His language is clear, at times almost poetic, and he provides both a glossary and a bibliography to protect the lay reader from drowning in technicalities. His historical review of the syndrome is of particular interest, starting as it does with Morton's differentiation of anorexia from other forms of "consumption" in 1689.

The parallel between the history of psychoanalytic theories and the changing psychodynamics underlying the treatment approaches to anorexia nervosa is of special interest. The earliest psychoanalytic formulations on anorexia nervosa in the 1940s and the 1950s were in terms of specific unconscious fantasies, such as the rejection of pregnancy wishes, and the reaction formation against oral-sadistic impulses. At that time, the symbolic expression of specific unconscious fantasies was attributed to a wide variety of other types of psychopathology as well. Psychoanalytic formulations then turned to regarding anorexia as a specific disturbance of drives (as in Thoma), again parallel with the psychoanalytic emphasis on the failure to neutralize aggression in severe psychopathology. Bruch's formulations of the 1960s, pointing to the perceptual and conceptual disorders in anorectic patients and to their interpersonal conflicts in the mother-child relation, corresponds to the formulations of ego psychology and the new interest in preoedipal conflicts. The early 1970s saw the anorectic patient as projecting onto her own body the image of a sadistic object (mother) who had to be controlled and dominated by savagely controlling and dominating her own body needs. This concept, proposed by Selvini Palazzoli before family therapy governed her thinking, reflects recent object relations approaches in psychoanalytic thinking.

It is this most recent view of anorexia nervosa that Dr. Sours stresses. He also draws attention to the prevalence of borderline functioning and narcissistic personality in so many of these patients, and to their need for control, mastery, and power.

In anorexia nervosa, the efforts to magically control one's own body (fantasied as a potentially dangerous enemy) coincide with the unconscious reprojection of that power struggle onto the surrounding environment. The patient's control over her own life and death assures her unconscious superiority and power over all those who try to control her—paticularly those who are concerned for her survival. Dr. Sours's description of the anorexia patients who aggressively try to force others to eat while withholding nourishment from themselves illustrates, it seems to me, the defensive "poisoning" of others as a development parallel to these patients' fantasied protection of themselves against being poisoned by food (which would strengthen the body, the internal enemy). The anorectic patient's primary goal is self-destruction; at the same time, she is identifying with a sadistic, destructive mother.

Dr. Sours proposes a treatment approach that focuses on the need for appropriate control and environmental structuralization in the early stages of treatment, an approach that has been advocated by behavior theorists such as Crisp (1965) and Halmi (1975). During the early phases, a psychotherapeutic relationship is initiated which later evolves into psychoanalytic psychotherapy. In the course of this psychotherapy the primitive distorted ego organization of these patients, particularly their defensive organization, which is so similar to borderline conditions and often reflects pathological nacissism, is explored and gradually resolved.

The treatment recommended by Dr. Sours is similar to the treatment program of the research unit dedicated to anorexia nervosa at the Westchester Division of The New York Hospital. The service includes setting up a social structure based upon behavior modification which provides firm yet flexible limits to the anorectic patient's control of environment, assures the gradual recovery of normal body weight, and transforms the fantastic, intrapsychic struggle into an interpersonal struggle with authority. This transformation activates the patient's pathogenic internalized object relations. Simultaneously, the patient enters a dynamically oriented individual therapy, in the course of which she gradually learns to explore and understand the current conflicts with hospital staff and family members as a reproduction of intrapsychic conflicts. It is then possible to eventually work through these conflicts in the transference. The results of this approach so far seem promising.

Dr. Sours's comprehensive, up-to-date survey of anorexia nervosa provides the reader with the tools for understanding this syndrome and its current treatment.

Preface

It would not be surprising for one to ask why twenty years ago a psychiatrist would have become interested in a disorder as obscure as anorexia nervosa. Then the disturbance was rare, and not many clinicians saw more than a couple of anorectics in a lifetime of practice.

During my medical internship at the New York Hospital–Cornell Medical Center in 1957–1958, I saw and treated several young women with this disorder, but I had little contact with the deeper psychological aspects of the disturbance. My main responsibility was for the physical care of the patients and to get them back to a reasonably healthy weight. When I went to London in 1958 for a year's study at the National Hospital, Queen Square, and the Institute of Psychiatry, the Maudsley Hospital, I had further experiences with this medical problem. At Queen Square I saw a number of patients who had been evaluated by the most precise neurological assessments, and at the Maudsley Hospital I began a systematic study of the disorder. It was there that I became familiar with the history of anorexia nervosa; for English psychiatrists, anorexia is a British psychiatric disorder, first thoroughly described by an Englishman in 1873.

When I returned to the United States in July 1959, I completed my adult psychiatric training at the Columbia-Presbyterian Medical Center and the New York State Psychiatric Institute, where Dr. Hilde Bruch was then a staff psychiatrist and in the midst of her lifelong research on schizophrenia, obesity, and anorexia nervosa. It was she who introduced me to the developmental aspects of the disorder, its neuro-psychological correlations with learning and perception, and who encouraged me to pursue my interest and follow these patients. I did several research studies on perception and cognition in anorexia nervosa, as well as a retrospective study of anorectics who had been admitted to the Columbia-Presbyterian Medical Center over a period of thirty years. Later, during my child psychiatry residency, I had an opportunity to treat anorectic adolescent girls at Babies Hospital at the Columbia-Presbyterian Hospital. In my subsequent psychoanalytic training, my dynamic understanding of this developmental disturbance became more refined.

I first became interested in anorexia nervosa because it struck me that although it was not a common disorder, it provided a panoramic view of clinical psychiatry. First of all, the history of anorexia nervosa is a history of world psychiatry. It clearly shows how psychiatry has advanced from descriptions of signs and symptoms, diagnostic formulations, studies on the interphase between body and mind, to psychoanalytic views of character and human development. Because of the anorectic's tortured and enmeshing family, the disturbance provides opportunities to examine disorders of family communication and structure.

And, in addition, now that the disturbance is becoming increasingly prevalent, it provides examples of the effects of culture on psychopathology, as well as transcultural transformations in the phenomenology and psychodynamics of this developmental disturbance. All in all, as we enter the 1980s, anorexia nervosa has become a symbol and leitmotif of the cultural forces in our society. The will to master and control one's selfhood and achieve absolute separateness and autonomy has become, for many Americans, the emblem of a safe existence. We find now a character style, exaggerated in the characterological structure of the anorectic, accentuating control and mastery with the central theme of realization of an ideal self, ideal body.

In order to understand this character style better—the ego style of control and mastery in the service of achieving perfection—I spoke with a number of people who, in one way or another, seek perfection. They include dancers, who must practice daily for long hours and are constantly aware of their body and its function. Likewise, swimmers and professional tennis players. In 1977 and 1979, I ran in the Boston Marathon (as a member of the American Medical Joggers Association), as well as the 1977 New York Marathon. Both the training for and the experience of marathon running gave me a better appreciation of the characterological traits needed to realize such goals, particularly the desire for perfection. I also pursued this study in discussions with fiction writers and poets at various writers' conferences, as well as artists and musicians I know—all people who strive to "get it perfect" and bask in the illumination of their achievement and creative product.

This book is written in the hope of bringing together a vast amount of literature for the clinician interested in treating the anorectic, without turning the book into an unwieldy encyclopedic collection of facts. Anorexia nervosa, a syndrome best defined by the patient's disturbed attitude toward food and eating, is presented as a heterogeneous developmental disorder with definite homogeneous subgroups, each with its own symptomatology, developmental background, and personality organization and style. The basic vulnerability of the anorectic is related to strong wishes for passivity and the resultant fears of surrender and, at times, body invasion. Confronting developmental issues of adolescence and early adulthood, the anorectic regresses to an archaic level of self-differentiation.

From the theoretical standpoint, my approach to clinical material is developmental, with emphasis on external-internal influences on ongoing development, phasic life-cycle transitions, as well as parental information about childhood and child-parent interaction. The developmental framework views clinical material from the longitudinal and epigenetic, the individual and intergenerational, conflict-free and conflict-laden, conscious and unconscious, interpersonal and intrapsychic, and somatic and psychologic. The developmental approach is complementary to the genetic reconstruction approach, which is based on recovery of screen memories and fantasies as well as the transferential enactments of early affective experiences, traumas, behavioral patterns, and somatic reactions. Since the genetic approach is predicated on the individual's perception of his traumas and developmental strain along with distortion of later developmental conflict—relying on evocative memory, secondary process dominance, and an introspective stance—it is not as useful as the developmental approach in the treatment of the dieting anorectic, who, partly because of the psychic dampening of starvation, is not inclined to report affect, memories, and fantasies. After the restoration of nutrition and the firm establishment of a working therapeutic alliance with the therapist, the genetic reconstructive approach can effectively be used. But until that time, the therapeutic thrust in the early treatment of the starving anorectic is toward developing a therapeutic alliance and treatment process by understanding the nature of the fixated, deviational, and atypical development of ego functions and self-object representations—a comprehension of clinical material facilitated by the emergence of a dyadic preoedipal transference, which is not the substance for interpretation of structural conflict (as is the triadic transference) but rather an instrument for facilitating development, warped by trauma and strain during the preoedipal period and freeing the enmeshed anorectic and her family from one another.

I have written this book in a style I hope will be readable for all clinicians and therapists in the mental health field. A medical glossary is provided for those who come to the mental health professions from outside medicine, or, because of a general interest in anorexia nervosa, simply want to understand the anorectic experience. I hope that this book will not, for parents of anorectics who might read the professional literature, substitute for psychiatric evaluation and treatment of their child. Nor should the book be used by parents as a probative device for understanding their frantic anorectic child.

In chapter 2 a fictional case study—a novel—of a mid-adolescent girl, an anorectic who starves herself, gorges and purges, describes how the psyche with its cruel imagination defends selfhood as it struggles to distinguish real from illusory dangers and finally succumbs to the real menace. The novel is an act of imagination; it is not a case report. Clinical cases, altered in details to preserve anonymity, are interspersed through the later chapters to give the reader an affective sense of anorexia nervosa and its clinical variations. From my clinical experience, I have also chosen specific clinical vignettes to illustrate various facets of the anorexia nervosa syndrome. Confidentiality has been maintained for these reports.

The chapters of this book have been written in such a way that anorexia nervosa is described in the first chapter in everyday language. Chapter 2, the novel, introduces the reader to the life of an anorectic adolescent and her family. Each successive chapter further develops the clinical description of the syndrome, so that by chapter 7 a psychoanalytic view of the disorder is reasonably comprehensible without a background in metapsychology. I want to use two languages and say what should be said in both. In this book there is a great deal of clinical material, which I want to synthesize but not devitalize; I want to clarify the disorder. I will be satisfied if I am able to present a working concept of anorexia nervosa which transcends any particular theoretical ideology. It will be enough if the conclusions of the study are ones the reader can understand, assimilate, and apply to the patients for whom he is responsible. There is nothing that a clinician can ask for other than more knowledge of his patients; this knowledge must be specific and vital for each patient and not applied as a theory too inert to help a person out of his misery.

At a time when patients' rights and confidentiality are the concern of all analysts, we must look carefully at the state of the case history in psychoanalytic literature.[1] Freud's clinical cases, which celebrate the use of language and sensitivity, have yet to be equalled by his successors; the depth of his clinical description and its lucid artistic expression won for him the Goethe Prize for Literature. His case studies, using the third-person point of view and sculptured details, give the reader the sense of being inside character, much in the same way that Thomas Mann, one of Freud's literary admirers, reveals Hans Castorp in *The Magic Mountain.*

The case history, even the clinical vignette, is imperiled by the increasing need for confidentiality. Psychoanalytic investigators are now reluctant to write about their patients. Increasingly sparse usage of clinical details—if they are used at all—is the stylistic trend in psychoanalytic literature. Often psychoanalytic evidence, such as conflict, dreams, fantasies, childhood memories, transference, and slips of the tongue—the analytic process itself—is lacking. The cases now presented in the literature are without space, time, and human form. Special language, new terms which border on neologisms, and the investment of ordinary language with unexpected meaning are commonplace. Mechanical sentences struggle to develop from clinical data objectal and structural formulations which dehumanize the essence of experience and the reality of life. Ambiguities flourish when no demarcation is made between analytic data, hypothesis, interpretation, and reconstruction.

The self of ego psychology, if it speaks at all, betrays only its anatomy

---

1. A few psychoanalysts have written about psychoanalytic evidence, metapsychology, and the state of the case history: Gill and Holzman 1976, Esman 1979, Waelder 1936, Schafer 1976, G. Klein 1976, Slap and Levine 1978, Sherwood 1969, Ricoeur 1977, Richardson 1978, Kohut 1959, and Loewenstein 1966. Several psychoanalysts have written case studies about anorectic patients. Binswanger's *Ellen West* (1944), Lindner's *Fifty Minute Hour* (1955), and Levenkron's *The Best Little Girl in the World* (1978) effectively demonstrate the suffering of the anorectic, but they do not portray the subtleties of the analytic process.

and physiology, hardly it flesh and passions. The use of scientific terminology for narrative description—often by psychoanalytic writers, who soon become self-imitative—tends, among other things, to hide the patient's identity behind a torrent of abstract language, often borrowed from medicine and transformed into metaphors and clichés beyond tolerable limits. Constructs are reified and anthropomorphized. For example, the phrase *metabolism of internal objects* is supposed to substitute for written language and human experience. Out of fear of exposing the patient, he is immediately described in medical and metapsychological metaphors which destroy his face and leave him imageless. Or, if described by a French structuralist who assigns a supreme priority to symbolism over cognition, the patient yearns for clarification in the poetry of the unconscious. This is a false poetry that fogs over as soon as one contemplates it. Poetry, with its true subject, selfhood, is telling, eternal in space and time, defending against the frightening by metaphoric language, defining, limiting, illuminating the self through interpretation. In its hunger for verbs, poetry bores into the imaginative, affective core of human experience and offers another means of psychological description.

It is not possible to return to direct clinical reportage in psychoanalytic literature. The patient's identity, as well as that of his family, must be hidden; yet the case must be rendered in such a way as to yield the empirical clinical information necessary for psychoanalytic research. Greater thought and skill are needed for case history presentations if there is to be a narrative structure of a life story with meaningful, affective sequences and connections.

To preserve the patient's anonymity, the psychoanalytic writer can change his patient's geography, his occupation or career, and, to some degree, his age and ethnic background as well as facets of the nuclear and extended family. He can add or subtract a sibling. If clumsily used, however, these disguises distort the phenomenology of the case, alter the internal landscape of the patient, and provide spurious facts for metapsychological formulation. For instance, an added sibling can blur, for the reader, the dynamic patterns of a family and raise objections that the case is based on "soft data," fantastic reportage, or is a false and fictive document. The reader is unwittingly apt to focus on the disguising additive. A discussant at a scientific meeting may decide to formulate a case largely on the basis of the disguise, using, for example, as psychoanalytic evidence, the "fact" that a sibling's birth at the time of the patient's rapprochement subphase had been a substantive, traumatic strain. False dates in the body of the psychoanalytic situation can vertically alter psychoanalytic knowledge, from the level of observation in Waelder's hierarchy (1936) to higher levels of theory and metapsychology. Asymmetric and fluid levels of organization of data and linkages can result, with clinical observation functioning at the same levels as clinical theory and metapsychology.

The technique of fictional nonfiction—the "new journalism" of Capote, Mailer, Wolfe, and others—suggests additional means of disguise, such as adding enriching details of status life, creating a realism of fictive facts which draw attention to the actual reality of the patient while preserving the essential factuality of the case. Using careful construction of scenes (going from one scene to another), defining character by selective dialogue, and employing the third-person point of view with occasional shifts to the first-person can add a richness that adumbrates the revealing realism that threatens psychoanalytic privacy in case reports.

Clinical narratives, however, cannot always be altered enough to shield completely the identity of the patient. It is not possible to disguise a patient if his life history or style of living is unusual and oddly characteristic of him, especially if the reader has had an acquaintance with the person. In reviewing Vaillant's *Adaptation to Life* (1977), Geoffrey Wolff (1978) challenges Vaillant's assertion that he prevents public recognition of his subjects; Wolff believes that he himself was able to recognize three of them. And of course the subject of a case report might well recognize himself in the narration regardless of the disguise. Philip Roth describes such a situation in *My Life as a Man*: The Jewish novelist Peter Tarnopol becomes enraged with his analyst, Dr. Spielvogel, when he reads the latter's contribution to a symposium. In his paper on "the riddle of creativity" Spielvogel has cast Tarnopol as an Italian-American poet, fifteen years older than he is in reality. Tarnopol attacks his analyst for being "somewhat dimwitted about matters of social and cultural background that might well impinge upon a person's psychology and values." He adds: "And while we're at it, Dr. Spielvogel, a poet and a novelist have about as much in common as a jockey and a diesel driver."

Usually a totally fictionalized case study is effective in maintaining confidentiality, even though Tarnopol may be unhappy with the fictive changes in his identity. Fictional narratives of our patients' experiences are possible without violating confidentiality, distorting factuality, and ignoring the principles of psychoanalytic evidence. The only tools of psychoanalysis are language and affect. Both must be preserved for psychoanalytic investigations. I hope that the fictive changes I have brought to my cases are effective in maintaining anonymity, yet powerful enough to sustain character and spirit.

I want to thank the many clinicians and investigators, knowledgeable about anorexia nervosa, who gave me their time to discuss with them various aspects of the syndrome. Special appreciation must go to Professor A. H. Crisp, St. George's Hospital Medical School, London; Professor Kai Tolstrup, Rigshospitalet, Copenhagen; the late Sir Aubrey Lewis, The Maudsley Hospital, London; Professor Anna-Marie Stovner, Nics Waals Institute, Oslo; Dr. Hilde Bruch, Houston; and to Dr. Lawrence C. Kolb, Professor Emeritus of Psychiatry, College of Physicians and Surgeons, Columbia University. And to Dr. Lillian Malcove and Dr. Ted E. Becker I say thanks; they taught me to listen to my patients. I am also indebted to Hilma Wolitzer, Seymour Epstein, and John Irving for their helpful critiques and comments on the techniques of fiction. Goeffrey Wolff's review of several nonfiction sections of the book was invaluable. And to Stanley Plumbly, I say thanks for helping me to appreciate the use of assonance, consonance, and surprise.

Rochester, Vermont
August 1980

1

Introduction

"I live on grapes and lettuce. I'm so afraid of putting on weight," she said, gazing longingly at a plump croissant that lay untouched on her plate one morning recently at breakfast at the St. Regis.

—An actress who had to fake
eating Chinese dumplings for
a movie (*New York Times*)

There is no disturbance in human development more enigmatic to clinicians and alarming to parents than anorexia nervosa. Typically adolescent girls, anorectics become morbidly fascinated with anything to do with eating—food, cooking, restaurants—to the extent of insisting that everybody, except themselves, eat heartily, while at the same time they remain deeply involved in a grim struggle to lose weight, beyond the expectation of any ordinary dieter. Usually of average weight, the dieting anorectic decides to lose ten to fifteen pounds initially but often goes on to drop to 50 percent of her body weight and sometimes dies. The common, self-starving pattern of the anorectic is a persistent need to diet; she manages to live on no more than 400 calories a day which eventually results in generalized body wasting, sunken, glazed eyes, a cage of chest bones, a hollow abdomen, and emaciated limbs reminiscent of the most gruesome photojounalistic reports of concentration camp victims during World War II. At the same time, she denies her skeletal appearance and insists that she is still overweight. She suffers from an encapsulated madness that makes her insist that she is not ill, never felt better, and sees no reason to be cured of anything.

Anorexia nervosa now affects tens of thousands of young women of high school and college age and appears to be increasing rapidly in most countries where there is an affluent, well-educated segment of society. Thirty years ago, a physician might see only several cases in his medical career; now, a clinician, especially if he treats adolescents, will encounter many anorectics within the first few years of practice. Often in private schools, at least two or three cases of anorexia nervosa can be found at any time in secondary grades. The developmental disturbance is also found in boys, usually of prepubertal age; but it is comparably rare, perhaps one-tenth the number of girls; and the disturbance is seldom found in older people, although self-starvation from other causes is well known in the aged and homeless.

The coercive quality of the anorectic adolescent girl who precipitously loses weight, sometimes over 50 percent of body weight in only a matter of a few months, brings about utter terror and chaos in her family and attracts attention in her neighborhood. She becomes a power-holder who recognizes that power is not a thing but a relationship. Yet, she is the pity of her community, a contrast to the family's affluence and the self-indulgent, ritualistic eating habits of the upper-middle classes.

These young girls, besides being bent on self-starvation and blind to their profound cachexia, are usually ambitious, perspicacious, and driven girls who seek sublime perfection, purity, and a sense of "specialness." Until adolescence, they tend to be sweet, compliant, bidable, and obedient; but a few months prior to the manifest onset of the anorexia, they may turn hostile, insouciant to the feelings of others, often greatly demanding, obstinate, arrogant, and irritable. They begin to fight constantly, especially with the mother; then, in an amazingly short time, if they are fanatically starving themselves, they look like walking skeletons with broomstick extremities, fallen shoulders with shoulder blades which stand up like little wings, and their bodies are covered with soft babylike hair over yellowish, tinted skin. They become caricatures of Modigliani sculptures with their gothic, ethereal verticality. They deny their emaciation, even though frequently reminded of it, because, they believe, it is their only protection against the humiliation of being fat.

If the starvation continues, their faces shrivel up like those of old, cancer-ridden patients; the eyes become more sunken and dead, the nose more sharply etched and pointed with the junction between nasal bone and cartilage visibly demarcated. When they smile beyond a set half-smile—which is seldom because they are usually humorless people—their facial muscles stand out in relief, creating an eerie image, like a skull on display in an anatomy laboratory. They flaunt their lamentable physical condition in the hopes of exhibitionistically drawing attention to themselves in an effort to derive gratification from their perverted sense of physical and mental achievement, their conquest of mind over body, and their exhalted sense of having risen to Olympian heights of perfection. Anorectics make themselves freakish in their own way, for they know that people are fascinated by freaks and tend to identify with them as expressions of their secret selves.

No longer does the adolescent girl need fear being common, average, or ordinary. No longer will she feel that she is treated with indifference. People will now notice her. Never sure what her parents want from her—or even if they value her for herself—before starvation she always did what she expected they wanted. The anorectic never feels that what she receives from her parents and other people is genuine; and, to add to her sense of ineffectiveness, she never knows quite what to ask for. Never is she brave enough to have a mind of her own, a sense of what is right to expect of her parents, or to know what right she has in living a life that she wants. The only thing that she believes in from her childhood is the persistent conviction, imparted by her parents, that the most important thing in life is to do something that is special. Throughout childhood, she pursued this hope in a lonely existence, looking for a place and a means whereby she can become special and remain aloof from ordinary people. Anorexia nervosa represents the oxymoronic ultimate in achievement, a conquest of the body by the self whereby the self achieves the illusion of supreme glory. This is an existence which, to the anorectic, has a special reality, even though it is isolating and self-absorbing. This is not the seeking of an adolescent identity, new role choices in the Ericksonian sense. Existence is not taken for granted. Instead, the anorectic is seeking a confirmation that she is alive, whole, and rooted in the present time.

A curious aspect of anorexia nervosa is that, during the height of their illness, relentless anorectic dieters speak, behave, and look as if they were all "cut from the same mold," as though they were designed by an obsessive, cosmic planner with only a single pattern in mind, which repeatedly produced the same stereotyped picture, the same broken record. They are usually amenorrheic. They either have not yet menstruated because puberty has been delayed by self-starvation; or their menstrual periods stopped before they began the diet, or after they had been dieting and their weight had started to melt away. As they lose weight, they often manifest an altered body image in the sense that they deny the fact that they are becoming increasingly thin. They cling to the belief that they still are plump, if not fat. They become increasingly obsessed with food and dieting, usually encouraging other people to eat what they want to avoid. Although they claim they are not hungry—this is how the word anorexia first came to be used for this developmental problem—they are indeed hungry and suffer intense hunger pangs which they manage to deny through superhuman willpower. They drink vast quantities of water and diet soda; in some instances, they binge ravenously and then vomit before the food is absorbed through the gastrointestinal tract. Often they are constipated and use this as an excuse for taking large doses of laxatives to rid themselves of food, feces, flatus, and fat—and sometimes a fantasied fetus. Striking is their remarkable energy and tolerance of fatigue. Always a surprise is the fact that they are in good health during starvation, sometimes even up to the time of death.

In many ways anorectics differ from the thousands of teenage girls who are obsessed with dieting and food fads. The most striking difference between the two groups is that the usual diet-conscious teenager abhors the idea of dieting, takes no pleasure in it, and derives little sense of superiority from the fact that she can lose weight. Furthermore, the willpower of the ordinary dieting teenage girl is a shadow of the anorectic will, the apotheosis of "the will-to-supremacy." The anorectic senses a potential for ultimate will-to-power over the enemy, which is the body and all that is mentally represented by the body.

The similarities in the clinical pictures of anorectics are due to the fact that, for many anorectics, there is a consistent, predisposing personality disorder which is intimately related to their early childhood experiences and interaction with the family. The anorectic's mother is typically perfectionistic, domineering, overwhelming, overcaring, and obsessively opinionated about her child, to the extent that the girl, as a young adolescent, is unprepared for youth. The mother of the anorectic is an emotionally immature woman who often continues to be dependent on her own mother, also a controlling woman who can only criticize her daughter and try to control her life—and later, directly and indirectly—the life of her granddaughter.

The anorectic feels that there is little she can do about an uncertain future, except to deny her needs and remove any suggestion of telltale plumpness and hints of burgeoning sexuality. She hopes to create a situation whereby her mother will continue to be responsible for her and, at the same time, be challenged, as she has never been challenged before, by the starvation of her daughter and the possibility of her death.

The anorectic is a caricature of will. She feels that she must control sensual enjoyment and delight, while at the same time, because of the heightened emotions of adolescence, she fears her secrets will be easily detected—her furtive, sensuous glances and impulses—and her private self revealed in all its desires. In addition, she believes that she must push away from the mother of her childhood and establish herself as independent, outgoing, resilient, able to put herself aside from the mother. Faced with the glimmerings of sensuous genital feelings, she finds herself longing to return to her mother for solace and guidance.

Although anorexia nervosa was described in the third quarter of the nineteenth century, it was not understood by clinicians until the last few decades. And there is still much confusion. Part of the difficulty in delineating the disturbance is that the developmental disorder ranges in its quantitative expression from minimal manifestations—commonplace teenage attitudes toward the self and the body, often fleeting and elusive—to a relentless course leading to self-starvation, cachexia, obliteration of the self, and finally death. Furthermore, the anorectic, on one end of the continuum, may steadfastly diet and starve herself to death; on the other end, she may binge and vomit in an unrelenting cycle, interspersed with periods of unnotable eating and constant weight. Then there are mixed anorectics who alternately diet, gorge, and vomit.

The disorder has fascinated and concerned clinicians for a variety of reasons. First of all, it is one of the few disorders in psychiatry that can lead to death. The mortality rate varies from 2 to 15 percent, depending on the severity of the illness and the commitment to and effectiveness of treatment. The morbidity rate is even higher, from 30 to 65 percent, in terms of chronic sexual dysfunction and gynecological, endocrine disturbances. The increased incidence of anorexia nervosa suggests the the rise reflects cultural and social changes: new styles in child rearing, effects of the "new narcissism," societal shifts in the investment in institutions, and basic changes in values, character organization, and structure.

The syndrome also interests psychiatrists because it demonstrates problems in diagnostic assessment. The question still exists as to whether anorexia nervosa is a neurosis, psychosis, or a "special entity." These diagnostic considerations are useful in the formulation of more traditional nosological categories, helpful in the statistical selection of patients for research studies. The anorectic disturbance also illustrates

the history of psychiatry. The developmental disorder was first considered a variant of tuberculosis, then a type of hysteria, and later a
manifestation of a pituitary gland deficiency. Its history has now come
full circle with the renewed interest in the neurophysiology and
neuroendocronology of anorexia nervosa. The illness is also a challenge
to the properly awed psychotherapist and psychoanalyst, for it forces
him to consider many technical issues, like those of countertransference
and resistance, and brings into view the fact that a one-dimensional
approach to psychological treatment is often ineffectual, if not dangerous. What most the anorectic fears advances, leaving her afloat, tiny
and lost, swaying unmoored. Its true name is what she must learn.

2

Starving to Death in a Sea of Objects: A Novel

In that this is a work of fiction, the characters are from the imagination.

PROLOGUE

Climbing steep trails, worn away over the years, crawling across fallen trees spanning white waters of mountain streams, the sun blazing down, making camp at the end of the day, singing with her friends by a campfire, steaks wrapped in white butcher paper, oozing blood on a grease-blackened pan—Kodachrome slides, dozens of them fresh from the summer trip, flash before them in Barbara's room—room 709—in the crow's nest of the Many Glacier Hotel.

"Here's to the summer and our group," Steven said, as he raised a bottle of Coors beer to his lips.

Barbara leaned forward, parting the white haze of Colombian Gold as she reached for her beer. She switched on a small tape recorder. Her eyes sparkled in the dim light. "The best part of the summer was meeting you, Steve," she murmured.

Steve lowered the bottle from his wet lips, half-startled, half-embarrassed. He winked at her reassuringly. The other couples, also teenagers, smiled at their partners, at one another, also musing over the end of summer. Tomorrow they would all leave Glacier Park and drive to Bozeman for their plane connections home.

A slide—eight rams gathered around their backpacks—brought back memories of their ten days in Glacier—the morning they awoke to find rams watching them. It was that evening when Barbara had heard the cries of timber wolves—not coyotes (which everyone preferred to think)—and became frightened, clinging to Steve all night. She and Steve sealed themselves together in his sleeping bag, like Siamese twins.

Barbara half-closed her eyes and thought about it. "To next summer, the West, us and the Many Glacier," Barbara toasted, her voice thin and reedy.

The slide carousel clicked to a stop, finished. The room grew darker and voices turned to inaudible whispers. Steven grasped Barbara's hand and drew closer. For a moment, she thought of the blackness outside, her empty bed 2,000 miles away, unslept in for the last two months. Hesitant, gradual, she leaned into Steven, and they lingered through the night, tender and loving.

I. AFTER THE SUMMER

Run away, leave them to ease.
What does it matter you wind up alone?
There is no finish; you can stop for no one.
—Marvin Bell, "Homage to the Runner"

Adolescence is the most passionate time of life.

Her eyes stuck together with invisible sutures, Barbara awoke to the news blaring from her radioalarm. She stretched her long, lean body and took several deep breaths to calm herself. Her blond hair spread out to the bars of the brass headboard, delicately entwining them with fingers of warm gold. The heat of her body filled the space between the sheets and invited her to linger in the calm light of her bedroom. She wished she didn't know it was Monday morning, and the beginning of a new school year—eleventh grade, the absolute end of vacation and an irrepressible reminder that another year had passed. Hesitating for a moment, she poked a leg out of the covers to test the world; she slid the rest of her tanned body out of the bed and walked toward the pink drapes which sealed her off from the other world. The second tug parted the drapes, making her step back from the harshness of the bright morning. The blur soon faded away into a resolution of light and colors: a dirty, tan brick wall across the back of her apartment building, a wall marked off by symmetrical windows, around which cleansing rains had etched black, shaggy patterns that would never melt away. The day would be another September scorcher, muggy and still.

She felt a heaviness in her thighs and buttocks, not the satisfying feeling of fatigue which she had experienced during the summer after hiking out West. This was different, almost like the early warnings of "flu," or the presentiment of tension over the unexpected. She knew that she shouldn't have looked out the window; the view would only make her think of sunrises in the Rockies—golden bursts between blue sky and green forest. The summer should never have ended. Now she had to go back to school, to teachers at Rockleigh School, people whom she had never gotten to know, to classmates whom she feared she might get to know.

She sat on the edge of the bed in a slouch; the skin drawn tight over her sculptured spine. Fearing another intrusion, she flicked off the alarm button, triggered to buzz momentarily, and switched the radio dial to WQIV and the Beatles' "A Little Help from My Friends."

"Are you up yet, Barbara?" her mother shouted from the kitchen downstairs. Her voice was cracked, a bit vague. It was difficult hearing her mother in her room—even when she wanted to—for her bedroom was at the end of the long, upstairs hall. When she was six, Barbara had resisted her parents' attempt to put in an intercom as a safety measure against her walking in her sleep, as though the device could monitor her footsteps on the thick carpet. Every night for weeks, she would go to her parents' bedroom where she ended up on the floor, next to her father's side of the canopied, queen-size bed. Her objection to the intercom was practical: too many of her friends would come over after school and want to play with the device; they would break it.

"Yeah, I'm just doing my exercises," she said, as she straightened up by her bedside table. She shook her head like someone trying to drive out a nightmare. "I'll be down for breakfast in several minutes, eight and a half, to be exact." She smiled, wondering if her mother had caught her mock punctuality. Nothing of the kind. She probably hadn't, Barbara suspected.

Barbara propped up her Royal Canadian Air Force excercise booklet and turned its pages to the next endurance level, almost one-third along the challenging columns of digits which three weeks ago looked as punishing to her as the Rockies had in June. Unrolling her pastel exercise mat, with care befitting a Persian rug, she slipped her nightgown off, letting it fall by the bed in a limp heap as she started her choreography of flexions, extensions, and lateral rotations. The boredom of exercise no longer bothered her. (Her father had once told her that boredom was the only predictable result from exercise.) She watched herself in a full-length mirror: her muscles still looked smooth and hard. Her belly was flat and firm, without the little mound which last spring had fit easily in the palm of her hand. But the skin around her waist was loose enough to be rolled, like worry beads, between her thumb and index finger.

"Barbara, come to breakfast!" her mother yelled from the bottom of the staircase. Sounding annoyed, she said, "I have to go to the office soon."

"I just have to finish dressing," Barbara said, calm, stopping to look at her face. When she frowned, little pouches gathered under her eyes. She rushed into the bathroom and splashed cold water over her face. The pouches remained; they had formed during sleep. She put her legs through cotton underpants, grabbed a loose peasant blouse and old irregularly faded jeans, scarred from the loss of embroidered red roses, ripped off by sliding along rocks during the summer. She kicked on scuffed leather sandals, a birthday present several years ago from her mother, and descended the spiral stairs, like a fallen leaf sucked into a vortex.

The smell of burning bacon led her to the kitchen; the smell that meant Rose, the maid, hadn't returned yet from vacation. Rose would never burn the bacon. Her mother was bent over the toaster with a fork in one hand, ready to stab a muffin if it didn't return to her quickly enough.

"Good morning, Mom," Barbara said after she kissed her mother on the cheek. She looked down, her rueful smile brightened. "Hello, Daddy . . . I didn't see you last night. Did you have a delivery?"

"No, no . . . just a staff meeting," he said, blinking and shaking his head in slow motion. He looked back to his bran cereal, floating on milk like old algae on a pond.

"Here's your orange juice and granola, Barbara. Do you want bacon and eggs?" She spoke precisely, carefully, in order that there be no mistake.

She looked away from her mother's gaze to her father. He was absorbed in the *Times*. He sat stirring his coffee, absent-mindedly, the spoon going around and around mechanically. He smelled of shaving lotion.

"No thanks. This is all I need," she said, considering again.

Her mother glanced at her.

"I have to meet Jill at the corner," Barbara said, shaking her head, thinking. "We're walking to school."

"Barbara, are those clothes all right?" her mother asked, suddenly staring at her daughter. She was a determined little woman with iron-gray hair, a pretty face, busy eyes. "Doesn't Rockleigh require something more substantial than that?"

"No, not really, Mom." Barbara's eyes grew narrow.

"Not even a bra?"

"Why should they care?" Barbara said. "I have to go now."

"There's a letter here for you, Barbara," her mother said, going out to the hall table to get it. "It came a few minutes ago."

Barbara ripped open the envelope.

Dear Barbara,

It's hard being back to school, even though I got on a sailing trip when I returned from Montana. The school work is building up already, and my PSAT's are scheduled for November. My parents are encouraging me to apply to Harvard since they went there, and I want to be a doctor, but I think I want Stanford, even though it's close to home. (I can keep the peninsula between me and them.)

We had a terrific summer together. Ours was the best wilderness group I've ever been in—including the one I was with in the Olympic Rain Forest, which reminds me of our plans to get together at Xmas here for our cross-country ski trip in Yosemite. I don't think we should continue to see each other.

It's strange. When we met in Denver last summer, we picked each other out of the group. We understood each other immediately, both of us lost our reserve and got close. Through the summer we were extraordinarily at one, sharing one outlook on life and destiny. But at the end of the summer I came away from you bewildered and at odds in some funny way with the kids at school. I don't understand it. Maybe it's because we're so much alike. I don't know what it is but when I'm with you, everything is deja vu.

We shouldn't go on. I couldn't anyway. You frighten me, Barbara, or maybe something deep down in me terrifies me. I'm sorry, Barbara. Perhaps we'll meet again, find ourselves in the same med school or hospital (? Mass General). Certainly, we must not meet at Xmas vacation. (I'm going skiing in Switzerland with a Sierra group in March.) Take care of yourself.

As ever,
Steven

Barbara, lips compressed, folded the letter up and stuffed it deep in her bag. Her eyes filled with tears, all at once. She pushed her half-finished cereal aside, kissed her father and mother, and flung her bag over her shoulder. "So long. See you tonight. Both of you be home tonight? . . . Good." She whirled around and slammed the door, leaving behind an unspeakable silence. Her parents said nothing; both looked down, she at her dry muffin, he at his fat paper, reading, eyes glittering.

"Barbara's bursting with energy, isn't she?" the mother said, sipping her coffee, looking at nothing.

"She sure is," he said, nodding to his wife. "The summer was good for her." He looked back to his *Times* and saw that Barbra Streisand was in a new movie; the critics liked it. They should go, he said to himself, the first evening he wasn't on call.

"Want another cup of coffee, Don?"

"No thanks. It will give me heartburn," he said, dead serious all at once.

She turned to look at her husband. He seemed tired and gaunt; he had aged over the summer as if he had been catching up on years before his forty-ninth birthday next week. His hair was grayer, especially around the ears, more noticeably now, since he wore his hair longer—one of those ironies of life for middle-aged men who want to look young. He hoped to get away from the Ivy League look, which had been his emblem from his Harvard days.

Dr. Donald Gordon wiped a tag of blackberry jam from his finger, remembered his coffee, drank it down at once, hot as it was, folded up the paper and left the breakfast table. His surgical day had already begun.

"I have to hurry, Susan. I'm in the O.R. at nine." He added, "I'll call later about dinner if anything should come up."

After kissing Susan, he put his hand on the back of her neck and pressed the side of her face against his chest. "It's right," he said to himself and then—in the subdued light of the kitchen, Barbara off to school, Peter still asleep upstairs, it did not seem a surprising thing to say—he murmured, "I love you very much."

"So long. I'll give Peter a kiss for you," Susan said, back at the table in the breakfast room, fiery with memories and sunlight from the casement windows. The front door slammed shut. I love him, she thought.

Susan climbed the stairs to stir her son, to remind the thirteen-year-old that his summer was also gone. The school bus would soon come, and he, too, could join the family in grieving for a summer slipped away.

Dr. Gordon's leather heels clicked in cadence as he walked through the lobby. "Matt, can you get me a cab? I'm in a hurry to get to the hospital." He looked up at the sky, wondering how muggy the day would be.

"Be glad to, Dr. Gordon," the doorman said. He added, almost without thinking, "It's a nice day, isn't it?" He went to the curb, straightened up like a good soldier and blew his silver whistle. A checker cab, going north along Park Avenue, swung across 85th Street into the south lane, abruptly swerving within inches of the doorman's left knee. A black Mercedes had cut the cab off.

"You goddamn pig," the Mercedes driver, a clean-cut Italian-looking young man, screamed at the Puerto Rican cab driver. "You want the whole fucking road," he shouted and then sped off; the cab driver needed his fare more than revenge, at least for the moment, and did nothing.

"Have a good day, Dr. Gordon," the doorman whispered. "They're funny damn things, human beings." Dr. Gordon slipped a tip into Matt's white-gloved palm.

"Maternity Hospital, please." He said it loud, crisply.

The cab started forward with a jerk. Dr. Gordon settled back and tried to ignore the cabbie's prattle about traffic. He wished the anti-mugging screen between them were soundproof. The taxi turned left on 79th Street, and, as it approached Lexington Avenue, he saw Barbara walking uptown. For a moment, he couldn't grasp why his daughter was in this neighborhood. Then it came to him that she had picked up Jill—probably at Jill's apartment down the street, instead of the corner—before going on to school. He smiled as he watched the girls walking fast; both looked as though they were being chased. Their silhouettes vanished as his cab lunged into a burst of traffic.

The two teenage girls stopped to look in a boutique window. Because of Barbara's height and figure and Jill's squatness, both were aware of their contrasting images in the glass. Barbara had always been close to Jill, who was her only real friend, her "go-between" with the other girls at school, toward whom Barbara felt only rivalry, which she tried, not always well, to hide in schoolwork.

"Jill, look at that new dress . . . the blue one." Her eyes were bright as the morning. "I love the way the waist pinches in. Should I get it?"

"Why not? You could wear it to the party Friday night. You're lucky you can get into things like that," Jill said, looking past Barbara, stopping to look in a window. She was fond, to the point of madness, of charm bracelets, brooches, pins, anklets and dimestore junk.

"We better hurry!" Barbara said. She seemed impatient to Jill, very rushed, although they had started out at least ten minutes earlier than necessary.

"What's the rush, Barbara?" Jill leaned into a trot to keep up.

"I think I'm starting my period. I'm not prepared," Barbara said with concern. "During the summer it was off and on. I missed completely in August."

Jill gave Barbara an impish smile.

Barbara could feel her jaws contract, as she smiled back uncomfortably. "I'd be quite happy to forget that nuisance," Barbara said. She talked on. "Hope it never comes back. It was great not having any pain or mess."

"My mother claims," Jill said, "that she had pain right up to the day she got pregnant with me, and then it never came back. She bets the same will happen to me."

"You're supposed to go out and get pregnant?" She threw Jill a look of panic.

"I don't know . . . but you know it's funny; she keeps bitching that my brother and his wife haven't had a baby yet." She grimaced. "She loves to have children around, the younger the better."

Barbara stopped to rub her left eye.

"Hey, come on. We got to hurry," Jill said.

"I got something in my eye," Barbara explained, looking pained.

They crossed 86th Street, the heart of Yorkville, once the center of the German community in New York. Over the summer the street had changed: a pizzeria instead of the Brauhaus, movies featuring sex, violence and machismo, a succession of hamburger places, each smelling greasier than the next, a store that sold big mounds of frozen yogurt, and, worst of all, gangs of young men, in odd assortments of denim and t-shirts with bizarre names inscribed on the front, standing motionless, watching, scrutinizing, sometimes muttering mocking remarks at people passing by. Jill pointed out a new pizzeria, its first day's opening still celebrated by strings of colored triangular flags.

"The mushroom pizza, Barbara, is magnificent." She smiled, eyes glinting. "Try some after school."

"Pizza is horrid junk food," Barbara said with an edge that surprised herself. "It's all mozzarella cheese and olive oil, you know."

"What do you want?" Jill asked, suddenly embarrassed, "a vitamin cocktail?"

They walked several blocks without a word. Jill stopped to look in the window of a bakery, to inspect the strawberry and peach strips, the Grand Marnier cakes and golden almond croissants, piled high. Even at this early hour, the Haitian clerks were scurrying around the small store, trying to speed up the line, stretching to the street.

Jill's face lighted up. "Look at those croissants! I haven't seen ones like that since Paris."

"Don't you ever think of anything besides food?" Barbara said, looking up, alarmed.

"Oh, sure: boys, clothes, movies and vacation, in that order today. Let's see," Jill said with feigned introspection, "did I *miss* anything?"

Barbara said nothing. They turned the corner of 93rd Street and entered Rockleigh. The sound of the morning bell greeted them.

"Hurry up, Barbara," Jill barked. "We'll be late for biology."

Barbara saw Nick Anagnostakis, sitting over on the right near the back of the class; he had been in her English class last year, and she found him disgusting. His acne was nauseating, purplish, milky-white with peaks that seemed ready to burst. He slouched. He was poor, a Greek kid from Hell's Kitchen, on full scholarship. She looked at him again; he seemed different. Over the summer, he had undergone a transformation—from a disfigured, crushed boy to a tanned, smooth-skinned, clean-shaven, blond young man who now acted like somebody who knew who he was. A girl sitting next to Nick was whispering to him; her face was only a few inches from his, and he was looking at her—straight on and confident.

Barbara hurried to an empty chair on Nick's free side and sat down and smiled at him. Her directness surprised her.

"How have you been, Barbara?" Nick asked. She could feel his eyes moving over her. "You look great. What did you do this summer?"

"I spent the summer climbing the Rockies, some of it on horseback." She bit her lip; her answer sounded pat and dumb. "How about you?"

"Oh, I worked as a lifeguard at a resort." He spoke with surprising enthusiasm. "An uncle of mine with Olympic Airways in Rome got me the job."

"Where was it?" she asked with suppressed curiosity.

"A little place north of Rome—on the Mediterranean at Porto Ercole." He took a deep breath. "Very few Americans know it . . . the I'l

Flamingo. You probably haven't heard of it either. Real neat people there. Jet-set type from the film business in Rome."

"Ah, I'l Flamingo! I know it well and love it." She listened to her last words; you better tone it down, sound more casual, she thought. "I stayed there three years ago. Then it was a favorite of the rich, British executives and MP's who arrived by yacht." She began to laugh, not meaning to. "My father said the British guests had more money than the Greek shipping people—certainly more charm."

Nick frowned, puzzled, taking in her comment and, after a second, to Barbara's amazement, he smiled.

She was struck by her last remark. And she could feel her face redden. Why was she attacking this boy? His comments about the jet set reminded her of a lifeguard there when she stayed at the resort. He was from Newton. They swam together, once took a sailboat out and went on a picnic to the other side of the peninsula. But after a few days he dropped her. Later, she became aware of Italian women who paid him attention—some in their forties, old enough to be his mother. At the bar one night she overheard several French women, commenting on his indifference to them: they attributed it to a contessa in Rome who visited him regularly and gave him money. For the rest of her vacation, she hated the lifeguard; she even refused to swim at the pool. Instead, she would dive off the rocks at the bottom of the cliffs, ignoring the shouts of her father who, certain of her imminent death, watched from the promenade.

The biology teacher interrupted her thoughts. He had a bush of reddish hair, almost all of it gone from the crown of his head, and where he was bald he had little clusters of freckles. He made an announcement: All the students should pair up with a lab partner; they would need dissecting instruments: a scalpel, Kelly clamp, scissors, two retractors and a dissecting microscope. Somebody wondered if they'd be doing open-heart surgery. Barbara thought she'd ask her father for the equipment. He certainly had extras at the office.

Her face felt like fire; her neck burned. Barbara wished she could look at herself in the mirror. Was she really beet-red? Nick seemed to be listening to the teacher. There would be a term paper on a research topic in biology—fully annotated, accurately supported by references, which had to be listed according to the style of *Science*. Looking down, she discovered that both Nick and she had crossed their legs; their feet touched for a moment. She uncrossed her leg and sat up stiffly, determined to concentrate on the teacher's instruction. She focused on his bushy red mustache, imagined him trimming it, tidying it up with his special Hoffritz mustache comb, then imagining how he'd look with a bare lip.

"Today," Mr. Blakely said, and smiled, grim, "we're starting the section on chromosomes and DNA. This material presupposes that you know something about biochemistry, particularly amino acids, which, needless to say, you don't."

Barbara wondered if she would have anything to say in class this year. She knew the essentials of biology. But often in class the word "nothing" would come into her mind, having arisen from nowhere. At Rockleigh, she had been consistently a B-plus student without much effort. In public school she would have been at the top of her class, possibly even at Bronx Science. After teachers' meetings at Rockleigh her parents would remind her of her potential for A's. Her advisor, Miss Green, said the same thing, even holding out to her the carrot of Radcliffe or Yale.

"DNA contains the messages of life," the teacher continued, tight-lipped, intruding on Barbara's thoughts. His voice was mechanical, like his words.

She listened more closely to the teacher. "Bright, successful parents," he said, "have bright, successful children; but many don't live up to their potential because they have emotional problems." He went on, dry, mechanical. "Many successful parents cannot tolerate their children's success. The sons of famous men illustrate this; most of them fizzled out. That's why environment must always be considered with the genotype. Great men are not merely born; they are shaped and embossed by experience." He repeated the sentence, almost in a whisper this time. "And only those who can anticipate their experiences have some control of the level of stimulation, see their way through the sensory-perceptual confusion of the world." She sat bolt upright in her chair, her head forward in rapt attention. "They are able to make the most of their DNA." As he talked and sounded more like an ethical culturist, Barbara found herself holding back snickers. Mr. Blakely looked "high" from his rhetoric. He had inspired himself.

She leaned over to Nick to glance at his notes. She had missed some facts on amino acids structures; it was all in the book anyway. The dismissal bell rang. Jill came over to Barbara and glared at Nick. He picked up his notebook and walked off with Connie Hollaway.

"Do you have a class now, Barbara?" Jill asked.

"No, I have two free periods, side by side . . . "

Jill looked at her and smiled.

"No, it hasn't happened," Barbara said, looking down. "I guess I'm in the clear. I think I'll go to the library. I have some reading to do."

"Really, Barbara! Well, if you say so. See you later."

Susan Gordon gathered together several books and her brief case, bulging with a manuscript she was proofreading, and checked the stove, to make sure she had turned the gas off, before she left for the office. The crosstown bus was crowded and hot, even at eight-thirty, but the uptown IND subway was almost empty, except for its usual derelict or two and the occasional slumped-over body of a drunk. When Susan got off at Broadway and 116th Street, the streets and walkways through the campus still looked fresh and beautiful to her, but not awesome, as they once had seemed. She had first seen the university as a child one Sunday afternoon. Her parents closed up the candy store early and drove downtown and around Manhattan, taking in the Christmas decorations, which she believed were the sole property of the goyim.

"Good morning, Mrs. Gordon," her secretary said doltishly. "Your mail is opened on your desk."

"Thanks, Sheila." Her voice sounded feeble, and she realized that she hadn't spoken for almost an hour. "Ring me when Mr. Rheinhardt arrives." She settled into her chair and lit a cigarette before confronting the mail, spread out on her desk like cards at the gaming tables at Monte Carlo. Her secretary had prepared an updated curriculum vitae for her; the Dean of the School had requested it for some unexplained reason. Susan scanned it to check for typos, and she liked what she saw.

Curriculum Vitae

Born Bronx, N.Y., 1934. Bronx Science High School, 1952. Merit Scholar, 1952. Radcliffe College, A.B., cum laude, 1956. London School of Economics, 1954–1955. Boston University, M.S.W., 1957. Caseworker, Massachusetts Mental Health Center, 1957–1959. Columbia University, D.S.W., 1962.

She broke off from proofreading, amazed that it had been fourteen years since she joined the school; then she returned to her reading.

Instructor, Columbia University School of Social Work, 1961; Assistant Professor, 1963; Associate Professor, 1968; Research Director, 1972. Member: Phi Beta Kappa, American Sociological Association, Orthopsychiatry; Consulting Editor, *The Family.*

She thought how she had wanted to be a doctor, probably a psychoanalyst. It seemed so absurd now. She was devastated—depressed for weeks at Radcliffe when she failed organic chemistry, enraged when her premedical advisor told her not to bother making it up at summer school. It didn't matter to her anymore; sociology and social work had been good to her. She read over the rest of her CV.

Publications: "Societal stratification and psychiatric disorders," *Am. J. Orthopsychiat.,* 70:445–490, 1961; "Child development patterns in France," *Am. J. Soc.,* 42:111–127, 1962; "Ecology of nutritional disorganization in Black and Hispanic cultures," *Am. Soc. Rev.,* 26:17–29, 1964; "Demographic factors in world hunger," in: R.A. Scott (Ed.), *Mental Health and Malnutrition: A World Survey,* New York: W. W. Norton & Co., 1968, pp. 109–121; "Coalitions in family structures," *J. Nerv. & Ment. Dis.,* 110:55–75, 1970; "Starvation and psychiatric disorder in Guatemala," in: T.E. Radborn (Ed.)., *Mental Health and Infant Development.* New York: Basic Books, 1974, pp. 91–113.

No typos. Sheila could send the CV right off to the Dean.

She flipped through her mail. It wasn't interesting. A population conference at Palm Springs in October sounded dull. She was no golfer. And those retired people who hide behind walls in their desert houses—off streets named Eisenhower and Sinatra—she had nothing in common with. How could Truman Capote ever move out there? She tossed a job inquiry into the basket. Meager qualifications for someone over forty. She was never satisfied with her research staff, who seemed to feed on her ideas and her energy. There were several letters from the West Coast about a research project in Guatemala. Jim Batten at UCLA was trying to get together a project on starvation among the natives. She didn't want to be connected with them; she picked up the phone and asked her secretary to call her home.

"Rose. Hello. This is Mrs. Gordon. We're delighted you're back. Have a good vacation? Good." She cleared her throat before preparing to go into the business of the day. "I'll be a little late tonight—probably about seven. Plan dinner for eight." She detected some weariness in her voice. "Tell Peter and Barbara when they get home from school. Yes, scallops are fine. No butter for Dr. Gordon. 'Bye."

The intercom buzzed, startling her.

"Mrs. Gordon . . . Mr. Rheinhardt is here."

"Send him in, Sheila," she said. She hadn't seen Tony Rheinhardt since her visit to Stanford in the spring. His research reports hadn't been good over the summer; the reasons she didn't understand. Alcohol, an affair, the "blues"—she wasn't sure. Maybe he had been tenured too young and had just burned out. Susan understood the academic world.

"Hello, Tony. It's so good to see you again." She walked over to him, gave him a kiss near the ear and noticed his beard was a bit shaggy and much grayer.

"I'm glad, Tony, you could get away from Stanford. Have some coffee?" Before he could reply she handed him the cup. "How's Ann and the children?" She left no time for a reply. "Are you comfortable at the Stanhope?"

"Yes, fine. It's a constant hotel," he said, snatching the first thing that came into his mind.

They sat on the deep, white lounge which she reserved for more informal meetings. On the coffee table were the several memo pads next to a bowl of white and heather chrysanthemums.

"Well." She lit a cigarette. "We have to do something, don't we, Tony? Our field workers aren't getting much data. And we're over the grant budget." Her hands stopped moving and she glanced at Tony.

"But Tyler," Tony sputtered, "has done well in the last quarter." Or so it seemed to Tony, smiling plump-faced, the lenses of his glasses blanking out his eyes.

"Please," Susan said, turning directly to look him in the eye. "Results have to go up."

"What do you suggest, Susan?" Tony said, glancing around the room.

"A complete reshuffling of the research people and data analysts in the Palo Alto office." She paused as though trying to deliver a calculated strategy. "Robertson shouldn't be in the field. He just doesn't have it."

"But, Susan," Tony exclaimed, hunching his shoulders in for warmth and sucking down his coffee.

"What are we to do?" She walked to her desk and glanced at a page of calculations. "Then there's Rothstein, your assistant. Tell me honestly, Tony. Do you really need her?"

"If she doesn't get married and pregnant," Tony said.

"Tony! Cut it out," she said, her eyes flashing. "I've drawn up an organization plan which I'd like you to put into effect when you get back."

"All right," Tony said. "What about the new child development project in France?"

"Helen, my new assistant—you haven't met her yet—will take you through the budget and other material." She considered for several seconds. "Look, I expect to be in California before Christmas. We should know by then if we can turn things around."

Tony seemed to think about it a moment. Then, slowly, carefully, not looking at Susan, he stood up. He smiled, but his eyes were still remote. He looked down at his folder of papers. *"Shit!"* he bellowed, and he hit her desk so hard the dust he stirred up hung in the air, mixing with the smell of coffee and cigarette smoke; then, very slowly, it settled. They looked at each other and then laughed.

"Good," Susan said, her voice quiet, so quiet it surprised her. "I got through to you. Now we can talk about other things."

Tony puckered his lips, then nodded, still smiling.

"Let's have lunch tomorrow at the Terrace," Susan said. "How's one o'clock?"

Susan switched on the intercom as Tony left.

"Sheila, can I have the Chicago research reports for last year?" Her look clouded a little. "The file on the demographic factors in world hunger," she said, scowling, annoyed. "Also, the report Miss Birnbaum sent me?"

Susan sipped at her black coffee. It was cold.

"Your husband is on the line, Mrs. Gordon."

"Thank you." She cleared a space on her desk. "Hello, Don. How was the morning?"

"Ver-y good," he said, sounding rather spirited. "The hysterectomy went well. I wanted to let you know I'll be home early." He paused, trying to recall what the rest of his day would be like. "I have residents' rounds after lunch and a delivery around four."

"I'm sorry," she said, arranging several pencils at right angles. "I can't get away at five. There's a staff meeting at four. I'm sure it will run till six or six-thirty." She rubbed the bridge of her nose, almost to a shine before she stopped herself. "I called Rose to have dinner at eight. I'll try to hurry home. 'Bye."

The old school hadn't changed. St. Stephen's looked like one of the first private schools in New York. The new wing, the high school, with all its dark, chocolate-brown windows and slabs of preformed concrete, like a diminutive, modern office building on Sixth Avenue, made fun of its Victorian mother-building, the home of the headmaster and the lower grades. Peter wasn't free of the old structure yet, since he was entering eighth grade. (He wouldn't "move up" until next June.) The vestibule of the old building still smelled dank; the halls were now perfumed by aromatic cleaning compounds, used in the last week. The smell would be displaced around Columbus Day by the old stale odors that lived in the woodwork.

Peter took his place in the chapel with the other eighth graders. He noticed that he was now a little taller than many of the other thirteen-year-old boys, one of the few things that distinguished him from classmates dressed in blue blazers with gold school emblems, gray flannels and black shoes. Except for his height and new steel-frame glasses, he looked like all the other boys, most of whom, like Peter, had blond hair cut by the same barbers on Lexington Avenue.

Peter felt a tap on his right shoulder. He turned around, vague and uncertain.

"Hey, four eyes." Someone said in a shrill voice. "You look funny in those goggles."

Peter grimaced as if about to cry. His gaze brought into view four, giggling boys behind him. Only Peter's left hand, middle finger, could answer; his voice stuck in his throat.

"Good morning, boys," the headmaster said with stentorian tones. "I want to welcome you back to St. Stephen's on the opening of our 130th year." Mr. Morgan, the headmaster, the bolt of cloth St. Stephen's boys were supposed to be cut from, had been a large part of thirty-five of those years. "We approach this new year with courage and love in our hearts—toward others, as well as ourselves." The shuffling of feet grew louder. "I have a few announcements. Mr. Jason Smith has joined our history department and will teach eighth grade ancient history. We are quite fortunate . . . Mr. Jason-Smith, will you please stand up." A tall, thin-lipped, young man with razor-cut short hair and rimless glasses, stood up and nodded an acknowledgment. "Mr. Jason-Smith is working for a Ph.D. in history at Columbia University. I also wish to announce. . . ."

This year would be no different, Peter thought. Nothing much had changed for him. A little taller, a lot more nearsighted, but that was about all. He even had "Bozo" Bozell—Mr. Lloyd Brian-Bozell, as it was printed on his schedule—again for Latin.

The 9:15 bell rang for the first class. Peter joined the line out of the chapel.

"There's the big owl . . . look at those glasses!" several boys said, pointing at him as though he were an anomaly.

Barbara realized that she had been in the library for two hours. She had read a *National Geographic* article on wolf behavior in the Northwest Territory. As a child, she had been afraid of wolves. A night light was finally installed—leaving the hall door open a crack wasn't enough—and kept on all night. That's of no importance now, Barbara said to herself.

She was well into the second chapter when her eyelids felt heavy. She put the book down and stared out the window, finally fixing on a glass and aluminum high rise going up on Third Avenue.

A faint whisper attracted her attention.

Lisa's little face beamed with excitement. "Barbara. How are you? Let's go to lunch. I got loads to talk to you about."

"No thanks, I'm really not hungry," Barbara said, with a look of indifference. "I've been sitting here all morning studying. What I need is some exercise."

"That's not for me," she said firmly. "We don't have time anyway. All right, I'll see you later, Barbara."

It was time to go to her English class. This year the class was being taught by a young woman, a new teacher who had only recently received a Master's from Columbia. Barbara had heard that she was working for a Ph.D. in comparative literature. This fact, by itself, had won Barbara's admiration for Miss Howard.

She looked around to find a seat by the window which would catch rays of the warm afternoon sun. A chilly northwest wind was now blowing, reminiscent of some of the frosty days she used to spend at Cape Cod, when she and her mother stayed on at the summer house until the day before school opened. Those were the days when her mother took a six-week summer vacation and did no work—just read novels. She found a column of sun by the window near the front of the class. Much warmer, more energetic, increasingly alert, she listened carefully to comments on the craft of poetry and did not take her eyes off Miss Howard.

"Hello, Barbara," Nancy barked as they left the classroom. She said, chewing gum, "Where are you going?"

"I have gym now. How about you?"

"This is my gym time, too, but I've worked out a different program this year," Nancy explained, looking at Barbara, watching her closely. "I'm interested in gymnastics so I've arranged to go to Barosky's on 46th Street three times a week to work out on the rings and trapeze." She smiled. "The instructors are Hungarians; they're very handsome."

"It sounds fine," Barbara said. "No thanks," she said, her tone so final it startled her. She heard her voice drop. "I have too much work to make the midtown trip."

"Nonsense," Nancy said, grimacing. "We both have gym at the end of the day, and we don't have to come back to school. You can take your books with you." Nancy squinted at her, suddenly aware now she was seeing Barbara clearly for the first time. "We'll share a cab so it won't take long. They'll give you a leotard; that's no problem."

Nancy had anticipated all her excuses, objections, rationalizations—mostly fears. Barbara found herself in a cab with Nancy, wondering if she had been seduced by this beautiful black-Japanese girl.

The gym was larger than Barbara had expected; in fact, it was four gyms with connecting doors, each painted a different pastel. The equipment looked new, clean and well-maintained. Women in black and blue leotards were in groups of six to eight in each of the gyms, and the clusters were taught and supervised by tall, muscular, young men in black pants and white, silk shirts, open from the throat to the navel. Barbara immediately noticed the ages of the women. Nancy and she were the youngest. The manager, an older, balding man, dressed in a fitted sweat suit, sat near the receptionist's desk. Five women were seated near him, regaling him with details of European vacations.

"Hello, Miss Okimo," the manager said to Nancy. He smiled, looking past her. "Let me see if Alex will be having a class at four-thirty." He looked at a master schedule. "Ah, yes. You're in luck. He'll be with you as soon as you can change." He tilted his head in Barbara's direction and said softly, "Perhaps your friend would like to join us?"

Barbara shrugged, looking at Nancy as though seeking permission.

"Yes, I would like to try the gym," Barbara said, with attempted heartiness. She was aware that she had swallowed the last word.

"Fine. We'd be delighted," he said as he looked her over. He polished his glasses. "We require a brief physical evaluation first so we can correctly place you. Olga will fit you with a proper leotard. Then I'll assess your physical status."

Olga, a dour, squat woman, Ukrainian in her origins, took Barbara to a dressing room and measured her body by eye and produced a black leotard. Barbara changed quickly, hanging her blouse and jeans on a hook in the stall. She stuffed her panties into her right shoe and returned to the reception area.

"Sensational. The advantages of youth," the manager said, when Barbara was returned to him. Several older women glared at him and then Barbara. "Please fill out this information card."

Barbara supplied the required biographical information and followed him into what looked like an examining room at her pediatrician's.

"Let's see," said the manager as he started his measurements. "Height, five feet six inches; weight, 115 lbs.; waist, 23; chest on inspiration, 35, on expiration, 33; bust, 33, and hips, 32." He stopped and rubbed the side of his nose, still thinking. "Now I want you to squeeze this gripper . . . V-e-r-y good!" He took out his ballpoint pen and clicked the head into position. "You are strong as well as muscular. Now I'd like you to pull yourself up on the rings. Like this . . . Fine. Your back is beautifully straight." He continued to scrutinize her body, fascinated, bending forward slightly. "Now hold on to the rings and put your feet under my arms. Great. Now do pull-ups on the rings until you get tired." He watched her hips move up and down.

Barbara wanted to stop. Her face flushed. She knew that she was blushing; she was a little dizzy now. (Yet, she puzzled, she hadn't been dizzy in the upside down position.) As she pulled herself up, she could feel her feet slide into his sweaty armpits.

"Splendid," the manager said. The man's eyes molested her thoughts. "You're as strong as a bull and sleek as a doe. How do you do it?"

"I spent the summer in the Rockies," she said, trying to think about something else.

"You look it," said the manager, laughing at her innocence. "I doubt if you now have an ounce of fat on that body of yours. And we're going to help you keep it that way." He laughed again, this time at his own determination. "Why don't you join Nancy's group? Alex can let the group practice a little until you are caught up with them."

Barbara went into the green gym. Alex was showing Nancy how to tuck her neck under for a tumble. He was as attractive as Nancy had said. His black eyes and mustache reminded her of a character in D. H. Lawrence's *Women in Love*. He excused himself from the group and showed Barbara the warm-up exercises, the handstands and tumbles.

"All right, ladies," Alex said, standing tipped forward a little with interest. "Let's do the rings and trapeze."

Barbara followed the class through the various maneuvers. Several obese women couldn't flip their legs over their heads on the rings. Alex, telling her to sit on the trapeze, watched Barbara take the position in two moves. Alex clutched the trapeze with his thumbs touching her thighs. She finished the session with a routine on the parallel bars.

"How did you like it?" Nancy asked in the shower room, her body covered with suds.

"Terrific. It really makes your body come alive."

Nancy warned, "You may be a little stiff tomorrow morning."

"I doubt it," Barbara said, shaking her head, knowing that Nancy was watching her thoughts.

"You better keep coming here, or you'll get flabby," Nancy added, thinking this comment would complete the recruitment.

The two girls stepped out of the shower together. Barbara glanced at Nancy's *café au lait* body as they dried themselves off.

Nancy flung her leotard bag over her shoulder and buttoned up her work jacket.

"What are you going to do now?" she asked, noticing that Barbara was taking her leotard home.

"I must get home for an early dinner. I'd really better get going . . . so long."

Nancy nodded, thinking.

As Barbara walked along the Avenue of the Americas, near the Hilton Hotel, she passed a tall, mulatto woman with blond hair, an azure blue dress and stiletto high heels. In a split instant, she imagined herself as a prostitute, cared for by a young pimp who arranged meetings with out-of-town and local businessmen, like the types flowing out of nearby office buildings. Barbara was curious about whores. Not me, she said to herself, very serious.

Five young men, residents in obstetrics and gynecology, followed Dr. Gordon from a patient's room to the solarium, where teaching rounds were to be held that afternoon. It was three o'clock. The operative schedule for Dr. Gordon was over; he had had a quick lunch of soup and cottage cheese, enough to take the edge off his hunger, and now he would spend an hour with the young doctors.

"Gentlemen, there is some fresh coffee if you're feeling a mid-afternoon slump," Dr. Gordon said, pensive in his manner. Warmth filled the solarium, and dust particles danced in the afternoon sun. "I've shown you some excellent examples of multiple pregnancies. I think we should discuss this subject to some extent." Scratching his nose, he thought for a moment. "As you know, the cararrhine primate, of which man is the most illustrious member, usually has only one young at birth, occasionally two or more."

He took a sip of his coffee. "There was a time when septuplets were most extraordinary—the most famous being from Hamlin Town, the locale of the thirteenth-century Pied Piper." He drew his coffee toward him and sucked at the edge of the plastic cup. "Then there were the South African sextuplets of 1903, and, of course, the Dionne quintuplets, born in 1934. With the fertility drugs, of course, multiple pregnancies of this order are no longer rare." Dr. Gordon clasped his hands behind his back. He was listening with the back of his mind to his thoughts coming out like the crackling of a radio. "Plural births are most frequent among blacks and rare among Mongols; whites are somewhere in between. Guttmacher demonstrated that single-ovum twinning is a matter of chance; but, on the other hand, double-ovum twinning is more a function of heredity, age and parity. In two-thirds of twin deliveries, only one sex is represented; in one-third, both sexes. In multiple pregnancies, as well as the rest of the life cycle, a differential mortality exists between the sexes. The mortality is always in favor of the female and against the male." For a moment he had the sense of having stepped unexpectedly from one world into another, having slipped away out of time. "Gentlemen, that is life! I should add that twinning, in fact, increases the individual's morbidity throughout life—from the fetal stage through the life cycle. This is particularly true psychologically for identical male twins."

Dr. Gordon looked at his watch. "Excuse me for a moment," he said. "I have to call the delivery room."

He first got a clicking tone and realized he had dialed too quickly. He controlled his impatience.

"Miss Reynolds? Dr. Gordon here." The fingers of his free hand played with the telephone cord. "How far along is my patient, Mrs. Beresford?"

"Dr. Phillips just told me the cervix is more effaced, one or two-finger dilation, but the contractions haven't increased." The nurse stopped and waited for Dr. Gordon's orders.

"Then tell Dr. Phillips to increase the Pitocin I.V. drip," he said, softly. "I want her in second stage by five o'clock." He slapped the receiver back into its plastic wall-holder and returned to the residents.

"Do you have any questions?" Dr. Gordon asked as he cleared his throat and tried to calm himself down.

"Yes, Dr. Gordon. Do you think we could discuss the management problems of multiple births?" a red-haired, first-year resident asked.

"There are some key things to know here," he said, rubbing his nose. "In about 75 percent of vertex-breech combinations, the first twin is the vertex presentation, and in around 85–90 percent of the longitudinal transverse pairs, the longitudinal child is the first." He was now pacing back and forth, speaking precisely, his tone hinting of hostility. "The usual plural labor is shorter than the ordinary single labor, and there is a greater frequency of unsatisfactory dilatory labors. A spontaneous delivery is desired because puerperal morbidity and blood loss are shockingly high in plural births. When you deliver the first twin, you should rupture the sac of the second and try to propel the fetus through the birth canal." Dr. Gordon spoke heavily, somewhat wearily, as though the lecture had begun to bore him. "Be careful of inhalation anesthesia: the fetuses tend to be small and vulnerable to lack of oxygen; gas may cause atony of the uterus after delivery. Saddle block or caudal anesthesia is safer, as far as delivery complications are concerned, but keep in mind placenta previa." He closed his hand around his lapels and looked at the floor. "Dr. Crammer, tell us about placenta previa."

A short, slight young man, sitting by the solarium window, straightened up. He had been watching a ketch bobbing up and down the East River, sucked along by the current of the ebbing tide.

His answer came at once, as if he had expected the question. "Placenta previa, Dr. Gordon, means that the placenta, instead of being stuck—I mean implanted—high up on the front or back wall of the uterus, lies low in the uterus and may touch or cover the internal os of the uterus. It's great danger lies in the increased chance of hemorrhage."

"Good, Dr. Crammer, and perhaps some day you'll own a ketch like the one that's been taking you away for the last five minutes. Perhaps in

ten years, when you're in practice and prospering, you'll be taking your
ketch down to Florida, through the inland waterway, following the
magenta line to the Blue Waters." Dr. Gordon was startled by the
harshness of his own voice. "Now, please tell us about placenta previa
in multiple pregnancies." His voice sounded softer to him now.

"I think they occur in up to 3½ percent of all multiple pregnancies—
higher at any rate than in single pregnancies." The resident spoke
guardedly, tonelessly. "The higher incidence is thought to be due to the
greater surface area of the uterus covered by the twin placentas." Dr.
Crammer sat back, lit a cigarette and crossed his legs. The professor had
asked him something he knew. The young resident hoped he'd be as
lucky next time.

"Premature separation of the placenta is to be feared in multiple
pregnancies," Dr. Gordon continued. The sun now in his eyes, he got up
and paced back and forth, like a panther behind glass. "This separation
is most frequent between the birth of the first and second child, since
the contracting uterus, after the birth of the first child, provides less
area for attachment of the second child. Other complications include
prolapsed cord, constriction rings of the uterus and postpartum hemorrhage." Life, for Dr. Gordon, was living with the statistics, holding the
right number.

Dr. Gordon stopped for a moment. He looked at his watch again.

"This week there should be a delivery of a multiple pregnancy," Dr.
Gordon said, his words muffled, just barely intelligible. "I intend to
deliver the woman, the Washington woman on Ward Four. We hear
two fetal hearts. Dr. McAndrews believes that he can hear a third. I've
asked him to assist me so he can have the pleasure of the third delivery."

The residents snickered, like little boys afraid of the teacher. Dr.
Gordon went on with his announcements.

"I'll expect all you men to be present. You'll excuse me now." He
smiled, earnest, serious, like a squadron commander before the dawn
attack.

It was still very warm for a mid-September afternoon. The subway
riders emerging from the 86th Street IRT Station on Lexington
Avenue looked limp and haggard, their faces drawn, lined and ashen,
but Barbara, still fresh and bouncy, walked quickly over to Park Avenue.
A little girl was roller-skating in front of her building. Her pigtails flew
behind her.

"Hello, anyone home?" Barbara asked, pushing open the door with her shoulder, her arms clutching several large bundles. The apartment seemed empty, but she hoped that Rose would be in the kitchen. "Rose, are you there?" There was no answer. "Rose? . . . Rose?"

The swinging door to the kitchen flipped open. "Here I am, Barbara." They rushed to each other, hugging each other, jumping up and down, joyful, relieved to see each other after the summer.

"Are my parents home yet?" Barbara asked.

"Only your brother. He's in his room doing his homework. Your mother called. Something's keeping her tonight. They should be home by seven-thirty." Rose pushed back a strand of Barbara's hair and kissed her. "How have you been?" Rose asked. "Your mother said you had a good summer."

"I bought some goodies," Barbara said, dumping them on the counter, like a sack of onions. "I stopped at Zellen's Coffee House and got apple strudels and pumpernickel bread. Mom and Daddy will be happy. Oh, Rose," Barbara added, earnest, "I want you to eat also."

Rose looked quizzically at Barbara, whom she had known since infancy. Then her manner relaxed and she said, "You look very healthy, Barbara." Rose always used phrases like "you look" or "I can see . . ." She went back into the kitchen to examine the purchases. Barbara ran upstairs to see Peter.

"Hey, Peter, what are you doing, sitting in your dark room?" Barbara asked in a challenging tone. "Didn't you get any exercise today?"

"We played dodge-ball in the gym," Peter answered, without looking up.

"Why don't you jog around the reservoir?" she said condescendingly. "That would really build you up."

"Why don't you?" Peter asked, still looking at his French book.

"I got a lot of exercise this summer—more than you got at that rich kids' camp you went to in Maine. All you did was rub tombstones." She remembered how she would say demeaning things to Peter when they were little.

Barbara said nothing for a moment. She couldn't believe how close Peter and she had been when her brother was about three and Barbara enjoyed getting in bed with him. They would hide under the covers, giggling and laughing. Peter would be happy for a few minutes and then shout for Rose, or his mother, to take him from the bed.

"And I plan to start jogging this week. Want to come?" Barbara asked defiantly.

She went back downstairs and burst into the kitchen. Rose was busy cleaning mussels. Even though Rose was Irish, she could cook well. As a young girl, she had left Galway for a year to work at an inn in Bantry.

"What's for dinner, Rose?" Barbara asked.

"Besides the mussels," Rose hesitated and looked around the kitchen as though she had not given much thought to the menu, "almond trout, asparagus, a green salad, and, of course, your dessert. You must be real hungry."

"No, not especially," Barbara said. "I just want the dinner to look good. What good is a meal if it doesn't do something for you, if it doesn't look like something out of a dream?"

Rose said quickly, "You mean you want pretty pictures," she laughed awkwardly, as if her comment had hurt Barbara. "Why don't you look at your mother's *Gourmet* magazines?"

"You miss the point, Rose." She smiled, her mouth open and eyes wide, expecting Rose—it seemed—to share her excitement. "Food is only beautiful if it's a temptation. The aesthetic experience lies in the temptation: you only taste it: never do you eat much of it."

Rose glanced at her with an uneasy smile. "If you say so, Barbara."

"Have you fed Angus yet?" Barbara asked. Her tone was an accusation.

"Of course not, silly girl. You know I don't have time to feed the dog until after dinner."

"Then I'll do it," Barbara said. "I can watch Angus eating by the hour. I love to watch the dog eating raw meat. He can't resist." Angus appeared by the door, ears lifted, watching.

Barbara looked at Angus. "I'm going to give you a great dinner."

She opened a can of dog food, a stew, adding some biscuits and topping it off with a half-pound of freshly ground hamburger. Angus attacked the mound of food. Barbara watched.

"Angus usually gets some milk afterwards," Rose reminded Barbara.

"I know, Rose, but the sight of milk makes me sick."

"You used to like milk," Rose said, puzzled by Barbara's remark. "When I took care of you, when you were a little girl, you drank your share of it. You seem upset, dear. Did something happen today in school?"

"It's nothing, Rose. I've had some diarrhea the last week," Barbara explained. "But, you know, it's strange. I've lost five pounds, and my face has gotten more angular and beautiful, like the models in *Vogue*."

"Beautiful?" Rose said with disbelief. "Poppycock!" Rose exploded. "I s'pose you don't want to talk about it, eh? . . . Don't be a damn mule. You better watch it. You'll be like a bean pole, flat up and down." She began to stuff the trout, laid out flat on the butcher block table.

"Remember Stella," Barbara asked, "the doll you gave me when I was four?" She tried to picture it. "She was beautiful: long blond hair, blue eyes and huge eyelashes. But the frills on the dress I didn't like. I think I made you take them off."

"You have a bad memory, Barbara." Rose shook her head. "You slept with Stella till you were six. It killed me, too, to see her fall apart. Don't you remember?" Rose decided for some reason to press the point. "We took her to the doll hospital near Bloomingdale's. They said she couldn't be helped and would die. You cried your little eyes out. They even promised to bury her for us." She closed the oven door.

"Stupid people!" Barbara said with a shrill. "But the doll was beautiful!" She stopped and listened. The front door had opened.

"Hello, Mom . . . Daddy?"

"Is that you, darling? her father asked.

"Hello, Daddy. How are you? Where's Mom?"

"She's still at the office . . . someone in from the West Coast. She'll be home soon." He was aware of a reassuring tone in his voice.

"Can I get you a drink?" Barbara asked. She sucked in breath. "Vodka as usual?" She went ahead and poured a drink without his reply. Barbara thought about being her father's favorite. "How's my little sweetheart?" her father would say and she would laugh and say, "Did you have a good day at the office, Dad?" Barbara looked like him—they both looked Nordic—and she walked like him. He used to tease her. She could eat anything and everything, he said. His "little garbage pail," he called her.

"Where's Peter?" her father asked.

"Studying in his room. You know how he is, Daddy."

"You mustn't be so hard on him, Barbara," he said sternly and added, "You've always been rough on Peter, right from the day he was born."

He glanced at the *Post,* lying on the coffee table, wondering how far to go with this.

"Stop it, Daddy," she said with a smile, her head cocked. "He's a little creep."

"Aren't you going to have something to drink, Barbara?"

"No, thanks, I'm not thirsty," her tone so final it startled her.

"Here's a letter from Max and Nanny," he said. "They're coming to the city for Thanksgiving weekend. Max has to see his publisher. They want to know if they can stay with us . . . they're so damn formal."

"Why don't you put them up at the St. Moritz?" Barbara asked. If she had been in their situation, she would have preferred it to staying with family.

"That wouldn't be very nice, Barbara." Don was puzzled. "Don't you want them here? You've always liked them."

"They simply talk too much, especially about the past." Her stomach jerked as if he'd jabbed it. "I get sick of hearing about my infancy . . . how 'cute' I was and what intelligent things I did."

"You used to love every minute of it." Don got up and patted her arm, then drew back his hand immediately and chuckled. "Here's your mother."

"Hello everybody. Sorry I'm late." She walked over to her husband and kissed him, standing on her toes. "Did you have a good day at school, Barbara?" She looked Barbara over carefully. "What happened to your hair, honey?"

"Nothing, I just went to a gym," she explained, nonchalant. "I guess it fell down when I was on the rings."

"Sounds dangerous. Glad you didn't fall on your head, darling," Susan said. "Don, can I have a planter's punch? Christ, it was hot today."

Don went to the bar, Barbara to the kitchen to get some orange juice. She found a pitcher of orange juice which Rose had prepared.

"Barbara," Susan said, clumsily, "I've noticed you're walking a little bent over with your shoulders rounded." Susan studied Barbara a bit more and said all at once, earnestly, "Straighten up and show your lovely figure."

"Yes, Mom."

"What's new with you, Don?"

"The same old thing," he said with a sigh. "Do you recall that director we met last spring at Doug Meskill's?"

"Of course, Robert Sineway," Susan said. "That David Niven type."

Peter walked into the room. He was wearing his school blazer, amply gold-buttoned, which was a little small for him. His brown hair hung a bit over his collar.

"Peter, my little darling!" Susan walked over to him, hugged and kissed him several times.

"Aren't you hot in that jacket?" she asked, blinking.

"No, just hungry," he said matter-of-fact. "I've done all my homework and have nothing to do. There is nothing on TV."

"My baby! We'll get you fed soon," Susan promised, sucking in her breath.

"Why," Don heard himself saying, "does the 'baby' have to be fed?" Don sipped on his drink, now watching Peter with no particular interest. He had admitted to himself many times that he didn't understand the boy.

Rose's footsteps came shuffling toward the door of the library. She hesitated, looking at everybody as though she were inspecting them. They were her responsibility.

"Dinner is served." Plodding goodness.

"Thank you, Rose," Susan said. "Don, did you see this letter from your parents? They're coming to the city for Thanksgiving."

"Yes, I know," Don said, stiff as an old knee. "What's wrong with that?"

"You know how funny Barbara has gotten about them." She threw a shadow over the room. "They're always embarrassing her by talking about her babyhood."

"I know now," Don said, assured. "When I told her about their visit, she was visibly pained and complained about them. I'll tell them to knock off their reminiscences. I also want to tell them to stop treating Peter special."

"Your mother is the one to talk to," Susan said. She grinned, troubled, thinking of Barbara. "She only had you: her son and only child. She just doesn't understand a teenage girl. Joel was something else."

"Nor does she want to," Don said.

The parents joined the children in the dining room. They were seated, staring at their plates of mussels and looking impatiently at their parents.

"Go ahead, kids. I know you're starved," Susan said, knowingly. "Your father and I still have our drinks."

Peter grabbed at the mussels, spooning up one after another. But Barbara just examined them, as though checking for sand.

"This French bread is great dipped in mussel juice," Susan said. "I could eat the whole loaf."

"I'm sure you could," Barbara said.

"There's a bitchy edge to your comment, Barbara." Susan's face was flushed. "I know it's hard to get back into the grind at school." She frowned, full of feelings.

"She sure is bitchy," Peter said, slipping another mussel into his mouth as he leaned down over his plate. Grich, grich, the sounds of a loud chewer.

"Peter, stop eating like a pig," Barbara said, distinctly. "And please wipe the juice from the corners of your mouth. It's atavistic."

"That's a nice word, Barbara," Don said with a gleam in his eye. "I like it."

"Tell me about your talk with Robert Sineway," Susan said. "Is his wife pregnant? Or the little girlfriend he keeps on East 66th Street?"

"Nothing so mundane as that," he said hastily, looking down. "He told me that he wants to do a documentary on life—not on death this time. There've been too many films on death. He wants to bring a crew to the hospital to do a two-part documentary on pregnancy and birth. He asked me to be both the narrator and obstetrician in the film," Don said, meaning it as a joke.

"Hey, that's cool," Peter said, looking up briefly from sopping up the juice of his mussels with a jagged chunk of French bread. "My father, the doctor and actor. Who's going to be your starlet?"

"Wise guy," Don chortled. "For that impertinence, I won't let you be the leading man."

"It doesn't matter," Peter said with a shrug. "It's not going to be a skin show anyway."

"Mmph!" Barbara said. "You're getting to be a bit too much, even for a thirteen-year-old brat."

"We fully agree," Don said with a faint smile.

"If I'm not bright and cute, who's going to notice me?" Peter asked.

The parents looked at each other. Susan passed the sauce Rose had made for the trout.

"When do you think Sineway will start shooting?" Susan asked.

"Oh, probably before Thanksgiving," Don said vaguely. "Would you kids like to come to the hospital when the film is being made?"

"Not me," Peter said, shaking his head. "I can see now this film is going to be an X-rated flick. I don't want to get my parents into trouble."

"Okay, stay home, kid," Don said. "How about you, Barbara?"

She seemed to consider it, looking at her plate. At last, having thought it out, she said, "I don't know about coming." Barbara stammered. "We're studying reproduction in biology. And we've started genetics, so maybe I should see it, I suppose."

"Who's doing the script?" Susan asked.

"I don't know, but I'm sure I can't get you the job," Don said soberly. But then he laughed.

"Don't you want some salad, Barbara?" Susan asked.

"No thanks, Mom," she said, dubious. "My throat hurts a little. I guess I'm coming down with a sore throat or something."

"Then you better go to bed early," Susan said. She closed her eyes, faking a smile, raising her finger in the direction of Barbara's bedroom.

"I'll be all right, Mother. I should be able to go to school tomorrow."

Barbara wondered whether her mother wanted her to stay home. All through grammar school she had fought this battle with her mother. What Barbara hated about staying at home was that no one, except Rose, was ever there. If she were ill enough, she would get a visit from Dr. Stimpson. She hated to see her pediatrician. It wasn't simply the repetitive shots which he had to offer; it was the sense that he would discover some terrible thing about her, tell her what she knew to be the truth: There was something basically wrong with her. He would take her temperature, feel around her abdomen and her neck, for some reason, and perhaps give her some antibiotic. She never understood what made him decide to give an antibiotic. Her father always objected to them. If she did have to stay home tomorrow, she dreaded Dr. Stimpson coming to examine her. She wished that she had switched to an internist last spring, like a lot of her friends. But it was too late now. What would she do if she had to stay home? Television was out of the question. She couldn't stand the soap operas. She could listen to some new records if she felt well enough to change them. If not, the FM radio would have to do.

"Rose, what do we have for dessert?" Susan asked.

"Barbara bought some pastries from Zellen's," Rose said, fascinated.

"Isn't that lovely, dear," Susan said, pausing for a second. "Let me pay you. I don't want you spending your allowance like that."

"That's all right. I have some money left over from the summer. It's nothing."

"Then let me serve you first," Susan said.

She thought for a split second. "No thanks, Mom. I don't think I want any dessert; I'll go to bed instead." She looked at her father. "You needn't examine me."

Don was surprised by the comment. His eyes widened; the corner of his mouth twitched.

"We understand, dear," Susan said. She hesitated, flustered, hunting for the right thing to say. "Why don't you gargle, rub Vicks on your chest and neck and take two aspirins."

"Yes, Mother," Barbara said, turning her head away from Susan. She wanted to shout: *Why don't you leave me alone?* She walked out without saying goodnight and went upstairs to her bedroom. As she unbuttoned her blouse, she noticed the room was warm. The air conditioner was off; Rose had been in her room. She flipped the switch to "low cool" and went into the bathroom, where she finished undressing and stood before a full-length mirror. Her breasts seemed large, as though molded from cold butter. Her nipples were darker, the brown circles about the nipples wider, like those of a woman who had had many children. Pubic hairs, once blond fuzz, now were black and curly, standing up stiff at the follicles. No longer could a finger pass along the space between her inner thighs.

Barbara turned on the shower, adjusting the hot water high enough to create a steam-mist. She pointed her face up into the pelting spray. In several minutes, she found that her nipples had hardened, the skin on her thighs had turned to goose flesh, and her belly and buttocks were heavy and throbbing. Perhaps she was about to have her period. She lathered and covered her chest, belly and flanks with thick suds.

Barbara stood directly under the shower to let the water run through her hair and down her back. Stepping back, she massaged a handful of shampoo into a frothy, white turban. She still liked her mother to wash her hair, to comb and dry it, although it embarrassed her to have to ask. She no longer would.

She dried herself off and reached for a dry towel for her hair. Her hair dryer was broken. She would have to stay up for a while, even though her throat now hurt her more. Her arms and legs ached. Perhaps she really was getting the "flu." She would read for a half hour or so. She slipped into pajamas, gargled with aspirin and went off to bed to read.

On her bedside table was a paperback copy of Mann's *Magic Mountain,* which she had bought in Boulder. Tonight she didn't feel strong enough—or alert enough—to start a long novel. She pulled the covers around her neck and reached for Mark Strand's volume of contemporary American poetry. Theodore Roethke's poem, "I'm Here," caught her eye. She read it with lukewarm interest until she reached the middle of the poem:

> So much of adolescence is an ill-defined dying,
> An intolerable waiting,
> A longing for another place and time,
> Another condition.

It seemed odd to Barbara that a man might view adolescence as death and waiting to pass into another existence. She had heard somewhere that Roethke had died of a heart attack after diving into a swimming pool. Maybe he had a premonition of death. The poem made her remember something, a poem she had written once about a juggler:

> She jettisons her body and her self
> and fingers metal
> as she floats on unwaxed wings
> sparkling an arc to the sun
> in an irridescent climb to a new birth.

Her hand trembling, she paged back in the alphabetical arrangement of poets until she came to a sonnet by Tom Clark. She always liked sonnets, even though they seemed a bit old-fashioned:

> The orgasm completely
> Takes a woman out of her
> Self in a wave of ecstasy
> That spreads through all of her body
> Her nervous, vascular and muscular
> Systems participate in the act.
> The muscles of the pelvis contract
> And discharge a plug of mucus from the pelvis
> While the muscular sucking motion of the cervix
> Facilitates the incoming of the semen.
> At the same time the contraction of the pelvic
> Muscles prevent the loss of semen. The discharge
> Makes the acid vaginal lubricant
> Alkaline, so as to not destroy the spermatozoa.

This was no sonnet, Barbara thought. Shakespeare never wrote like this. She reread the poem twice, cautiously, until she had calmed down. Her eyes filled with tears. The poem was a mockery of anything beautiful and romantic. Pornography was the creation of the ordinary male mind. Love could not be reduced to something mechanical or molecular. In fact, the poet sounded like a gynecologist. She was indignant and angry; the anthology no longer interested her.

She set her alarm for seven a.m., snapped off the bedlamp, and curled up into a ball to wait for a deep sleep.

Barbara lay there awake, or lay there believing she was awake. Already an hour had passed. She considered turning on WNCN, listening to the all-night concert, majestic, lovely, but interrupted every hour for news, the same news over and over again, the same voice: Fleetwood's mellifluous tones. That wouldn't help. She couldn't turn her mind off; her thoughts were like phosphorescent fireflies. She tried to conjure up a fantasy which would lull her to sleep. At first, there was nothing but black space; no sounds. Barbara watched the shadows on the walls and ceilings move about. She discovered that if she moved her legs back and forth, as though bicycling, the shadows danced about, reminding her of the horse she had ridden during the summer out West. There were silhouettes of pines where they rose out of the fog, which lay all around the meadow. She saw a girl running along an overgrown path, crisscrossed by blackberry bushes, poison ivy and sumac; the girl tripped on a rock and fell into a space between several boards. It was a well. She tumbled into darkness, like a limp body caught by gravity. She awoke with pains in her neck, back and legs and lay motionless, sweating, her heart madly pumping blood through her body. Her forehead was hotter now; her throat hurt worse. A persistent throbbing threatened to burst the back of her throat.

Barbara couldn't tell what time it was. Darkness enshrouded the room and even covered the fluorescent numbers of her radio alarm. She guessed the time was between two and four; she pushed back the sheet and made her way, like a sleepwalker, to the door, which she opened for the cool draft of the long hall. Her parents' bedroom door, at the other end of the hall, was ajar. Their room was dark. She returned to bed, peeled off her nightgown and lay exposed to the black of the hall. In point of fact, she couldn't afford to waste more than a few hours on sleep. Her face and neck were cool and dry. She waited to drift off into snowy images. Finally, she lost consciousness.

It seemed hours later when she awoke with a start, scared. Sweat dripped from the silky, blond hair under her arms. Her stomach burned and her head throbbed. She had dreamed of a trout swimming frantically back and forth near the shoreline of a lake. Several times its tail slapped at the black surface of the wind-swept lake. A fisherman in waders, pulled to his armpits, cast a fuzzy, black-green fly toward the fish. The trout would not rise; it turned and darted into deep water, where it met a large pike, resting near the rocky bottom. Suddenly the trout attacked the pike in a convulsive thrust, butting its snout against the fish's belly. The pike swam several yards away, turned, briefly puzzled, looked back at the trout and plunged into a school of minnows. The pike opened his mouth. Small fish, one after another, as though drawn by a magnetic field, entered a cavernous tooth-lined mouth.

Barbara lay motionless. Suddenly, her abdomen tightened. Acid sprayed her stomach and sent fire up her gullet. In a reflex, her throat convulsed, the cords of her neck pumped, and she vomited everything in a projectile spurt over her pillow and eiderdown. An acrid stench of sickness filled the room. Flecks of blood in the vomit frightened her. Wiping her mouth, she sensed a second gastric rush was approaching. She ran to her bathroom, sat before the toilet with her legs embracing the pearl-white bowl. It happened again. Her eyes were like rocks, ready to pop out with the next explosion of her stomach; her hands were white and cold, as they grasped the rim of the bowl.

"My poor little doll; you're sick," Susan said, as she stood over Barbara, sleepy, kissing her forehead, not knowing quite what to do.

Barbara sighed. Susan had appeared from nowhere. But Barbara wanted to take care of herself. She braced herself for the next regurgitation. She recalled that during her nursery school years, frequent vomiting attacks—they were called "bilious attacks" by the pediatrician's nurse—would wake her up with a start. Her mother would suddenly appear from nowhere, wash her face, give her sips of ice-cold ginger ale and take her to her parents' bedroom. For the rest of the night, she would sleep next to her mother, on the edge of the bed, which gave her a reason to hold onto the mother's arms and shoulders. Her father was never disturbed from his sleep. Sometimes he wasn't even there; he was at the hospital, bringing another baby into the world.

"Oh, Mom, I don't know what happened," Barbara whispered to her mother. Her throat felt scalded. Susan took a large wad of toilet paper and wiped Barbara's face.

"You must have had some bad mussels at dinner," Susan said, shaking her head, trying to drive out sleep. "They can make you deathly ill. Rose should be more careful and sort out the bad ones."

"I saw Rose cleaning the mussels," Barbara said. "They looked okay to me. I don't know what caused it."

"Never mind. You'll be all right now."

Susan wiped Barbara's face again and went to the kitchen for some ginger ale. Barbara vomited again, but now only strands of mucus, slight rewards for the effort, and they hung there from her pale, trembling lips, as though put there to make her ugly.

"Try to control your vomiting, Barbara," Susan said, returning from the kitchen. "Here, drink this; at least you'll have something in your stomach to work on."

Barbara sipped the ginger ale after wiping her mouth dry. The cold glass against her sweaty palm distracted her for a moment from the pains in her stomach. Susan combed and brushed Barbara's hair, tied it in a ponytail and had her get into clean pajamas. She sat on the edge of the bed and waited for her daughter to fall asleep.

"Mom, I'd like you to sit here. It's been a long time." Several tears rolled down her face. "Remember how I used to get sick as a little girl during the night and have to come into your bedroom?"

"Those were the days," Susan said. Her eyes closed tight oozing a few tears. "You were in kindergarten and determined to learn to read. After dinner we would sit for an hour or so, learning phonetics. By the time you reached first grade, you were the best reader in the class." She bit her lip, moist-eyed and grim.

"I'm getting sleepy now," Barbara said, yawning. "I won't kiss you in case I have something."

"Good night, Barbara."

Susan turned off the bedlamp, leaving Barbara alone in the dark. Resting on her propped-up pillows, she could look out her bedroom window and see far into Queens. An occasional blue light flickered over an approach to LaGuardia Airport, an approach she knew well. Only a couple of weeks ago she had flown from Denver in a DC-10, which she feared might miss the runway and land on the mud flats of Flushing Bay. She was too young to die.

Barbara felt a little better. Her stomach no longer hurt; only the abdominal muscles were sore. The ginger ale had soothed her throat. A dull headache lingered above the eyes. She would be well enough to go to school; there was no point in staying home. She hated the "soaps" and quiz shows on TV. Only Rose would be home, anyway. And she didn't want to fall behind at school. She turned over on her left side, closed her eyes and almost instantly she was dreaming.

Solemn-faced, her right arm sawing across the front of her as she jogged, Barbara entered the reservoir path by pushing aside a secret panel under the astrodome. The water was an azure blue in the early morning light—a delicate blue she connected with Cape Cod. Along the running path were fruit and nut trees. Peaches and pears hung from sagging branches, and opaque, purplish grapes, sparkling with dew, lined the path. Little children hid in the bushes, watching runners go by. She waved at them, not knowing what else to do, and started to run. Along the west side of the track a white stallion cantered past; a rider in a black body suit waved at her. It was her mother, partly hidden by wisps of fog in the hollow.

She awoke and turned off the alarm, missing it at first. If she went back to sleep, the dream might continue, but it might also be another dream. Jumping out of bed and peeling off her pajamas, she went through her calisthenics but decided to forego stationary running. Although she had no outfit, she would start running the reservoir track today. She put on a baggy white t-shirt, old jean-shorts from the summer and her sneakers. She walked briskly to the front door.

"Aren't you having breakfast, Barbara?" Rose asked, stirring the porridge. She smiled, motherly.

"Yeah, of course," she said, noncommittal in tone. "I'm just going for a little run. I'll be back in about thirty minutes."

Barbara could feel the doorman's eyes on her. His smile hid curiosity. She walked over to Fifth Avenue and entered the park near the 86th Street transverse. The sky was lead-gray, full of blackbirds; and the stands of trees were dark, still misty from last night's rain. She passed several old men, walking mongrel dogs, hesitated for a few seconds before running through early traffic on the circular drive, and ascended a gentle hill to the jogger's path at the southeast corner of the reservoir. She swung her long legs over the rusted top strand of the wire fence and stepped on the dirt path. The sky began to open, and the sun hit the dew like music; now the trees were silver and gold, still and breathless. Barbara began running north, counter-clockwise, along the heart-shaped course. On the east stretch, strength began to build up in her legs. Not since the summer did she feel so competitive. She increased her speed to pass a young, black man and sprinted to the north corner. Two paunchy, bald men looked around at her with surprise; they sped up for ten yards and then, fatigued, discouraged, they drifted to the right to let her pass.

Her breathing was near perfect. Each inspiration was deep and smooth, in rhythm with the world. She felt no pain in her body. Her skin was warm and moist with droplets of sweat resting on her neck and a trickle running between her shoulder blades.

She turned west and ran along the top of the "heart" of the reservoir path. Two runners, in their thirties, were hanging on the chain-link fence which enclosed the reservoir. Both were gasping for breath, like prisoners trying to break away. She caught up with another runner, dressed in a loose sweat suit, who, on hearing her quick steps, accelerated a few yards to keep ahead. She looked more carefully at the runner, noticed the runner's curved hips, and realized her competitor was a thin, young woman. Barbara ran faster to exhaust the woman, to run her into the ground, repeating the maneuver until she assumed her competitor had depleted her energy. With a deep breath, she shot past the woman, who threw up her arms with a shriek of "Oh, shit!".

Turning south, Barbara saw a middle-aged woman, dressed in a black pantsuit and a short, black seal jacket, coming toward her with mincing steps. A miniature white poodle paced the woman. A flock of mallards, taking flight over her head, startled Barbara. Further along were half a dozen Canadian geese, bobbing unperturbedly on the reservoir. She recalled some remarks made by an ornithologist in Boulder last summer: fewer Canadian geese are now migrating south of New York and Long Island. She wondered whether these geese would stay on the reservoir through the coming winter. What would they eat when New York was frozen in January and February?

Barbara slowed her pace when she reached the south end of the reservoir; she continued toward the south pump house. A group of people was near the house. Several men rested against the stone wall. A couple of young black men, probably boxers, were running backwards. Three Hispanic teenagers with black berets were doing push-ups; they seemed to have lost count. The rest were motionless, watching Barbara run past.

"Hey, José! Look at that blond cunt," a young man, shirtless, said in a voice loud enough to be heard across the reservoir.

There were catcalls and laughter. One youth, a green beret perched on his head, held his middle finger up at Barbara.

"Yeah, look at those tits bounce up and down," another yelled, his eyes like a crazy toad's. His friends bent over, convulsing with laughter.

Barbara pretended that she had heard nothing; she increased her speed.

"Man, look at that nice, little, fat ass wiggle," another said. His face was lumpy; his eye lids swollen and red-rimmed.

An older man in a gray windbreaker and a brown center-crease Brooks Brothers hat—much like her father's hat—darted past her in a clockwise direction. She knew the boys at the pump house wouldn't comment on how funny he looked.

Barbara sprinted down the pedestrian path to Fifth Avenue, shot by several three-piece suited businessmen who were waiting for a Wall Street express bus.

"A good run, Miss Barbara?" the old elevator man asked. His bony hand whitened at the knuckles as he slid the door closed.

"Beautiful, Mike, beautiful!"

At the apartment door Barbara realized that she had forgotten her key. She rang the bell gently.

"Good morning, Mom," Barbara said, forcefully.

"Barbara! How could you run after having been sick most of the night?" Susan asked, disbelief written across her face.

"Oh, I feel fine. In fact, I'm hungry," Barbara said, going to shower and dress. "I'll be with you and Daddy in a few minutes."

Barbara pulled off her soggy t-shirt and shorts. While she adjusted the shower, she wondered why she had told her mother how hungry she was. It wasn't true—just a silly remark a little girl makes to a mother to please her. She was a big girl now; really, a young woman who should know better.

"I'll only have a cup of tea, without milk," Barbara mumbled to herself. She continued washing between her legs. A lot of sweat had collected.

"Hello Luigi," Susan said, with a half-nod, as she and Alice entered the restaurant. "We have reservations for one-thirty . . . Mrs. Gordon." They were seated by the *maitre d'*, who nodded to a young waiter to take the drink order.

For a moment, the two women sat starling at each other. Alice's angular face and black hair speckled with gray contrasted with Susan's graying blond hair and slightly heavy jowls. Both knew their differences. Alice put on her black-rimmed glasses to read the menu. Only then did she look as though she might be part of the publishing world.

"No pasta for me," Susan said, tipping her head down and looking up from under long, heavily made-up eyelashes. "Ah, veal and a tossed green salad—and a new Vouvray."

"That sounds good," Alice said. "It's good getting away from the office, " she added, sighing. "I can't wait for the weekend. What a dreadful day. We commissioned William Blackworth to write his experiences at the White House when the Watergate thing broke." She splashed her hand out with disgust. "We gave him a $50,000 advance. Today he delivered the manuscript: it's boring, trite, partisan and stupid!"

"What are you going to do now?" Susan asked quizzically.

"We can't demand the money back. His book is unpublishable. I'm sure it will go to court, and the lawyers will be richer."

"They always are," Susan said with a shrug. "Do you have anything good coming out this fall?"

"A curious commercial novel is just going into galleys. It's by a young English doctor, a Harley Street type, Royal College of Physicians and all that stuff." Alice now spoke rapidly and loudly, her diction precise, as always—the diction of the stage. "The story line takes a young man—a poor London kid from Elephant and Castle—through London University, St. Thomas's Hospital and his ascent into English society. He finally becomes the Queen's physician. He's a Mayfair snob—a classy Marcus Welby." She began to laugh, without meaning to. "I finally persuaded him to put a sex scene in near the beginning, a little perverse—some 'S & M,' as the kids say. He has literary aspirations—a Somerset Maugham or something. The novel will appeal to doctor freaks, Anglophiles and voyeurs."

Susan looked up with new interest. "I wish Don would write something original, at least interesting. He keeps cranking out dreary medical articles on high blood pressure in pregnant women." Anger was in her voice. "He writes the same stuff over and over, saying what other people have said, sometimes adding his own two cents, but mostly old wine in old bottles."

"You don't think his work helps people?" Alice asked with a twinkle in her eye.

"Eschatologically speaking, it's bullshit! He claims his blood pressure research got him his professorship." She found a sardonic grin. "Maybe so, but it would have been smarter for him to have done the early work on the pill. He'd have an international reputation, and, I'm sure, a large block of stock in a drug house."

"Well," Alice said, half-turned from Susan, engrossed in tearing off a piece of bread. "At least, he's happy doing what he wants."

"Happy? Hell, no! He's the most desperate man I know." She emptied her glass of wine, "All he thinks about is survival. He worries about keeping his professorship, getting Federal grants, his clout with the president of the medical center—whom he wouldn't ordinarily have a drink with—his Nielsen ratings with medical students, his credibility among the residents, the reliability of his tailor, the likelihood of Gucci discontinuing his favorite slipper-shoe, and the possibility of Xerox plummeting. Christ!" She hesitated for a moment. Her hands were pressed to her face as if to keep it from shattering. "He also worries about his twin brother, Joel. He's the one who flunked out of Harvard Law School and now works as a guard at a museum."

"What can I say!" Alice flagged off the waiter. She put her glasses back on, brushed a crumb from her cheek, and then she leaned her white stiff hands on the edge of the table. "I hate Italian desserts—so unimaginative," she said, speaking rapidly and loudly, her diction again like that of an actress. " . . . George fussed all summer. At the West Hampton house we saw a lot of publishers and writers. Did George help me with the entertainment? He couldn't understand I had to meet people." She kept thinking how men become weird after their fortieth birthday. "He only complained, whined, nuzzled me all summer for affection. Men are little boys masquerading as warriors."

"Perhaps George had nothing of his own to satisfy him during the summer," Susan said, feeling smart about her interpretation.

"Exactly, that was part of the trouble," Alice said, putting down her coffee. Her wide-open eyes were like a doe's. "He had planned to do some painting on the beach—he has a show opening at the Rapoli gallery on 79th Street—but all he did was to buzz around me. It could have been a productive summer for both of us." She half-heartedly picked at some lint on her sleeve, not cognizant of her pained grimace. "Cedric was off to camp for eight weeks. But tell me, darling, how was your summer?" Alice waved and smiled at a middle-aged man at the far table. "That's George Solomon of Cartax Productions . . . Sorry, go on."

The Palisades Parkway lay ahead, a maccadam corridor cut through a forest bursting with the colors of fall. The sky was an amazing blue and the morning danced with sunlight. The Gordons had already passed through Englewood Cliffs, beyond the smoked-glass, aluminum corporate headquarters which had taken flight years ago from New York City. The transition from the city to the country seemed sudden. Yet it was deceptive, for beyond the corporate strip, hidden behind a wide barrier of trees, were rows of costly ranch and colonial houses, set on two-acre plots of zoned isolation. The Gordons were now approaching the next protective zone where the mental and retarded communities of Rockland State Hospital and Letchworth Village sequestered the state's less successful citizens.

Harriman and Bear Mountain State Parks lay ahead, worn-down mountains covered with autumnal colors. After the wet summer and light frost several days ago, the Columbus Day weekend came at the peak of fall foliage.

"What a terrific weekend to be going up to Cornwall," Susan said as they turned off Route 9W to 128. "I'm glad we didn't go to Stowe," she said. "Vermont leaves must be past their peak." She lit a cigarette. "You're right, Don. The cliff road above the Hudson will be nicer."

Don slowed down as they drove by the north gate of West Point. Cadets in their blue and gold uniforms were drilling as usual on Saturday morning. Families, friends and lovers were gathering around the drill field. Station wagons were filled with children and shaggy dogs who stared out the back windows as the cars turned to park. Some children waved at them, hoping for a little attention. Angus growled at a German shepherd that poked its snout out the window at him.

"Come on, Dad," Barbara said, pouting. "Let's keep going. There's nothing I hate more than West Point . . . stupid place."

"That's because you can never be in the service—not even the army," Peter said. His friend, Jeremy, a guest for the weekend, chuckled.

"He's such an insufferable bore," Barbara replied. She rubbed her ear. "I can't wait to get to the house so I can go for a walk in the woods. Black Rock Forest will be beautiful this weekend. Next weekend all those crazy deer hunters will be out. Let's hurry."

"Look who's talking," Susan said, slightly smiling, revealing her overbite. "We got a late start because of your running."

Barbara looked back to her book, which she had started to read after crossing the George Washington Bridge.

"I thought you read *Death in Venice* several summers ago when we were in Italy," Susan said. A muscle began to twitch in her cheek. "Why does it fascinate you so much now?"

"It's a fascinating example of how two people can be so involved with each other—never before knowing each other—to the point of being together as one human being. Once Aschenback could do this with

Tadzio, he felt almost reborn, created new and whole, so it didn't matter if he died of cholera."

"I never thought you cared much, Barbara, about such stuff," Don said, watching her in the rear view mirror. "Your mother and I raised you two kids as non-religious Jews," he said, still looking straight ahead as if Barbara were merely some annoying stranger. A minute later he decided to say what came to his mind. "Barbara, my girl, human beings are animals, just the same as a dog or cat." He was feeling more angry. "Religion is strictly a gimmick people use to get power over other people."

"You can't stop me from thinking about God," Barbara snapped. "We've been reading Descartes's *Meditations* in philosophy class."

Don opened his hand on the steering wheel, making a kind of shrug. He had never been interested in philosophy at Harvard. He had missed Santayana and Whitehead by some years, but his parents had met and admired them. Any intellectual European Jew would. They used to tell the story of Royce and Santayana, sitting all night before a fire in the library, both silent and meditative, and at the end thanking each other, for the interesting evening. Philosophers always struck him as introverted types. Even John Wild's course in existentialism didn't excite him; it did Barbara's mother. Don's mind, as he himself knew, was not theoretical but practical. It never struck him that it might be of value to wonder what he really believed in for the simple reason that belief was obviously of no practical use. For him, philosophy was simply the transformation of emotions into ideas, vague ones at that.

Barbara decided to lecture: "Descartes says that he possesses an idea of God, the character of which involves all perfection. Now, among the perfections which the idea contains is existence, because it is perfection to exist. Therefore, Descartes says, bad exists." She smiled, satisfied she had remembered the tricky rhetoric.

"Do you believe that?" Don asked

"Are you kidding? Of course not!" An awkward silence fell between them; she quickly broke it. "To say that bad actually exists because one has an innate idea of God which involves the idea of God's existence is to confuse the ideal order with the real or actual order. It's a lot of crap. Do you want to hear his other arguments?"

Angus stood up to find a more comfortable spot on the back seat. Susan took a nail file out of her purse and smoothed a rough edge. "So I can conclude," Susan said, "that you don't believe in God. Well, neither do I, Barbara." Susan half-expected a voice to come out of Don. "Your father still does, in his quiet New England way, but he can't defend his position, certainly not against your metaphysical big guns." Barbara's mother turned her head to stare blindly, perhaps irritably, in Barbara's direction. "I never realized you had such a fine philosophical mind. You talk like something out of Plato."

"Please, Mother," Barbara said in a high, thin voice.

Approaching a small farm outside of Cornwall, they stopped to let sheep cross the road. The herder was driving the animals toward a barn. She watched the sheep move; some darted across the road, others wandered, some just stopped.

After they drove past the farm, they entered Cornwall-on-Hudson, one of many diminished Hudson River towns. The old Exxon station had closed down in the last few years because fewer cars now used Route 128 since the Thruway had been built. A boarded-up movie house would never be painted again. And the old gourmet delicatessen had finally shut its doors. Some S.S. Pierce canned goods, covered with dust, were still stacked in the dirty window. Don made a sharp left and began climbing Mountain Road to their house. A deer bounded off into the pines, as they turned into the white, pebbled driveway.

"It's strange for deer to come this close to the house, even in dead winter when they're hungry. Do you think," Barbara asked, "the deer season is already open?"

"No, not yet," Don said, wondering.

"I hope not," Barbara said. "Angus and I want to go for a hike in the Black Rock Forest."

"Are you and Jeremy going?" Don asked Peter, perfunctorily.

"No, not us," Peter replied. "We're going over to Alan's, going bike riding instead."

"Don't you want some lunch first?" Susan asked, concerned. "It won't take much time. We won't be long at the supermarket."

"No, I'll find something in the refrigerator," Barbara said. "Don't worry."

The parents took the luggage into the house and then drove off to the shopping center. Barbara helped herself to a carton of plain yogurt and had some clear tea. She took her lunch out into the backyard and stretched out on a chaise. Sitting under a dark-leafed maple tree, now ablaze with red and orange, she studied the yellow-green valley that once had been a glacial river, a graveyard of terrifying beasts. Angus lay down next to her and watched her eat. As she finished her yogurt, she felt sorry for the old sheepdog; she returned to the kitchen and brought out a box of Ritz crackers, which, one by one, she fed the animal until they were all gone.

The backyard had been one of her favorite places in past years. She'd sit in the gazebo in the middle of the garden reading or meditating or dozing, or maybe watching crows make circles high above her, or she'd look at the mountains that rose up, awesome, like God, beyond the highway, or the old copper beach tree in the yard. The landscape always fascinated her; it was transformed by changes of light. Her parents' fifteenth anniversary party had been in the yard. Streamers of bright papers and clouds of confetti had filled the air that night. A huge tent had been erected for the bar and buffet in case of rain. A rock band had played into the night until the masters at the local boarding school complained to the police chief, Mr. Morrison, that the music was keeping their boys awake. Barbara sipped her tea. Angus looked up to see why the crackers had stopped. She recalled her eighth birthday party in this yard. A dozen girls from the city had been invited. Her father had blown up balloons and made crepe paper displays. All the girls played "hide and seek" while her father put the hamburgers and hot dogs on the grill. Barbara went to hide in a thicket of small spruce trees. For an instant, she knew with a part of her mind that behind her, motionless, was a living creature. Suddenly, something moved and tried to grab her by the leg, sending her screaming to her father. It was a chimpanzee, standing by the edge of the lawn and watching them with great interest. Her father took her by the hand. He had heard at the hospital about chimpanzees biting people. Scared by the onlookers, the animal scrambled up an oak tree and then swung to a tall pine.

The monkey had stared at them and made little grunts as though hoping for some consideration. Her father tossed a hot dog toward the animal; but the monkey let out a shriek and swung to the next branch.

No one knew where the monkey had come from. The nearby zoo had no monkeys—only the indigenous animals of the Hudson highlands. No neighbors, they knew, kept monkeys. One of the girls—Barbara remembered: it was Janet—asked what the monkey would do when winter came. They all agreed that he would die. Sometimes it went down to –20° F in the woods.

Don decided to call the local police; and when the police chief arrived, he grumbled about the monkey and all the calls there had been. Barbara

would never forget how the policeman walked slowly over to the tree
and peered up at the monkey. It yelped and jumped to another branch.
The chief explained to her father that his men had not been able to
catch this monkey. Pointing to white spittle about the monkey's mouth,
the policeman warned of rabies and the danger to all the little girls. He
knew about such things. The chief then drew his .45 revolver and shot
the chimpanzee from the tree. Barbara felt weak, sick to her stomach, as
she again saw the monkey falling head over heels to the ground. He hit
with a dull thump and twitched for a few minutes. The police chief—it
was Tim O'Malley, the cop who used to beat up his wife and probably
still did—tossed the bloody carcass into the trunk of his patrol car.
Barbara never forgave O'Malley. She probably would see him this
weekend. To this day, she gave him dirty looks, even though he
probably had no idea why. Or perhaps he thought that Barbara was
some hippie kid who hated cops.

"Let's go, Angus," Barbara said to the dog. "Remember, you're not to
chase rabbits." Angus looked back at her, as though hurt.

It was a warm afternoon for October. They walked up Mountain
Road toward the main highway. The boarding school came into view
just as a Ford station wagon stopped in a cloud of dust.

"Get in, Angus. It's Mrs. Snyder."

"Hello. Thanks for stopping." She gazed at the old woman, solid and
warm. "How have you been? I haven't seen you since last spring."

"That's right, Barbara," she said. She had a red face, curly silver hair,
prominent teeth. Her hands, clutching the steering wheel, were fat. "I
was in the hospital for my gall bladder. How have you been?"

"Just fine, thanks."

"You look a bit thin, Barbara." She leaned toward her, smiling, but
failing to meet her eyes. "You should stop by and have some of my lentil
soup . . . maybe even some cherry cheesecake."

"No, I'm as fat as ever," Barbara said tartly.

"Angus and I are going for a hike in Black Rock. Could you drop us off
near the yellow trail?"

"Glad to. How's the family?" She watched the road carefully as they
came to the busy highway. "Your father still delivering scads of little
babies?"

"He's cut down his practice a little. He says he wants more time for
research."

"Hey, look at that woodchuck over there," the old lady said. "Cute
little feller, ain't he? How's this, honey?" Mrs. Snyder asked.

"Great," Barbara said, turning away from the woman. "The trail starts right over there."

"Be careful," she said, pointing her index finger at Barbara to emphasize her point. She drove them on to the beginning of the trail. The car jounced over ruts and rocks and clattered over the old wood and iron bridge. "Mr. Johnson told me the other day there's been a lot of rattlesnakes in the forest."

"I will. Thank you. 'Bye." She shoved in the clutch, shifted to second and lurched forward.

Barbara and Angus ran across the highway to a gravel road leading into the forest. A semi whined up the hill and disappeared. She went under the gate, kept closed, except to the forest master and workmen. A sign, BLACK ROCK FOREST, HARVARD UNIVERSITY SCHOOL OF FORESTRY. Another sign, NO HUNTING, FISHING OR CAMP FIRES, announced their entry into the Harvard forest. With Angus running a few yards ahead, Barbara walked toward the mountains. The stream that paralleled the road was rushing white, foamy water toward a creek that would take it to the Hudson River. A blackbird whistled. The pine forest was dense here, but, off to the left, beyond centuries-old piles of boulders, she could see fresh dirt and rock sprawled over an embankment. For some reason, the highway workmen had dumped truckloads of fill; part of the dump had slid into the shadow-filled stream, diverting it through a small hollow. A fish hawk flew over and registered a shrill that sounded like a complaint.

She walked beyond the curve in the road where the stream was dammed, forming a muddy, silted pond with high, dry grass, seaweed green, along its banks. Willow trees hung motionless, their tips still. She and Angus climbed over a crumbling stone wall and a snarl of old barbwire. She bathed in the feeling of leaves against her face; the ache of her cramped legs, the smell of the moist earth felt good. An old man sat fishing next to the spillway. Smoke circled about his head from his stained meerschaum pipe.

"Catch anything, Mister?" Barbara asked.

"Just a couple of old, hungry eels," the wizened man grunted through yellow stumps of teeth. "There're a couple of pickerel in this old pond, but they ain't going nowhere."

Angus finished smelling the man's cuff and ran ahead, maintaining his usual path-finding distance from Barbara. She was pleased the old man had killed the eels. If he hadn't, they might have reached the

Hudson River and fed on the spawning striped bass in the deep channel by Storm King Mountain.

The road narrowed to a two-rut lane and ended; Barbara had to choose now the "yellow" or "blue trail." She decided on the latter; she could follow the stream to the upper reservoir. The blue circles on the trees along the narrow trail contrasted with the autumn yellows, reds, magentas and tans. Evergreens and maples and birches with chalk-white trunks scarred with black stood on both sides of the trail. Their branches, interdigitating overhead, strained the sun's rays and made dark lines, like scratches, across the sky. A foot bridge, its bark long worn away, spanned a small, rocky tributary of the stream. Angus crossed the bridge; but, near the other side, his front paws slid between the logs. She grabbed Angus under his chest and lifted him to safety.

"You silly dog." She squeezed Angus's head to her bosom. "You wouldn't last ten minutes in Scotland. You'd run a flock of sheep right off a cliff and then follow them."

The trail climbed and made its labyrinthine way to the top of Honey Hill. Next to a clump of rocks, red and white flowers were singing with honey bees. Stepping over a snarled old root, Barbara noticed bits of tan, gray fur and skin. A large animal had fed on a racoon. Or perhaps wild dogs—coy dogs from the Adirondacks—were in the forest. The rangers supposedly had killed one in March. An old bushwacker behind Dorn Crest in Mountainville had once told her about local black bears and mountain lions. But she had doubted his stories. New York City was only sixty miles away.

She came into the meadow by the upper reservoir and paused in the shadow of a hundred-year-old oak. A group of men dressed in Tyrolean greens, apparently Austrian refugees, waved to her, as they disappeared along the trail leading to Mt. Misery.

Barbara stopped. She couldn't decide which branch of the trail to take. To follow the Austrians meant going south to Rattlesnake Hill and then out through Glycerine Hollow to Route 9W. There she would have to hitchhike back to Cornwall. She felt more like hiking to the Hudson River.

Barbara looked at her watch. It was two o'clock. She wasn't tired. Her new boots were not blistering her feet. She could keep going until dinner time. Angus lapped up some water from a spring.

Climbing over a fallen tree, Barbara was confronted by a large, white sign. The black letters were unfriendly, TRI-STATE POWER CORPORA-TION. NO TRESPASSING. BLASTING IN PROGRESS. Last spring the conservationists had defeated Tri-State, she thought. She saw some huge, yellow machinery, partly hidden by trees. She would do more than trespass; she would inspect. Several dozen bulldozers were lined up, one after another, all quieted by the long weekend. A swath of fresh dirt and rock stretched all the way to the highway. Already part of the mountain had been gouged out. She looked for the gas tanks of the bulldozers; she could put sand in them and stop them in their tracks. But a watchman must be in the area, she thought, and if caught, she would be made an example of the "crazy kids" who supported the conservationists' cause.

She walked on to the east peak of the mountain, where she could see New York to the south, Kingston to the north. Survey markers were everywhere. Axmen had already moved into the woods and cut oddly shaped, geometric patterns on the trees to be felled. Now she understood why there were deer near their house. In the rocky cliffs were drilled holes, painted bright red—blasting sites for attacks on the mountain.

She whistled to Angus to turn to a precipitous path, which dropped to the bottom of the mountain and the Cornwall Marina. She tripped as she made a sharp turn down the mountain; she grasped a tall birch and bruised her right shoulder and breast. She continued her descent by clutching some scrub brush by the side of the trail. Finally, she could see the tracks of the Penn Central below. She had forgotten about the West Branch trains; they were so few now, even across the river on the main line from New York to Albany. The railroads were dead. And there was only one tourist boat a day, passing Cornwall-on-Hudson. Several Victorian houses, once guest hotels for boat passengers at the turn of the century, now suffered from abject neglect.

The last few yards of the trail ended in a sheer drop. Barbara slid the rest of the way on her buttocks and walked to the tracks. She noticed that there wasn't much rust on the rails. There was still an occasional freight train from New York. She put a penny on the rail, hoping a train might come along soon, something she and her father used to do; and, after the train had passed, they would compare their squashed pennies. His was always larger.

She walked down the tracks toward the marina. The sky had turned a green gold, and the trees, now darkened by the approaching stormy weather, took on a new intensity, like space in a three-dimension viewer. Angus ran off into a thicket; he didn't answer her whistle. Out of both curiosity and concern, she followed Angus, pushing blackberry bushes aside, circling around the poison ivy and bending over to avoid branches of young maples. She walked back toward the base of the mountain. Still she couldn't see Angus ahead. There was a crack of a branch. She whistled to Angus. There was no sound now, only the croak of a frog, alone. She went on. The brush was now denser; gnats swarmed about her face. There was a green bog ahead, which she could barely make out. To the right was a pond covered by algae, a rough, green carpet, extending almost to the other side. She then crawled through the underbrush to a small meadow.

Barbara looked around again for Angus. It occurred to her that the dog might have circled back to the tracks and gone to the marina to beg for handouts from the yacht crews and dock hands. She was tired. There was a brisk south wind and a flickering of lightning in the west. The air was weighted and the storm much closer. She lay down in the deep grass by the edge of the pond, stretched out in the "corpse position" of yoga, and closed her eyes.

Suddenly, a heavy weight fell on her, making her breathless. She looked into the pale face of a young man, in his late twenties, dressed in a blue polo shirt and white duck pants. He must have come off a cabin cruiser at the marina, she thought.

"We're going to make love, baby," he whispered, leaning closer. "You're a beautiful girl."

The man brought himself to a kneeling position over her. As he tried to move her legs out, she jabbed her thumbs into his armpits, a karate blow she had learned at survival school during the summer. He shrieked in pain and fell back on the grass, limp for a moment. He began a second approach. She leaned back, pretending to be hurt and exhausted. She awaited his charge. As he flung himself toward her, she brought her knees to her chin, rolled back on her hips and let her feet fly at his chest. The force knocked him off center, sending him into a spin to the left. He tripped and fell forward, off the grassy embankment, face down into the green pond.

Barbara jumped up; and, knowing she had only a few seconds' advantage, frantically breathing in huge gulps, heart hammering, she ran through the brush toward the marina. Twigs and brambles scratched her arms and face. She heard the man crashing through the brush after her. Reaching the tracks, she ran to the marina. Angus was sitting on the dock by a sailboat, where a cocktail party was underway. Several girls were feeding him Fritos.

Barbara slipped into the clubhouse bathroom. Thunder shook the walls; lightning filled up the windows. Several open scratches on her cheeks, oozing blood and sweat, ran from her hairline. Bits of twigs and grass were stuck in her hair. She would never tell anyone about the incident. She had simply fallen into some brambles and scratched herself. That was enough.

Barbara walked out of the clubhouse and shouted to Angus. The girls on the boat smiled and turned back to their party.

"Let's go home, Angus. It's time for your dinner," Barbara muttered. Rain started up, whispering in the leaves, and then it came hard and all at once as though it had been raining for hours. She felt old as the world.

It was one of those nights when a person shouldn't try to sleep. A vague worry, or some question, enigmatic, kept coming into Susan's mind and then escaping. Susan and Don had been to a dinner party at the Merriweather's. Several of the wives, hoping for a comeback in their old careers now that their children were off to college, had questioned Susan about her work. Flattery always excited her, and the two espressos after a rum cake dessert did nothing to calm her. She lay next to Don's tense body. Occasionally, a faint flash of light flickered across the ceiling as another jet made its descent into the approach pattern to LaGuardia. She lay back and closed her eyes again. There came to her mind—in full detail, she believed, though to concentrate now on any part of it would blur her thinking—images of a weekend once spent some years ago.

That evening they had met Mark and Jane Buckley, whom they hadn't seen in ten years, since the weekend they had spent with them in New Haven. Mark was working then as an editor at the University Press. Since the Buckleys also had a little girl the same age as Barbara, Susan and Don had taken her along for the weekend. On Saturday night, they had sat up late drinking with the Buckleys, and because of a hangover and the need for some exercise, the two couples took their daughters out for ice skating.

Susan remembered the Sunday afternoon well. Never would she forget it: Barbara was already up and playing with Miranda Buckley when Don and Susan went downstairs for brunch. Barbara looked more beautiful that day than ever. Rose had dressed her in the Austrian snowsuit her grandparents had sent her for Christmas. Her long, straight, blond hair had been combed, and she seemed light-hearted and

calmer than usual. Susan knew that this Sunday afternoon with the
Buckleys at the ice-skating rink would be more than just fun for them; it
was to be for Barbara a new experience with people. Susan welcomed
the chance to show Barbara how to skate, something which she had
enjoyed as a teenager.

In the early afternoon, the six of them drove into the parking lot by
the Yale Ice Rink. The Saarineen shell looked like a huge, white ladybug
with stripes, instead of spots running down its back. The rink was
crowded; the cold afternoon had driven a lot of faculty families to
indoor skating. After fumbling with Barbara's laces for a few minutes,
they took to the ice. Don and Susan had expected to creep around the ice
with Barbara. But they found her a strong, little skater; she never
seemed to get tired.

By late afternoon, the skaters were numerous, like flies on a piece of
candy. A continuous phalanx of skating figures, tall and short, broad
and narrow, slow and fast, steady and shaky, made up the constant,
undulating circle, moving clockwise. The ice had softened to the point
that the maintenance crew announced a refreeze in the next fifteen
minutes. Barbara caught her skate in a rut for the second time. She fell
spread-eagle on the wet ice. Although she complained of cold slush
against her skin, she insisted on continuing. Susan admired her and
suggested to Barbara that she skate a few feet ahead of her. If Barbara
fell again, Susan could catch her by scooping her up between her legs.

The three skaters enjoyed their last turn around the rink. Susan was
telling Don how tired she felt—mostly in her legs—when suddenly
Susan saw a small form, prone, with outstretched arms several feet
ahead of her. She couldn't stop in time; instead, she spread her legs
wide, hoping Barbara would pass through the safe triangle. Unable to
stop immediately, she turned to smile reassuringly at Barbara and
found her lying on her side frozen in fear and pain. Susan wondered if
she had struck her face against the ice and cut her lip on a tooth.

"Oh, my God, Susan," Don screamed, as he reached Barbara first.
"You've cut her little finger off."

Susan's body went numb. She saw Barbara's little finger, sharply
severed just below the last joint. Its tip lay in a red puddle on the ice.
More and more people encircled the sobbing child. Susan's impulse was
to scoop Barbara up in her arms and protect her.

"We've got to find the fingertip. Move back everyone," yelled a tall,
gray-haired man. He bent over Barbara, pulled out a fresh, white
handkerchief from his back pocket and wrapped up the pink tissue.

"I'm Dr. Stone." He put the small bundle in Don's jacket pocket. "Take your little girl to Yale-New Haven Hospital immediately. Dr. Fielding, the plastic surgeon there, is on call today."

Don drove so Susan could maintain pressure against the bleeding stump. Except for Barbara's moans, no one said anything. Susan could only think of getting the finger sewed together. What effect would this have on Barbara's life, she wondered.

Dr. Fielding and a surgical resident were waiting for Barbara and the blood-stained bundle. Someone had called from the rink. There was nothing to do but wait in the emergency room, full of shadows, chemical smells, and doctors and nurses moving about endlessly.

The end of October always brings a sadness to the city. The foliage of Central Park, now past its peak, faced its end and everyone knew, not only the birds and squirrels, that cold winds and rains would soon blow across the Hudson.

An iron grayness hung over the city. Susan Gordon felt chilled as she walked down the street. Her day was full, too full, because of several unexpected meetings. She was tired, perhaps a little down; a trip to Bermuda would probably snap her out of it. Or a meeting in Barbados. But neither was in the offing.

Susan looked across her desk at her visitor. A short, plump man of sixty or so, an old Marxist who weathered the McCarthy purges of the fifties and went on to be the head of the School of Social Work, Charles Gross had just asked her to be the Elvina Livingston Professor of Research.

"Charles. Please excuse me," she said, all joy now, eyes bright as daggers but a little uneasy in his presence. "I have to make a call." She believed she owed him an explanation for this interruption; he might think her rude. "It's Don's forty-ninth birthday, and we're having a family dinner party for him.

"Sheila. Please call Dr. Gordon at the hospital. Better use the page operator.

"Charles. Your offer is sensational," she said, holding the receiver away from her ear. She stayed at her desk. It didn't seem appropriate to make this meeting less formal. "I'm pleased you think this well of me. I think I can handle it, but only if I have your support.

"Excuse me . . . Yes, Sheila. Thanks. Hello, Don! I just wanted to check with you about dinner. Are you sure you don't have a meeting tonight?"

"Yes, that's fine." She smiled into the phone.

"What a nice birthday present I got this morning." Don sounded excited, happier than he had been in months. "I've . . . I've been elected president of the International Obstetrical and Gynecological Society and asked to give the Stanley Lecture at the annual meeting in Paris this February. Will you come with me?"

"Sure, I can visit some Sorbonne people in Paris when you're at the meetings. Maybe we can go later to the South of France for a few days." A sudden emotion, almost like fear, leaped up into her stomach. "Have to hurry now, dear. We'll talk tonight. 'Bye."

"Don had some good news. He's been elected president of the International Society."

"Mmmm," Charles said, rubbing his chin. "But tell me, Susan, how does he feel about your career?"

"He's glad I'm happy." Her mind was clicking like a Geiger counter. "When Don was still a resident at Mass General, I was so depressed one morning I couldn't brush my teeth. Everything seemed so complicated. Barbara was a tiny baby." She reflected a moment, wondering how much to reveal. "I thought I had no talent for the academic. If anyone said I did, I wouldn't have believed him. A fool or ingratiator, I would have thought."

"How did you get out of it?" Charles asked, watching Susan closely.

"Don urged me to get into university work. He wanted me to be successful, like himself. He reassured me that Barbara would be all right, as long as we had a good nanny. Don's pride in me has helped Barbara be a confident young woman. She's doing marvelously in school, showing remarkable independence. We expect her to go to Radcliffe."

"Like Mom, eh?" Charles said with a smile. "I gather Don is thinking of dropping his teaching and administrative responsibilities. He made a remark at the party the other night."

"Don claims that after twenty years he's reached the top of the academic mountain and finds it barren and wind-swept." She sighed, eyes moving away, her mind far away for a moment. "'Above the timber line,' he says, 'not much grows.'"

"Isn't he practicing anymore?" Charles asked. His nose moved a little like a rabbit's nose, and his eyes met Susan's.

"Oh, yes, to a limited degree. He raised his fees to support his research. Our style hasn't suffered." She paused, flickering her tongue across her lower lip. "He hopes research will be his real contribution to the future."

"I want you to be frank with me, Susan." His hand moved slowly as he, squinting, reached for a cigarette. "How will Don feel about your new research job?"

"He's always encouraged me in the past, but I've noticed recently he seems lonely, wants me around a lot. Seems to resent my interest in the children, particularly Barbara." Her voice was more tentative than she felt. "But I guess this is all part of his mid-life thing."

Charles was distracted as he listened to Susan. He knew how he had been in his forties, how he had made all the usual mistakes, like shedding his first wife of nineteen years because she wasn't exciting in bed anymore. Five years later, his second wife turned out to be a young duplicate of the first. And not a very good one at that.

"Well, Susan, I have confidence in you—and Don for that matter." He said now, suddenly, "I want you to start January first. Will you be ready?"

"Of course, Charles," Susan answered.

Charles went over to Susan and kissed her on her cheek. Charles gone, she stared out the window, perfectly still.

Deeply in a journal and absorbed in some statistics, Susan jumped when her secretary buzzed her. "Mrs. Gordon here . . . Yes, Rose. I just wanted to go over the menu for tonight." She looked again at the white paper before her, her small cursive writing in black ink, and she touched the side of her reading glasses. "I thought we'd have the rack of venison Baden Baden with sauce Grant Venent. You remember how to cook it from last year?" He loves it, she thought to herself. "What about the rest of the dinner?"

"Barbara has planned everything, Mrs. Gordon," Rose said.

"Barbara? What do you mean?" Susan asked, perplexed.

"She made up a fine menu." This is crazy, Rose thought, swearing under her breath. "We start with a salmon ring, then go on to venison, rutabaga and carrot puree, chestnut puree and boules de neige tutti-frutti with creme Anglaise. She even picked the wines."

"Which ones?" Susan asked, alarmed, fingering a letter opener on the desk.

"Let me see," her tone was dark with hostility. "She wrote down the names. Bernkasteler Schlossberg '71, Nuits-Saint George Les Vaucrains '66, and Sparkling Vouvray. Sorry about my French."

"Oh, she thinks of everything. Is she there now, Rose?"

"Yes, she just came in. I'll put her on."

"Barbara? Hello dear." She spoke slowly, somewhat wearily, as though the whole thing had begun to bore her. "That's quite a menu. I couldn't have done better myself!" And then Susan said all at once, earnestly, "Could you make sure Rose gets it all together. Perhaps you should call the wine store so Rose doesn't get the names mixed up."

"Yes, I planned to," Barbara said. "I also thought I'd stop by at the hospital around six-thirty to make sure Daddy comes home on time. He might forget his birthday."

"Don't worry about that." Then, gently: "He'll be the first there. But why don't you stop at Bloomingdale's and pick up presents from you and Peter."

"Any ideas, Mother?" Barbara asked.

"Oh, maybe some ties—you know, designs like Liberty prints, or a turtleneck sweater." She heard her comments with the detachment of a benevolent god. "He could use a burnt-orange for his tan jacket."

"Yeah, I'll do that. We should be home by seven-thirty. And you?"

"The same time." She said, cagey, "Both Daddy and I have good news."

"I can't wait. Tell me now . . . Oh, okay, goodbye."

Don, after another dreary education committee meeting with the medical school deans, walked from the hospital board room to the self-service elevator and went up to the delivery floor. The clock in the nurses' station read 4:05; he checked the delivery board. It always reminded him of the old train arrival board at Grand Central Station: its little chalked numbers in neat boxes, a reminder of the times he traveled as a child with his parents back to Boston, after shopping trips to New York.

"I see Mrs. Beresford is still farting around," Dr. Gordon said to Miss Reynolds, the head nurse, a tough old-timer from Queen Charlotte's in London.

"We increased the Pitocin drip as you directed," she said, her jaw firm.

"She's still not dilating very fast. I'll go in and see her," he threatened. "Perhaps that will do the trick."

"She's in 802, Dr. Gordon."

Don walked down the long, green corridor. On the left were two delivery rooms, now occupied by groaning women. An Italian woman was screaming out in pain. Her doctor kept shouting at her, trying to get her to push her baby out. From the other room there were no sounds. He always believed it was a bad omen if neither shouts of pain nor cries of joy come from a delivery room. He knocked perfunctorily on the door of Room 802 and went right in. "Mrs. Beresford, I understand you're doing well," he said, trying to be positive. "Dr. Phillips tells me that we can expect the baby by dinnertime. How is your pain now, dear?"

"My back feels so tight and sore. Oh, oh . . . here comes another one." The woman, a thin brunette in her late twenties, grabbed at the sheets. Her back arched. "It's going to break." Her face reddened, her eyes fixed on the ceiling, and spit stuck to her lower lip.

"Your contractions should get stronger," Don predicted, as he sped up the I.V. Pitocin drip. The drops approached a trickle, like a slight leak in an old roof during a cloud burst.

"I'm going downstairs to tell your husband things are going well." He spoke with a senseless, grim smile. "Dr. Phillips and I will be with you so we know exactly when you're ready." He wondered why he was promising so much. The great Doctor Osler wouldn't have approved of this compliance to a patient. "You'll be all right, dear."

Don walked down the hall toward the doctors' lounge.

"Miss Reynolds, will you please call down to Mr. Beresford and tell him his wife is progressing as expected. He can join her in the room, if he promises not to get nervous."

The nurse smiled indulgently.

"I'll be in the lounge." Sadness, tension, anger, God knew what filled up his chest like fluid. "Tell Dr. Phillips to let me know when she's ready to pop. Tell him that I must be home by seven and have no intentions of returning tonight."

There was no other doctor in the lounge. Don went to the large bay window that overlooked the Queensborough Bridge and the East River. The tide, having turned against the current, white-capped the river. A coal barge, its bow hidden by spray, was being pushed up the river by a puffing tug. Traffic was accumulating early on the East River Drive, bunches of cars every forty to fifty yards. They were men who could go home after four. A young couple walked along the drive by the river. He wondered why these simple activities of life now appealed so much to him. An Airedale ran ahead of the couple, trying, for a minute, to keep up with the barge. Don turned; he noticed the clock now at 4:15. He sat down on the leather sofa, worn thin by generations of impatient obstetricians. Fatigue settled in his legs, but his mind remained busy. The *New York Magazine* caught his attention. He paged through an article on "The Unsinkable Barbara Walters Talks" and settled on the crossword puzzle at the back. That it had come from the *London Sunday Times* appealed to him; but his enthusiasm was dampened when he bogged down on 9 across. They were probably right, he thought; this must be the "world's most challenging crossword." More than his legs were tired now; he propped up several leather cushions from a chair and stretched out. His back muscles relaxed a little—but not his jaw muscles—and he knew that he wouldn't go to sleep. This was the best he could do until Mrs. Beresford was ready for him. He hated to wait for women, more than he hated to wait for other things in life. If he could justify it, he would induce every delivery. He saw no reason to keep three people waiting.

Don picked up the first section of the *Times*. There was the usual Watergate news. He had watched the hearings over the summer; he was pleased by the roundup and then bored by it all. The baby he was to deliver would also be disillusioned some day. He was glad that he hadn't been fooled by that Kennedy idealism of the '60s. He suspected Kennedy had tried to kill Castro. And Mayor Lindsay had proven to be more ineffectual than the worst party hack. Administration was the same anywhere, whether in Washington, New York, or a university medical center. There was always a permanent government that never changes.

He finished the first section of the *Times* and turned to the family page. He was always interested in reviews of new restaurants. An article on single mothers caught his eye. Sheer crap, he thought; any woman needs a man to help with the children. Beneath the article was a two-column description of Michelin-starred restaurants in Great Britain. The nine designated restaurants in London interested him; he knew most of them well. Rules, Walton's and the Connaught Hotel were old friends; Le Verité was a questionable acquaintance. He and Susan would have to visit the place again and meet the owners, the Jacon brothers. A friendship might develop.

He picked up the phone and called the delivery room.

"Dr. Phillips?" He hoped he didn't sound frantic—just properly impatient. "What's happening with our Mrs. Beresford?"

"I'd guess a little more dilatation is needed," the young doctor said. "I'll call you, Dr. Gordon, as soon as we're ready to go."

"Thanks. But try not to guess."

Don sighed. How nice it would be if the doctors' lounge were like the Harvard Club and a waiter could take his order for a vodka on the rocks while he waited for that prima donna in Room 802. His thoughts went back to London and the six months he spent there at Queen Charlotte's Hospital. He had found himself transported from midway through a Mass General residency to London, where he was the young, rich American doctor, generously provided for by Queen Charlotte's, looked upon by the staff as a fascinating oddity, and even shepherded by the Queen's obstetrician, Sir Anthony Mason, who saw to it that his young Boston bachelor was invited to the more interesting parties in London. Those were the days: the excitement of residency life in a hospital, the doctor-nurse games over midnight coffee, kooky dinner parties in the West End, visits to private "after-hours" clubs. This is how he had met Susan.

He had been invited to dinner at the American ambassador's near Regents Park. It was part of a Fulbright-Marshall student exchange program. The whole evening was still very vivid to Don. He had immediately noticed Susan talking to the ambassador. Her figure and poise—the way she held her head when she talked—prompted him to ask for an introduction. He was told that she was a Radcliffe junior, doing a stint at the London School of Economics. He found her bright, as he had expected. They immediately were fascinated with each other, probably because they were so different in many respects. Susan was from Brooklyn and a Polish-Jewish background. Her ancestors had come from Silesia, where they had worked for decades in the coal mines. Her parents owned a candy store, a Momma-Papa operation; the family lived upstairs. He didn't question her ability to escape from this background. He spotted her extraordinary energy, apparent in her face, speech and manner, the first time he saw her; it got her out of the store. Likewise, Susan was intrigued with him. The son of a history professor at Harvard, a well-to-do refugee from Vienna in the early thirties, was a novelty to Susan, as were the intricacies of the Cambridge establishment. Don knew from the beginning that he could offer Susan a new life, as well as a guarantee she would never have to go back to the Bronx. And Susan admired his eagerness to explore new places and ideas and meet interesting people. He had changed parts of his own past that he found burdensome, like his name, which had been Gudonowski.

Now he liked the name of "Gordon." It had taken a long time to get used to it. Still he had to laugh when he thought of the "Gordon family." The "House of Gordon"; it sounded like a gin ad from *The New Yorker*.

Quarter to five. How many times had he looked at *that* clock over the years. "Come on, lady," he muttered to himself out loud. "Let's get on with it."

He lived four months with Susan in London. They had a pleasant little flat off Chandos Place. What seemed like a happy affair turned out to be marriage. When he finished his elective in May, he returned to Harvard, leaving Susan at the London School of Economics until July. During the summer he was swallowed up by his work as a senior resident. One weekend in August, they managed to go to Provincetown, but he spent most of the time sleeping on the Wellfleet Beach while Susan read for a course which she was taking at the Harvard Summer School. They both wanted to marry in the fall; they knew that they wouldn't see much more of each other, but the prospects of loneliness at night and her distaste of dormitory life made them go ahead. His parents objected; they hadn't married until their mid-thirties, until his father had established himself as a historian and his mother had received her doctorate in art history. They reminded him that he earned $200 a month as a resident. The hospital would give them food tickets for the cafeteria, but who would pay the rent on an apartment? Susan's parents couldn't help them.

A rich girl? Maybe he should have married one! He would often think about it when he was tired, when he was annoyed with Susan. He'd met a lot of unattached heiresses. But he knew he couldn't stomach dancing to their moneyed whims: going to the opera every Thursday night, summering on Fisher's Island, going to Sunday brunches at the River Club. He was too independent; he knew that.

They agreed to postpone the wedding until the following summer. Then she would have her Masters of Social Work and probably have a job as a caseworker, and he would be a research fellow on a government grant. His salary of $600 a month, augmented by her $85–90 a week, would be enough, as long as Susan didn't get pregnant.

Her parents insisted on a religious wedding in a neighborhood temple in the Bronx, but they were equally fixed on a reception at the Plaza Hotel. His parents found the contrast amusing, but they could understand the clashing worlds which Susan had faced.

They worked out a three-day weekend for a wedding trip. One of the residents at the hospital agreed to cover for him as a wedding present. Their honeymoon was at the Chatham Bars Inn at the Cape. It rained all weekend. By Sunday afternoon, they were eager to move into the new apartment Susan had frugally furnished and decorated from her "dowry." The apartment was filled with an odd assortment of old Macy furniture, donated by her uncle and aunt on the Grand Concourse. Some of the junk was still in the attic of the Cornwall house, probably ruined by the mice they had had over the years. It was hard to throw out. The apartment, ugly but comfortable, amused Don, probably because he only occasionally ate and slept there. He was usually at the hospital. It was only one and a half rooms, above a short-order restaurant, the Rena Nova, which the hospital staff had renamed the "Inferior Vena Cava."

Don looked at his watch. It was five o'clock. He was now hungry as well as thirsty. He'd go down to the cafeteria if it didn't take so much effort. He often wondered how Susan and he could have lived so simply in their little apartment above the restaurant. They had stayed there until he had finished his fellowship year. Only with the guarantee of an increasing income from private practice did Don dare move to New York, to a one-bedroom apartment in a red brick building, built before the Depression. The rent was $125 a month. He shook his head. That was a lot of money then. Susan could now spend that on a pair of Bendel shoes; he, on a couple of custom-made shirts.

Don broke out of his thoughts and checked the time. The wall clock said 5:10.

"Dr. Phillips?" he asked, holding the receiver tightly in his hand. "Is that goddamn woman ready yet?"

"Yes, Dr. Gordon." The voice was infinitely younger, infinitely more gentle, and more patient than his—the way he used to speak to older attendings when he was a resident at the Mass General. "I was just going to call you. She just went down the hall. We're ready for you, sir."

"Be right there," he said, slapping the phone down.

Don went to the dressing room and scrubbed. He extended his arms while a student nurse slid a gown over his muscular arms and shoulders. She tied it tightly behind him and helped him with his mask and gloves.

"You're doing magnificently, Mrs. Beresford," Don said, as he entered the delivery room. His dimple flickered into sight and then faded into his cheek. "Breathe deeply and push hard and steady when I say so."

With a scalpel, Dr. Phillips made a small, lateral episiotomy incision into the wall of her vagina. The cut bled profusely.

"Now we can push, dear . . . splendid." The aching muscles of his arms and the beads of sweat forming on his brow took the place of thought for a moment. "A little more . . . one big push and that's it." She clamped her lips together and said nothing as the cords of her neck tightened, her face turned red and sweaty and eyes squeezed shut. "Wonderful, Mrs. Beresford. You have a bonny, big, blond boy. See the handsome fellow." He passed the baby to the nurse, who vanished into another room. "Now your work is done. You can go to sleep and spend time later with your son."

Don nodded to Dr. Phillips, whose hands were enmeshed in umbilical cord, and disappeared through the door to the dressing room.

After locking her bike to a No Parking sign, Barbara made her way to Bloomingdale's. A huge, blind black man, dressed in a dirty herringbone coat, stared into her eyes for money. Transfixed by his opaque eyes, she tripped over his guide dog.

"Sorry, sir," she said. "I didn't see your dog." She plopped a quarter into his cup and went into the store. Instead of walking straight ahead to the men's department, she veered to the right to look at what used to be inexpensive wrist watches—Timexes and Tissots. She asked herself why she needed a new one; her old Bulova kept accurate time. But it wasn't good enough for running. She needed a digital watch to keep track of the seconds. She smelled the gourmet shop. Aromas of breads, cakes and candies greeted her at the door. She entered the food fantasia. There was everything—even Fiuggi and Evian bottled water, reminders of vacations to Italy and France. She inspected the canned fish section: herring in various kinds of mustard and tomato sauces, from France, Scandinavia and Japan; shark from Achill Island; turtle from the Pacific; both Russian and Iranian caviar; long tubes of anchovy paste and cans of Scottish salmon. She imagined herself in Fortman and Mason's, browsing through the food department, like Julie Christie in *Darling,* helping herself to every whim. But she was no shoplifter; she hadn't been raised that way. Anyway, she wanted more than she could ever stuff into her pockets. She picked up a wire shopping basket; she collected a dozen types of sherry soups and four decorative tins of German and Dutch cookies.

"I'd like to charge this," Barbara said, "and have it sent."

A frail-looking saleslady puzzled over Barbara's selections.

"Cash or charge, Miss?" she asked, blinking.

"Oh, charge, please," Barbara said. "But I'm sorry, I don't have the card." She pretended to search for her charge plate. "It's under Dr. D. Gordon, or Mrs. S. Gordon. I forget which."

The saleslady went to the phone to confirm this information at the credit department. She seemed to whisper into the phone more than a name and address; she looked back at Barbara with curiosity and then came back to her.

"Yes, Miss." The saleswoman looked at her again, blankly, pausing for a second. "It will take one day for delivery. Do you want me to write up the order now and give you the receipt?"

"I don't need the receipt," she said with a shrug. "Just send it as soon as possible. Thank you."

Barbara walked toward the men's department. She passed through the cosmetics and perfume sections and stopped for a moment in the game section to see a backgammon set. She liked the game, but it had become, for her, too *de rigueur*. Last winter, while at dinner at Mandel's with her parents, she saw a hippie selling $100 sets to chic couples, people whose only interest in the game was to display their sets on stainless steel coffee tables.

In the men's shop, young men wandered around, some talking to one another in a party atmosphere, some painfully self-aware, holding themselves stiffly, as though their spines had been fused. Shirts and ties were striped or multicolored; display counters looked like fruit and vegetable stalls in a Caribbean natives' market. She couldn't buy this plumage for her father; he already dressed too young, too self-consciously for a professor.

She went over to the toiletries, where there were dozens of men's perfumes and toilet waters, some magnificent scents; and lovely English shaving brushes. Ornate, French shaving mugs were displayed to tempt the flamboyant male. She noticed an odd-looking white razor, a combination safety and electric razor. A clerk, dressed in mauve and tan, told her that it was a "Firem," a new Italian razor that promised no cuts or nicks, only endless, clean, smooth shaves. Her father used an ordinary silver safety razor, which left at least one cut a week on his chin. She hated to see him bleed at breakfast. And the razor was only $19.95. This would do for Peter's present.

Barbara moved on to the sports clothes department. An attractive, white-haired man in his fifties waited on her. He looked like the type that she saw at the Harvard Club at New Year's buffets. Had he been a

Wall Street broker whose firm went bankrupt in the late sixties? She
wanted something conservative but casual. He showed her a blue
blazer. But her father already had two, a single and double-breasted.
Then maybe a smoking jacket, he asked. Barbara explained that her
father had wanted to give up smoking. It didn't matter. He claimed a
man needn't smoke to enjoy a silk, burgundy smoking jacket. He was
right. Her father would look dignified in this jacket—like one of those
men in *The New Yorker* whiskey ads. She selected his size and hoped it
was the correct arm length. He could return it for alterations, if
necessary, the salesman said.

At the corner of Lexington Avenue and 60th Street, in a public phone
box, she dialed her father's private office number. He would probably
be there, seeing patients at the end of the day.

"Hello, Miss McArdle? This is Barbara Gordon." She put her left
hand to her other ear to block out the traffic noise. "May I speak with
my father? . . . He just came down from the delivery room? Good!"

"Hi, Daddy . . . Yes, it's Barbara." Her father, she was reminded,
never seemed to recognize her telephone voice. "I'm on Lex at 60th.
What if I stop by and pick you up?"

"Yes, that's a good idea, except I'm with Robert Sineway." Her father
sounded tired. "You know, the TV director who did the film on *The
Cost of Dying*. We're just leaving. We're going to the Bemmelman's at
the Carlyle. You've been there before. Meet us in fifteen minutes."

"I have my bike with me and I'm in jeans," Barbara said, not knowing
how formal she should be at the Carlyle.

"That's okay. Chain the bike to a parking meter." He mumbled
something about meters being stolen. "Afterwards, I'll ride you home
on the handlebars. See you, honey."

Barbara peddled over to Madison Avenue and rode north, stopping
occasionally to look in the windows of boutiques. She didn't want to
wait for her father in a bar. She saw the Carlyle marquee and headed for
a space between two parked cars. A car screeched to a stop.

"Hey, you stupid little broad." A gray, heavily-lined, slightly shaking
face had emerged over the top of a Cadillac. "You can't put your bike in a
perfectly good parking space."

Barbara pretended the driver didn't exist. He cursed her and sped on.
Her bicycle locked up, she pushed open the door to the bar.

"Excuse me, Miss. But you have to be eighteen to be served here," the
maître d' said.

"Yes, I know," Barbara said. "I'm meeting my father, Dr. Donald Gordon."

"Yes, of course." He leaned slightly forward. "The doctor and his friend are over in the corner."

Barbara made her way through the dimly lit room. She bumped into a young woman in a black cocktail dress, and would have collided with her escort, a burly, older man, if he hadn't caught her by the arm. She peered into the corner. There was her father waving at her.

"You were looking right at us, Barbara," Don said, turning slightly to his right. "You know Robert Sineway?"

"Hello, Barbara. Nice you could join us," the director said. He was in his early thirties. With his tan bell-bottom suit, he wore a chocolate turtleneck and brown leather boots. "Your father and I have been going over details for the shooting—the film on the birth of a baby. We hope to do it soon."

"Sounds great," Barbara said, looking away.

"Do you want a coke, Barbara?" Don asked.

"No, thanks. Just a tall glass of club soda and a twist of lime."

"Don't tell me you're on a diet, Barbara," Sineway said.

"No, of course not," Barbara said, serious. "I just adore food." An awkward silence fell between them.

"I recently got back from London," he said. He cleared his throat. "I kept meeting these tall, stringbean models who starved themselves. Real Twiggy types. They call it some disease." He turned his head to stare blindly, perhaps knowingly, at Don. "There was a big article on it in *The Sunday Observer* by some doctor at the London Hospital."

"That's interesting, Robert," Don said, half-turning to Barbara. "I think I know what you mean. Strange. We don't see that sort of thing much in New York."

Barbara looked at him with obvious distaste; her look clouded, and she smiled unhappily. "Tell me about your film," she asked. "Who's the leading lady?"

"We star Miss Maria Gonzales, the prima of Spanish Harlem. No subtitles. Fortunately, she doesn't say a word—just grunts and groans."

"You see, Barbara," Don said, "one of the ward patients will be used for the film."

"Does she know a movie will be made of her bottom?" Barbara asked, with a terrible smile.

"Of course. She'll sign a permission form," Don said sharply. "There's no legal problem."

"I think this film is terribly important," Sineway said, watching Barbara. "We've had a lot of medical programs on NBC, CBS and educational TV—oh, things like open-heart surgery, the artificial kidney, old age and death, all real grim stuff—but nothing as positive and optimistic as birth." Sineway wondered if he were speaking pompously, too cockily, with the wild look that can come to someone's eyes when he's had two too many vodkas. "Do you think, Don, our leading lady will be ready Friday?"

"Oh, sure. No problem." Don was dead earnest. "We can have the camera crew all set up in delivery room C by nine."

"Wouldn't you like to come to watch the shooting, Barbara?" Sineway asked.

"I have school that day . . . a test in biology." The color in her face left. "I shouldn't miss school."

"You're a lucky girl," Sineway said, "having a father who delivers babies." He smiled, dimples and ivory-white rodent's teeth showed, and his eyes twinkled. "Your husband will be the lucky one."

Barbara looked at her empty glass. She felt like a woman being spied on through a mirror.

"So, what's in that Bloomingdale parcel?" Don asked.

"Birthday presents," she answered.

"Who's birthday?" Don asked, absent-minded in his manner.

"Yours, silly. And I think it's time to go home for your birthday dinner," Barbara said. She couldn't hide her impatience any longer.

"It's seven o'clock." He signed his name on the check with a flourish. "Sorry, Robert, duty calls. Give me a ring tomorrow, if you have any questions about Friday."

"Goodbye, Mr. Sineway. The best for the shooting Friday."

They left the director ordering another vodka. She unlocked her bicycle while Don flagged down a cab.

"Where did you find him?" Barbara asked, bitterly.

"What do you mean, 'find him?'" Don asked. "He's one of the top documentary directors in the business. He came to me because he knows my interests in medical education and public TV."

"He knows what a showman you are!" Barbara snapped, full of doubt and revulsion.

"What's eating at you, Barbara?"

"Oh, nothing," she said, exasperated. "I just don't think he's a nice man and I don't want you to get mixed up with him."

"'Mixed up with him?'" Don asked. "Why, he's half my age. We don't have much in common."

"That's the trouble," Barbara said, staring at her father with a look of disbelief.

They didn't say anything for the remaining blocks. Still, they felt close to each other.

"Happy Birthday, Father," Susan and Peter bellowed as they entered.

"Happy Birthday, Dad," Barbara chimed in, forcing her way between her father and her brother, pushing her present to his chest. "You'll love this."

"Where's my present to him?" Peter asked.

"Oh, it's here somewhere," Barbara said, vaguely looking through the bag as Peter glowered at her.

"If you kids could give your father a little room," Susan pleaded, "maybe he could enjoy his present and have a drink. In fact, why don't you kids wash first?"

"You always take the fun out of things," Barbara said, disgruntled.

Susan and Don ignored the children and went to the living room. "Oh, hell," he thought to himself and then turned away from Susan, too preoccupied to waste the words on his tongue. "All I mean to say," he mumbled, directly challenged, trying to straighten out his mind, re-nounce cynicism—the idea growing in his mind (a fixation, maybe)—"was that . . . " He met Susan's eyes, saying nothing more. All that was beside the point now. He, too, (but he was only now thinking of it) knew. They looked at each other, frowning, then looked away. He said to himself, she doesn't need me anymore; then he glanced at her, knowing that she was thinking the same. He went over to the stereo and switched on the power. Unbeknownst to Don, Susan moved, and coming up behind him, put her hand on his arm. He drew back, spying on himself, as though he could not trust himself. Still Don said nothing. Then he said, aloud, but not quite so desperately as he feared, not because he absolutely believed it, but to reaffirm their mutual existence, "I'm nuts about you." And in the half-darkened room it didn't seem a surprising thing to say. But then it struck Don, things seemed different now between them.

"Happy birthday, Dr. Gordon," Rose said. "What would you like to drink?"

"Scotch on the rocks, Rose. Tell me, Susan, what's the good news?" he asked.

"Can I have some of that Beluga caviar?" Barbara asked, coming into the room and staring at her mother, who barely nodded.

"Charles has asked me to take the research professorship January first." Susan waited for him to say something; he didn't. She wasn't sure of his silence. "This will mean more involvement in departmental and school research. I'll have to travel more."

"I'll be traveling more, too, because of the International," Don said. "Perhaps we can coordinate our travel schedules. Let's buy a little place in the South of France, like that one we saw a few years ago near Menton. We could sneak down there for a few days at a time."

He looked at the headlines on *The Post*. "I wonder what the jury will do with Mitchell and Stans."

Barbara had been sitting on the side in one of the overstuffed chairs, sheepishly licking the caviar off a wafer cracker. She looked over at her parents. "Do you really think we need another house . . . particularly, one we'd go to a few weeks out of the year?"

"Don't be so practical," Don said. "Your mother and I need a little place to get off to during the winter." He laughed anxiously. "We must think of our retirement years."

"What a laugh! You two retire!" She was abrupt, as if wanting to affront them. "Mother has just become professor of something; you, of an international something or other. You'll never be able to stop."

"Barbara, Barbara, calm down," Susan said. She frowned and thought about it. "You're on edge tonight. I know—and your father certainly knows—that there are a few days every month when a teenage girl feels uptight." Susan looked at Don with remarkably tranquil certainty. "When you get into your twenties, it won't bother you so much. I never had any trouble after you were born. Pregnancy is the best cure."

"You make it sound as easy as popping a pill," Barbara said.

"Barbara, about the house in France." Susan wanted to get down to facts. Vagueness was always intolerable to her, overcome only by details. "I'm going to be traveling to Europe more because of my job. Your father also, with all his medical meetings. We'll have many chances to use the house." Her voice was now unctuous, high-pitched, apt to crack, Susan thought, if she weren't careful. "And you can use it, too. In summers, school vacations. Who knows? You might want to take your junior year of college in France. The house could be a lovely weekend place for you."

"Are you serious?" Barbara asked. Ideas flooded in and she began to seal her mind against them. "Who can work in the South of France besides, maybe, Picasso and Calder?"

"Dinner is served," Rose announced.

"What have you thought up for the birthday boy?" Don asked Rose. He hoped he'd be moved by it. Perhaps even touched.

"It's your favorite, Dr. Gordon. But don't thank me; it was Barbara's idea."

"You'll love it, Daddy," Barbara blurted out. "We spent hours planning and cooking it."

"You've all read my mind—rack of venison! Wonderful." He kissed Barbara and Rose on the cheek.

"The meat has a funny smell," Peter said.

"Nonsense," Barbara answered. "You're used to hamburgers and junk foods. I'm going to teach you, Peter, what real eating is all about."

"I think you're going to teach all of us," Susan said. "You've memorized my *Gourmet* magazines."

"That's quite a magazine," Barbara said, wide-eyed. "There was a fascinating article on Les Baux-de-Provence and that great inn—the Outstande Baumanierre." She wet her lips and looked down, as though reading from a menu. "I'd love to have their mousse de saumdi."

"That is a great place," Susan said. A groan of dissatisfaction. "Jeff Richter went there last summer. Isn't this venison good!"

"If it's so good," Peter said, "why isn't Barbara eating?" He broke wind as he spoke, but not noticeably. And then he laughed, "Ha, ha, ha."

"I am, Peter. Have some more rutabaga and puree." She nodded to Rose to help Peter. "He'll take more, Rose. Daddy, let me give you some venison." She spoke rather loudly, as if to defy the silence of the group. "Don't worry about dessert. It's light and fluffy and won't take up much room."

"All right, but I'll have to go back to my gym class," Don said with resignation. "I've gained a few pounds this fall."

"Not enough exercise, Daddy," she said, full of nervous energy and troubled thought. "If you ran every day, you could eat to your heart's delight, like me."

"I don't see you eating very much," Don said. "You've hardly touched your food; you've been so busy telling Rose to feed us."

Barbara watched her mother and father eat the venison. She was struck by how her father sat solemn and uncomfortably erect, so expressionless one might have thought him lost in fantasy. Suddenly she put down her fork. "I was very naughty today," Barbara said. "I had three blackberry tarts at Bloomingdale's bake shop."

"And then you feed us this fancy junk," Peter said.

"You won't say that when you get to the dessert: boules de neige Tutti-Frutti with creme Anglaise. For your information, Peter, that's snow eggs with glazed fruits and English custard."

Don sipped his wine, looking over the rim at Barbara, and then he said, "A nice, low-calorie, low-cholesterol dessert."

Peter picked around the eggs and custard, trying to separate out the bits of fruit. Then, suddenly, arrogantly, saying the word with all the force he could find, he said, "Shit." And then: "Why can't we have Baskin-Robbins' ice cream for dessert, like a normal family?"

"Don't be plebeian, Peter," Barbara said, turning away from her brother.

"Let's not hurry," Barbara said, smiling. "I got my homework done this afternoon. I think I'll have some coffee with you. Please, Rose. Can I have some black coffee?"

"How was school today?" Susan asked, somewhat patronizing.

"Philosophy was great," Barbara said. "I really have a feeling for it. I might even take it in college."

"They have a fine department at Harvard," Susan explained. "It goes way back to Royce, Santayana and Whitehead."

"I'm sleepy," Peter said. He kissed his parents goodnight and ignored Barbara.

"We've been reading some of the early philosophers," Barbara said. She turned sober, pressed her hands together, elbows out, like a man praying. "Today we discussed St. Augustine's *On the Immortality of the Soul*. It's an odd little book." She continued, "Very obscure and confusing; and, in fact, some forty years after its printing, St. Augustine regretted it had been published and admitted the proofs he developed to prove immortality were so obscure that he himself couldn't understand them." Barbara laughed, admitting to herself the whimsicality of philosophers.

"Sounds like the cynicism of an embittered old man," Don said, proud of his insight.

"What were his proofs?" Susan asked. She glanced at Barbara and then looked away.

"They're rather complicated and wordy; but, if you really want to know . . ."

The Gordons found themselves alone after Barbara had gone to her room. This seldom happened.

Don sat on the sofa. One afternoon (it was the end of August, a sultry, muggy day), Don had said to himself that his life had become a coma; the world had changed for him. It didn't seem right, but he was no judge. "Jesus," he thought, troubled by a memory he couldn't contact, "something is wrong." But he could not tell himself what he was struggling with, however subtly he tried to think it out. It all seemed now beside the point. He picked up a book. "Have you read this book, *Alive?*" he asked his wife.

"You'd like it," Susan said. She gave him a smile. "It's high adventure, about the survivors of the plane crash in the Andes." Susan went back to scanning an issue of *People Weekly.*

"I recall the story now," Don said, jerking his head in a nod. "Wasn't that the soccer players who ate their dead teammates after a plane crash in the Andes?"

"Yes, they turned to cannibalism," Susan added.

"The poor bastards!" Don said. He looked at the curling hairs on the back of his fingers, the wide gold wedding band on his left ring finger.

"It saved their lives. Why not?" Susan said.

"The whole thing disgusts me," Don said. "Perhaps after a crash in the Andes it has its place." He knew, without needing words for it, that Susan's practicality was triumphant.

"What do you mean?" Susan asked.

"You know what I mean: dog eat dog." His chin tightened. "I see it in my colleagues, friends, patients and . . . "

"Why don't you say it: in your wife?"

"Don't put words into my mouth," Don said with anger. He looked at her, trying to guess exactly what was on her mind. "You're right about one thing. You're making the same mistake I've made. You think work can solve everything."

"What do you mean?" Susan asked.

"Just what I said." He hesitated, thinking to himself: Christ, don't you get anything? "I've put all my energies into being the best 'whatever that is.' I thought it would make me feel good for the rest of my life. I've gotten to the top in my profession and find myself surrounded by types like myself, not very interested in people at all, only themselves." He was silent for a moment, his lips trembling. "I know I'm one of them, but I'm different in that *I know what I am* . . .

they don't!" Don sat silent for almost a full minute, lost in his anguished thoughts, probably still going over his monologue and not yet cognizant that he had ceased to speak aloud.

"You're depressed," she said. "It must be those terrible birthday feelings people have after they turn fifty."

"Don't be flip with me," he said, after a deep breath. He pretended to read a magazine but instead, he thought of the creases of flesh under his eyes, his graying hair and the new bifocals that he was having trouble getting used to.

"You do mind my career?" Susan asked, fixing her gaze on Don's face.

"Of course, I do," he snapped. "I feel I'm alone." He looked baffled, hurt. "You'll be only my imaginary companion; I used to be able to see you as mother to our children. Yes, to me, too." He swallowed, then looked Susan in the face. "You're not even an ally anymore. It's plain to me that you and I are going in different directions."

"Don, I wish you could hold together for the next few years; maybe, you'd feel better then."

"I can't pretend anymore," Don said, stubborn. Don recalled what good sex they used to have. In the last few years he would hold Susan next to him at night; he had to touch her to go to sleep. They had become morning lovers. He would awake before Susan, clutching her, feeling his penis growing against her leg. Now he could only mythologize their sexual life.

"What do you want to do?" she asked.

"Simply continue what I'm doing at the hospital: teaching, research, some practice. I can work that out for myself." His mind raced, not sure it would ever stop. It hit him: "It's you that frightens me. At last, I'm ready to be a person with you, and you're running in an opposite direction."

She frowned, not getting it at first. "Frankly, Don, I'm going to continue in that direction," she said, sitting up straight. "I refuse to join you in your anthropomorphic misery and depression."

"All I ask," he whispered, senselessly now, "is for you to be available."

"Fine, there's always space available for you." And then, suddenly, seductive, her eyes wide and unblinking: "Let's make love. It's only ten-thirty. I'll get ready."

"Go fuck yourself," Don bellowed.

Susan threw her magazine on the coffee table, got up and sat on her heels. "You're making me sick," she said. "I wish you'd grow up and realize there's a big world out there for both of us."

Don went over to the liquor cabinet and poured himself a Drambuie. He picked up a copy of *Watership Down,* which a colleague had lent him.

"What are you reading?" Susan asked.

He said nothing at first but then decided he wouldn't pout.

"It's a new novel by an Englishman, a book about rabbits," he said, trying to keep his distance.

"Please don't get any ideas about raising rabbits in Cornwall," Susan said. "Mr. Trumball couldn't take care of them during the week." She sat staring at her husband with a look of disbelief.

"You're too concrete," he said. He looked back at Susan. "But I must be concrete with you about Barbara."

"What do you mean?"

"There is something bothering her. She's acting funny. She's . . ."

"But she's never done better in school," Susan interrupted. She shook her head, thinking to herself that he didn't know what he was saying. "I've never seen her so excited about learning. Her midterm report was all A's."

"That's it, Susan," he said, leaning closer. "She's just too damn good, too bright, too energetic—too everything—too perfect for this world." He couldn't make out what it was that frightened him. "She'll get into Radcliffe—don't worry—but what kind of life will she have?"

"Her brains will take her far," she said. "For you even normality is a perversion."

"And she shows no interest in boys," he continued. "In fact, I can sense her hostility to men, especially me, which hurts my feelings." He choked up and looked out the window.

"Stop worrying, Don. She got a letter from a boy she met in the summer. She's not going to be a bull dyke . . . the feminist impact will wear off."

"You're missing the point," he said. He felt exasperated. "Haven't you noticed how thin she is? She's lost weight in the last couple of weeks—after losing a lot over the summer."

"She was delighted to shed her baby fat this summer," Susan pointed out. "Now she wants to keep thin."

"I can't stand to see her eat," he said, somewhat annoyed at her dismissing the whole thing so lightly. "She pecks at her food like a little bird on the edge of being startled and ready to fly away."

"Oh, she is becoming a bit fussy about what she eats, but I think it's part of her gourmet thing."

Don picked up his book and went up to the bathroom to dental floss. As he pulled the unwaxed string through the spaces of his teeth, he thought how complicated his life had become. He went to his gum brush, the *tour de force* urged on him by Dr. Toms, his dentist. His life was now cluttered with health chores, supposed to guarantee his physical status quo and postpone the inevitable.

He heard a noise in the hall. At first, he thought it was Susan coming to bed. He stepped out into the hall.

"What are you doing, Barbara?" Don asked. "It's past midnight. You need your sleep."

"I'm not sleepy," Barbara said uneasily. "I'm going to the library for a book. Good night, Daddy."

"Goodnight, Barbara. And listen, remember what I told you, get some rest. Don't read now."

Barbara moved down the tight circle of the stairs and slipped into the kitchen. She squinted at the pure white appliances, staring back at her, like robots awaiting her command. She pulled open the door of the refrigerator, inhaled to smell the food and prolong her pleasure. Like a skinny buzzard, she stood still, neck stretched, looking straight ahead, with the refrigerator door open, throat and temples throbbing. A wish from one part of her divided mind concentrated on the food; another part thought of calories and calculated the amount of food energy in watercress. She felt a mysterious, painful excitement, almost like pleasure, something beginning to rise in her stomach, and she cringed and put her fingers to her mouth. Caught between pleasure and fright, Barbara froze, shame mushrooming inside her. Everyone who ever knew her said her self-control was amazing. If she could crack open her skull, she was certain she'd find a perfect image. Barbara sat down, leaning forward, neck craned, motionless, watching the food, searching for thoughts—distractions. Her lips stopped moving, and finally she turned to the cabinet where the digital clock sat. Its numbers were fuzzy, too blurred to read. A smorgasbord stood before her. She started to eat. A piece of creamed chicken dropped from her lips, and she tried to catch it with her hand, missed it, and it spattered her robe a little. Several slices of venison caught her eye. She tasted a piece. At dinner, it had been very gamey; now it was tender and sweet. She ate one slice after another until only bone and juice were left on the platter. A bowl of spaghetti from somebody's lunch, probably Rose's, tasted spicy; it warmed her stomach. The white clam sauce was still fresh. Cheeses in a tightly wrapped Zabar bag turned out to be a triangle of French Brie and a cube of Stilton. She cut the latter into thin slices and slid them, one after another, into her mouth; the Brie, oozing its cream, melted on her tongue, and a little trickled down her chin.

Back in the corner of the refrigerator, behind a large jar of Vita Herring, concealed to be a treat for somebody, was a neatly wrapped bag. She felt it; there were squares several inches thick, slightly soft and crunchy. She couldn't resist. It was baklava, her favorite Turkish dessert, those multilayered honey cakes to which her father first introduced her. She ate all six of them and then drank a Tab. On the bottom shelf, behind two grapefruits was a half-moon of cherry cheesecake; she ate most of it, hiding the rest from the next visitor to the refrigerator.

Gnawing feelings in her stomach persisted, even though she was bloated, to the point of bursting. Her gut growled with periodic contractions. In the kitchen cabinets she found an unopened package of granola; she poured herself a double serving and added a half-pint of heavy cream. It was chewy—fruity, flaky and nutty; she had to resist eating the rest. Barbara was now hot and sweaty. She looked at the clock; it was one-thirty, too early to go for a jog around the reservoir. A cop might stop her. Or worse! Sleep was impossible. She was too keyed-up. Her mind raced from one thing to another; and she felt restless, like a seagull before a storm. What could she do with all this energy? Only working on something could stop this mental momentum. She would write her term paper now, at least pick a topic and start the outline. What could it be on? Not biology. More her own ideas.

Barbara had recently finished Hobbes's *Leviathan* and Machiavelli's *The Prince*. She would compare the two thinkers. She sat down at her typewriter and reached for a box of typewriter paper. She wouldn't need the erasable bond; she was confident about what had to be said. She sucked in a deep breath and started:

"Hobbes's theory of power is, in some ways, very near to that of Machiavelli's with one important exception: he has none of Machiavelli's profound observations and none of Machiavelli's limiting wisdom." She hesitated as if she could find nothing to say. "That this is true is shown by a critical comparison of the view each philosopher takes in regard to basic life motivations."

Barbara paused to read over her opening paragraph. She read it aloud. It was musical; it was strong but hardly overwhelming.

"Machiavelli takes a dim view of man, who, to him, is, as T. S. Eliot says, a fickle, false, mean and covetous individual." She congratulated herself on remembering this line from Eliot. "In *The Prince,* Machiavelli speaks out as a philosopher, intent upon the development of ideas, to give substance to a systematic view; his utterances are those made by an empiricistic philosopher (she wondered if she really knew what she meant here) seeking to define the goals of man's activities; i.e., these activities by which one man can maintain order, rule and authority in a state through the exercise of power. His corruption of power, the analysis of which is made around"—no, she better change her fancy language, she thought—"in terms of unscrupulous politics, is the substance of his philosophy."

She paused for a few moments, reread the paragraph and then forced herself back to her writing.

"There is little or no developed theory of human nature; specifically, the nature of man in Machiavelli's analysis of power. He merely accepts things as he finds them and then suggests ways and means by which a prince may successfully function within the limits of that analysis."

Barbara thought that she better get down to hard facts. She returned to the essay, but her fingers wouldn't do their little dance on the typewriter keys. She went to the kitchen and ate the rest of the cheesecake. Its crumbs still clung to the sides of her mouth as she went back to her typing.

". . . and since men, wicked and wild, will not keep faith with the prince, the latter must act reciprocally. 'The end is all that counts.' These are but a few of the princely rules, enough to show Machiavelli's belief that power reigning over potential power is essential for the survival of a prince."

Barbara sat closer to her desk, chin on her fist, musing, lapsing into reveries of what medieval Florence must have been like. She could see herself in a castle overlooking the Arno, a deep blue instead of its present yellow-mercury, watching armored soldiers march across the Ponte Vecchio. On the last visit to Florence, she had a fine veal dish for lunch at Sabatino's after a long morning in the Uzzi Hall. . . . Now she had to compare Hobbes.

An hour later Barbara searched for an ending.

"But one must acknowledge that the philosophic value of Machiavelli and Hobbes's work lies in the impetus these men gave to subsequent philosophical thinking, which sought a resolution of sovereignty and human motivation in conflict."

She added a footnote: "We are reminded of Watergate—the gluttony of power—a clear indication of political decadence, long ago prophesized by Lord Acton's dictum that 'absolute power corrupts absolutely.'"

She entered another footnote, this time from a recent book, *Anarchy, State, and Utopia* by Robert Nozick, on his concept of the minimal state. Nozick was about the same age as Mr. Jones, her philosophy teacher. Perhaps they knew each other at Columbia.

Barbara yanked page five from the typewriter, almost crumpling its bonded texture, and stapled the pages together. She wrote "Barbara Gordon, October 30th," at the top left corner. She wouldn't have to write the paper over the weekend, but she would read it again to make sure it was perfect. She wasn't tired; her mind was a little dulled but not sleepy. No more of these word games, she thought. She would seize life by the neck, grasp control in her hands; quintessential control was the *sine qua non* of a life well-lived. She undressed before the bathroom mirror and was shocked when she saw herself the first time, turned to profile. It told her, cruel and unforgiving, bold and unrelenting: she had abused her body. She was fat and sloppy, sticking out everywhere, like a picture that she once saw in Eastman's *Text of Obstetrics and Gynecology:* a young girl, no more than eighteen, also in profile, with a swollen abdomen. The caption said something about teenage girls seldom showing a pregnancy at four months unless they are in poor physical shape. She pulled her scale out of the closet. The numbers spun before her burning eyes and stopped at 98 pounds. She looked at her clock. Its hands made an irridescent, pie-shaped wedge at four-thirty.

She vowed that she would rid herself of every last thing she had consumed during the night. She suspected that the debris was still high in her gut. Milk of magnesia, after she vomited, would push the rest through by morning. She searched for the trigger in her throat, which would release the stagnant pool of food. A rush of warm, viscid fluid shot into the toilet bowl. The first spurt was creamy white, flecked with chunks of meat, cereal, raisins and coconuts; the second, dark brown streaks interspersed with snippets of spaghetti and lumps of white cheese; and, finally, the watery, white slime of unrecognizable origins. She pulled herself to her feet; and, although chilly and clammy, she got on the scales again. Now the scale read 92 pounds. Barbara expected her weight would fall to 90 pounds if the milk of magnesia purge—after jogging—eliminated the food which had escaped the reaches of her index finger.

Barbara gargled, rinsed her mouth and went to bed.

II. ON THE WAY

Living well is the best revenge.
—Old Portuguese Proverb

Barbara enjoyed long, hot baths. She would sit, submerged to her neck in iridescent bubbles, and close her eyes and imagine herself swimming in a thermal spring in Idaho, where she had spent hours last summer with her friends. Now, she lay in her hot bath, her legs still aching from an eighteen-mile-long run. The lethargy that enveloped her wasn't upsetting; she knew that she had earned it; she would run and exercise tomorrow.

Rose stormed into Barbara's room and blurted out something that she didn't understand. Often Rose's Irish accent was difficult to grasp, more so if she were upset.

"What's that, Rose," Barbara said from the bathroom. "Speak slowly, I can't understand you."

"Nanny from Boston is here."

"Oh, why didn't you say so in the first place?" said Barbara. "Did you take her things into the guest room?"

Rose nodded. She never liked house guests; less so relatives, the least, these grandparents.

Barbara finished her bath, dressed and ran out to the living room to greet her grandmother.

"Hello, Nanny," Barbara screamed as she hugged the tiny white-haired lady. Barbara looked carefully at her grandmother to see if age had brought any more change. She found her hair whiter, a few liver spots on her temples, more skin crinkles about the eyes, deep lines at the corners of her mouth—and, perhaps, a little shorter for some odd reason. She would often wonder why old people seemed to shrink, dry up and bend over. But she was as lively and petite as ever in her fur-trimmed, tweed suit.

"Did you have a good trip from Boston?" Barbara asked.

"Max drove the speed limit all the way along the New England Expressway." She leaned forward, put a magazine she had just picked up on the chair arm and stood up.

"Where is he?" Barbara asked.

"He's putting the car in the garage." A vague fear, or perhaps some regret, came into Nanny's mind. "We wouldn't think of driving around this city, especially on Friday, with all the shoppers and college kids home for the Thanksgiving weekend. Where's your parents?"

"They should be home soon," Barbara said. "School got out early for the holidays, so I've been here all afternoon. Studying and writing." She smiled with unnatural eagerness. "Also, helping Rose with the Thanksgiving dinner."

"Aren't you good," Nanny said. "You work as hard as your father. Is he still killing himself at the hospital?" She had given up trying to make her son slow down.

"No, not really." She wondered if she should let the topic trail off. "He did have a delivery this afternoon before he signed out to Dr. Sullivan. But it's my mother who's working like a fiend. She's been made some big shot research professor."

"That's all Donald needs!" Nanny murmured to herself. "I suppose she'll be at the office Thanksgiving eve."

"Probably," Barbara said, her blue eyes smoldering. "Or she'll likely stop at P. J. Clarke's with some people from the office—'holiday cheer' she'll call it. Is that the door? Yeah! It's Max."

Her grandfather kissed Barbara and put his arms around her. She drew back, a little embarrassed, and stared at the spry old man, whose faded blue eyes smiled at her from behind his trifocals. With his white hair, dark leathery skin and Cambridge gray suit, he looked more like a retired ambassador than a Harvard professor emeritus, just recently turned seventy-eight.

Max stepped back from Barbara, slowly taking his hand off her shoulder. He spoke in a German accent, which years in Boston hadn't changed.

"Barbara! You don't treat yourself well these days," Grandfather said. "Ridiculous! Jesus!" he would tell Nanny later. "What's happened to her?" "Your bones stick out, crying out for some flesh. You must eat to keep up with your growth. Isn't that son of mine worried about you?"

"Max, you know I'm on the fat side. You always called me your 'cute little fatty!' " She put her arms behind her head, making her breasts rise. "I eat well and get plenty of exercise. But look at you; you've been thin all your life; and now you're in super shape."

"But my bones don't stick out," Max said. "I'll take you to Luchow's and fatten you up like a Christmas goose."

Barbara averted her eyes from Nanny and Max for a moment. She was reminded of how Central Europeans used to fatten geese for the market, stuffing food down their gullets for weeks, to the point the birds' livers became rotten.

"How's your book coming along, Max?" Barbara asked.

"I accomplished a great deal this summer at Wellfleet, but the sculptor next door kept distracting me," Max said, reflecting a moment and turning back to Barbara. "He's using iron now instead of Vermont marble. Noisy guy! But your Nanny did a great deal of acrylic painting with his wife. You remember Maria?"

"Yes, she's that cute, little woman."

"How has school been?" Max asked.

"My best year," Barbara said, proud and strong. "Straight A's thus far." Barbara seemed to think more about the question, less spontaneous now. "My philosophy course is terrific. It's a survey course but not too superficial."

"Are you going to be a doctor, like your father, or a historian and philosopher like Max?" Grandmother asked.

Barbara felt something booming in her mind. "I'll be both, Nanny," Barbara said, smiling at her grandmother.

Nanny did not care for philosophy; she was a practical woman and had become more so after she and Max had escaped from the Nazis. She would always say that if a young person under thirty had no social awareness, he had no heart; and if he had a lot of concern for social problems after thirty—idealism which she equated with philosophy— then he had no brains. She wore her heart on her left sleeve, her purse on her right.

"Hush," she said to Barbara. She shook her head. "I can't stand it."
Fixing Barbara with a stare, she told her to go into medicine like her
father. "Why, the next Depression will make the last one look like
nothing."

"O.K., Nanny," Max said, watching his wife closely, at once repelled
and fascinated, like a man watching a tarantula. "That's crazy," he
murmured. "You can't take hope away from youth." He turned away,
the problem still there, but not white-hot in his mind.

"Well, Max, it's almost five o'clock," Nanny said. She sighed, voice
falling off, her mind far away for a moment. "We should rest and then
dress for dinner. Will you excuse us, dear? Your grandfather and I get
tired this time of the day."

Rose knew this meant the old lady wanted her tea.

"See you later," Barbara said. She went in the library and paged
through *The Atlantic Monthly*. The articles were dull. She decided to
take Angus out. They walked down Fifth Avenue, past the Pierre Hotel,
to the pond near the Plaza. Barbara sat with Angus on a bench. Two
dogs suddenly ran past her; their masters nowhere in sight. Angus
considered joining them but Barbara pulled him closer. The shaggy
sheepdog and the Irish terrier rolled in the grass, nipped at each other
and poked each other with their snouts. Suddenly, the sheepdog
mounted the terrier; Barbara watched the animals playing, the male
panting.

A chilly wind started to come off Central Park. Instead of walking
along Fifth Avenue, she turned onto Madison and went north. Traffic
was heavy, slowed by people double-parked to pick up Thanksgiving
parcels. She paused at a meat market to look in the window. The display
reminded her of the Tenth Avenue slaughterhouse, which one of her
friends once took her to.

She crossed the street and went into a bookstore where she bought
Ezra Pound's *ABC of Reading* and continued down to East 79th Street.
Several times she stopped to look in gallery windows, all displaying
monochromatic canvasses with no images on them, priced up to
$50,000.

The breeze off the park was gone. Barbara walked over to Fifth
Avenue and the Metropolitan Museum. On the long, flowing steps
were clumps of young people, like students on the Spanish Steps in
Rome. A gypsy woman was playing a guitar. Some boys watched a
French juggler, waiting for his first mistake; several nannies gasped at

the juggler's tricks. Two girls waved to her and shouted when Barbara didn't wave back.

"Hey, Barbara. Aren't we intellectual enough?" asked a freckle-faced girl in a tentlike Ecuadorian poncho.

"Hello, Jane . . . Molly," Barbara said, a bit flatlipped and stoop-shouldered. "I didn't see you. Guess I was distracted. How have you been?"

The second girl, myopic and frizzy-haired, spoke up. "Not very good. What a drag coming back to New York and school. I've been miserable these last two months." Which she wasn't. "I guess it's gotten to you too."

"What do you mean?" Barbara asked.

"You're thin as a scarecrow," Molly said. "Are you sick or something? Or are you just skinny-smart these days?"

"No, I'm fine," she nodded, remote. "I gained some weight over the summer, but I'm managing to get it off now."

"We'll come to your funeral when you're finished," Jane said," with a heart the size of a pea. "Are you going to the Rolling Stones concert Friday night?"

"No, my grandparents are visiting," Barbara said. She half-turned to leave. "I really better get going. See you around."

The girls watched Barbara walk down the steps.

"Wow! Has she become weird!" Jane said, with her mouth like an inverted U. "Did you notice? She has no ass now! I bet she has leukemia, or something, and doesn't know it yet."

Barbara walked briskly up Fifth Avenue with Angus panting behind her. She thought that she had aroused the envy of the girls. In fact, she liked nothing better these days than making girls resentful of her thin hips, long legs, finely boned face, and blooming mind.

She found Rose looking for her when she opened the door of the apartment.

"Where have you been?" Rose raised her arms above her head, prepared to speak, but she murmured something and let her arms drop. She couldn't think of anything to say that would match the gesture. "I need you for the marinated lamb breasts. After all, it was your idea! How long do I baste the lamb with marinade?"

"You've cooked it eight hours, right?" Barbara asked. "Now you bake it at 375° F., basting it with marinade for thirty minutes; then sprinkle it with salt and repeat it for thirty more minutes. Okay?"

Rose shook her head and took another sip of tea.

"Where's everyone?" Barbara asked, still angry.

"They're all in the library having cocktails," Rose said with a scowl. Her father and his two brothers, like so many Irishmen, drank themselves to death after the Great War.

"Barbara, dear. You're just in time," Don said. His fingers closed lightly around his tie, fiddling with it. "Can I get you something to drink?"

"Just a diet coke," Barbara said. Her eyes came partway to life.

"We were just talking about the Watergate mess," Max said, glancing very approvingly at Barbara. "I feel sorry for you young people." He looked at her with perplexity. "I don't know how you can have any confidence in adults when you see what they're capable of doing. I tell you; Nanny and I have recently experienced fear and despair similar to what we felt in Vienna when the Fascists began to move into power."

"Thank God it can't go that far in this country," Don said, challenging the old man—something he'd only been able to do in recent years, now that he regarded himself as archetypal of a less awesome generation of fathers.

"Don't be too sure of that, Don," Max said. He looked at his son calmly with an incredulous twinkle in his eye. "I can point out historical examples of how democracy couldn't stop the growth of destructive power."

"The thing is," Susan interjected, "most politicians are power gluttons. They have no genuine character. Assassins kill the wrong ones. Yet with all the internal economic problems this country has, business remains good." The uneasiness in her chest abated, and she was now sure of her voice. "In some ways it's a booming economy."

"That's what is so alarming, Susan," Max said. He touched his upper lip with the knuckle of his index finger and looked directly at Susan. "Do you realize that many less endowed universities may have to close down because of this crazy economy?"

"Well, that really won't affect us," Susan said. She drew back reassuring herself that Don and she were with highly endowed universities with trustees who were experts in investment. "Barbara and Peter will be going to Harvard."

"Let's hope so," Max said, clearing his throat. "Don, how's things at the hospital?"

"As you said, there's no money for research."

"That's distressing," Max said.

"Dinner is served," Rose announced with a pinched face.

"Come everybody," Susan said. She touched the ends of her fingers together. "Let's see what Barbara has prepared for us tonight. You know, Nanny and Max, Barbara is our resident gourmet chef."

"I understand, but I wish she'd enjoy some of her dishes," Max said.

"Stop worrying, Max," she said. "I'll always be your 'chubby Barbara.'"

"I feel sorry for you and Peter," Max said. He raised his eyebrows. "Being a child is complicated these days."

Barbara looked at her grandfather with fascination. He was the wisest man she knew.

"Max, you old hedonist," Barbara said. She smiled whitely. "You're talking about fun and pleasure."

"I know it goes against the American work ethic. Henry Wadsworth Longfellow suggested delayed pleasure:

> 'Let us, then, be up and doing,
> With a heart for any fate;
> Still achieving, still pursuing,
> Learn to labor and to wait.'"

Susan glanced at Barbara, who was smiling. It was a poem Barbara hadn't realized she knew.

"Well, Max, I guess we know what your next book is about," Susan said.

"Yes, dear," Nanny said. "You've just heard his introductory chapter, 'Working to Death in America.' But the funny thing about Max is that, although he talks a good game, he works like a madman, even since he retired."

"Work is different now for me," Max said. "These days keep me young and busy. It leaves little time to think of my arthritic hip."

"One pays a price," Susan said, "for everything you do."

Don thought of Ken Smith, his old college roommate from Harvard, who was now a cardiologist in Beverly Hills and convinced that another Great Depression was coming. A misogamist, dedicated bachelor, a machine of a man who worked sixteen hours a day, doing insurance physicals at the end of the day and even locums at posh resorts during his vacation, Ken couldn't forget the stories his mother told him about

Black Thursday, 1929, when Ken's father plunged out the window of his apartment and hit a car on Lake Shore Drive. It struck Don that Ken had changed, from a liberal do-gooder to a money-hoarder, after his mother had suddenly died of a heart attack. Or so it seemed to him.

Susan turned to Barbara. "We've been so busy talking I haven't complimented you, Barbara, on the dinner. It's delicious."

"Yes, I second that," Max said. "You should enjoy it too. You've hardly eaten a thing, Barbara."

"How could I?" Barbara said to Max. "Your comments are right to the point. I wish I could enjoy the simpler things in life."

"Nonsense," Max said. "I remember you as a little girl. You were the happiest, nicest little girl I ever saw." He laughed, and the laugh sounded sharp to Barbara. "If your parents bring out the home movies from those days, I'll prove it!"

Barbara glowered at her father. "No, Dad. Don't get them. I can't stand it."

"Don't be that way," Don said. Barbara's attitudes gave him the willies. "You embarrass too easily."

"Let's take our coffee to the library and see the movies," Don said. He began to set up the equipment.

"There's nothing I like better," Max said. "I enjoy movies, home or commercial, any kind. Well, Donald. Lights out."

Max immediately took the best chair for viewing the screen. The rest of the group settled in the nearby chairs. Peter stood by the door.

"Here's a film taken back in summer of 1960, when we spent a month at Wellfleet. This was one of the hottest summers at Cape Cod," Don said. He was clearly enjoying himself. The only thing better than going on a vacation was reminiscing about a past vacation. "Our cottage was a tiny bungalow, one of four in a row on top of a sand buff, looking across the harbor. Barbara was only a toddler; she had just started to walk well enough to get around on the beach. There she is by the water!"

In the film, Susan stepped back to pick up a shell. Barbara tried to go further into the water, but her mother apparently said no. She came right back.

"Barbara had the sweetest disposition I've ever seen," Don said. Don was speaking slowly, as if thinking it out for the first time. "She always obeyed and was agreeable."

"She was so easy to take care of," Susan added. "Breast feeding was no problem—in fact, I enjoyed it." She let herself slide into vague thoughts about the past. "She weaned without a whimper."

"Please Mother," Barbara said, now looking glassy-eyed, "don't bore Nanny and Max with all the narratives. They've heard them before."

"Never you mind, Barbara," Max said. "There is nothing more fascinating. So on with your documentary, Donald." Max sat back, beaming, thinking how his son's narrations could turn a picture of the Zagreb railroad yards into the Riviera.

"Oh, I was going to say that here's where a crab bit Barbara's little toe." Don looked at Barbara, dubious, rather annoyed at her dismissal of his pleasure. "Look at her trying to control her tears. Always such a stoic. Here she's eating dinner. Look at her wolfing down her duck. We'd just returned from the Mayo Duck Farm in Orleans. Remember their great deli?"

"Stop talking about food, Daddy," Barbara snapped. A sudden emotion almost like fear leaped up in her.

"Interesting you would say that, Barbara," Don retorted, ignoring Barbara's request. "Here's a sequence of Barbara and me coming out of a Howard Johnson's in Chatham." He put his finger to his lips. "Oops, there goes Barbara's top scoop of ice cream. It fell on her new sneakers, which added insult to injury."

Everyone, except Barbara, laughed. She stood up.

"Here's some shots of the Wellfleet beach. Isn't it called Newcomb Hollow?" He glanced at Susan, thoughtfully, then smiled. "Remember how cold the water was, Susan? Beautiful, sunny day, though. A lot of lovely, young girls on that beach—almost as good as The Excellior on the Lido." Don remained bent forward, looking at the screen. "Barbara's sandcastle being washed away by a wave. She cried, and I had to make another one for her. Here we're walking down the beach toward Orleans. I wanted to bring Angus but Barbara wouldn't let me. She knew dogs weren't allowed on the Wellfleet beach so she figured they weren't welcome anywhere at the Cape. What an iron-tight conscience that girl had."

"You mean 'has,'" Susan said, sarcastically.

"Let's see some movies taken a few years later," Max suggested.

"Okay." Don reached into the cabinet, quickly looked through the film and slide collection for the next few years and picked a reel, marked "Family Vacation, August." The projector began to whir again. "This is one of our vacation in the South of France. You can turn the lights off again, Nanny." He found himself searching unsuccessfully for a clever, snappy introduction to the next batch of slides. "This is the Grand

Hotel Cap Antibes. A grand place to stay; they think of everything. Fantastic gardens. That path leads down to Eden Roc. Barbara's twelve there. Hey, there's Peter sitting in the corner. Peter's first trip with us. There's Barbara by the pool. Susan's diving off the high board."

"Aren't you ever in these movies?" Max asked, looking up at him, perhaps concerned.

"Sometimes I make it," Don said. "Speak of the devil! There I am at lunch at Eden Roc. Susan must have taken this one of me, downing my bouillabaisse." A little pompous now. "Lots of artists go there. And here's Barbara on the gym stuff that hangs over the water beyond the pool. Barbara on the rings, now the trapeze. I wish she had kept up her gym lessons."

Don turned to Barbara to discover that she was no longer at the doorway; she hadn't sat down.

"I guess Barbara was tired and went to bed," Don commented, knowing her separateness from him and the whole family, hoping this rift would never become a gulf. "Here's some pictures of Nice," he said. He leaned closer, pointing at the screen. "We stayed at the Negresco Hotel. Remember that movie, *Day of the Jackal?* That's where the assassin phoned Paris, only to learn his plan to kill de Gaulle had been blown. It's one of the great hotels. The doormen dress up in the damnest outfits . . . "

Barbara had to study.

Her grandparents had returned to Boston after the Thanksgiving dinner, which, like most turkey dinners for Barbara, was dull and dry. She had wanted to have pheasant and quail for Thanksgiving, but her mother ruled them out, insisting that wild fowl was too strong for the stomachs of old people. Turkey was always safe, she said; no one would be repelled by it. Barbara also resented the dessert, a tasteless pumpkin pie, which might just as well have been made with old summer squash. It really didn't matter to Barbara that her suggestions were turned down; she wouldn't have eaten much of it anyway, no more than she did of the mother's bland dinner.

She was relieved that her grandparents had gone home early. They had planned to leave Friday afternoon, but Max was restless and wanted to return to his book. Nanny really didn't care about family reunions, less so, her daughter-in-law; a fact Barbara had known for several years. Her grandmother was a cold fish.

Barbara felt uneasy about her grandparents. Perhaps she should have spent more time with them in the morning. Max had hoped to go to the Macy's Thanksgiving Day parade; he wanted to see Evel Knievel do his "wheelies." "Only in America," Max had said, "could business profit from a crazy man's jump across a canyon." But she hadn't offered to go with him. By the time she returned from her twelve-mile run in the park, it was nine-thirty. Furthermore, the parade seemed silly to her. Debbie had called her about a party which several boys were having Saturday night at an Amagansett beach house. Barbara had declined because a ride back to New York that night couldn't be guaranteed. Nevertheless, the phone conversation had taken almost an hour. And she had been abrupt with her grandparents Wednesday night by suddenly leaving the movies and not saying goodnight.

Perhaps they weren't too angry with her. In the spring, she wanted to visit Boston and stay at the grandparents' house, if they had not gone to the Cape yet, and, if she were still in their good graces, they might take her to dinner at the Ritz-Carleton.

Mahler's Ninth was being played by WNCN, as Barbara settled down on the sofa. She wouldn't do any school work tonight. There would be time on the weekend. She listened to the music and stared out the window at the park, still angry about her father's movies last night. Barbara increasingly resented her father being at home these days, or anywhere in her presence. She was happiest when he had to go on trips; she knew that her father could humiliate her again by bringing out his movies. He had done it before when the Michelsons were over for dinner. After that, she had hidden the movies, but Rose had found them. If Rose hadn't, they would have been lost and forgotten forever. Never again would she have to hear how cute, sweet and nice a baby she was. Barbara knew what she had to do. Hide them permanently. Even better, burn them.

She went to the library, uncertain where her father stored the films. At the bottom of the large, oak cabinet were dozens of loose 35-millimeter slides, mostly taken in the last few years. Her father must have shown them to the grandparents. Taking the photograph albums down from their shelf, she cut out all the pictures of herself. She found the movie films, about six reels in all, behind the slides. Since she couldn't see and hesitated switching on the lights—she wasn't certain whether her parents were in bed—she couldn't tell whether the reels were chronologically marked. They would have to be examined in her room.

Barbara crept back to her room and locked the door. The reels were not well marked. She would burn them all immediately; they were probably all of her. Methodically, she unrolled the first film into her bathtub, making a mound of celluloid which stood out sharply against the white marble. She had no matches; there were some in the kitchen. Stealthily, she made her way in the dark to the kitchen; and, guiding herself along the counter, she came to the drawer next to the stove. There was a box of wooden matches, exactly the kind she had used on camping trips. They always lit. She retraced her steps. Her tremulous fingers struck the match, transferred its flame to the celluloid, which burst into flames, so old and dry it was, leaving behind a clump of white ash and a ring of char.

Banging on the door, her father shouted, roaring, outraged. "Open the door; I smell smoke!" She opened it a crack. Then he flung it open, almost hitting her. "For Christ sake! What are you doing?" Don clinched his teeth, trying to put a stove-lid on his anger. "You're not going to burn my movies. Who the fuck do you think you are?" He thought to himself: she mistakes her omnipotence for strength.

Barbara could say nothing in either denial or explanation; nothing came into her mind. She waited, expecting more.

"You didn't like me showing your baby movies to Nanny and Max? Why? Do you think you're too big to be a kid any more? If you want to be a woman, act like one." She frowned, as if to say, What's next? "You better start eating and get some meat on your bones. And get your periods back again. I'm sick of your sneaking around the house, all hours of the night, cleaning out the refrigerator and then throwing up. It's the goddamnest thing I've ever seen. I bet you're down to 90 pounds by now." He pointed his finger at her, and his eyes shot fire.

"No," Barbara said with a shrill in her voice and a smirky smile. "I'm down to 88 pounds and finally have most of the fat off me." She bit her lip to white, and tears came. "It's taken me five months to do it, and you're not going to get me fat again."

"And what's that silly sign hanging over the headboard of your bed?" Don asked. He squinted, more than curious.

"If you weren't so illiterate, you'd know that's Mr. Squeers' comment in Dickens's *Nicholas Nickleby:*

Subdue your appetites, my dears,
and you've conquered human nature.

"I don't know what you're trying to do, Barbara," Don said, "but I know you're acting nutty. You've turned into a Prussian field marshall." Enraged more by what he considered sheer impertinence, he stopped speaking for a moment and stood pouting, hurt to the marrow. "You boss Rose around. She has no say anymore. We pay her $500 a month to cook and you do all the work. She has no authority whatsoever. I never get my fried eggs anymore, because you want me to have poached shad or scrod—or, creamed kidneys on toast—and you stand over us watching us eat and pushing the food on us like a Jewish mother." Suddenly, unbelievably, he found himself on the verge of parting with all controls. "I can't stand it—I don't need another Jewish mother." He stood there, shoulders hunched, shaking his head.

"You're an intolerant old man," Barbara said. She scowled, studying him critically. "I've tried to learn what it is to be a young woman, how to prepare interesting meals, run an efficient house; and all you can say is that I'm a nuisance."

"I'm sorry, Barbara," Don said, "but we're all worried about you." Noticing Barbara's lips were now a thin, tight line, he tried to guess what she was thinking. He continued, then, remote, professional. "You're not your old self. Besides looking like a scarecrow, you're acting funny . . . always tense, rushing around, no friends anymore and turning into a phony intellectual who talks about stuff I can't understand."

"I've reached the point of breaking out intellectually," Barbara said, now smiling pleasantly, pausing momentarily to pick her words, "I used to be afraid kids wouldn't like me if I acted smart, especially boys, but now I don't care." She thought, "Another year I'll be in college and find people there with the same interests."

"In the meantime, you'll drive me crazy," Don said. He touched his chin, looking past her, wishing he could end this conversation. "I'm sorry, Barbara. As a father, I can't understand you anymore; and, as a doctor, I can't help you."

"Mother doesn't seem so worried," Barbara said. She smiled a little absently.

"I'm afraid you're right. She thinks you're going through some teenage phase. Apparently, she lost weight and tried to look like a *Mademoiselle* model when she was your age. But she forgets that she never got under 105 and continued to menstruate." He shook his head angrily. "It's your amenorrhea that really gets to me. A good gynecologist should be able to get you back on cycle."

"What's so wonderful about being 'on cycle,' as you call it." She laughed with delight. "Now I have no cramps, no worry about staining my clothes, and no bothering with tampons and napkins. No thank you. Forget it! I'll worry about it when I get married . . . if I ever do." She smiled and blushed very faintly. "And as far as children are concerned, I don't want any. It's not right to have children. Everyone in my generation knows having children is ridiculous."

"That's stupid!" Don said, part of him wondering whether his daughter was right. He paced back and forth. His face looked grayer. "You've gotten me off the subject, Barbara. My original question was why you burned the movie film and what's with you in general?"

"It's simply," she said, with an incontestable shrug of her shoulders, "the only way I have of stopping you from showing my baby pictures. Why can't you understand they humiliate me? And, also, why do you have to give such sappy middle-class narrations? Your parents must wonder what's happened to their son."

"What they wonder about is *you*!" Don said. The sound of his own voice alarmed him. "They were so upset by your appearance they went home early." He winced, trying to think. "They tried to convince your mother to let me send you to a doctor."

"Did they succeed?" she asked, alarmed.

"No, but, frankly, this movie burning of yours tonight tips the balance." There was a tear on his cheek. "Your mother will see my point in the morning. I'm insisting that you see a gynecologist and a psychiatrist, as soon as possible."

"Oh, no, I'm not exposing myself to some friend of yours." Barbara scowled, but inwardly, not a muscle of her face stirring now. "If I did that, I'd really be nuts."

"What's wrong with my friends?" Indignation crossed his face. "They're among the best physicians in New York. Bill Daniels is a top gynecologist."

"And he's also a good friend," Barbara said, laughing. "A person I know, someone you often invite to dinner here and to Cornwall for the weekends. Don't you think that's a bit too cozy?"

"Then go to someone at Methodist Hospital." He was willing to make this concession; Susan wouldn't think he'd given in. "I know of a good man there. You'd have to see him at the Davis Pavilion. He doesn't have an office downtown."

"I know the IND subway," Barbara said. "But I want to know what he's going to do. He better not try to give me any pills. There's enough chemical junk in the foods we eat."

"That's for him to decide, not us," Don said, with an attitude of detachment. "I'll call his secretary in the morning and make an appointment."

"I'll go under one condition: that you speak only with his secretary and only request an appointment." She said this with a settled conviction, not open to question, as sure as the seasons. "I don't want you giving him some history on me, concocted out of your own fears and fantasies. Agreed?"

"Okay," Don said with some hesitation. "But I want you to tell me what he said." There was weariness in his voice. "You must consider my feelings."

"All right."

"About the psychiatrist . . . I don't know any psychiatrists there."

"Don't worry." She said, not because she believed it, but just to say something, to feel she didn't have to sit back and be passive during his verbal torrent. "If there's a problem, your colleague at Methodist Hospital will be able to handle it."

"But I really think you should speak to a . . . shrink. Isn't that what the kids call them these days?"

"'Stretch' also, depending on your point of view," Barbara said, feeling very smug.

"Oh, of course! Tom Evans is practicing psychiatry in New York now. He's a good man. No, he's not a friend now. We were once friends at Harvard. He was the only guy in my class who did well in biochemistry and went into psychiatry."

"What does that have to do with psychiatry?" Barbara asked, considering again her father's arcane assumptions.

"A great deal. Drugs have been a real breakthrough in psychiatry." His voice was irritatingly sweet to Barbara. "I give all my neurotics Valium and Librium."

"Wouldn't it be better if you talked to your patients?" she asked. "You say Tom Evans did well in biochemistry, but can he talk to me like a real person?"

"I don't see why not," Don said.

"How long has he practiced?" Barbara asked.

"Probably a good ten years." Don tried to make up a curriculum vitae for Dr. Evans. "He did some research in Washington, at The National

Institutes, and practiced in Chevy Chase. He recently came to New York. He has a good mind. You should like him."

"I should?" Barbara asked, at a loss to know why.

"And I hope," Don said, "you don't give him all this philosophy folderol of yours." He began to shake, and, much to her surprise, he sensed that fury was in his eyes. "I'll give his secretary a call tomorrow. Maybe we can set up both consultations the same afternoon, so you don't have to miss too much school."

"Lovely," she said with more than a hint of sarcasm.

"I'll take the rest of my film now," Don said, with a senseless, grim smile. "Please promise me you'll never do this again. I'd feel silly locking up the family movies in our safety deposit box."

"Only if you promise never to show them." Their eyes locked.

"It's a deal," he said grudgingly.

Don kissed Barbara on the forehead, hugged her and patted her on the back of her head with fingers like wood. They smiled, then chuckled and said goodnight.

Barbara did her fifty evening push-ups, washed and went to bed.

Barbara spent hours, making neat, miniscule entries in her journal, which she had started during the summer. Since being back to school, the journal had become more personal, the record of her most intimate thoughts, dreams, fantasies, and feelings, almost too sensitive to be even on paper. Her dreams and fantasies seemed like semiconscious thoughts, acts of creation, imaginative works of selection and arrangement, hovering between consciousness and unconsciousness.

It struck Barbara that her mother had once told her that she kept a journal, really an expanded baby book which she had started after her daughter's birth. Looking through her mother's desk, Barbara found the book in the top drawer. She hated the family 8-millimeter films. The baby book, however, was different: it was private, kept within the immediate family, and no outsider would ever read it. But Barbara also liked the tone of the entries, the warmth and care that seemed to flow with her mother's words. Barbara knew that her mother savored every little detail of her childhood. She compared her baby book with Peter's. Hers had more entries than Peter's. The firstborn child, Barbara knew that her parents had many hopes for her. She was to be the brighter of the children: better educated, more cultured. She knew this from the days when she shared St. Stephen's Nursery School with other toddlers;

her mother and father looked at her in a special way. But Barbara always wished that her mother hadn't cared so much about her manners.

She began to page through her mother's journal:

December 10, 1958. Born at midnight. Weight: 7 pounds, 10 ounces. Perfect timing. Don able to be there. A pink, crying little girl. Buzzing, blooming confusion for both of us. Fluffy blond hair. Blue eyes. Looks like me but has Don's blue eyes. Pediatrician wants me to breast-feed. Ugly thought. Fat cow. Episiotomy incision hurts. Now I have a child I can't lose it. Something might happen. Nothing permanent in life. How happy can one be in this world. But I feel a bit blue. It is an irrational, wordless unhappiness, an impenetrable mood caused largely by the monotony of infant feedings and the suspension of challenging activity.

December 15, 1958, Finally at home. Baby nurse will help for several weeks. A German woman—Fraülein Eva Neustadt. Bossy type, but I can handle her.

January 2, 1959. Returning to work today. Very excited. This is long overdue. Returning to work during the Christmas holidays didn't make much sense. Now I feel better, more alert. The colors of things are brighter. Now I hear people laughing and, for the first time in several weeks, food tastes the way it used to. Dr. Stafford said I'm getting over my "blues."

Barbara wondered how any young woman could remain home, take care of a house, wash her husband's shirts, feed a baby every few hours and acquiesce to everybody's wishes.

January 7, 1959. Breast milk running out, so I've switched totally to bottle. It's just as well; it is too embarrassing to have Rose hear Barbara sucking my breast. Although I hate the ugliness of breast-feeding, I miss the closeness to Barbara. It's a loss. The baby nurse is now getting possessive of Barbara; she resents me. I shall give her a week's notice Friday and look for an easier nanny.

Reading her mother's words recalled a dream she had had the night before, a dream in which pain was intense. In the dream, she knew that she was pregnant and starting labor; and, as this fact revealed itself, she gave birth to a baby boy who got up, walked toward her and began to talk to her.

Barbara liked the dream. Sometimes she could press the fingertips to her eyes and the memory of a dream would come back, a memory not only of concrete images, but also of formal relationships—a dream she enjoyed both at the time she dreamed it but also afterwards.

She paged ahead to her first birthday.

December 10, 1959. A wonderful birthday. Her new doll, Zelda, is always with her. Even takes it to bed at night. It is encrusted with milk and "up-chuck" stains. Smells awful. I hope her birthday doll, a cute German tiger, becomes a substitute.

An entry in early spring caught her eye:

April, 1961. For the last several months, Barbara has seemed aware of somebody else. It turns out that she has an imaginary companion, Penelope, whom she watches over and takes good care of. Barbara says that she loves her a great deal. And, for that reason, she takes her to dinner every night. Rose has to make another place-setting and serve an entree to her. Don and I think this is only a phase, as does her pediatrician. If it continues, we will get Barbara a dog. Besides being a companion, the dog will help Barbara with her sense of responsibility.

She noted an entry on constipation:

June 21, 1961. Barbara has been badly constipated. She holds her BMs back as long as four days. Dr. Stafford feels she might have megacolon from the holding back. She should be checked for Hirschprung's disease, according to my pediatric book. I read about it also in *Cosmopolitan*. But I don't think she has that. All children have spells of one thing or another, some children worse spells than others; she'll grow out of it. Don agrees with me and thinks she is just a willful child. There's awful spillage in her panties. Disgusting! When she does go, they're big clumps in her panties or in the corner of the room—never in the toilet. Dr. Stafford put her on big doses of oil; it leaks everywhere. Stupid man!

Whenever traveling, Barbara had always been aware of constipation. In her younger days, she was stopped up when she visited grandparents in Florida. Her mother told her it was the water; hard water bound things together. She could still hear her mother's opinion, but the same thing happened in Italy, France . . . everywhere she went. And now it was happening in New York. Ignoring the fact that she now ate little, Barbara seemed unaware that she was holding onto everything: old papers, books, clothes, all sorts of things that should have meant very little to her. She had decided to take laxatives; and after looking through her father's book on pharmacology, she bought Senokot, preferring its action over other cathartics. Senokot was natural. Ex-Lax contained chocolate, was fattening and would increase her blood cholesterol. She would take a teaspoon of Senokot every night.

Eager to get out of infancy, she flipped the pages almost a year.

> *May 21, 1962.* Barbara has always found it difficult to play with friends. In kindergarten, she seldom plays dolls with other girls, only play-acts family scenes, like mother-father-baby, and mimics Rose, Don and me. Usually she plays alone, avoiding the doll corner and reading and drawing in close range of the teachers. She's always disappointed when the boys won't let her join in their activities, especially building forts and playing "Cowboys and Indians."

There was a dim memory, probably around age seven, of a vacation trip to Italy. She couldn't have said what it was that made her remember. They were staying in a little town with a protected seaport, which their hotel overlooked, a hotel with a fancy name—the Splendido. She was frightened there by a bad dream. Rose was asleep in the next room, and her door was locked, much to Barbara's surprise. She ran down the hall to her parents' room and flung open their door. Her parents were naked, lying on their sides, facing each other. Her mother gasping, seemed sick. Her father pulled the covers over them and said that her mother had a stomach ache; she had eaten too much. Barbara should go back to her room; her mother would be all right by morning.

Barbara stopped short on seeing the entry for Peter's birth; she swallowed, bit her lip and began to read:

> *December 20, 1962.* Peter was brought home from the hospital today. Five pounds, nine ounces. Overdue. Skinny and wrinkled. Not as cute as Barbara, who danced with delight, proud of her new brother. He's to be circumcised tomorrow. Don wants a mohl to come in and do a neat job. He said the medical students, who do circumcisions for a small fee, often get results that aren't neat. I suspect Don wants a religious ceremony to placate his mother and confuse his father. I don't want Don to fight his parental battles through my children.

What a lot of crap, Barbara said to herself, heavy in the stomach. She turned the rest of the pages, as if in flight from a memory burning in her head, and returned the book to the desk drawer.

The dismissal bell had just rung. Lines of students flowed out of the classrooms, mixing in the center of the wide hall, like the turbulent confluence of several rivers with many tributaries. Someone brushed against Barbara.

"How about going down to Bloomingdale's with me after French class?" Jill asked.

"Sorry, I can't," Barbara said. "I have a dental appointment at two."

"If it's not a big job, I'll wait for you."

"Thanks, but I have to see a root canal dentist over on the West Side," Barbara explained.

"Some other time. Goodbye," Jill said, dubious.

Barbara went into the library to work on a philosophy paper. It was a quarter to twelve, three hours until her appointment with the gynecologist and five hours until the psychiatrist. She decided against having lunch. She wasn't hungry, and, anyway, she wanted to get some work done.

"You're just the person I want to see," a black girl with an Afro said. "I want to pick your brain for my paper. I'm not sure what Mr. Thomas means by the 'general will' and democracy. What philosophers have you written about?"

"It's kind of tricky, Martha," Barbara said. The question seemed to please her. "The greater power men obtain in society for the presentation of society is called 'political power' by Locke, the 'general will' by Rousseau, 'autonomy of will' by Kant, and the 'Leviathan' by Hobbes." She went on, trying not to be pedantic, even worse, condescending, but forming her words carefully. "The 'general will' is really a metaphysical, ideal principle. It is general in that it expresses the will of the generality and it contemplates only general 'goods.'" Barbara found her words so unspeakably eloquent that she felt that she had stepped unexpectedly from one world into another. It was, even though she knew this feeling was absurd, like slipping away from time into the boundless. She continued: "The concept is a substitute for the old idea of natural law presiding over governments."

"I get you, Barbara. Good girl. You really understand this stuff." Her glasses cocked up onto her forehead, Martha responded, her words muffled, just barely intelligible. "I don't remember you being such a brain last year. You've really changed. But anyhow, thanks, Barbara."

As Martha left the library, Barbara could feel only resentment for the girl, who had made too much of her weight loss. Just that morning,

Barbara had spotted a roll of fat along her inner thighs. And her cheeks still puffed out, like Nixon's used to before Watergate. Certainly she still had her fat pads from infancy, and she doubted if she would ever lose them. They would turn into sagging pouches later in life.

The more she thought about being fat, the more she thought of food. She would be busy in the afternoon, burn at least 350 calories, just enough for a lunch. She decided to spend her calories on a baked apple with skim milk at the Empire Deli.

It was the height of the lunch hour at the Empire. Well groomed, silver-haired women in their late fifties sat at a large table, talking about going south to Miami Beach, complaining about the maintenance of their co-ops going up. An overly dressed grandmother showed no concern. Waving a hand in front of her, like fanning away irksome gnats, she said it didn't matter to her. She had signed up five years ago for a senior residence in Tarpon Springs, where she could move whenever she wanted; she was at the top of their waiting list.

Barbara saw an empty double-table in the far corner by the window. The "take-out" part of the deli didn't appeal to her. She would be exposed to public view, both in and outside the restaurant, which was next to the crosstown bus stop. People gawked through the long windows at the food while waiting for the bus.

"East Side tomatoes went up ten cents more this week," a wizened lady said to a young girl, physically her daughter, who looked up at her mother with a shrug of her shoulders.

"Don't worry, Mother," the daughter said. "You have more than your Social Security to live on."

Barbara sat with her back to the two women; she couldn't look at them. The idea of humoring an old mother irritated her.

A dark Middle Eastern waiter put a huge menu in front of Barbara. It listed fancy club sandwiches, with names like "The Empire State" and "The Reconstruction," as well as a variety of dairy dishes and French pastries. Barbara forgot about her baked apple, she ordered cold borscht, thin enough, she calculated, to be no caloric threat, followed by Nova Scotia salmon, with cream cheese on a plain bagel. The waiter asked her if she wanted a dessert with her coffee. She ordered cherry cheesecake.

"Best cheesecake in New York," the waiter said, as he set the huge red and white triangle in front of her. Her fork slid through the creamy, cherry-filled cake. The buttons on her jeans seemed to tighten in protest. Nevertheless, she ate all the cheesecake and spooned up the cherry juice. When she got up to pay the check, she thought her guts had fallen into her pelvis. Her legs were leadened, her face puffed up; fingers felt like balloons. She imagined a woman's fingers, grotesque like her own, coming toward her. People sitting behind her sounded far away. As she left the table, her buttocks moved up and down in rhythm with her breasts. Turning sharply to the right, she went into the ladies room, relieved to find it empty. Almost painless now, it took only a minute.

Barbara washed out her mouth with cold water. Now she looked thinner; her eyes less puffy and the contour of the cheekbones more visible. She adjusted her jeans, relieved that her body was returning to size.

A crosstown bus was at the stop; she ran for it. All the seats were taken. Her legs felt a little unsteady as the bus lurched through the Central Park transverse. Her throat burned; she needed a piece of scented chewing gum. At West 86th Street, she descended into the IND subway station. An "A" express train screamed by the local station, heading north into Harlem. The token booth attendant shouted directions in a melodious Jamaican accent.

"Take the 'AA' train to 125th Street," he shouted at her. His eyes were sad, half-closed. "Then change to the 'A' express to 168th Street."

She realized that she was the only person on the platform. Her helplessness was made worse by another passing express train, producing a clatter which hurt her ears. She remembered reading in the *Times* that this station had the worst noise level in New York. She would go deaf if she had to wait here often. Leaning over the platform, she saw no lights from an oncoming train. A black rat, more than a foot long, ran down the track, stood up on his hind legs to look around and vanished behind a pillar. Barbara turned to read graffiti on the walls. "José 108" was in brilliant red, ornate letters. There was an ad for karate, with a guarantee of self-protection after three weeks. Next to the karate ad was a picture of Gatsby and Daisy, both in white, announcing the coming of *The Great Gatsby*. Under the ad was scribbled: "Gatsby Sucks." On the other side was an ad for Alka-Seltzer.

The floor of the station began to quake. A white light appeared down the track, an incandescent glow inching up the rails of the track. It was an "AA" train, almost empty, as though catching its breath before the rush hour.

Barbara picked a car—her mother once told her to do this—with the conductor. As soon as the doors closed, he locked himself in his compartment, leaving Barbara across from the only other passenger, a plump English-looking woman in her late fifties. The woman carried a brown leather attaché bag, on which she rested a thick book which absorbed her interest. Barbara turned to her own book and started chapter four of *The Magic Mountain.* At each local station she glanced up, wishing for 125th Street to appear. Finally, she was there. She walked across the platform to a waiting "A" express, slipped into the nearest car and continued her reading. She lost her sense of time until the train stopped at 135th Street and broke off her feeling of being inside the character of Hans Castorp.

Returning to her book, she soon sensed eyes focused on her. She looked up, into the desperate eyes of a swarthy boy—about sixteen, she imagined. He was leering at her as he sat forward in his seat, moving up and down. She felt panicky and angry at the same time. Would he come over? Make her hold it? Would he try to rape her? She would run to the next car; but, just as she got up, the older woman with the attaché case appeared from nowhere.

"All right, young man," the woman said, firmly, intolerant of recalcitrance. "I know that thing of yours isn't working right. You need a doctor to fix it up." She spoke firmly but softly, holding out her hand to him. "Come with me at the next stop. I'm a doctor, and I have a doctor friend who can make you not afraid of girls."

The youth pulled himself together, and compliantly followed her off the train at 168th Street. The woman smiled at Barbara and disappeared. When Barbara reached the street, they were out of sight. Relieved, she swallowed hard.

She paused to get her bearings. She passed the main entrance to the hospital and managed to find the Davis Pavilion. The hospital looked overgrown, unplanned for, like weeds ignored and now gone wild. The medical office building, all glass and plastic, looked like the tallest weed, sure to fall after the first heavy frost. She wouldn't intern here, she thought—not at Mass General either, if Steven were there. A receptionist directed Barbara to Dr. Ronald Berg's office. It was large, modern and looked like an overpriced doctor's waiting room. A middle-aged, sedate woman, the secretary, took Barbara's name, acknowledged the appointment hour and asked her to be seated with five women already waiting.

Barbara paged through an issue of *Nova,* without even thinking about the pictures. She wished that she had asked her father what gynecologists really do in a routine exam.

"The doctor will see you now, Miss Gordon," said the nurse. "Come with me, please."

The nurse had her lie down on an examining table and told her to remove her jeans and underpants. Then Barbara covered herself with a white sheet. Like a corpse, Barbara thought, puzzled, faintly smiling.

She waited for Dr. Berg, wondering what his first move would be. She couldn't decide which would be worse: his weighing her, or sticking a finger into her vagina. It didn't matter. She would refuse both.

"Good afternoon, Barbara. I'm Dr. Berg." He leaned against the white instrument table, taking her in with every glance. His round face and circular, rather surprised-looking eyes reminded Barbara of a cautious rabbit.

"Tell me how I can help you," he asked.

She smiled in spite of herself. "Well, my father thought I should see you because I haven't had a period since last spring."

"Had they been regular before?"

"Pretty much so . . . since I started at twelve," Barbara said. "I think I'm just off my schedule. I was out west, you know, mountain climbing last summer and didn't get much sleep or good food as I guess I should have. And this fall I've been working hard to raise my grades for college."

"Good for you. What school do you go to?"

"Rockleigh, eleventh grade. I love it."

"What college do you want to go to?"

"Radcliffe, like my mother."

"You can't go wrong," the doctor said with a look of approval. He wished his own daughter were as bright. "Are you interested in a career?"

"Yes, theoretic physics, especially particle theory. I hope to do some elective work at M.I.T." She thought that would give him a thrill.

"Unusual for a girl your age to have such a . . . specific interest."

"My uncle is a physicist. He was with J. Robert Oppenheimer in New Mexico during the war."

"Really? . . . Have you had any bleeding or discharge?"

"No. Only occasionally from my nose. I have allergies."

"All right. Let me feel your tummy," the doctor said. "Hmm, not an ounce of fat on you. It makes it easy. I can even feel the tip of your spleen."

Barbara blushed.

"Well, young lady, I think you're just off your cycle. Nothing serious. I'll give you some pills to start things up again. Here's a prescription. Follow the directions. I suggest you take it easy over the Christmas holidays."

"I'll be in Jamaica for two weeks during the holidays getting a lot of rest and good food."

"Let me see you in several months. Miss Pomeroy will schedule your next appointment."

In going to the elevator, Barbara thought next of Dr. Evans, a more difficult opponent to handle, since she couldn't anticipate his questions. She read in the reception area until the time for her psychiatric consultation.

Dr. Evans's waiting room was empty; she was his only patient. There was a Miro print on one wall. No magazines or ashtrays were evident. The room lacked a personality; it might as well have been an in-transit area at an international airport. Barbara stood there, trying to find nuances in the Miro, thinking of what to say, or not say, to Dr. Evans.

His soundproof doors suddenly opened. A young man in a white coat stiffly strode out, shutting the outer door after him. For a brief moment, Barbara feared this man was Dr. Evans. He was too frenetic, too young; he must be a medical student or resident, Barbara thought. The door opened again, and a chunky man nodded to her.

"I am Dr. Evans." He had a round face, curly red hair, prominent teeth, slightly spaced apart.

A foam mattress couch was in one corner, an executive desk, perhaps from Zopkin's, and a black Danish chair, obviously intended for patients. Industrial chic, she thought. Dr. Evans waved her to the chair.

Barbara sat back, crossed her leg, resting the calf of one leg at right angles to the knee of her other leg. Did she look tough enough? She noticed that she was chewing her right cheek. Primitive, she thought. They glared at each other. She broke the stare and focused on his Gucci loafers for a few seconds. Finally, Dr. Evans spoke.

"Your father called me last week, as you know, and said he was concerned about you." He rubbed his upper lip with the inside of his index finger. "You've lost some weight?"

She hoped to throw him off. "Yes. That's quite right. He's been very concerned all fall. He's been desperately dieting so he can get into more youthful clothes." She smiled, her mouth open and her eyes wide with excitement of the challenge. "He hasn't been very successful, though. He's talked so much about dieting he thinks he gave me the idea. I simply don't know why he's so guilty."

"How much weight have you lost?"

"About ten–fifteen pounds since last summer. Most of it was lost in Wyoming—the Tetons—mountain climbing. And then this fall I lost a few more pounds, bringing my weight down to 100. I feel best at that weight." She smiled sweetly, even radiantly, as though it were a moment of great significance. "I find daily exercise is all I need to maintain it. All the girls at Rockleigh do this."

"Are some of them dieting too?"

"Oh, yes, I'm afraid I've started something." She straightened up, seeing a chance to move him away from her. "Let's see; there's Peggy, Vivian, Ruth and Dorothy. I should add Ann. They all want to lose weight so they'll have a better chance at dating." She shook her head in dismay.

"Are you sure you haven't dieted, too?" Dr. Evans asked.

"Oh, I hope not. I don't want to get sick." She looked at him, absolutely innocent and blank. "I just wanted to get rid of some baby fat so I could wear the new styles. I bought a beautiful bikini I have to fit into for our trip to Jamaica."

"When are you going?"

"In a couple of weeks, for the Christmas holiday. I'm looking forward to it so much." Her manner, she sensed, was too conciliatory, artificial, as if mimicking someone. "There aren't many boys in Port Antonio, but there might be a few rich ones at Frenchman's Cove."

"How will your parents feel about that?"

"They're great," she said cooly, avoiding his eyes. "They give me a lot of freedom because I know I won't abuse it. My mother has great confidence in me; she knows I'm just like her: think things out, nothing reckless."

"And your father?"

"He's a doll. A real d-o-l-l! Very generous and trusting." She was becoming increasingly aware of how she was trying to please the psychiatrist and she didn't like herself one bit. "He's one of the few fathers I know who doesn't try to compete with his children. He's a devoted father and physician. I love him very much."

"Have you had any traumatic experiences?" Dr. Evans asked, looking very sympathetic.

Barbara thought for a minute. Searching for an answer, distracted by her heart racing like mad, she felt silly, clumsy, inept. Dr. Evans was getting anxious, she decided.

"Yes," she said with an air of discovery. "This summer I almost fell when I was mountain climbing." She shuddered, hunching her shoulders, clasping her hands behind her head and then turned her face to him again. "I was going up a sheer cliff, had my left foot planted on a ledge and reached for an overhanging rock above my head. As I held on, I stepped up with my right foot. Just then the rock let go, and I was left hanging until I could find another footing." She hoped her face showed the terror she had felt at that moment. "I kept my strength until I reached the top. Then I collapsed out of exhaustion . . . I could have been killed." She sighed with relief.

"Have you dreamed about this experience?"

"No. I never have bad dreams," Barbara said. "Last night I dreamed I was in Jamaica. I swam out to a little island offshore and spent the day snorkeling. It was beautiful."

"Do you date much?" the psychiatrist asked. There was a note of impatience in his voice.

"Date? . . . I'm sorry; young people don't use that word anymore." She hoped that she didn't sound too condescending, too smart-assed. "Yes, I go out. We go to movies, stop at Blimpie's for something to eat, that sort of thing. I try to keep it simple for the boy. New York is so expensive."

"For everyone," Dr. Evans said. "Have you ever had any difficulties with your menstrual periods?"

"Yes, I have. In fact, I just came from seeing Dr. Berg." She studied Dr. Evans for several seconds, wondering what kind of impression she was making on the man. "They've been irregular since last summer, and he said not to worry."

There was silence. Dr. Evans looked hard at her. The silence grew and struggled with itself. Barbara could tell he was trying to figure out how to get back to the question of her weight loss. She decided to let him flounder. He made the next move.

"How has your health been in the last year?"

"Oh, so-so," she said. "I used to be one of those kids who got every cold going around." Did she sound fragile, she wondered. "When I was in eighth and ninth grade, I missed a great deal of school. In the gym I was the first to get winded. The kids used to call me sickly; I was so pale and flabby, as I said earlier." Her voice suddenly changed, becoming infinitely older, infinitely more adult but yet frantic, as though it were indeed the voice of a child. "But last summer I went to Outward Bound, lost some of that baby fat and got my body in shape. So far this fall, I haven't missed a day in school."

"That's curious," Dr. Evans said, "because I was just thinking you looked a bit pale. Did Dr. Berg order a hemoglobin?"

"No, he didn't." She shook her head, knowingly. "I imagine he figured my red cells were okay since I haven't been menstruating much these days." She thought her remark was perceptive. "The whole family is rather ghostly at this point. That's why we're going to Jamaica."

"Then, too, I suppose you've been working hard in school," Dr. Evans said.

"Yes. They really do work us." The sudden animation of her voice emphasized her seriousness. "I'm in the eleventh grade and feel the pressure of SAT's and college interviews coming up."

"What are your college plans?" Dr. Evans asked.

Barbara thought that she had seen a suppressed yawn come over his face.

"I hope to go to Radcliffe," she said, bending forward to him and rubbing the tip of her nose with her index finger. "My mother went there and had a wonderful time. I want to be a comparative literature major. I know that doesn't prepare me for anything much, but a woman has the luxury of not having to worry about making a living. Maybe I'll meet a successful young man at Harvard."

They both smiled.

"It's unusual to hear a young girl talk that way these days," Dr. Evans said. His voice was clear, a bit reedy, and Barbara noticed that his fingers were twitching.

"Oh, women's lib!" Barbara said. "I really don't believe in it except for equal work opportunities. Women should be paid the same as men." She trembled a little inside from the blow she wished she could inflict on Dr. Evans. "But the rest of it is nonsense. I hope to be a woman who can enjoy depending on my husband and, at the same time, feel whole and complete."

Dr. Evans looked over Barbara's shoulder to the digital clock that sat on a shelf behind her. He moved his feet several times; he was searching for a smooth closing. She would remain silent and let him fish for a while.

The silence seemed endless. She restrained herself from giggling.

"Well, that's fine. I really don't think we need to get together again." He held out his right hand and said: "I hope you get a good rest and get a nice tan in Jamaica."

They shook hands and Barbara left Dr. Evans alone in his office. She walked to the street, reached into her pocket, crumpled up the prescription and stuffed it in a mailbox. Then she hailed a cab.

"Bloomingdale's, please."

Barbara had seen her doctors. Now it was time to do her Christmas shopping. The stores would be open till nine.

Don was upset by a phone call from Chicago. Invariably, long-distance calls from Chicago frightened Don, for it meant an emergency from his twin brother, Joel, who constantly struggled to keep his job as a guard at the Chicago Museum of Modern Art.

"Yes, Joel," Don said, with mock interest. "How have you been?"

"Pretty good," Joel said. "But I'm thinking about quitting this job. It's getting heavy . . . very heavy."

"What do you mean?" Don asked.

"It's the gun . . . the damn gun," Joel said. "They want me to carry a gun."

"Why?" Don asked.

"There have been a lot of art robberies this year," Joel said. "Last week a Degas, worth $500,000, was pinched. Now they want us to carry guns."

Don said nothing, knowing that Joel was looking for an invitation to come to New York—even a job at the hospital. Don could have placed his brother in a variety of jobs: a security officer (guards carried no guns at the hospital), a laboratory assistant (his college sciences would have qualified him), a male practical nurse in the recovery room (Joel's heterosexual urges, Don suspected, were slight), or, after some training, on the ambulance (but he was afraid of blood).

"Can you get me a job, Don?" he finally asked.

"Of course, I can," Don said, trying to be positive in his tone. "But you like Chicago, have friends there and favorite haunts. Can't you switch to some other job at the museum?" The room was very quiet. Joel said nothing, and into the silence Don asked: "Maybe, a *maitre d'* at the restaurant there?"

"That's not the kind of change I have in mind," he said. "It would be nice being back in the northeast; after all, I grew up in Boston."

"Have you considered museums in Boston?" Don asked. Don was silent, and he could hear Joel's breathing in the receiver. He couldn't wait any longer for an answer from his brother who seemed to be in the same room with him. "The ones in New York, I'm afraid, probably have more security measures than the Chicago museums."

"Boston museums pay nothing," Joel answered. "New York has more possibilities for me."

"Well, okay, Joel. It's good hearing from you. I have to run now. We're going to Jamaica over Christmas. Let us know how things work out in Chicago. Susan and the kids send their love. 'Bye."

Years ago—so long ago he could hardly remember it—someone told Don that Joel and he were "as like as two peas in a pod." Somebody else had said that the two of them were exactly alike, like snowflakes or crystals. His face drooped to the form of upside-down V's as he considered the comparisons. It wasn't true: some peas were cone-shaped; some were square; others were hexagonal. Only a few were round. And in every pod, Don thought, there was a pea, runted and pushed to the side. Nature favored variety rather than duplication.

It was a long and tedious flight to Kingston. There had been a delay at Kennedy because of heavy Christmas travel. The Pan Am 747 was completely filled with Jamaicans, mostly women, returning home with presents, many carrying religious statues, gold-embossed and wrapped in plastic bags. Others clutched large dolls and stuffed animals, intend-ed for children, cared for by grandmothers, too old to work in New York.

At Palisados Airport, Don picked up a BMW rental car and loaded the luggage and Christmas presents into the trunk. As they drove out of the airport, he found himself at the roundabout, drifting to the right of the center line. He would have to remind himself that English "left-hand" driving was the custom here.

He recalled what had happened to a New York anesthesiologist last year before the unlucky man had driven two minutes away from the airport parking lot. At a roundabout, probably the same one he was passing, a truck had hit him head-on, killing the man and his family.

The outskirts of Kingston were ugly. Several cement plants belched dense smoke, which disappeared in the gray smog. Nevertheless, Don was still glad that they had landed at Kingston. He objected to Montego Bay and Ocho Rios; there were too many American businessmen at these resorts, loud and vulgar, spending money ostentatiously.

He looked forward to the two-week vacation. No one could reach him in Jamaica. He was tired before the winter had ever arrived. His research assistants had fumbled his new project, and he wondered if he were seeing too many patients. His last vacation had been in August and was not particularly restful. The young gynecologist covering his practice had called him a number of times. He hoped this time Dr. Rothstein would show better judgment. After a night in Kingston, they would drive to Port Antonio, where they had rented a house in San San through a retired British colonel, who devoted himself to real estate in the northeastern corner of Jamaica.

As they drove through Kingston, they decided, seeing urban poverty and decay worse than in Harlem, not to drive any more around the city. Instead, they would go directly to the Blue Mountain Inn, which some friends had recommended. They drove through a middle-income residential section, mostly pastel, stucco split levels, and past the campus of the University of the West Indies. The Blue Mountains lay ahead of them—a striking mountain range, over a mile high and stretching along the center of the elongated island, like a wall separating the north and south coastlines. The road started its ascent and began to disappear into the jungle.

"There's the inn," Barbara shouted to her father who hadn't seen the entrance, mostly hidden in bougainvillea.

The inn was built into the side of a mountain, next to a rushing stream. While the porters took the luggage to the rooms, Barbara followed the descending rocky foot path to the stream. Below a falls, the stream formed a pool filled with clear, cold water. She took her shoes off and waded up to her knees. Her feet hurt; they were red and swollen. In fact, she noticed that the contour of her ankles wasn't apparent because of swelling, which she attributed to sitting for most of the day.

She slipped on her sandals and climbed the steep stairs to her room. The exertion tired her and made her short of breath. She blamed the fatigue on the altitude, lay down on her bed and fell asleep, just before her parents looked in to see if she wanted to join them in the garden for cocktails before dinner.

"Let her sleep, Don," Susan said. "She's looked so tired in the last few weeks."

"I agree," Don said, "but you know what Dr. Evans said." He was shaking his head gloomily. "Adolescent girls go through these things for a while. I hadn't realized that some of Barbara's classmates are also having their troubles."

"She still hasn't had a period as far as I know," Susan said. "But I don't dare ask her. And she's got downy, blond, baby hair all over her, just like a new-born monkey."

"I wonder if she took Dr. Berg's medication," Don said. "He thought her amenorrhea was a simple functional problem. Before we left, I checked at our drug store to see if she had the prescription filled." After a few seconds, he said—too loudly, as though his voice had to be loud to penetrate the folds of darkness that lay over the garden—"There's no record of it."

"Perhaps it was filled somewhere else—maybe near school."

"Well, we'll just have to see how she is after the vacation," Don said.

They pretended to be engrossed in the gardens of the inn. Don looked at the menu and made some approving remarks about the food.

"What time shall we leave tomorrow?" Susan asked.

"It depends on how you want to go." He was distracted for a second by the low, monotonous whistling of a bird in the bushes. "If we take the coastal road east and around to Port Antonio, we'll be going the long way. And some of the road isn't very good after Port Morant; there's one spot called Flat Bridge, which is just the road running through a stream; no bridge at all. If there's a heavy rain, you don't get across. Beyond that, there's less traffic, but the road is pot-holed, jaggy and passes through pockets of poverty, little towns like Hectors River, Manchioneal, Long Bay and Boston Harbor."

"You make it sound exhausting," Susan said. "Maybe we should fly." She raised her glass of sherry, upset by the prospects of the journey, and she absent-mindedly touched a button on her blouse with her left hand. She wished that she could read her long novel, which she resolved to get through on this vacation.

"It would be better to go by way of Hardware Gap." He cocked his head, grinning. "All we have to do is follow the road we left in coming to the inn and head north over the mountains."

"Over the mountains!" Susan said. "Why . . . they're over 7,000 feet."

"The road is safe," Don said. "When the British first held Jamaica, they cut the road out of the mountains, named it Hardware Gap and mapped out its hairpin turns." He laughed, but not wholeheartedly.

"You see, I've done a lot of research on it. Driving this road in a BMW and hearing its gears spin will be great fun."

"Barbara doesn't want to come to dinner," Peter announced, matter-of-factly. "She's still tired. She wants me to get her a hamburger and coke."

"Will you be a good boy," Don said, "and get it for her. Your mother and I will go to our table."

Calmly, purposefully, the parents left the patio bar and walked into the outdoor restaurant area.

"Good evening," the *maitre d'* said.

"There are three of us. Our daughter will not be joining us," Don said.

"Don't you think we should get another opinion on Barbara?" Susan asked, inclining her head and crossing one leg over the other. "She looks like hell. Her cheeks are really sunken; far beyond Katherine Hepburn's, one of her idols, you know. Rose told me an odd story: When Barbara helped her with the Christmas cards, she wouldn't lick the stamps. Rose thought Barbara feared the calories in the glue."

"We should wait and see what she's like when we get back to New York." Don dismissed the subject with a wave. "Let's order."

The three of them said little during the dinner, except to comment on the French and Jamaican cooking. They had never had plantains before, although Susan had seen the vegetable displayed in Columbus Avenue markets in New York. After fried bananas for dessert, which none of them could finish, they went to bed early.

Barbara was the first up in the morning. She did her exercises on the veranda and jogged a mile up the road, to the point where the road climbed the mountain at forty-five degrees.

After leaving the inn, the mountain road rose quickly to 5,000 feet. The mountains stretched like a spine almost the length of the island; they could see the ocean on both sides of the island. Past Irish Town and Redlight, they drove in the heat.

Two motorcycles hummed behind them for several hundred yards; then they roared when they accelerated, popped, and when the drivers, ebony-black young men in Hawaiian shirts, cut the spark for a right angled turn, the motorcycles crackled on the crest of the hill.

The tropical beauty was shattered for Susan when they reached Hardware Gap, for there the road became single-laned with partly washed-away shoulders, which had lost their dirt and gravel over the precipice by the side of the road. Susan screamed when she realized the road fell off by the side of the car.

"Don, you damn fool, stop the car." Her face had blanched.

"We have to go on. I can't back up on this road," Don said, glancing up, slightly surprised and then said: "Be happy we're not in our station wagon. If the Jamaicans can do it, so can we."

Barbara laughed when she looked out of her window. She could barely see Kingston now. The idea of falling had no meaning to her. She would probably be unconscious before the car crashed into the forest. And her remains would be scattered through the jungle and soon eaten away, she imagined, by land crabs and vultures. She was glad her father was fearless. That she admired in him.

At Sylvan Hill, the road widened to two lanes and the rest of their descent was easy. The next town was Tranquility, which made them all laugh. At the north coast, near Buff Bay, they turned onto the A4 and drove east to Port Antonio and San San, which they finally reached by nightfall.

The cook and houseman had seen the car lights coming up the road. They were standing at the gate. Inge and Javin introduced themselves in their best English accents and then took them into the large courtyard, past a bubbling fountain, to the north side of the house that overlooked the sea. Don went with the cook and houseman to the kitchen where he inspected the food supplies and general conditions. He instructed Javin to stock up on Schweppes tonic water and Inge to use margarine, if she must fry their foods.

Susan liked the open, airy rooms and the oak and white stucco construction. Peter ran from the living room to the patio and swimming pool, and Barbara lingered over the view of Frenchman's Cove and its beaches. It excited her.

Going to her room, bending over, Barbara got out her tape recorder from the desk where she had hidden it, threaded the tape on the machine and locked the bedroom door. She bent over and plugged it in and then stood, motionless, squinting, wondering, enclosing herself in silence. She lay down in her bed, her hand under her head, warm under her sheet, listening, almost drifting off into sleep.

Steve: *I'll miss you very much. Wish you could move out to the Bay area.*

Barbara: *So do I! It will be awful without you.*

Steve: *I love you.* (He breaks off for several minutes.) *Maybe we can see each other over the Christmas vacation.* (Puzzled murmurings. The voices fall away to silence, then after a moment begin again, rapid and light.)

Barbara: *What do you love about me?*

Steve: *Your hair, face, sense of humor.* (Loudly, slightly pompously.) *Your sculptured body, your Dionysian pleasures.* (His voice grows distant, and then there are peals of laughter.)

Barbara: *That's great! Beautiful . . .*

Steve: *Right there for me.*

Barbara switched off the tape and absently sank into thought. She tried to clear the images from her mind, but struggling against the weight of exhaustion, feeling herself sinking into drowsiness, she closed her eyes and permitted herself to fall off into sleep, almost instantly dreaming, for what seemed like hours until her mother woke her for dinner.

Around nine-thirty, a bit sleepy after a heavy dinner, Don went to the patio. There was no moon; the night was black and humid. He could see the top of Alligator Head, as it disappeared into the darkness. The lights of Frenchman's Cove shone forth in defiance of the tropical night. It was a surfless night with only occasional faint noises from the undergrowth near the pool. In the afternoon the gardener had macheted the growth around the wall of the garden. Don wondered if the Jamaican had disturbed some animal life. The pamentoes had just blossomed. Could these faint sounds be land crabs making their annual pilgrimage for pamentoes? He lost interest in his speculations. Finally, almost all the lights which dotted Alligator Head faded into the darkness. The bubbling of the pool's filter made Don sleepy.

Don walked along the open corridor of the Spanish house. Barbara and Peter were asleep (the Biot sounds of their sleep-breathing told this fact) after their long swim in the Blue Lagoon. Entering the master bedroom, Don was pleased that their room was cool. The houseman had left open the doors to the balcony; and, with the window shutters pushed back, there was a cool breeze coming off the bay. He took off his clothes and slid under the fresh sheet, falling asleep in what seemed like a fraction of a second.

Unconsciousness knows no time. Don had no idea of how long he had been asleep; or, for that matter, exactly when he had awakened.

There was a deafening buzz which made his inner ear vibrate. For a moment, he thought it was part of a dream—a strange sound, perhaps from the day residue of power boats and water skiiers in the Blue Lagoon. What could it be? He could see out to the terrace. Nothing was out there. A gentle breeze was coming into the room. He was no longer asleep.

The noise was now eclipsed by increasing vibrations which seemed to pass through the bony structures around his ear. It was no dream; it was some frantic insect trying to free himself from the warm, sticky wax in his right ear. The bug let out a convulsive lurch. Don jumped out of bed with a shriek, which woke Susan up. She looked at him with disbelief, as he hopped about on one foot and then the other, expecting to dislodge the thrashing bug. The activity only sent the insect into more of a frenzy. Don dug for the bug with his little finger, but he feared that would slam him against the ear drum. His finger was as effective as a billiard stick. He would drown the bug mercilessly. Shouting instructions to Susan, he ran to the bathroom, shoved open the shower door and slid to the chilly tile floor.

"Go ahead," Don shouted to his wife. "Turn the shower on fast." And he pointed his buzzing ear toward the shower nozzle.

The water was cold. How could water in the tropics be cold? The water source in this part of Jamaica was rain. He knew that rain water was collected from the roof and went to a water tank under the house. What had happened to the hot water heater? Peter must have turned off the heater switch thinking it was the switch for the hall lights. Don had no choice. What else could he do in the middle of the night to kill the insect but drown him in cold water?

Don lay there, shivering on the tile as torrents of water pelted one side of his head and face. The flapping and buzzing rose in crescendo, then diminished for a few seconds, only to return with new vengeance. The cycle continued for what seemed like hours. Finally, the bug quieted. Gradually, Don made his way back to bed. The noise in the ear was an agonizing contraction, as though he had turned over several times after a seizure. He was surely dead. How could any bug live through a flood of cold water? Don pulled himself from the floor of the shower. His left foot had gone to sleep, and he was exhausted and shaky as he stepped out of the shower. Susan helped to dry him off. He turned to go back to bed and saw Barbara standing in the doorway; he put the towel around his middle.

"What's wrong, Daddy?" Barbara asked. Her voice was quaking.

"Your father has a bug in his ear," Susan said, rolling her eyes up. "He'll be all right; go back to bed now."

Gradually, Don made his way back to bed. The noise in the ear was entirely gone. But the ear was blocked, as though the bug had dove to the depths of the sea. The insect and his bath water remained. Perhaps the bug would come out in a torrent of water and wax during the night and lay dead on his pillow in the morning. With that thought, he went to sleep.

In the morning, the ear took his total attention as it throbbed, as though something was pushing the water back and forth in the ear canal. There was no sign of the bug. It had either died in the ear, or made an escape into the darkness. What good was he to himself, stuck in Jamaica with no otoscope and a bug in his ear? No eardrops or antibiotics! And a week to go before getting back to New York.

Don drove to the beach and did the sidestroke across the bay with his aching ear in the water, hoping to wash the bug out. Next, he ran along the beach, trying to shake him free. He took his little finger and shook his head, like a dog just out of water. Eventually, he admitted to his family—and himself—that he needed a doctor. He asked Inge about a local physician; she told him to call Dr. Calaban in Port Antonio. He had given her family good care over the years. He could only imagine Dr. Calaban annointing him with oils and herbs while dancing around him with a snake coiled about his arm. He called the manager of Frenchman's Cove to learn that the club's physician was on holiday in England and his substitute had been delayed several days.

Don sat on the terrace; he thought about the hot, dusty ride to Kingston along the coastal road to the University of West Indies Hospital. The British trained doctors could extract the bug, probably even identify the insect as to species and toxicity. The houseman approached him, cleared his throat and addressed Dr. Gordon with deference.

"Do you wish a drink, Doctor, before dinner?"

"Yes, please. I need something strong to help my pain." His voice was intense and reedy. "One of your island's insects got into my ear last night and is driving me nuts. He wants to go back to New York with me."

Javin smiled. "If you can get me a working visa, I'll go with him . . . But that won't be necessary, Doctor." Javin folded his arms and squinted. "We folks here know about the banana cockroach. Just pour a little of this brown rum in your ear. That will make him come out with the wax and dry up the infection."

Don took a bottle of Appleton's rum to the bathroom. He felt silly; he didn't want Susan to know what he was doing. As he poured himself an earful, he wondered what his New York doctor friends would say. He cocked his head to the side to let the rum settle around the insect.

"Don, where are you?" Susan called out. She repeated the question several times, loud, finally expecting an answer.

He said nothing. He hoped that Susan would be distracted by the children in the pool.

She tiptoed along the hall to the door of a bedroom. "Don, what are you doing in the children's room?"

"Here I am, Susan. Just doing something to my ear," he said in a thin voice.

As Susan approached the children's bathroom, Don was bending over to let the rum trickle out of his ear. He put a towel to his ear as she entered the bathroom.

"Don, you reek of rum!" She laughed, horselike. "Are you sneak-drinking?"

For Don to be accused of alcoholism was worse than admitting his need for Javin's homespun treatment.

"Susan, I told Javin about my ear. He felt sorry for me and mentioned a local treatment—rum in the ear." He pushed out his lower lip, then sucked it in again and said: "I'm embarrassed to admit it; like a damn fool I tried it."

"You are a goddamn fool, Donald." She leaned toward her husband, perspiration on her forehead like dewdrops on a pale mushroom. "Nincompoop," she shouted. "Your miserable bug is in the sink, pickled with rum, lying on his back, dead to the world. If you hadn't been so proud, that witch doctor Inge told you about could have gotten the bug out and prevented your ear infection. Your stubbornness cuts through every part of your life." Susan turned to hide her tears from her husband and left the room.

Don picked up the bug with a piece of tissue, dropped it in the toilet and flushed it away.

The rain fell with no forgiveness, making small lakes in the road along the way to the airport. As Don swung into the rental car return area, he splashed several construction workers. They glared at him and said something about roasted pork.

"Those bastards," Don said. He slammed on his brakes and came to an abrupt stop. "Thank God we're getting out of this place."

Don rushed ahead of Susan and the children. A porter went to the car for the luggage.

"Don't tell me!" Don said, seeing the crowd in the waiting area. "They're all going to New York on our plane. I'll get the bags from the porter."

They pushed their way to the Pan American check-in counter.

"Good afternoon, Mrs. Gordon," the airline clerk said. "You're a party of four." He smiled faintly. Then: "Your tickets are in order, but there will be a charge for alien exit permits."

"We have to pay to be sprung from this country?" Susan asked. Her narrowed eyes and tight mouth left no doubt about her anger. She threw a twenty-dollar bill at the clerk.

"Customs and Immigration is to the right," he said, without looking up.

"Thank you," she said, with an edge to her voice.

"You all set?" Don asked. "Good, let's get our boarding passes as soon as we can."

They were waved on by the custom's officials who seemed only interested in Jamaicans flying to New York. Don rushed up to the boarding gate.

"Four seats together, please, in the non-smoking section." He waited, nonchalant, but fretful beneath the surface.

"Sorry, sir. I'll have to give you two sets of two, separated by a few seats." The check-in clerk didn't look up while fastening seat-assignment labels to the tickets. "This is a heavily booked flight. Seats 10 and 11 and 14 and 15. Have a good flight, sir."

Don helped the family on board the plane. Peter and he sat together, leaving Susan and Barbara together for the flight. Barbara considered various schemes which would allow her to switch with Peter, for she knew she couldn't talk with her mother for four hours. She reached for a magazine and opened it to an article on gourmet restaurants in New York. She read for fifteen minutes.

"Oh, look, Mother, we're flying over the tip of Cuba. You know Castro is still having a lot of trouble. Some of the kids at Rockleigh are going down there next summer to help with the sugar cane harvest." Without thinking any further, she blurted out: "I'm thinking of going."

"That's ridiculous!" Susan said. "The heat gets up to 110° F. in the fields and, anyway, you're not strong enough to slash away at sugar cane." She said aloud, now even more angry. "You'd die."

"I don't know about that," Barbara said. "I did pretty well out West."

"No comparison, and you know it."

"Don't get angry, Mother."

"I do get angry, Barbara. You're acting like a loony bird these days." She cleared her throat, felt more anger, but she tried to keep it out of her voice. "You hardly ate anything for two weeks in Jamaica. You ran for hours on the beach each day. You swam your head off, not because you enjoyed it—just to take off mythical fat." She winced, tears forming in the corners of her eyes. "You were aloof from me; and, with your father and his damn ear, Peter and I almost went out of our minds."

"Peter didn't complain," Barbara said.

"He didn't. But I know how he felt."

"You mean like the way you always know how I feel."

"Shh, dear. Your voice is getting loud and abrasive. That's a trait of the Gordon's—part of their Austro-Hungarian lineage." She looked around; except for a man sleeping, the passengers near them were reading. "I know one thing, Barbara: You are ruining your body and your mind. It's true you did well at Rockleigh this semester . . ."

"All A's, Mom."

"But the energy you spend dashing around Central Park, doing push-ups, sit-ups, et cetera, should be put into your creative efforts." Suddenly, ferociously, she asked: "Don't you realize that A's are not enough? Colleges, like Harvard and Yale, require applicants to submit examples of their creative work. What will you submit, outside of some old gym shoes and a beaten-up, sweaty, warm-up suit?"

"You're wrong, Mother," Barbara said. "I've written some good philosophy essays I can send in." Barbara shuddered. They'd been through this many times before.

Susan shook her head and gazed at the endless blue of the sky and ocean. She guessed that they were now flying off the coast of north-eastern Florida.

"Would you care for a drink before lunch, M'am?" the stewardess asked.

"Yes, please. A vodka martini, extra dry with no garbage?"

"And you, Miss?"

"A Tab," Barbara said.

"Sorry, Miss. We have no diet drinks."

"Then, just club soda and a twist of lemon, please."

"You're hopeless, Barbara. Do you expect to live all day on a twist of lemon?"

"Don't talk to me," Barbara said. "You're killing your liver cells with all the booze you drink."

"I don't drink much. In fact, if it weren't for your father, I wouldn't even drink wine. Probably just have a drink before dinner and that's all." Susan looked at Barbara indifferently, as if from infinitely far away, and began sipping her drink, uneasy. "He wastes so much time and energy on food and wine and other little entertainments.

"Ladies and gentlemen," the pilot blurted out. "We have some ripples up ahead; it might be more comfortable if you fastened your safety belts." His voice disappeared with his swallow.

Barbara did nothing. Instead, she started to sip her drink in silence. Her mother, who never unfastened her belt until after landing, began to talk to Barbara when suddenly the plane lurched and fell a few hundred feet. Barbara's drink spilled over her lap as she rose several inches off her seat.

"It serves you right, you silly little girl," Susan said, aloud above the noise of the pilot's calming Southern voice over the PA. She finished her martini. "This is what I mean when I say you waste your energy in being defiant. You were going against the pilot's orders. You could have knocked your head on the ceiling. I tell you: you're spinning your wheels."

Barbara sucked in the cold soda and said nothing for a minute. "What do you want me to do?" Barbara asked, grittily.

"Could you please remove your drinks from the tables?" the stewardess said, as she extended lunch trays to Barbara and her mother. "Would you care for some wine with your meal?"

"Yes, please," Susan said. "Chablis, a little chilled, would be lovely."

"Nothing," Barbara said, looking hard at the young, dark-complected stewardess, who was trying to be pleasant, smiling through her long, thin front teeth.

Compressing her lips, Barbara studied the tray.

Susan looked at Barbara's unfinished tray. Her eyebrows lowered, and her mother grew taut.

"Barbara, this nonsense has to stop. You won't listen to me." Her chest was so full she felt like someone drowning. "Your father and I must talk to you and this time talk hard. I'm sick of this." She gave her handbag a shove.

Susan had noticed the window seat empty since lunch.

"Miss," Susan said to a stewardess. "Has that lady vacated her seat?" Her eyes narrowed.

"Yes," the stewardess, a henna-red-haired young woman with gypsy eyes, said, crisply, pointing to the right. "She's joined a friend in the first class lounge."

"Would you be so kind to ask my husband in seat ten to come back and join us?"

"No problem at all," the stewardess said. She went ahead and bent over Dr. Gordon. He spun around in surprise to look for Susan, fearing something was wrong. He looked at Peter and excused himself.

"What's up?" Don asked.

She barely ate a thing," Susan said.

"What else is new?" Don sat down between Barbara and Susan.

"Barbara is getting out of hand," Susan said.

"I've been cognizant of that for some time," Don said, bitter.

"Barbara, I want to tell you something," Susan said, thinking how her daughter's life had become a nightmare. "We saw Dr. Evans. He said you are only passing through a phase of development. You will outgrow that menstrual problem, start eating and dating by the time you go off to college."

"Did he really say," Barbara asked with astonishment, "that I would start dating? He's dumber than I thought."

"See, Don. We need another opinion."

"They're all dumb, Mother."

"Quiet, Barbara," Susan said. "There must be another good psychiatrist in New York. Don't you know any, Don?"

"Not really."

"Do you remember Rick Carter, the actor," Susan asked. "He was in terrible shape. I fell in love with his grief. His third wife had left him; he was drinking and hadn't worked in six months."

"No!" Don said, glad he didn't.

"Well, anyway. He went to an analyst, a well thought-of man in the upper sixties. Fantastic man. Brilliant, charming. He used to teach human development to the social workers at the university."

"How do you know all this about his practice?" Don asked. "Does he show people his credits?"

"And he's written widely," Susan said. Instantly, she wished she could pull her last words back.

"Is *How Your Neurosis Can Make You Money* one of his best sellers?" Don asked. It was all coming clearer in his mind: Susan wanted a celebrity. Panic flooded him.

"He's more sophisticated than that," Susan said, shaking her head. "He writes about neurotic and developmental conflict and the creative process." Abruptly, almost before she knew what he was thinking, Susan exclaimed: "His special interest is da Vinci. He spends a month every year in Florence and Vinci, doing his psychoanalytic study of the painter."

"What does this have to do with Barbara's eating."

"You miss the point," Susan said. She glanced at Barbara with a look of disgust. "You know what Barbara's real problem is." Susan turned mock-solemn. "She's blocked. I think Dr. David Jonas is the best bet." She scratched her leg absent-mindedly, producing, with her nails against her nylon stockings, a sound that always, no matter who the woman, made Don's spine tingle with electricity. "Rick is back to work and is off alcohol."

"Has he found himself a workable marriage yet?"

"No, but he'll get around to that when he's really made it. Let me make the consultation appointment this week."

"What!" Barbara said. Her mother's voice stirred up in her a churning of strong and confused emotions. "You won't even let me call the man, Dr. Jonas or whatever his name is." Nothing of the kind, she thought. "You're the one who needs to see him—not me."

"I quite agree, darling," Susan said, tipping her head, all innocence. "I look forward to meeting him. I'm sure I'd be much further ahead now if I had treatment when I was your age." She threw a ghastly smile intended to evoke compassion and guilt. "You see, Barbara, my mother never knew anything about psychoanalysis. Like I said, before your father sat down, life for me was entirely a matter of survival—nothing more, nothing less."

"Ladies and gentlemen." The PA cracked and faded and after what seemed like a long time, the stewardess said: "We're twenty miles due east of Philadelphia."

"That's close enough!" Susan interjected, as the stewardess stopped her patter to swallow.

"We are preparing to make our descent to John F. Kennedy International Airport." Barbara glanced at her mother. "Please fasten your seat belts and extinguish all cigarettes. We hope you enjoyed our flight as much as we did, and hope you'll fly Pan Am real soon again."

Barbara climbed the steps of a brownstone and rang the bell for the doctor's office.

"Miss Gordon?" a man asked, as he entered the waiting room. "I'm Dr. Jonas." His smile was warm, his handshake firm but not overdone.

Barbara entered his office expecting to see some original art, or, at least, a few good reproductions. Instead, she found his office rather bare, unlived in, with only a dark abstract impressionist painting over his couch. It wasn't clear which of the three chairs in the room was the one she was supposed to select. They all looked equally expensive. She sat opposite the chair behind the couch, hoping he wouldn't surprise her by selecting the third chair, only several feet from her, much too close. Until he took the chair by the couch, her heart flapped against her chest wall. There was something about Dr. Jonas that was different from the first psychiatrist. For one thing, he was more attractive—tall, conservatively dressed, and he looked like a real person, even though her mother had described him differently. Although he had been friendly in the waiting room, he didn't look that way now. He watched Barbara expectantly. She could do nothing but cross her legs; she pushed back a cuticle. She was sure that she was naked.

"I really know nothing about you, Miss Gordon." Barbara nodded thoughtfully. "Your mother phoned me and wanted to see me about you. I told her you are now pretty much an adult and I expected you would prefer to see me without your mother." He leaned forward with a glint in his eyes. "She thought I needed background information, but I told her, if I did, that could come later."

He stopped talking and waited for her.

Disconsolate, Barbara sighed and, like an aged, slow lizard, re-trenched into silence. "I'm . . . I can't put my words together now for some reason . . . I'm amazed my mother didn't insist on seeing you first." She raised her hands and smiled, angry.

"She did."

"Oh . . . I don't know what to say . . . " She half-closed her eyes.

"Whatever you think I should know," he said, grinning a little.

"That's it." She smiled ironically. "I don't know," she said. But she knew. "I'm not sure what's interesting about me. I don't even know why I'm here. My mother would say it's because I don't eat, and I'm wasting my life."

"Wasting your life?" Dr. Jonas repeated.

"Yes, wasting my life. She wants me to do more."

"Like what?"

"Be a writer—maybe a screen writer. Get some experience in the theater." She knew her blush was unmistakable but, in spite of herself, she smiled. "Go into film making after I get out of Radcliffe."

"That's where you want to go to college?"

"Yes, my mother went there . . . I know it's hard to get into." She winced with feelings of humiliation, then stopped talking, musing for a moment, trying to think. "My mother says I should be doing more extracurricular things to make sure I can get in."

"You agree with your mother?" he interrupted, breaking her train of thought.

She was sweating. Pitiful it sounded. "Yes and no . . . that's the trouble. She's probably right, but how important is that anyway? . . . She's very successful. She can do anything."

"And at home?"

"She tries too hard at home." Her hands, awkwardly resting in her lap, were slightly shaking; she steadied them by grasping the arms of the Danish chair. "She runs the house, like a general. Our maid is programmed. Mother calls her several times a day to check on her." She was having trouble keeping the words straight in her mind, and she strained to think. "She's a super gourmet cook, but she has hardly gained much weight. She has a figure of a twenty-year-old woman."

"Why age twenty?"

"Maybe because that's the age when I hope to finish college, start a career and be on my own." Barbara now felt like a person being spied on through a one-way mirror. "My mother looks, in fact, like a girl just out of college, and successful overnight—a starlet, just discovered."

"You keep going back to your mother."

"I guess you're right . . . She's hard to get away from. I feel she's always with me, like a tick under my belly skin."

"Like a little girl who needs her mother by her side?"

"Exactly," Barbara said. The psychiatrist was looking at her hard, searching for something, or expecting something; she wasn't sure which. "It's very odd. My mother worked when I was little, yet I remember her vividly. My nanny was usually with me, but it didn't seem to matter. She treated me the way my mother wanted. I remember my mother taking me to museums when I was four. I can't step into the Museum of Natural History now." Her nerves jangled with the thought. "She used to con me into going to the Museum of Modern Art by promising lunch there. I'd, in turn, promise to be good, if I could have chocolate Napoleon. On weekends, she would take me to lunch at the Metropolitan and then walk me through the Egyptian Wing. Now I can't stand anything Egyptian, including King Tut. Saturday mornings, I had to take painting classes with her. She'd get disgusted with her own painting, lean over toward me and start criticizing mine."

"Has she never been satisfied with herself?"

"God, she should be." Barbara sat motionless for a minute, as if thinking about the question, but, in fact, she wanted to let it drop out of her mind. "She's very successful in what she does. Perhaps that's the trouble. She wants to excel in everything and so must I. Christ, I hate her!"

Barbara's body stiffened. Her face grew redder, the room insufferably hot.

"You don't like to be angry with your mother, do you?"

She nodded, then hunted in her purse for a tissue and blew her nose. Then she turned her face back to his. It gave her a crick in her neck to be constantly looking away from his omniscient gaze. "On the plane back from Jamaica, I had to sit next to her all the way. I couldn't keep her away from me. When I got off the plane, my body felt blown up, tight—ready to explode. When I got home, I had to do my exercises and jog around the reservoir four times."

"You felt less angry with your mother after jogging?"

"I wasn't so angry with her."

"Well," said the doctor, "can we get together tomorrow at three-twenty?"

"Yes, sure," Barbara said, surprised that he would want to see her again. He stood up stiffly. She jumped up, smiled a little at him and rushed ahead to open the door. She felt exhilarated, like somebody slightly drugged.

The afternoon was cold and damp. Snow had started to fall. Some first graders from the Brown School were being collected by their nannies. When they saw the falling snow, they rushed out of school to make snowballs.

She looked at a clock in a jeweler's window. It was four-fifteen. Her mother had told Rose that she wouldn't be home until eight. Dinner would be late tonight. And only she and her mother would be eating. Peter was staying overnight at a friend's; Father was in Boston giving a lecture at the Peter Bent Brigham Hospital.

She saw the T & M Bakery in the next block. It had been her mother's favorite until she had switched to Silverberg's, further up Madison Avenue. Barbara did a quick inventory of her eating during the day. Breakfast had been 200 calories; lunch, 100. She could afford several hundred calories, as long as she didn't eat too much at dinner. She had weighed 81 pounds that morning—and that was with her nightgown on. Her true weight, she was sure, was 80 pounds.

The bakery window was full of cakes and pies. She remembered the Napoleons that she enjoyed as a child. As best she could recall, the Napoleons had come from the T & M.

She took her number in the line. Several young women bought meringue shells. Barbara glanced around. There were the Napoleons. A whole tray of them, sitting in the corner, undisturbed, a rectangular block of chocolate and cream, symmetrically together.

"I'll take a Napoleon," she said to the saleswoman.

"How many, Miss?"

" . . . a dozen, please."

Barbara put the change from the twenty-dollar bill in her pocket. She hurried through the snow, avoiding delivery boys and superintendents shoveling snow. Sweat fringed her hair and ran down her temples; her nose dripped from the cold, stinging air. Headlights against the falling snow lit the dusk. There was no chance of meeting her mother. But what could she do about Rose, who might see the T & M box and regard it as a contribution to dinner. She went back to Madison Avenue, bought a copy of *Mademoiselle* and *Ladies Home Journal* and sandwiched the box between them.

The precaution was unnecessary; Rose didn't come out of the kitchen. Barbara retreated to her room. She flung off her coat, put on Mahler's Fifth, and flopped in her leather bat chair. The string around the box broke easily against the tension of her index finger. She bit into the first Napoleon. Chocolate cream spurted over the sides. Each mouthful of chocolate cream she washed down with a sip of Diet Pepsi. After the fourth Napoleon, the creamy filling was smeared over her fingers and lips. Some of the filling spilled on the carpet and was licked up by Angus. She ate further into the box of Napoleons; and as she bit into the tenth Napoleon, she scooped the chocolate cream up with her finger and rubbed it over her face. It made her skin tingle. She removed her shirt and bra and took apart the last two Napoleons, dug out the cream and rubbed her breasts with the creamy goo. Stripping off the rest of her clothes, she went to the bathroom.

Perhaps some of the Napoleons had been absorbed, enough to give her 50 calories. She turned on the shower to hot and lay on the floor, ready to be pelted.

"Good afternoon, Miss Gordon," Dr. Jonas said. "Come right in, please."

He looked relaxed. He gazed at Barbara with his large, calm eyes. Although she had no idea of what she would tell him today, she knew that the doctor would wait for her to speak.

"In walking down here—along Madison Avenue—it occurred to me that I didn't tell you anything about my fear of being fat. Funny, I forgot it. Did my mother mention it to you?"

"Yes, when I spoke to her on the phone the other day . . . That seemed to be her main concern."

She gave him a long look. "She thinks I spend too much time thinking about my weight. I can't convince her I'm still on the fat side. She never really gains weight. How can she be sympathetic with me? I still have a roll around my middle, and my buttocks sag a bit. I wouldn't dare wear a string bathing suit."

"When you were in Jamaica," Dr. Jonas broke in, "did you feel very comfortable on the beach?"

"Not very much so." She was dismayed that her voice cracked. "I liked the Blue Lagoon better. There I could slip out of the car and dive right off the dock before anyone saw me. I wouldn't hang around the beach and be observed. Instead, I jogged along the beach, sprinting hard whenever I passed any people."

"You enjoy exercise?" he asked.

"Yes, very much. I greatly admire Mishima."

"Mishima?" he said, curious.

"Yukio Mishima. He really understands us . . . I mean teenagers." She spoke in a quick, feathery voice. An uncanny feeling passed over her. "He has a sense of perfection of both the mind and body."

"I recall," Dr. Jonas said, "that he recently killed himself with a sword."

"He did—a show of complete domination over the body. He couldn't bear to watch his body grow old, wrinkled, stooped, sagged and decrepit. He did what he had to do; otherwise, his spirit would have shriveled up." She could imagine his face, inexorably aging, eroded by a life that would be more senseless, useless—stupid as he grew older.

"There is great power in starving. By fasting, Gandhi was able to bring the British to their knees. Look at what Jesus Christ did with his self-control! Only a few people are entitled to absolute power; around this fact hinges a lot of history."

"You know a lot about this," Dr. Jonas said, looking at her gently, as if the tone of her voice had touched him.

"I want to study philosophy and political science at college. I'm doing a paper now on the history of sovereignty; it started in the Middle Ages with John of Salisbury, who tried to place an undivided sovereignty in the church. And it ended with Jean-Jacques Rousseau, who, realizing that the day of Louis XIV was past, gave sovereignty over to the people."

"Then what happened?" the therapist asked.

"Up to this point," Barbara continued, "sovereignty was absolute and indivisible. The classical theory of sovereignty received its first real blow with the existence of the federal state." Dr. Jonas smiled at Barbara, took his hands from his sides and rested them on his stomach. "For instance, Calhoun, in his book on the constitution and government of the United States, speaks of a high sovereign power which is the sovereignty of several states, absolute and indivisible."

"He sees sovereignty as divisible but yet consolidated into one sovereignty?" Dr. Jonas asked.

"Yes, but a difficulty with this position is that if sovereignties can be combined, why can't one sovereign be divided. Calhoun doesn't answer that . . . But I think history does answer this point."

"So you don't believe in the monistic theory?" he asked.

"Absolutely against a monism," Barbara said, determined. "If one follows Spinoza's thought, one must agree on a single sovereignty for the entire world. I think sovereignty is divisible, just as it is combined in a federation."

Barbara felt tired but still excited. Dr. Jonas had heard every word, and he understood.

"I've always thought, Barbara, that basic political and philosophical ideas came from people's experience with their family. You know, families tend to be monistic or pluralistic."

Barbara was surprised. " . . . I suppose you could call my mother an absolute sovereign."

The therapist looked at his clock. "Well, we have to end the hour now. Barbara, I'd like to be able to get together with you four times a

week,"—looking at his appointment book—"starting in two weeks."
He continued: "I have in mind Mondays, Tuesdays, Wednesdays and
Thursdays at two-thirty. How would that be?"

"Yes, those are good times for me." Her face tipped up.

"Let me plan to start seeing you on Monday, January 29th. Since I
haven't met your parents, I suspect they will want to meet me," he said,
leaning closer. "Is that okay?"

"Yeah, as long as you don't tell them very personal things about me."
She brought her gaze back, looking at him without smiling.

"That is always understood," he said, closing the door.

The traffic was still heavy on Fifth Avenue even though it was six
o'clock and the January darkness had descended over the city. From the
window Susan and Don could see fountains of the Metropolitan
exploding into geysers and then retreating from the freezing chill of
the evening.

"I wouldn't let my daughter go to him," Susan said. Her jaw was set
like rock. "He's a dreadful man."

She stared out the door of the bar into the lobby of the Stanhope
Hotel; her vision fixed for several seconds on an attractive, young
couple walking up to the reception desk. The atmosphere at the hotel,
especially the advertisement for George Feyen, the pianist, made her
recall college vacations, when she would come with her friends to hear
Feyen at the piano.

"He seemed fine to me," Don said. "His view of Barbara is accurate."
He looked pensive. "She's an articulate girl but with a remarkable
capacity for intellectualizing her feelings."

"You don't have to be a Freudian analyst to know that. He is so drab.
He's out of the fifties."

"What bothers you, Susan, is that he didn't spill Barbara's guts to
you." Don chuckled. "*You* don't know what went on *between* them, and
neither one of them will ever tell you."

Susan nodded to the waiter for another drink.

"Do you think I'm going to let my daughter go to that man four times
a week?" Disbelief, indignation; it was written all over her face. "Do
you really think I'd let her waste her precious time on that fool!"

"But he said that she has to go four times a week since her resistance
to feelings is so strong. Look, she only weighs 79 pounds. Don't you
understand." He pounded on the table. "She's lost over 25 percent of
her weight!"

"Look, Don, it's mind over matter. She could reverse things if she wanted. Why don't we take her to Europe with us?"

"What good will that do?" Don asked cautiously.

"We'll be in London for a week, go to Paris for a couple of days and then to the South of France. We'll take her to three-star restaurants in France." Susan looked at Don, then past him. "She'll not be able to resist!"

"She will, but I won't," Don said, sighing.

"This is perfect," Susan said after checking her calendar. "Barbara will be getting a two-week vacation at the time we planned to go. She won't miss much school."

"Where's Barbara?" Don asked.

"She's probably home. Jill and Barbara were going to work on a term paper."

"Good," Don said. "When we get back to the apartment, we'll tell Barbara about our plan for the trip." Don fell silent, exploring the odd sensation he was now experiencing, a pleasant numbness of emotion.

"Good evening, Rose," Don said. "Is Barbara in?"

"Yes, Dr. Gordon. She and Jill are in her bedroom. Do you want her?"

"Ask her if she'll excuse herself for a minute and join us in the library."

Don pulled back inside himself; his face became pale and seemed to close up.

"Hello, darling. How are you? You and Jill getting a lot done?" Susan asked.

"We're just outlining our paper." Barbara swept her glance toward her father, wondering what he was thinking. "We're doing the same topic."

"Barbara. Your father and I want to talk to you about Dr. Jonas. As you know, we saw him today."

"Did you like him?"

"Yes, he's a charming, intelligent man." Her voice was vibrant with sincerity. "I can see why you're fond of him, but your father and I don't quite understand why he should need to see you four times a week."

"Yes, it does seem a bit much." She looked at her feet, then the corner of her mother's mouth drawn down. She said, after a thick silence: "I felt the same way when he first told me. But he seems to have a good reason."

"But four times a week so you can gain weight?" Susan asked. Her eyes narrowed to needles of ice-blue. "Did you discuss your eating with him?"

"No," Barbara said.

"What do you mean? What *did* you talk about?"

"A lot of things."

Susan spoke more rapidly, patting the table. "Your father and I—I think you know—are going to London and France next week. You'll be on vacation then. Why don't you come with us?"

"But I have to get this paper done," Barbara said. She sat with her arms around her knees, scowling. "I still have research to do."

"Look, you can go to the British Museum for your research. I bet they have volumes on your topic."

"I suppose you're right," Barbara said. Before she knew she would speak, she said, "You know, I'd love to go skiing in Switzerland."

"I think we could go to Grundelwald or Klosters for a few days. Don't you think so, Don?"

"I don't see why not." He laughed loudly, the way people do at a wake.

"But will you promise me, Barbara, one thing?" Susan asked. She squinted, watching Barbara's face and listening for an affirmative answer.

She stood staring, pursing her lips. "What's that?"

"Will you try to eat a little more?"

"Yes, of course, Mother. I think my passport is still valid, but I'll check anyway."

Barbara got stiffly to her feet, looking at her parents wearily.

III. BRIEF RETURN

We forget that we are all dead men conversing
with dead men.
—Jorge Luis Borges, "There Are More Things"

Dr. Gordon put down his *Herald Tribune* and turned to Barbara by the window; she was watching the approach to Heathrow. Between them was her mother, who was flipping through a copy of *House Beautiful*.

"According to the *Trib*," Don said, "a Palestine terrorist group has threatened to blow up the International Terminal at Heathrow." He shook his head doubtfully. "Wilson has soldiers ringing the airport, and everybody is being searched."

"There's always some damn thing," Susan grumbled.

"The only real trouble," Don said, "will be delays in customs—maybe not even that, now British customs is on a voluntary basis."

They glanced at one another as the jet bumped several times on its touchdown.

"Now to get to the hotel," Don said, reaching up to the overhead luggage rack for their coats.

The black taxi moved along Mount Street, past a butcher's shop with a stuffed pheasant in its window, and swung left onto Carlos Place. The taxi driver went beyond the Connaught Hotel, corrected his mistake by making a sharp U-turn, but stopped short of the hotel entrance. At first, Barbara thought the building was an embassy. A doorman in a morning coat opened the taxi door and directed the baggage boys.

"I'm glad we didn't go to White's Hotel," Susan said. "Remember that American woman at tea there; she kept talking about how cheap things were in Minneapolis? This place has real charisma."

"And good food, too," Don added. "Good afternoon," Don said to the desk clerk, softly. "Dr. and Mrs. Gordon . . . and Barbara, our daughter."

"Yes, of course, sir." He nodded, remembering. "You are fully registered. Everything is in order, except I must inconvenience you for your passports."

"Sure," Don said, extracting them from the bottom of his attaché case, from under a copy of *The American Journal of Obstetrics and Gynecology.*

Barbara followed the desk man down the hall. They stopped at a large suite with two bedrooms. She turned to her mother, upset. "You didn't tell me my room is next to yours! Christ, there is even a connecting bathroom. Can't I have some privacy?"

"The travel agent did this and quite naturally," Susan explained. "Wouldn't one expect that a family would want to be together?"

"No!"

"Well, it's too late," Don said with finality in his voice. "By the looks of things in the bar and restaurant, they can't make any changes, at least right now."

"Thanks!" Barbara said. Her sarcasm was not subtle.

"Oh, Barbara," Don said. He pondered what he could say, could do to relieve Barbara's burning rage. Not much, he was afraid. "I've made reservations here for dinner at nine." He couldn't directly invite her.

Barbara slammed the door.

"Her mood turned foul," Susan said, "as soon as we arrived at the hotel, before she saw the room." She was both amused and depressed by Barbara's behavior. "I think she is upset because the hotel is so posh."

"What's wrong with that?" he asked, puzzled.

"She can't enjoy anything, Don. She's some kind of socialist, but I'll be damned if she'll ruin my fun in London." She began to cry, half-smiling, embarrassed.

"We have a dinner engagement tomorrow night with Sir Geoffrey Pinchon," Don said, trying to reassure her. "He's the consultant from the Maudsley."

Susan started to unpack her cosmetic case. "Who recommended him anyway?"

"Michael Bennett," Don said. "They met in Boston; Michael was very impressed."

"I hope he can tell us about Barbara's starvation . . . I wonder if she will eat tonight."

"Who knows," Don said, lying down to close his eyes for a few minutes, to shut off his mind.

Don resented Barbara and Peter when they interfered with his vacations with Susan; he would prefer to go away with Susan alone, to have her all to himself; but on the other hand, he knew how little the children actually saw their mother during the year. Nevertheless, he would catch himself expressing these feelings to Susan in front of the children, and he wondered whether Barbara, always quick to pick up comments from them, remembered how many times she had tried to entice him to play, talk, or read to her when she was small. Her overtures were seldom heard. He was always too busy, called to the phone by colleagues, preoccupied with the family finances (bank deposit statements, tax diary entries for professional entertainment— IRS cosmetic work as he called it—and investments and professional papers he was at various stages in writing. Those things he did in the evening when he didn't go to professional meetings at the hospital or the Academy of Medicine.

The *maitre d'* glared at Barbara as they entered the dining room. Don had spoken to Thomas Ivor, the managing director, who had asked the head chef, Heinrick Tobas, to prepare something "especially splendid or recherché" for the Gordons. Barbara's baggy blue jeans and white peasant blouse offended the staff.

The Gordons were led to a small corner table, obviously chosen by the *maitre d'* after he had observed Barbara. She walked to the table in perfect posture, like the Queen at Ascot, graciously smiling at the people who turned to her. A waiter approached.

"Good evening, Dr. Gordon." He smiled at Susan, who was dressed in a new black suit, cut long and sleek. "Would you care for a drink before dinner?"

"I think not," said Don thoughtfully. "But we'll have a bottle of Saint-Emilion now."

"Do you wish to proceed with the dinner now?"

"Yes, please." Don paused for a moment to gather some tact. "I think Monseiur Tobas has made the selection for Mrs. Gordon and me."

The three turned to Barbara.

"I shall have . . . " She looked panicky for an instant and reached over to the next table and took a menu which she pretended to study. "I shall have American cheese on Wonderbread with French's mustard and a Tab."

The waiter swallowed; a slight tic appeared in his neck. "I'm sorry, but sandwiches are only served in the Grill Room." The waiter, an oldish man of years' experience, offered no other suggestions or substitutes.

"Steak, kidney and mushroom pie is excellent," Don said. He smiled vacantly at the waiter.

"And lamb from the pres sales of the South Downs is divine, darling," Susan said.

"I shall have," Barbara said, smiling sweetly at the waiter, "fish and chips."

"Would mademoiselle prefer Dover sole or turbot?" the waiter asked, glancing at her father for a second.

"It doesn't matter—any old flounder you might have back there will do."

"I'm sorry," the waiter said, "but we do not have plaice."

"I shall leave it to your discretion," Barbara said with mock charm.

The waiter flicked his head back and left.

"I can see you plan to be naughty," Susan said. She drew her whole face in to give intensity to her eyes.

"Suit yourself, Mother. I was just goofing on that poor man. Such a sap! He needs a little spunk!"

"He's not submissive," Don said, not looking at Barbara, watching Susan. "That's his profession." The muscles round his eyes were tense. "His job is an art he learned at a Swiss hotel school."

"Is that what they do to you in Switzerland?" Barbara asked.

"I only hope you enjoy London," Susan said.

"I expect so," Barbara said. "After dinner, I want to take a walk around Mayfair."

Susan flashed a look at Don. She sighed, wondering what Barbara would do next.

"That's a good idea," Don said. "London is safe at night, at least in Mayfair." His forehead wrinkled as though he were debating the point with himself. "We'd join you, but we're tired from the trip."

"In fact, I think I'll go now," Barbara said. "And you needn't be my guide." Abruptly, she stood up, head thrown back. "I know London quite well."

They watched Barbara rush out of the dining room. The waiter approached them with the wine.

"I'm terribly sorry," Don said, "but can you cancel the young lady's dinner? She is not feeling well tonight."

"Of course, sir."

Turning back to Susan, Don made a comment he had meant to make earlier in the evening. "I saw in the paper that Ken died." He tightened his lips, concentrating. "The UPI release said he had a coronary in his office. He was only forty-three." Ken was dead, leaving behind, he imagined, an oversized safety deposit box stuffed fat with gold stock certificates. It was of no importance, Don thought. "Dust to dust."

Barbara marched up Mount Street, past Berkeley Square and along Berkeley Street to Piccadilly. A clock in a tobacconist's read 8:30, and the theater traffic had stopped. Her steps increased to a slow jog as she crossed New Bond Street. When she reached Regent Street, she could see Piccadilly ahead; she made a quick left and walked up Regent Street, where it curves toward Soho. As she passed an airways office, she saw a restaurant sign along a short alley. It was the Viraswami, an Indian restaurant. She had never found Indian curry dishes in New York very good. The curry was always too subtle, never hot enough. That was why Szechuan restaurants, she imagined, were so popular back home. She climbed two flights of stairs and was greeted by a red-turbaned Sikh. With a flourish, he took her to a table for two by a window overlooking Jaeger's.

"Will the young lady have a drink?" the waiter asked.

"A bottle of Heineken, please. May I see your menu?"

She stared out at Jaeger's window. Many of the Rockleigh girls got their cashmere sweaters at the London Jaeger's. She used to be tempted. But she couldn't see herself walking down Park Avenue for all the old doormen to ogle.

"Would you care to order?" the waiter asked, as he poured her beer.

She hesitated and turned to the door. She cocked her head, concentrating on the faces of people coming into the restaurant.

"I'm sorry," the waiter said, "but I thought you were alone."

"I am," Barbara said. "I'll have a tandoori dish and special dahl, your lentil dish."

"Yes. And do you want any Indian bread?"

"Is that the thin, crispy bread?"

"Yes." .

"A double serving, if you don't mind!"

She could not rid herself of extreme uneasiness; it seemed more a physical sensation than an emotion, as though the whole world was rising up against her.

"Take me to Kings Road in Chelsea," Barbara said to the taxi driver. She had considered taking the underground to see whether she could sneak in free, perhaps give the West Indian ticket-taker a bogus ticket and run for the train. A few weeks ago in New York, she had found herself slipping through the subway exit gates without paying. Once the token vendor spotted her and shouted, but no transit cop heard his cries. She could have bought a token if she had wanted, a dozen, for that matter. Sneaking into subways was exciting; it was daring. Furthermore, it was always nice to have something for nothing, like the things she had taken from department stores last fall: combs, buttons, needles, pencils and notebooks.

The taxi moved slowly past St. James's Park, around Buckingham Palace, through Sloane Square and to Kings Road. Many people were walking along the streets. Young girls were dressed in peasant-style dresses of cheesecloth or calico. She paid her fare and walked for several minutes. A young man, dressed in an old brown suit, shouted something at a girl about a "dolly for the night." Along the side streets were endless boutiques, still open and crowded, featuring both mod and Elizabethan clothes. The pubs were already crowded with people, mostly in their early twenties: shop girls, students, tourists, prostitutes in Harlequin colors, pimps, clerks, upper-class, lower-class, blacks and whites, and occidentals and orientals. Barbara sucked in the smells from a pub. The odors of beer, wine and rum, mixed with those of sausages, cheese and bread, made her want to eat again.

She pushed her way into the Roebuck on Kings Road. Young couples, three deep, lined the bar. Several young men spoke in what sounded, to Barbara, like BBC accents. A transvestite, who reminded Barbara of Sarah in *Upstairs Downstairs,* pinched her on the bottom as he walked by her.

"Excuse me, Miss," an older man said. He looked like some kind of manager, portly, gray and dressed in a black suit. He looked a bit petulant. "I know you are American, so perhaps I should tell you that we prefer women to be escorted."

"She's with me, mate," a young man, several bar stools away, told the manager. The expression on his face—the thin, wide lips, large eyes set far apart, nostrils flaring—was grimly serious. "You needn't worry. I've got her in tow."

The youth inched over to her and put his hand on her shoulder. His shaved, shiny head glistened under the overhanging lamp, and his work clothes were wrinkled and dirty. His shoulders were like hangers. Beneath the sawdust that clung to his boots—more to his boots than to anybody else's—Barbara could see scuffed steel toes. She drew back, out of reach of his extended hand.

"You're not a dolly, just a bony chick," he mumbled. "Might break mine against yours." He went away, disgusted.

"This is no place for a high school girl," an American man, probably in his thirties, said. "I've seen too many kids like you get hurt here." He stood by the bar, hands in coat pockets, scowling and looking like some kind of policeman. "Beat it and don't come back unless you got a guy with you."

"I won't . . . I won't," she said, trying to reassure herself. She fled into the street and jumped into an empty taxi, waiting for a light.

"Take me to Soho," she said to the driver. She had heard that Soho was like Greenwich Village and Chinatown thrown together. These districts in New York were very familiar to her; she always felt safe there. The driver finally reached Oxford Street and stopped several feet beyond the Circus.

"Just down the street is Soho," the driver said. "Is there any particular place you wanted to go?"

"A Chinese restaurant?"

"There's a good one. Many Yanks go there." He swung around to face her, curious to see what she looked like. "I'll find it for you."

The taxi turned the corner and went along Gerrard Street. The driver came to a stop at Lee Ho Fook.

A grinning waiter guided her to the back of the restaurant where there was a single table. The menu, to her surprise, was Cantonese, and in a few minutes she lost herself in shrimp, pork, beef, rice and egg rolls. The food wasn't as good as Bo Bo's in Chinatown. She didn't care. She wanted volume.

Going up Gerrard Street, she knew the price for her gluttony. She turned into a darkened cul-de-sac and knelt over a wide-mouth cement pot, filled with ivy in front of a Georgian house. Afterwards, she looked up at the black February sky and was very alone.

"Sir Geoffrey," Don said to the tall, stout man with preternaturally white hair, the man standing before him like God looking at one of his children. "We're very grateful you could join us tonight." Don grinned with his teeth clenched and stood stiffly, self-consciously, fearing this man might consider this introduction an intrusion on his life. "Yessir. Michael Bennett said you know more about self-starvation than anyone else in the world."

"How is Michael?" Sir Geoffrey asked. He got up quickly for a man of his proportions. "I've been a friend of Michael's for years. I enjoyed the three months I recently spent with him in his psychiatry department in Boston."

"We are dreadfully worried about our daughter," Susan said, unable to control her anxiety, her fists locked together.

They walked into the lounge at the Connaught. Except for a group of unoccupied chairs by a window, the room was filled with people having drinks before dinner. Sir Geoffrey chose a center chair and put Susan on his right. He opened his briefcase, resting it against his prominent stomach and looking down as best he could by pulling up his chin. A silver fringe encircled his head and emphasized his full mustache, a bit stained by years of constant pipe-smoking. His grey eyes were steady, and beneath his austere appearance were warmth and timidity.

"I'm sorry," Sir Geoffrey said, "I wasn't able to see you yesterday." He spoke solemnly, a little pedantically. "I just returned from a meeting in Australia and was rather tired. Those Australians are a hardy lot. Never seem to sleep."

"It is also a long flight," Don said, reassuringly.

Sir Geoffrey said firmly, hands in his pockets, his eyes locked on Don, "Now tell me, will I have the opportunity of meeting your daughter?"

The Gordons hesitated. They had the impression that Sir Geoffrey's consultation was to be informal, just a chat without Barbara. "Nothing can be simple," Don would say later, again and again.

"We thought," Don said, "that it would be better . . . " He laughed, but it was like laughter coming from a stove. "Sir Geoffrey, would you like a drink before dinner?"

"Mmmm! Scotch and soda."

"And two extra dry martinis," Don said to the bar waiter.

"As I was saying, we thought it would be better if we spoke with you first. If you feel that you need to see her, a visit to your Harley Street office could, of course, be arranged."

"Yes, certainly," Sir Geoffrey said, soberly, shaking his head. "Excuse my silly curiosity, but where is she now?"

"Oh," Don stammered for a moment. He remembered how he used to stammer at boarding school when the headmaster asked him a question. "She went up to Cambridge Sunday—yesterday—and will be back tomorrow. She has a friend there."

"Is she your only child?" Sir Geoffrey asked.

"Oh, no," Don said. He studied the man's bald dome. "We have a son, a younger child we left back in New York with his nanny. He's a fine young lad, cocky and alert. He hasn't given us a minute's worry."

"Tell me a wee bit about Barbara," the old man asked. "Whatever you think I should know." He sat back, patiently rubbing the fabric of the upholstery with his middle finger.

"She is a beautiful and talented young woman," Susan blurted out. "We love her dearly. But she is such a worry now. Last week I put my arm around her, and I felt nothing but bones. The bones began to quiver, like those of a frightened bird. She eats nothing now. The other day, when Barbara was helping me mail some letters, she wouldn't lick the postage stamps. She's so strange now . . . "

There were traffic noises on Mount Street. Don suspected that some of the clatter was made by delivery trucks to the hotel. Scotts down the street, the butcher's and the continental deli probably accounted for the rest of it. He knew that he wouldn't get back to sleep; it promised to be a difficult day. Barbara wouldn't go to Sir Geoffrey's office; she probably wouldn't see another psychiatrist after her choice had been denied her.

He got out of bed and went to the enormous, white bathroom. He was relieved to empty his full bladder. Since his last birthday, he had noticed an intolerance of any bladder pressure; he feared this was a sign of early aging. He did some stretching exercises, shaved and showered under a huge Victorian nozzle. It was no point in delaying the confrontation. He tapped Susan on the shoulder, told her that it was time, and he called the desk to tell Barbara that they would see her at breakfast in thirty minutes.

Susan moved about slowly.

"Susan," Don said, "I'll wait for you in the sitting room. I want to read the paper."

"Okay. I'll be down in a few minutes."

The sitting room was empty. He was relieved; he wouldn't have to talk to anyone. The lead story in the *Trib* was Nixon's refusal to leave the White House if he were impeached. He thought about Barbara and how to sell the consultation to her.

"Good morning, Daddy," Barbara said.

"How is my beautiful daughter today?"

"Just fine." She hadn't slept a wink all night. "How about some breakfast?"

"Good," Don said, with a note of surprise in his voice.

"Did you have a good dinner?" she asked. "Who did you have dinner with?"

"Sir Geoffrey Pinchon," Don said. "Some friends in New York suggested we all get together."

"Why?"

"He's an extraordinary man," Don said.

"He's a psychiatrist, too, isn't he?" Barbara asked, knowing the answer.

"Yes, as a matter of fact . . . and a good one, too. We mentioned, of course, some of the adolescent difficulty you're having. He's seen a lot of young girls like you in London."

"As bad as me?" Barbara said with a laugh.

"Yes, and real tough ones," Don said, trying to smile. "Oh, here's your mother. Let's have breakfast."

Don sat between his wife and daughter.

"The young lady," Don said, "if I'm not mistaken, will have orange juice, oatmeal and a kipper." He looked at Barbara to get her agreement. She nodded.

"And the lady will have orange juice, poached eggs and toast with marmalade.

"And for me . . . orange juice and stuffed mushrooms on toast. And three teas, please."

"You also enjoyed your dinner with the English shrink?" Barbara asked her mother.

"And you know, Barbara, even with all his accomplishments, he is still down to earth. You would never think," Susan added, "he's *the* Royal psychiatrist—the Queen's psychiatrist, if she ever needed one."

They sipped their orange juice, studying each other. Barbara spoke up. "What did he really have to say about me?"

"He couldn't really say much," Don said. "He spoke in generalities."

"What were they?" she asked.

"He feels very strongly," Susan said, "about weight loss—if it falls below 50 percent of the body mass."

"Does he, really!" Barbara said.

"Yes," Susan said, nodding, looking up now. Her eyes were ice. "In fact, he suspects you might have to go to a hospital to regain your weight and health."

"A hospital . . . weight and health?"

"Not exactly a hospital," Susan was quick to say. She slid her lower lip over her upper, cautious, pensive. "It's more of a sanatorium—more a medical resort. Anyway, Sir Geoffrey would like to see you this afternoon."

"See me this afternoon! That's a lot of nerve!" Her eyes were glittering, her face flushed. "Who does he think he is? How does he know how much I should weigh?"

Don looked at Barbara, searching for a way to distract her. He thought of a kipper, split apart and wide open before them. He shifted his food into his left cheek and said, "That's a fine looking kipper you have there."

"You eat it." She rushed out of the dining room.

An old man, reading his paper in the corner, cleared his throat.

"The tea is cold," Don said. "Shall I order some more?"

Susan didn't answer. She pursed her lips and acted noncommittal. She held back her tears and drank her tepid tea.

"Let's go back to the room," Don said.

They stopped at the mail desk. There was one letter for them, and on the envelope, unstamped, was written, "Dr. & Mrs. Gordon." Don opened it, his hand unsteady.

Dear Father & Mother,

I'm sorry to run out on you, but I can't face another consultation. Furthermore, I think I'm old enough to travel in Europe without you. I've felt like the girl in *Daisy Miller*, traveling with her mother through Europe and being gawked at all the time by men. I'm going to the continent for a few weeks. Then I'll fly back to New York on my own. No need to worry.

Love, Barbara

P.S. Daddy. I took my Pan Am ticket out of your attaché case. Got my passport back from the desk. I didn't want you to think you had lost the ticket.

Don handed Susan the letter. She read it twice.

"Such nonsense! Daisy Miller!" She exploded into laughter. "She has illusions of grandeur—a Jamesian heroine being pursued by handsome Italian men."

"Where do you think she'll go?" Don asked.

"It's simple," Susan said, reassuring herself. She collected her wits. "She'll run to Paris and go to her Aunt Flossie in Nuilly." She spoke rapidly, with precise pronunciation. "Old Flossie has always been her favorite aunt, probably because Flossie's so much like me."

"She has an entirely different character," Don said in protest. He straightened up, eyebrows lifted, annoyed. "She's a hysterical Auntie Mame who loves to have kids around."

"Whatever," Susan said with a tone of closure, "that's where she's going, and we better leave this afternoon for Paris. You have to be in Paris anyway for the International Society."

Don was tired as he gathered the luggage together for the porter. He had called Sir Geoffrey. Because Barbara had run off, even though only to an aunt's in Paris, the doctor was alarmed. He told them that hospitalization at the Einfurt Sanatorium near Klosters was now necessary. The sanatorium was a well-established institution, founded by a Swiss analyst at the turn of the century—Professor Eduard Kurzwinger, who still ran the sanatorium. The famous psychiatrists Kraepelin and Bleuler used to consult there back in the old days. Kurzwinger's two sons, both analysts also, helped to continue the sanatorium in an impeccable manner. Sir Geoffrey suggested that they present the sanatorium to Barbara as a mixture of ski resort and convalescence home. Although not particularly honest, this approach might make it more palatable for her.

The traffic snaking out of Orly moved slowly, even though the peak congestion should have passed.

"Isn't there a shorter route to the Ritz?" Don asked the driver, who made no response. Perhaps, Don thought, he didn't understand English. The taxi left the expressway and made its way through small, twisting streets on the Left Bank. Suddenly, the Seine was in front of them. The taxi sped across the bridge, into the Place de la Concorde, then up to Place Vendôme.

"Let me call Flossie," Don said, "as soon as we register."

"Room 927, Cambon side," the deskman said to the porter.

"Flossie was dumbfounded," Don said, when he joined his wife in the room. "She's heard nothing."

"Well," Susan said. She smiled and tipped her head. "Not much we can do about her tonight. She'll probably go to the Left Bank and try to meet students." It sounded false, but everything was sounding false. Time, like truth, seemed to have stopped. She glanced at Don, then away. "She speaks very good French, you know."

"You're probably right," Don said, "but I wonder if we shouldn't drive around a bit—to the usual tourist spots. But she wouldn't go to tourist places like Café de Deux Magots." The blood drained out of his face. "I've notified the police, anyway. They've put out a missing person's report. Every gendarme in Paris will be looking for her."

"Great consolation," Susan said, frowning. "Her description matches probably half the young American girls in Paris. We'll look for her early tomorrow morning. Oh, by the way, the concierge got us two tickets for the ballet tonight."

Barbara had arrived in Paris in the early afternoon. A coach from Orly had taken her to the bus station near the Invalides, where she checked her suitcase, a large bag with toilet articles and a few clothes. Although she was aware that she had come to Paris because of Aunt Flossie—she always liked her father's sister and admired her for leaving New York years ago to work as a legal secretary in Paris—Barbara vowed not to call the woman. She would stay in Paris until her two hundred dollars was gone; she would look into the Sorbonne and find out about student life in case she ever wanted to spend her junior year abroad.

She walked across the Esplanade des Invalides. She stopped abruptly, avoiding a covey of motorcycles, whirring, screeching and skidding as they turned the corner. There were a few people strolling through the esplanade, mostly shop girls and students, passing time after lunch. A small group of German tourists were explaining things to one another. She asked a young girl what the tourist interest in the Invalides was. "Son et Lumière," she was told, a light and sound show recounting the Napoleonic Wars. The poster read: "Napoleon's generals pay homage to Bonaparte, the Eagle . . . and at the end his son goes to his father to live forever with him at the Invalides. The eaglet returns to the eagle."

Barbara made her way along Rue Saint Dominique, past the Square Rousseau and the Ministère de la Guerre. When she came to Boulevard

St. Germain, she reminded herself that this part of Paris was the Left Bank; this was where French students lived and worked. A wet snow had begun to fall; it stuck to everything, like confectionery sugar, making Paris even more beautiful. As she crossed Rue des Saints-Pères, she noticed the Faculté de Médecine and thought of her father. He would be hurt by her running away and would never understand why she did it.

The sun was fading fast, and it was getting colder. Ahead was a small street, Rue de Buci, on the left with many cafes and shop after shop of foods: pastries, vegetables, cheese, fruit, meats and fish. The smells of foods were just beyond freshness; they were perfume to her. Why couldn't those scents be bottled? Most of the pleasure of good food, Barbara thought, came from the aromas. It would be better if people could release these odors and simply enjoy them, instead of gorging themselves.

Her toes and fingers stung with the cold. She went into a little restaurant for hot coffee. The waiter suggested onion soup, beef ragout, selections from the cheese board and a blueberry tart. The last meat Barbara had eaten was a blood-red cube steak a few weeks ago in New York. She had soaked the meat in vinegar for several hours. (She had read somewhere that vinegar eliminated fat and broke down protein.) After the vinegar process, she had covered the meat with mustard, salt and cayenne pepper and then boiled it.

"I'll have a croissant and coffee," Barbara said. The waiter nodded. Her face grew sober, and she began to sip her coffee, not sure that she intended to drink it.

The coffee warmed her insides. She couldn't keep her eyes off a woman at the next table, eating a coq au vin, covered with a delicious smelling sauce with a green salad on the side. And a bottle of Chablis even appealed to Barbara. She began eating her croissant. To prolong the pleasure, she dissected it and ate it, layer by layer, until only a few crumbs were left. She arranged them in a little pile, wet the tip of her index finger, against which she crushed them before putting her finger to her tongue. She paid her bill and left.

The cold went to her bones, and trying to keep warm, she jogged down St. Germain. No one paid her any attention. She reached Boulevard Saint-Michel; across the street was the Musée de Cluny, which she had read about when a tapestry show was at the Metropolitan Museum. The museum had borrowed some medieval tapestries, part of the unicorn series, from the Cluny. She entered by the Rue de Cluny entrance. The Sorbonne, she noticed, lay behind the Cluny. Groups of students, talking and laughing, were in the vestibule. She wished that she could join them, at least for the evening.

The Cluny was dark, only slightly warmer than outdoors.

"Are you American?" a young woman asked in a half-whisper. Unknown to Barbara, the young woman, motionless, hands on her hips, staring into Barbara's face, had been behind her for a few minutes.

"Yes, I am," Barbara said. She scrutinized the woman, who was dressed in jeans and wore a black leather jacket. At first, Barbara thought she was Algerian, but after she had spoken to Barbara more, she realized that the woman was probably Parisian French.

"What part of the States do you come from?" the woman asked. Her English was slightly accented and a bit aristocratic, not the kind of English a French girl learns from a summer's stay with a family in Devon.

"New York City. I've lived there all my life." She would never have said "New York City" to an American, she thought. "By the way, I'm Barbara Gordon."

"I'm Brigitt Dreyfuss," the young woman said. "Are you a student, too?"

"Yes, I go to a little school in New York." She frowned, then thought better of it and smiled. "I'll be going to college soon."

"Which one?"

"A girl's school in Boston."

"Oh, yes, I know Boston. You mean Radcliffe?"

"You're at the Sorbonne?" Barbara asked, shifting the conversation away from herself.

"Yes, I'm reading philosophy there."

"What kind of philosophy?"

"I'm interested in post-Existential philosophy—contemporary philosophy, really. Structurallsm."

"I don't know much about it," Barbara said. "I've only recently read about Lévi-Strauss. Before that, I thought he made jeans."

"We must talk. Are you spending much time in Paris?"

"A week, I hope."

"Where are you staying?" Brigitt asked.

"I just got in from London. I haven't decided yet."

"Oh, you can stay at my place," Brigitt said. "I have an apartment with a girl who's at the Côte d'Azur with her friend for a week. She's a comparative literature student. You'd like her. Perhaps you can meet if she gets back in time. Her name is Anna Margot."

"That's nice of you." Barbara studied the young woman with alarm. "I had thought of a pension near the Sorbonne."

"You mustn't," Brigitt said. "They're terrible and filled with old perverts. That settles it. You must stay with me." She smiled, mechanically flashing teeth, and rolled her eyes. "It's not elegant, but it's comfortable and interesting."

"You're very kind," Barbara said, not really feeling it.

"Not at all. Shall we get out of here? The Cluny is charming, but not on a February afternoon." She stood up with her back sightly arched, her weight shifted to one leg, her left hand pressed to her waist, bent at the wrist. "Let's go to a little cafe on the Rue des Beaux-Arts. Then we can go to my apartment, and you can be comfortable."

Brigitt took Barbara by the arm and pointed her toward Boulevard St. Germain.

The snow was several inches deep; footprints would remain until other feet blotted them out. She paused to look at her own footprints until Brigitt tugged at her.

In the warm air of the cafe hung the smells of stale wine and smoke. The afternoon gathering appeared to be Sorbonne students, mostly drinking an unlabeled wine, what her parents called cheap jug wine. It was not chilled; she had a glass for warmth. She couldn't possibly remember all their names, she thought. Unable to speak French, without translating from English, she had little time to think about anything else. Nevertheless, she was struck by the odd combination of young people. They looked like a random sample of youth from all over Paris. She looked for stereotypic Sorbonne students: the black-haired, leather-jacketed young men throwing street bricks at gendarmes and attractive blondes who looked like Françoise Sagan. She found none. Some looked like peasants from the Bordeaux area; others, clerks in retail stores, a couple of possible junior executives, several prostitutes, a fashion model, an old junkie on heroin and a banker's daughter with beaded hair from Avenue Foch. The crowded, smokey cafe, filled with unfamiliar, nameless faces, made her feel unreal. She couldn't be friendly, but they might accept her anyway. They didn't. One student, a scraggy, acne-marked youth who, apparently as a matter of habit, looked over every woman in the cafe, murmured that Barbara was an "odd American bird who needed a good meal." He returned to talking to some students about Robbe-Grillet and reality. She wished that she could have talked to them about *Last Day at Marienbad*. She had liked the movie.

Barbara moved away from the bar. Brigitt was putting out a cigarette on a boy's jean leg. He didn't seem to mind. In a corner was an art-deco jukebox, like something out of a 1940s movie, only it had classical selections. She put a franc in it and pulled the lever for a Satie selection. She must have looked, she thought, pathetic, lost and homeless, for Brigitt left her friend and came over to her with a cognac.

"I think you've run away from your parents," Brigitt said. "But, so have we all, more or less. Some succeed; others fail. But here. You need this cognac to come to life."

"Thanks," Barbara said. "I should have thought of this, instead of wine."

"It doesn't matter who thought of it," Brigitt said, looking up, her head forward like a hawk.

Barbara sipped her cognac. Her eyes, large and white, were glued on Brigitt's face.

"I like you, Barbara," Brigitt said. "You mustn't be afraid to trust me." She sighed and slipped her hand into Barbara's. "I don't think you've ever had a sister. You treat girls like they're mothers."

Barbara knew what Brigitt meant. But could she trust her? After all, hadn't she really been picked up by Brigitt? Why did the young French woman want her to stay at her apartment? Why was she so suspicious? What right did she have to doubt the woman's intentions? If she had seen a lonely looking French girl in the Metropolitan Museum, wouldn't she have done the same? Certainly.

"It's not that I don't trust you, Brigitt. It's simply that I'm not used to people caring about me like this. I'm used to people who take care of me to take care of themselves."

"We've been here long enough," Brigitt said. "You're still cold and you must be hungry . . . Let's go to my apartment."

"Goodbye," Brigitt said to her friends. She said nothing to Barbara.

The two young women, hand-in-hand, walked down Rue des Beaux-Arts and around the corner to Rue Visconti. The streets were deserted, everything seemed asleep. The two-block trip took over four minutes, but, for Barbara, pierced by the bitter cold of the snow, turned to needlelike sleet, the journey was endless.

"This is my flat," Brigitt said, pointing to an apartment above a used book store. "It's very comfortable."

Barbara tried to romanticize her situation. Here she was, in the heart of French university life. Yet all she could now feel was a deep chill. The building was a dirty brown; the paint was chipping, revealing white-stone patches, like unsightly depigmentations. The hallway smelled of old wine, probably, Barbara thought, from drunks who slept and urinated there during the early morning hours. The first floor hall was illuminated by only a dim light.

A door opened, and a young man and woman peered into the darkness. They recognized Brigitt immediately. Whispers were exchanged. Barbara could only make out the word "later." The door closed, and Brigitt went to the adjacent apartment.

"Here we are," Brigitt said as she swung open the door. "This is where I live and study." Brigitt put her hand on Barbara's shoulder. "Why don't you take the bed nearest the radiator. It's softer. I'll get dinner."

In a few minutes, Brigitt produced a meat dish which tasted like a beef ragout. Barbara found herself eating a second helping. Still her stomach seemed empty. She had a second glass of burgundy.

"What's that knocking on the wall?" Barbara asked.

Nothing was said. Barbara looked again at Brigitt. She wanted an answer.

"That's Jacques. He's a crazy painter next door." She nodded, smiled, as though knowing what Barbara was thinking. "Very surreal, but you'd like him. He can be witty."

There were two knocks. Barbara pretended not to hear.

"He must be putting up one of his paintings," Brigitt said. "They're really fascinating. He's able to blend one form into another. Surreal fusion that loses one object to another."

There was the third knock, loud as a gunshot.

"I can't resist," Brigitt said, laughing and startling herself. "Let's go next door and see Jacques. He loves company. He always has company so we won't be bothering him."

Barbara's natural impulse was to decline; she just wanted to go to bed. She thought more about it, chin tucked down, mouth wry. At last she said, "Yeah, please introduce me to Jacques and his friends."

Brigitt smiled. They went into the hall. The apartment door snapped locked as they left. The only light was in the entry way. Brigitt made her way along the hall. She knocked; the metal door flew open.

"Brigitt! Come in," Jacques said, prepared to embrace her. Barbara observed his bare chest and wondered, since she couldn't see in the faint light, if he had anything on.

"Jacques, I want you to meet my American friend, Barbara Gordon, from New York." He turned his head, slightly tipped.

They shook hands. She furtively looked down. He had pants on. As she glanced around the large apartment, her eyes settled on nude forms, two young women wrapped about each other, in the shadows of the corner. She watched.

Brigitt's hand touched Barbara's arm as her other hand released the buckle on Barbara's belt. Barbara turned to flee but stumbled over Jacques, sitting on the floor in a cloud of pungent smoke. She drew back from Brigitt and moved to the door. Brigitt seemed surprised.

"I am leaving now, Brigitt." She raised her hands protectively, shaking all over, collecting her thoughts. "You will let me get my coat and bag."

"Why rush, Barbara?" She brought one finger to her lips, like a mother hushing her small child. "Yvonne and Denise are just good friends. They mean no offense to you. And Jacques—poor Jacques—his child-wife, who was like a fawn, died only six months ago. He's still grieving. Every girl reminds him of his lost wife."

"I must go now," Barbara said. And her voice said, inside her mind, "You must walk out of this place now."

"But it's almost midnight." Brigitt bent forward slightly, and in the glow of a lamp her eyes looked dangerous to Barbara. "Where can you stay at this hour on this miserable night? It's freezing rain now."

"I have relatives I can call on in times like this."

"Oh, you are very fortunate," Brigitt said.

Barbara waited in the hall for her few possessions.

"Thank you for your kindness." She ripped the coat from Brigitt's hand and slid into it quickly.

Brigitt was correct. The sleet had turned to freezing rain which coated everything with a film of ice. She would have to call Aunt Flossie.

At the southwest corner of Rue de Rennes, near Rue Gozlin, she found a telephone kiosk. She huddled in one corner, after slamming the door against the rain and searched for coins. The warmth of the kiosk was mixed with the smell of urine.

She dialed 53419. The ring was faint but seemed to continue. She guessed the call was going through. No answer. Perhaps Aunt Flossie was on vacation.

The phone rang about a dozen times. There was no point in holding the receiver, except to stay out of the rain. She went back on the street. She proceeded south along the Rue de Rennes to Montparnasse.

Barbara had no idea of what she would do now. She could walk all night, or take cover in the Jardin du Luxembourg. From a friend she had learned of a small hotel near the Place des Invalides. It was called the Dijon.

The lobby was well-lit and attractive, recently redone in white. The upholstery on the furniture had no sheen or bare threads. But there was no one about, not even a desk clerk.

"May I help you, Mademoiselle?" a voice from nowhere said in a Brooklyn accent.

Barbara couldn't find the face. She giggled. She laughed, dry as a dog's laugh, vigilant as she looked around the lobby.

"I'm sorry," said a man standing behind the desk. "I thought you had seen me when you came in. I was sitting at the side of the switchboard, reading this great book." Barbara noticed the book was Benchley's *Jaws*. She was thinking—not seriously, just playing with the idea—that if the hotel clerk were another "crazy," she'd turn on her heel and walk out. "You want a room, don't you?" he said. "Please register. And I'll need your passport."

"New York, eh?" He clasped his hands on his rotund belly. Out of his elephantine ears, as well as his nostrils, like black holes of a .410 shotgun, grew white hairs. "You must live near 84th and Park. Right?" As he talked he would rise on his toes with his eyes closed, as though required for clear thinking.

Barbara nodded, surprised.

"I used to work at a florist on Madison and 72nd Street. Made many deliveries in your building. I wish I had a buck for every poinsettia I carried into that building at Christmas time. That's what I hated about the job—blood-red poinsettias. Can't stand the damn things and Christmas, too, for that matter. His vision fixed on the bitten-off end of a pencil; he thought for a moment and laid it down on the counter. "You're a real adventurous girl. I don't see many teenagers traveling alone in Paris. And at night! Real spunk!" He reached for the key but kept it tightly gripped in his large hand. "I was a G.I. here after the war," he continued. "Paris was a great place to be then. After my discharge from the army, I stayed on, got into the perfume business and made a lot of dough." He paused for a moment, slightly muddled, bit his lip and then wiped his forehead with the back of his hand. "I got tired dealing with my old New York distributors. They kept taking more and more of the profits. I met a French widow, a couple of years older than myself. She had inherited this hotel, and I was tired of running around. So we got married, and I took over. Never spent a day at Cornell's Hotel School. Smartest thing I ever did, but, Christ, I wish I could get a dependable night clerk. I can't stay up late, like the way I used to."

Barbara reached for the key. He slowly handed it to her, teasing her, reluctant to let her go.

"Yeah, I'm glad I stayed here." He held up his book. "I think it's gotten worse in New York. This book is about New York—all those kooks who go out to the Hamptons to rip each other off. A lot of bullshit." He stood with his hands in his coat pockets, scowling fiercely. "Great book Benchley wrote. It's a modern *Moby Dick*—an allegory: a shark against New York piranha fish . . . But you look tired. I better give you the key."

"Thank you."

Barbara went to Room 214. After turning on the lights to check the room for cockroaches, she flipped the switch off, fell onto the bed with her coat on and, with effort, crawled under the blankets. She lay there, nose pointing at the ceiling, arms at her sides, inert, exhausted. The room was silent, like a sealed tomb, no sound except for the heavy swishing of blood in her head. She became one with the mindless silence of the room.

It seemed hours later when she awoke. She sat on the bedside wringing her hands. Today was . . . she thought for a moment. The wallpaper had the look of softness about it. The weight of wordless unhappiness was in her head, and several lines of a poem by William Stafford came to mind:

> Animals, rocks, breath, people: Listen to us!
> Listen! Like you, we are alone

Her legs ached, and now everything in the room looked misty and out of focus. The room was full of distant sounds, muffled, far off. A ray of sun penetrated the frosted window; it fell on her pillow, next to her face, and as she lay there too tired to think about anything in particular, she watched the sun move to the edge of the pillow and eventually to the floor. She looked at her watch, remembering that she hadn't undressed. It was three. No. Twelve-fifteen was the right time, she discovered, when she looked carefully at the silver hands of her watch, bold against its black dial. For a moment, she was dizzy when she sat up. The room was chilly; it must have been near zero outside, possibly even below. She combed her hair and left the room.

"I'm checking out now," Barbara said to the woman at the desk. She was a large red-haired woman, heavy lipped with clownlike mascara. "How much do I owe you?" She must be the owner's wife, Barbara thought; she wondered why she cared at all.

"That's thirty-five francs."

"Thank you."

"Have a good day," the woman said, as she returned Barbara's passport. "Hope my husband didn't talk you up too much last night." She laughed. "He enjoys talking to New Yorkers and telling them how lucky he is."

One p.m. She looked out, unseeing, at the street. It was sunny when she reached the street. Passing cars splashed pools of slush against one another and pedestrians on the curbs at the corners. She made her way back to the Rue de Buci, where she had seen food specialty shops yesterday. At Rue St.-Dominique, she decided to take a taxi because of the deep slush, but she knew her impatience was due to her hunger.

She left the cab at the bottom of the street. Boucheries displayed cuts of meat full of marble-grained fat; pâtisseries, grand marnier and rum cakes; and charcuteries, pâtés, salads and fish. She went through them all, smelling, touching and tasting. She bought one grand marnier cake and let a piece sit in her mouth for several minutes, until it was so soft she feared it had melted. In a corner of the store, she spat the brown mush into a paper napkin.

Back on the street, she passed a bar tabac, where people sat enjoying their coffee and croissants.

"There she is!" a woman shouted.

Pedestrians turned to look, uncertain what was happening. There were murmurs from several old ladies standing by the curb. They suspected a shoplifter had been spotted. Or maybe a kidnapping was happening.

Barbara looked up and froze to the steps of the shop. The shrill New York accent, with upper East Side intonations thinly covering Bronx inflections, could only come from her mother.

"Barbara! Barbara!" Susan shouted, her hands closed like claws.

"There she is, Don. There's my baby! Grab her, Don. She's starting to run."

Four men with ruddy faces stood watching, motionless, like birds at the rim of a birdbath. It was like a dream.

Barbara sprinted down the street and tried to lose her parents in the crowds on Boulevard St. Germain. But, as she leaped over some cabbage crates, she slipped on the ice and fell flat on her back. She struggled to get up, slipping, twisting, turning her head to look past her shoulders, her face as white as bleached flour. She pulled herself to her feet, but her father was standing over her. He clasped her under the arms and pulled her to her feet.

"All right, Barbara." Don held her by the collar. Then he grasped his chest with his two hands to keep the pounding of his heart from breaking through his chest. "Enough of this crap. You're coming back to the hotel with us."

"Don't let her get away, Don," Susan warned. She took a deep breath and walked toward them with exaggerated caution.

Barbara looked out of the spotless window of the train as it gained momentum in leaving Zurich. Her eyes had searched the platform, the corridors of the coaches, the compartments for young American skiers, before they found their seats. For a moment, she thought she saw Steven; then she remembered a line from his letter last fall: "I don't know what it is, but when I'm with you, everything is *déjà vu*."

The train was full of skiers; she was going to a sanatorium. Some Dutch students sang folk songs while a group of Danes laughed at jokes which she couldn't understand. A British family sat together across from them; the two teenage daughters played bridge with their parents, occasionally teasing their mother about her foolish bids. The father, heavy and ebullient, wearing sunglasses, and the mother, stout and black-haired, dressed in a bright red dress with white flowers on it, helped themselves to food they carried in a bag. The father rubbed an apple until it shone bright and then ate it, down to its bright, black seeds. Then he dropped the core by his feet.

Her parents read, hardly distracted, even when the train, now leaping toward Klosters, shot through black tunnels. Barbara propped a pillow behind her head; and, as the train passed into another tunnel, she closed her eyes.

When she awoke, she was alone in the compartment. It was 3:47

p.m., and dusk was falling on the deep recesses of the valleys. The mountains were now much taller; and, although some were yet no higher than the Green Mountains of Vermont, which she knew well from her childhood, Barbara was diminished by the vastness of the Alps. A sheet of paper lay on her mother's seat. Its black print, against the whiteness of her mother's monogrammed stationery, was difficult to read. Barbara squinted at her mother's small printing: "Gone to the dining car for tea. Join us if you like."

Just then a conductor walked by. Barbara, glancing up, almost apologetic, signaled to him.

"Excuse me. But when do we get into Klosters?"

"We will arrive at 16:23, Fräulein."

"Thank you." Her eyes clenched tightly shut.

Never had she been called "Fräulein." "Miss," "Mademoiselle," but not "Fräulein." It didn't seem appropriate, for Barbara couldn't imagine herself as a little German girl. It sounded too dainty and petite. She leaned back, closed her eyes for the remainder of the trip and fell into a deep slumber, taking her many miles beyond Klosters, to a desert where the hot winds met the blue of the Mediterranean. Four large tents, blue and red striped, were erected on a bluff overlooking the water. She was in one tent, a large rectangular structure, not unlike tents in a Berber village. Her tent was filled with Berber women, some of whom were nursing babies. There was a woman, diagonally opposite her. She looked up, offered Barbara her plate of couscous and smiled.

The click of the compartment door closing woke Barbara; it was her parents. Her mind seemed flooded. One moment she was like iron; the next, she was collapsing into despair, destroyed and helpless.

"Did you have a good nap, Barbara?" Don asked.

"Very good," Barbara said.

"We're getting into Klosters," Don said. He studied her, smiling with only his mouth. He ran his hands through his hair and then slid his hands into his pockets. "We better gather our things. Dr. Kurzwinger is sending a man to help us with our luggage and take us to the sanatorium."

"Don't forget your book, Don," Susan said. She felt her old, dull hostility and weary heaviness in the heart. "We're coming to a stop... Look. There's the village lights. Pretty how they fan out and extend up the sides of the mountain."

Barbara pulled her bags down from the overhead rack. The train had stopped, and skiers were struggling with their equipment. From the darkness stepped a broad-shouldered man without a coat.

"Dr. Gordon?" he asked. He leaned toward Don.

Don nodded.

"I am Kurt, Dr. Kurzwinger's driver." He nodded and touched his hat brim politely. His face was a mask. Drawing himself up, Kurt took Barbara's bags first, slid them out to a waiting porter; and shouting German commands, he cleared a path for the Gordon family. "The car is parked near the entrance of the Bahnhof. Please follow me." He pushed through a phalanx of skiers, some sitting on their bags and packs; others, silent and waiting, were standing around. They seemed confused about their connections.

"Dr. and Mrs. Gordon," Kurt said, "I want you to meet Hans." The short, fat man bowed, his brown eyes looking past them, unalive. Barbara looked out of the car into the darkness, trying to ignore the center of her unrest. "He'll provide the transportation wherever it's needed."

The car sped through the main streets of Klosters. A swatch of the headlight flew ahead of them. Kurt and Hans were silent as though withdrawing into stone.

"There's the Vereina Grand Hotel," Susan said. "Isn't that where we're staying?"

"No, the Pardenn," Don said, petulant. "I've told you three times." He pursed his lips as if to spit.

Suddenly the car made a sharp right into a thicket of fir trees, depressed with snow, and entered a long, gracefully curving driveway. It was a little after six.

"*Ja,* here we are!" Kurt said, kindly authoritative.

The main part of the sanatorium was a stone structure, which looked like an administration building at a New England college. On the left was a wooden wing, painted white, which Barbara took at first to be the living area for patients. And scattered around the grounds were eight or nine—she lost count—two-story houses probably belonging to the staff.

Don nodded, glancing over at Susan and Barbara, faintly smiling. His stomach made a turn.

Barbara stepped out of the car first. She looked up at the sky, now cloudless. The moon was a ball of fat. Kurt led her, without waiting for her parents, to the director's office. Don felt momentarily nauseated, involved in the insanity of what life had become for them. Dr. Kurzwinger's secretary had left for the day; the director was waiting for them in his office.

"Dr. Kurzwinger," Kurt said, "Miss Gordon and her parents are here."

"Good evening, Miss Gordon." His English was heavily German-accented. "Did you have a good journey from Zurich?" He cocked his head, smiling; his eyes humorously watching her. Barbara smiled back.

Barbara assumed this was a rhetorical question; she studied his face and was fascinated with the doctor's black mole on his left cheek. She wondered how Dr. Kurzwinger shaved every morning without cutting himself.

"Welcome to Einfurt," Dr. Kurzwinger said to the parents. In his white coat, he looked every bit the professor and director, younger looking than she had expected. It was all hardly more real than a dream.

"Kurt will take Barbara to her quarters where Frau Schein, our head nurse, will settle her into her quarters and introduce her to the patients. Abruptly, the director slung out his jaw and frowned, judicially. "May I speak with you for a few minutes?"

The director, mustached like a cat, led the Gordons into a large room, where before a stone fireplace were high-back, leather chairs, arranged in a half-circle before a blazing fire. "Your daughter looks gravely ill as do many anorexia nervosa girls we admit to Einfurt. Sir Geoffrey has spoken with me. I think quite rightly, he has suggested that several consultants see Barbara and confer with the physician who will be her therapist." With a sermon voice, he continued: "I have called— expecting you would approve my action—Dr. Heinz Kabat in Zurich and Dr. Pierre Luchan, an analyst in Geneva. Both men are very experienced with anorexia nervosa and could save precious days in Barbara's treatment. Dr. Frieda Weiss has been chosen to be Barbara's therapist. She is a fine clinician, trained medically in Frankfurt and psychiatrically in Zurich and London, where she was a British Council Fellow at Queen's Square and the Maudsley Hospital. I should add that she is a mature woman, a mother with adolescent children; I have no doubt she and Barbara will be able to relate splendidly."

He stopped and looked up at the massive oak beams which had traversed the roof of the imposing chambers for a century.

Don said nothing. As always, his mind turned in on him and filled him with indecision. He could feel his eyes, turned inward, feelings washing over him.

"Now," he continued, solemnly. "I would like to meet with you Monday morning to summarize the consultants' views and our treatment plan. That means a three-day weekend for you in Klosters. I hope you don't mind."

"Not at all," Susan said, meeting his eyes. "I suppose we could ski in Davos." Her voice thick from disuse, she was aware that her voice wasn't in control. Susan's heart sped up.

"Or Klosters," Dr. Kurzwinger said, steely, after a moment. "We have some magnificent runs. And the snow now couldn't be better."

"We shall have to try both," Don said. He sounded conciliatory, a little uneasy in his presence. "I understand one can ski from Klosters to Davos and return by bus."

"Yes, but I advise you to ski this trail only on a very clear day." The director spat his words out so fast that Don stared at him, uneasy. "Storms are known to arise without warning."

"Thank you." Don said, happy to change the subject. "We'll be staying at the Lorelei in Davos. Would nine Monday morning be all right?"

"Fine." the director said. "I shall call Kurt to drive you to your lodgings." He shot up, standing erect, his hands extended and opened, his heels pointing slightly inward. Don thought of Jesus at the Last Supper.

Barbara was struck by the size of her room. In all respects, Switzerland seemed massive to her. She sat on the double four-poster bed, made of heavy oak, and kept rubbing her hand over the silky eiderdown. Against the far wall was an ornate dresser which reached to the ceiling. A French provincial desk was next to glass doors, which opened to a terrace.

Barbara prolonged her unpacking. She began to put her clothes in the dresser drawers in a geometric pattern of an inverted T. She looked at the geometry. What trivia she could imagine; in a few minutes she would be meeting all the patients. She chose a long black satin skirt which would hide her body and be severe enough for this German-Swiss hospital.

Barbara could wait no longer; she left her room, noting the absence of a lock, and went to Frau Schein's room. As she walked along the hall, she peeked over the ornate wooden railing of the balcony, squinting, unbelieving: she was now part of another world.

"I'm ready to meet your patients," Barbara said, wringing her fingers and sniffling.

"*Sehr gut,*" Frau Schein said in a low tone. Her face was white, powdered looking, her nose flat and wide, and there were liver spots on her temples.

The two women walked down the high-arched hall, crowded into a metal-cage elevator, like the ones in old Parisian hotels, and descended to the first floor. They entered what looked like a drawing room with deeply upholstered maroon sofas and chairs. Over the fireplace hung a portrait of Sigmund Freud; and along the side walls were other portraits: E. Bleuler, Zurich; K. Jung, Zurich; and L. Binswanger, Krenzlingen. She assumed they were portraits of regional psychiatrists, displayed so local physicians wouldn't feel slighted. Over their heads the beams creaked a little and she could hear feet shuffling, organ music playing a hymn and a constant murmur of voices.

"We enter now," Frau Schein told Barbara, staring, slightly confused.

Barbara studied the patients, some fifty or more she guessed: men, women, a few teenagers, many nationalities. They were seated along two long tables, at least a hundred feet long, with their backs to the wall. In the middle of the room, a smaller table was positioned equidistant from the two patient tables, dominating the center of the room. Around the table were a dozen men and women—physicians, Barbara judged by their demeanor; and, at the head of this table, somewhat removed from the other doctors, sat Dr. Kurzwinger.

"It is my pleasure," Dr. Kurzwinger said, "to announce the arrival of Miss Barbara Gordon, age seventeen, from New York City, the United States." He looked down. Then: "We expect that she will be spending the spring with us and hope you will help make her comfortable." He repeated the announcement in German and glanced at Barbara, uneasy, then away.

A stout woman from the center table came over to Barbara. Unlike the director, she spoke English with only a trace of an accent.

"I am Dr. Freda Weiss, your therapist." Barbara felt a sudden, inexplicable leap of hope; but soon the sensation of freedom passed, and her jaw grew stubborn. The woman had straight, brown hair parted down the middle, a fleshy face, droopy, mascara eyes, soft, smooth hands and fingers obscenely warm. "Permit me to show you to your place at the dinner table."

"Frau Berta Meister, I want you to meet Miss Gordon. Frau Meister is from Munich." The woman smiled with malice. "And," Dr. Weiss continued, turning to her left, "this is Herr Anton Beiser, a medical student from Groningen." Barbara's immediate impression was that he was a German hippie because of his longish hair and turned-up collar. "Now I shall leave you, but tomorrow morning at ten-thirty, we shall get together in my office. *Guten Nacht.*"

"Hello," Barbara whispered to her dinner companions as she sat down. She put her hands in her lap to hide the shaking. Frau Meister said nothing. She shook her head and glanced at the waitress. A lentil soup was served. It looked watery. The woman picked apart a large chunk of black bread; she arranged the crumbs carefully in her soup plate to make patterns that had no perceptible meaning to Barbara, except at about two o'clock, where there was a design which could be taken for a human face. Each time Frau Meister would spoon up the pattern and with a noisy swallow gulp it down, more times than Barbara cared to watch.

The medical student snickered and turned to Barbara.

"Don't you know this is a Krankenhaus, the most Kracken of the Hauses where Krankenheit ist heiss and heiss can be kranken? *Eins, zwei, drei und so weiter! Kranken, kranken, kranken, nein kein Mutter.*"

Barbara couldn't listen to any more of his clanging. Only a few patients were talking to one another. A man, with a small goiter pushing against his collar, sat studying his food. A waiter went up to him, put his hand on his shoulder; and, Barbara suspected, encouraged the man to eat. He shook his head. The light from a nearby candle was reflected in tears which clung to his beard. She watched to see what the waiter would do. What strategy would the doctors use if he refused to eat? Would force be used on this man? She took a few sips of the soup, smiled at the waiter holding her main course, and then passed the soup bowl to him.

"*Danke schön,*" he said, surprised by her quickness.

"Would you like my dinner?" Barbara said to the medical student, turning away as she spoke, looking up at a painting on the wall.

He continued to chew for several minutes, finishing his food. "*Ja wohl!* Essen ist gefessen and don't you forgessen," he said as he pulled the plate from her hand. He bent forward, chewing, forking in the food, eating like a ravenous hound dog.

Barbara picked at the salad. She ate with her head low, eyelids

lowered. Her eyes were filled with tears, puddling in the corners so that
the candles were a blur of yellow and white. Her heart now beat lightly
but quickly. She knew that Dr. Kurzwinger could easily see her from
where he sat. Before she had finished the salad, a meringue dessert was
brought to her. She was glad to see that the waiters didn't linger
between courses.

She kept thinking about being locked up with people who were
either mute or incoherent.

Forming the words with her lips, Susan said to herself, "It's done."
She had to face a new reality: Barbara was gone. After seventeen years,
she was gone. She was finally in a hospital. Now she would be treated. It
had all happened too quickly. Only ten years ago, Susan had driven her
to camp in New Hampshire. That had been in the early summer, when
the leaves were bright green and still fresh, the sun warm; and it
seemed the summer would never end. Barbara had cried when it was
time for her mother to leave. They had kissed, said goodbyes, and
Barbara had turned away. And when Susan drove off, she could see her
daughter's tears in the mirror. Barbara was seven; she hadn't seen the
camp before, and Father and Peter were back home.

Now she was gone. In the evenings no one would ask Susan how her
day had been. There would be no discussion, not even an occasional
argument about whether Angus had been fed. No telephone calls from
Barbara's friends would break the quiet of the night. A reminder about a
forgotten allowance the past week would never be spoken. No longer
would Susan wonder if her daughter smoked pot in her bathroom.

The limousine had turned the corner; and, by the time it reached the
village, Susan knew what had happened. But she didn't know why. And
as Susan and Don drove back from Einfurt to the hotel in Klosters, she
silently cried, which she feared might confuse, even hurt, Don, sitting
next to her. He might not understand; he didn't comprehend, perhaps
never would, a mother and daughter. Susan had taught Barbara how to
use a sewing machine and to think about being a wife and mother.
Fathers didn't have to think about their daughters, their needs and their
future—things a young woman must understand to be an adult woman:
those parts of the feminine self that must ride high in the sea.

As they drove to the hotel, Susan wanted to think of other things: a
walk in the chill of the February air, a dip in the heated hotel pool, the
need to cash a traveler's check. And when they reached the hotel, Don
took a nap and Susan went off to jog.

Along the mountain road the breeze had turned to harsh bursts that made her eyes water even more. She could smell snow in the air. The runted pines and scrub oaks waved as they had each winter when she and Barbara went for walks in Cornwall. And twirls of snow spun round and round, turning over and over, as the blown snow rolled down to the meadow. And soon she saw other joggers, mostly young and tanned, running alone. She greeted each one, even after the fifth had passed without a word. Susan was alone.

She ran and ran, cold air sucked deeply into her lungs, until she noticed a church. A sign indicated that she was in another village.

Thirty years ago Susan had gone off to a hospital, too. No one had much cared. She had had a virus infection of the nervous system, Guillain-Barré syndrome; she was paralyzed from the waist down and stayed in the hospital for six months.

Now Barbara was gone. She didn't need much holding anymore.

Dr. Weiss hadn't been able to see Barbara the day before because of a personal matter. Cancellations by therapists there were always put in those terms. She was relieved and suspected Dr. Weiss would soon say something about her eating, as soon as the waiters reported her calorie intake.

She was made aware of how hard she squeezed the doctor's door handle; her hand blanched with her grip. Two psychiatrists had seen her an hour before; she had already forgotten their names. They had asked her many silly questions about her childhood.

"Guten Morgen, Herr Doktor Weiss," Barbara said, as she sat down in an overstuffed chair next to the doctor's desk. Next time, she thought, she would goose-step in.

Dr. Weiss returned no greeting. Silence for a few minutes.

"Did you sleep well, Barbara?" she asked in a low voice, squinting at her.

Barbara said nothing. She observed Dr. Weiss's towering, brown bun near the top of her head and smiled. She was wearing a different hair style today. Maybe a sign of flexibility, Barbara mused. But the German woman looked inane in her loose, black dress, tightly belted through a roll of fat. How could this woman possibly take herself seriously? Or be taken seriously? Was this "Hausfrau" really a therapist? She would sit motionless and stare her down.

"I would like to set up a therapy schedule with you, Monday through Friday, at nine." She smiled, a bit falsely. "Is that all right?"

"Sure, why not?" Barbara said. The questioning would continue, endless, she thought.

"Fräulein Gottlieb, the recreational director, will arrange the remainder of your day." The sobering thought filled her chest with a coldness. "But I think you should also take part in Dr. Weiner's group therapy. That meets daily."

"Is there anything else?" Barbara asked. How sarcastic could she be, Barbara wondered.

"Just that we shall start tomorrow . . . Oh, yes," moving on, oblivious to Barbara's building anger, "there is one other thing. It has been called to my attention that you aren't eating. On account of your condition, we cannot let your weight drop. You are so thin you look made out of sticks." She stopped talking, apparently to translate her German into English. "Food is now a medicine for you. A high protein concentrate will be added twice-daily to your diet. Because of your weight, you must eat what is given you. If you don't, then your physical activities, including your morning exercise, will be curtailed. Do you understand?"

Barbara imagined clapping her hands over her head and hissing with rage. She considered how much better it would be if food were totally supplied in capsules containing protein, minerals and vitamins, as well as a gelatin coating that could cover fecal matter in the large intestine, turning it into cylinders neatly evacuated without smell.

Barbara left the office and went to the ski room. She wondered if Klaus, the ski instructor, would be there.

Silhouettes of pines rising out of the snow surrounded the sanatorium, and snow lay all around the buildings, sealing it up like a box. As they entered the administration building, Susan and Don saw their reflections in the great glass doors. They both looked tense, expectant; they said nothing to each other. But there were murmurs of voices from the other side of the doors. Inside, they found Dr. Weiss talking to the receptionist, a small, lean, beak-nosed older woman. The huge grandfather clock began striking, a whir of gears, ten quick notes. They were on time for their appointment.

"Did you have a good weekend?" Dr. Weiss asked the Gordons. She looked them over more carefully than she had on their first meeting. She forced a smile.

"Excellent," Don said. He nodded and swallowed. "The skiing at Davos was superb."

"And we met some New York people—in the same field as I," Susan said. "We hope to see them in Cannes."

"Can I see you alone, Dr. Gordon? Please excuse us, Mrs. Gordon." She directed Susan to the waiting room. "I must tell you what our consultants felt about Barbara," the psychiatrist said. She was brusque.

"They concur with the London psychiatrist and our staff that your daughter has anorexia nervosa. They, too, fear for her future," Dr. Weiss said. She shuffled some papers on her desk.

"What do you mean?" Don asked. His eyebrows lowered so that between the smoothness of his forehead and the hollows of his cheekbones his eyes were like slits, too narrow to be penetrated.

"What worries us is that we are not sure what is behind her starvation. Do you have any idea what precipitated the dieting?" Dr. Weiss asked. She sat back to listen, nothing moving now, not even her eyes.

"Well, the fact her periods stopped makes me suspect she's afraid of sex," Don said. "I know this is the usual reason." She said nothing; he began to be anxious. "But I'm not sure I can go much further than that."

"How does she act around you," Dr. Weiss asked, shooting the question at Don. "Nervous?"

"She's very uncomfortable." Dr. Weiss nodded, faintly agreeing. "Again, I think it's her fear of sex. If I look admiringly at her, she blushes. And if I touch my wife affectionately, she seems angry."

"Perhaps so," Dr. Weiss said. She looked at Don again, squinting. "We will learn more about Barbara once she's engaged in treatment. We'll certainly be in a better position," Dr. Weiss said, "to discuss Barbara's situation when you get back."

"I hope so," Don said, sighing. "We'll be back in a month, at the end of March." He rubbed his chin and straightened up a little. "We'll be at the Negresco in Nice for a few days, the Hotel Cap Antibes for several weeks and in Cannes, if you need us. Susan may have to go to Rome for a while." Don stood up, abruptly, surprising himself. He rejoined Susan, reading a copy of *Match* in the waiting room.

It was snowing lightly as Barbara reached the ski room. Klaus, the square, muscle-headed recreational therapist, a bull of a man who had been a ski instructor in a Nazi Alpine training school, wasn't there, but the ski equipment was unlocked. Against the wall were a number of skis of various lengths, both downhill and cross-country. Boots were scat-

tered along an oak table with goggles and mittens. She clamped on a
pair of fish-scale Trak skis. There was no time for waxing skis.
Trembling, Barbara fled from the sanatorium.

The trail passed along the base of the mountain behind the sanatorium. It began to snow harder as she climbed the trail. The sun, still
low in the winter sky, tried to burst through the clouds.

On a trail map she had found a course from Klosters to Dorf. By her
calculations, she would reach Dorf by four in time to get the returning
bus and be on time for dinner at the sanatorium. The trail increased its
ascent. The limbs of the fir trees along the trail sagged more under the
burden of falling snow. The trail grew narrower. Only three sets of ski
tracks were visible in the new snow. After a quarter of a mile, the trail
opened up into a meadow and then sloped abruptly down into a narrow
pass. She could only stop herself by falling sideways into the snow. In
front of her lay a long, curving trail carved out of the side of a mountain
wall which looked down on the toylike village of Klosters. She skied
along the ledge, only a foot away from her right ski. The top bar of a
hand railing, intended for summer hikers, stuck starkly out of the snow.
She looked up at an endless wall of snow jutting out, like an old man's
bushy eyebrows. She knew these accumulations of snow gave birth to
avalanches. She increased her speed. As she climbed higher, the tracks
ended; she passed into the sky. The wind blew harder, scattering the
snow around her.

She came to another meadow. An indentation in the pine trees
suggested the continuation of the trail, but she couldn't be certain until
she had glided down a slope to a clearing where she found a goat
herder's hut. Two trails fanned out from the hut; the wider, by a few
feet, appeared to go down the mountain. The narrowed trail remained
at the same altitude and looked like the trail to Dorf. She told herself to
follow it, even though it was one o'clock, and the sun had long
disappeared behind a solid cover of black clouds. She knew by the dirty
gray of the sky that a blanket of snow was soon to cover her. Surprising
herself, she laughed at the snow as it fell like confectionary sugar, blown
from the sky by a madman. She slid her goggles down over her eyes.

Barbara knew storms in Vermont, where it snows sideways and turns
to ice. But this snow was different—it blew at her from all directions, as
well as twirled about her head. She whistled some sections from
Beethoven's Eighth, but the cold wind nipped at her lips and made
them numb. She skied on. Now her goggles made no difference; the

world had turned solid white. Should she go back to the goat herder's hut? Should she try to build a fire in a clump of pines? Either way, a frozen death. Only activity could keep her alive. She pushed across the meadow. Lost in the snow, she became part of the vast whiteness. She thought how good it would be to lie down, only for a little while, and rest. She giggled and laughed; now she wanted to fall down, clutch the snow to her chest and cry. A new-found serenity surrounded her; no longer did she feel that she needed to know, to be certain of anything. Snow, now covering her body, crept under her collar and went down her neck. Her numb fingers could barely feel the ski poles. Her mouth could only open slightly, her cheeks felt stuck in the hollows of her face, and her eyeballs, fixed straight ahead, were frozen into their sockets.

She sensed her direction was off. The storm had started from the west. Either she had turned north—which would be unlikely since she now wasn't going up the mountain—or the storm was now coming out of the northwest. If the latter, she must continue skiing across the meadow to the trees. Then there would be a trail which would turn to the right and drop down to Dorf. Her eyes clamped shut, wincing from the exertion, sweat pouring off her like rivers, her arms and legs mush from exhaustion, she trudged on, her mind now almost a blank, except for the awareness that her ankles ached from twisting and turning and that an area of raw flesh on her right foot from the rubbing of her boot stung with every step.

She was right. The trail was precipitous, and a crevasse ahead might swallow up her body. Controlling her speed would be difficult. The blades of her skis weren't sharp enough for safe snowplowing, and the trail not wide enough for stem christies, even if she had been able to do them. Suddenly as she turned a sharp right angle—she feared a precipice ahead—she came into a clearing, flooded with sunlight. The storm had passed on to the next mountain and left her in a half-moon of an iridescent rainbow. An unspeakable weariness passed through her body; the strength had gone completely out of her legs.

The village of Dorf looked up at her. The thrusts of her poles were bolder. And as she descended down the mountain she felt warmer, stronger, strangely relaxed and agile. She skied into the village, where the van from Einfurt was waiting for skiers in front of a Gasthaus.

The hall leading to Dr. Weiss's office seemed longer today. She was more aware of muscle pains in her legs, arms and shoulders. Her teeth hurt from grinding during the night. Everyone at Einfurt had heard about her survival. Even the mumbling patients—those who listened only to themselves, like ham radio operators, bent over their sets—watched her at breakfast. She was an Olympic athlete, returned home with a gold medal hanging from her neck.

There would be no gold medal from Dr. Weiss. "Please come in," the therapist shouted through the door. Dr. Weiss remained seated. She read a neatly typed chart, which Barbara knew was her medical dossier.

An uneasiness, until this moment only in her stomach, began to rise in Barbara, a kind of premonition. There was a stab in her throat, as if her heart were lodged there and was hurting. She drew back a little, preparing to leave.

"Barbara, please sit down," she said. She stared at Barbara with mindless eyes, and she showed, as usual, no overt signs of emotion. "I'm relieved you returned safely from your ski hike. Last winter two Norwegians took the same trail and weren't found until May. They had skied off a cliff."

For one reason or another, Barbara said nothing at first, merely watching the thing build up. "They must have panicked," Barbara snapped. She clenched her fists and made herself calm.

"Perhaps." Dr. Weiss closed her eyes tight for a moment, then opened them. "At any rate, you are back. The exertion of the trip took five precious pounds off you. This is now my main concern. We must reverse the weight trend. It will be necessary for us to put you on bed rest for the week." Her eyes narrowed just perceptibly, and a hint of a smile crossed her face. "And I must insist that you eat what is given you."

Barbara stared at her for several minutes. Dr. Weiss was serious about her new plan. As if speaking to herself, she said, "You must be off the wall!" She thought it was some lunatic joke, although she knew at the same time that it was not. "I can't get away from food," Barbara said, adamant. "It's on my mind all the time; I'm always eating." She winced as the words fell out. "I just can't get away from it. I say to myself every day: I'll have granola for breakfast, chicken soup for lunch and a piece of roast beef for dinner. I think about menus all day: what I'll have." A chill went through her. "How much of it I'm to eat—to the point I get sick of food?"

Dr. Weiss lit a cigarette and inhaled deeply, relaxing a bit after a few moments.

"Yes, I think," Dr. Weiss said, "that I know some of the anguish you live with." She paused, compressing her lips. "But, before we can really understand your pain, we must keep you alive."

Barbara glared at her, feeling the therapist's eyes watching her critically, perhaps amused or scornful.

"You are physically sick," Dr. Weiss went on, straightening up, "and you are unable to take care of yourself. We must take care of you, as long as you can't do it for yourself." She looked up at the corner of the ceiling and drew out another cigarette. "Each day will be regulated for you in accordance with your capacity to take care of yourself."

"I understand," Barbara said, trying to think about other things.

"I hope you won't again elope from Einfurt." The muscles of her face squeezed inward around her eyes. "I'm sure at any time you can run off. We are not a jail, and you can prove your superiority, if you wish." She glanced at Barbara, then grinned. "You desperately need to feel in control of all situations, don't you?"

"I sure do," Barbara said. She turned her head, then went on, raising her voice to avoid interruption. "If I'm not, then someone else will be. That's the way it's always been." She closed her eyes and gave out a tiny whimper. "I used to be a good little girl who did what my parents wanted. I always saw my mother as my best friend, my companion, even though she was usually at work. I was always well-behaved and always knew what to do. I was the nicest one in the family—certainly better than Peter." It all came to her suddenly, with perfect clarity, as though someone next to her had whispered it into her ear. "I really wanted to impress my parents with my dieting—they never could do it as well. I could never get angry with my parents—it always made me feel so imperfect, frail. Whenever I'd get angry with them, I'd sense a voice in me telling me to behave myself, control myself before every good thing in me was lost. For me, things have to be perfect in order to be good."

"Why were you so good?"

"I was afraid . . . they wouldn't love me anymore." Her chest filled up, then her eyes.

Barbara studied the patterns in the oriental rug. She started to count its purple rings. She looked for a sign, but she knew better. But still she cried. Suddenly she straightened up like someone who had reached a decision, ready to turn on her heel and stalk out of the room. But she settled back into her chair, sobbing.

"I've always been worried my parents would die, get a divorce or stop loving me. When Peter was born, I thought I had disappointed my mother. She had exchanged me for Peter." She shuddered once, so violent she imagined her teeth rattling.

"You've worried a great deal about letting your mother down," Dr. Weiss said, her voice full of pressure.

"And I have in many ways," Barbara said, confessing. "She's fed up with me. I'm not going to complete this school year. My transcript will have withdrawals on it."

"What else has she wanted from you?" Dr. Weiss asked, as if with scorn, but only by accident.

"She's always expected me to be beautiful, a Cybill Shepherd, like in *Heartbreak Kid.*" Then, firmly: "But I don't want that kind of burden. And if I really start eating, I'd eat all the time. I need a voice around me, telling me not to eat, warning me. The voice is always there, critical, harsh and exacting."

"You are right. You hate yourself down to your bones. You punish yourself with your worries about eating and getting fat." Dr. Weiss looked away, compressed her lips and made an entry in Barbara's chart. She looked up, wet her lips and said, "And you're paranoid."

Pure rage tore through Barbara's mind, hurling her back into her cage of doubt and misery.

Barbara enjoyed the sauna at the sanatorium. She would lie in the dry steam on a wooden bench with Fräulein Mittwock, a slow-witted, suspicious, cowlike girl with thick, square ankles, doing isometrics of her arms and legs, leaving the room periodically to drink water, plunge into a cool bath and walk naked in the snow-filled enclosure behind the building. As the days went by, the ritual was a purification, which left her limp and sleepy. In the mornings, Barbara would go to hydrotherapy between her therapy sessions and lunch. She could have happily made hydrotherapy and the sauna her whole day, spending long hours floating in the hot bath and, even though heavily sugared, sipping hot tea as she watched her body. Her skin would tingle. When she closed her eyes, images of the Mediterranean appeared. After hydrotherapy, she would swim thirty laps in the pool, although she had been forbidden this activity—all physical exertion, for that matter—by her therapist when her weight again fell. Deceiving Dr. Weiss became another pleasure: playing cat and mouse with her therapist—teasing, cajoling, threatening, jibing, and tormenting her—excited Barbara as long as she didn't sense that she had pushed beyond the limit. She wanted to arrange her appointments to allow time for walks, hydrotherapy, sauna baths, jogging and gymnastics; no time should be lost.

From the beginning of her stay at Einfurt, Barbara knew that Mademoiselle Theroux, a cachectic brunette from Nice, was always worried about weight. Oddly enough, Barbara regarded this young woman with a low opinion. She saw her as arrested at about age seven and felt alarm when she looked at the woman's face, blank and long, drawn out, she suspected, by demons and terrifying hallucinations. She never, however, spoke to her, felt concerned for her, or thought that she should worry that the petite French girl would capture the attention of everyone at the sanatorium. They only had in common stratagems for hoarding partly chewed food: letting it drop from their lips to the napkin or the floor or wrapping it up in tissue. Both of them had no intention of eating. Both were amused by the attendants when they searched their rooms for caches of food in an endless game of hide and seek.

What irritated Barbara the most about Einfurt was having to eat in the dining hall with the other patients and staff. She never seemed to have enough time to arrange portions on the plate, cut them into small pieces with the dull knife after she had stabbed the pieces repetitively with the fork, put them into her mouth and then start the whole ritual over again. And they wouldn't let her drink fluids through a straw, for fear she would linger further over meals. The nurses and attendants at Einfurt found Barbara interesting when she first arrived; then they could even be empathic—something rather rare at the sanatorium. They saw her as a youngster who deserved compassion and help because of abandonment by her parents. But soon Barbara's will and pride over having conquered her body and tamed its spirit irritated the nurses, even made a few openly envious, and when she began patronizing them—sympathizing with them over their obesity and woeful physical shape, even making ethnic comments about "fat Swiss-Germans" and their fattening diet—they came to loathe her.

The infirmary was a rectangular room, large enough to accommodate ten beds with only room for a nurse to move around with a medication tray. Its walls were green and yellow, pictureless—drab colors, unmatched by several couches that would see no immediate repairs. The infirmary offered Barbara no haven from the people who wanted to feed her; even if she intended to gain weight, the lack of space, the closeness to other bodies, and the sight and sound of people eating would nauseate her. She now watched the other patients, most of whom seemed to be able to get out of bed; they had finished their breakfast and were going out to the solarium. Outside, the light was yellowing after the early gray of dawn. A few patients, including Hans, chose the snow-covered veranda. Several were talking in muffled voices, except for an occasional shrill laugh. She joined them, wrapped herself in several furry blankets, put her head back, closed her eyes and pretended that she was on a beach, a crescent lagoon, where there was no one else.

Suddenly, Hans, who usually sat bent double, his eyes clamped shut, got up from the chair when the attendant was not watching, and lay down, ecstatic in the fresh, fluffy snow. His eyes were not fully shut, the whites fecking out as he blinked. He was an angel, could dance on the head of a pin and had seen Beatrice and Dante. Quickly, he was picked up by several attendants and returned to the infirmary. Barbara leaned back. With eyes now heavy, closing, she sank into the chaise-lounge, half-asleep, her mind cobwebbed with dreams. A chilling breeze struck her face. Voices faded away from her; a total darkness enclosed her and, as though an executioner had thrown a circuit switch, her back arched, sending her headlong into an abyss . . . People were speaking to her in French and German, but their faces were blurred by a white-flecked haze. Her tongue was sore; her spit, salty. And as she was pulled to an erect position and pink froth wiped from her mouth, she saw a circle of urine on the blanket that had been wrapped around her.

Someone spoke in guttural English. His voice exploded. "Give her air to breathe. She's had an epileptic fit."

In a few minutes—it seemed like hours later—she was in her bed, immobilized by heavy blankets, tightly tucked under her. A nurse on the veranda had injected something, probably a barbiturate, in her upper arm. Her limbs were heavy, eyes dazed—the eyes of a sleepwalker; all substance had drained out of her. Drifting off to sleep, she dreamed that she was a little girl on a swing in Central Park, moving back and forth, higher and higher, under her own power without any concern or fear. She ignored the danger that she might fall off, or, if her momentum increased, make a full circle. Her mother sat on a park bench, talking unconcernedly to other mothers.

"*Guten Abend,* Fräulein Gordon," Dr. Perlmutter said, shaking her by the shoulders. A young man, sullen and arrogant, quick to sneer, he stood several feet away from the bed, as though he feared contamination.

"You've been asleep six and a half hours. How do you feel now?" he asked, thoughtfully, looking at her carefully.

"Sleepy," Barbara said, her eyelids like lead.

"I'm afraid you've had a fit this morning," the young doctor said. "Sometimes this happens when people starve themselves and brain chemicals are altered." He said something more and she studied his mouth, trying to concentrate on his words, but her mind would not obey her will; she could not make herself listen to anyone. "I see from your record that you never had fits before. *Ja wohl?*"

"Yeah, that's right," she said, abruptly, "and no one in the family."

"I think we should get an electroencephalogram just to be thorough. But you must eat." He put his hand on her arm. "Your weight is down to 33 kilograms—that's about 66 pounds—to the point of danger. We will start hyperalimentation tonight."

"Hyper what?" she asked, her flesh goosepimply and white.

"Hyperalimentation, extra calories, delivered by intravenous feeding." He took a deep breath, then another. "We must build you up to 90 pounds. The nurse will start this tonight. This means bed rest, as well as eating the regular diet."

"Does Dr. Weiss know about this?" she asked. A pain like a hot ember in her throat made her voice crack.

"Yes," Dr. Perlmutter said. "We concur in this matter. We must keep you alive so you and Dr. Weiss can finish your work."

"Oh?" Panic seized her for a moment, then passed.

"Ja wohl. Guten Nacht," he said mildly.

"Ciao," Barbara said, her lips snarling. She sat up and put her pillow behind her head. She would read since she couldn't sleep. None of the books on the bed stand seemed interesting. She got out of bed to check if the nurse was in her office. It was empty; she had probably gone to the pharmacy.

"Operator? You speak English! Great! I want to call Dr. Donald Gordon in Nice, France." She cleared her throat. "He is staying at the Negresco Hotel." Barbara waited, wondering if her parents were still in the South of France, if they were at the hotel which they seemed to like so much from past trips.

"Your call is ready now," the operator blurted out. A pain shot up through Barbara's belly and chest.

"Hello, Daddy, it's Barbara." Her eyes filled with tears.

"What's wrong? It's eleven p.m.," Don said, sleepy and distant.

"Nothing really," Barbara said, weeping. "I just thought I'd call to see how you are." She compressed her lips, a flood of strong but vague emotions channeling into anger.

"How are *you?*" Don asked. "Your mother and I spent the afternoon in Nice after the morning at the convention in Cannes." He could feel the abyss between them.

"How long are you going to be on the Riviera?" she asked. She frowned, expecting nothing certain.

"Oh, another week," Don said, hesitating a bit. "We planned to call you tomorrow to let you know we want to stop at Einfurt on the way back to New York." He knew it sounded like a lie, but it was true. "Your mother has to go back to her research projects for a few weeks; I'm going to visit some maternity hospitals in Sweden and Denmark. Next Wednesday, April 18th, we'll see you."

"Good," Barbara said. Her reeling thoughts began to make sense, as though she were thinking clearly all at once, and more efficiently than ever before. "Tell Dr. Weiss. Permission is needed. How is Mom?"

"Just fine," Don said. He thought his heart would break. "She's in the shower now. Okay, see you next week. Our love to you, sweetie."

"'Bye, Daddy." The line went dead.

Barbara heard the door open down the hall. The nurse would be upon her in seconds. She ran back to her bed and pretended to read. She sat primly erect, her hands folded in front of her book.

"Fräulein," the nurse said, coming immediately up to her bed. After what seemed like a long time she said, "The doctor wants you to have this I.V. He also wants you to take this Largactil."

"Largactil?" she asked. The muscles of her face tensed, and she wanted to shake her head. "What kind of medicine is this?"

"It's a tranquilizer," the nurse said. "Maybe you know it as Thorazine, its American name. It will calm you down and help you eat." The nurse ripped off the plastic envelope to a long needle and attached it to a syringe. "This will only be a mosquito bite," the nurse said. Her speech meant nothing; it was out of a nurse's manual. She extended Barbara's arm and slid the needle into the vein. The saline in the syringe turned burgundy red, as the column of blood snaked into the syringe chamber. The nurse unscrewed the syringe and attached the I.V. tubing. She turned to face Barbara, dead serious.

"So gut," the nurse said, pleased with her skill, "and now these pills."

Outside, the wind was howling; the pines moaned, a kind of mindless choral singing.

Barbara read for thirty minutes, snapped off the bedside lamp, dozed and dreamed something about loving her demons, smelling the wonderful smoke of her demons. She awoke with a start. Quiet everywhere. All the other patients seemed to be asleep. Throwing the blanket on the floor, she left her bed, after disconnecting the I.V. tube. Wandering down the dimly lit corridor to the rooms of other patients, she stopped at every patient's room, rifled the lockers and bureau drawers and, like a cat burglar, took candy and cookies. In several rooms, she found Swiss francs, which she took for reasons vague to her. Her parents had left her ample money for shopping; she could buy anything she wanted. Nevertheless, it was always good having some extra money available, and the candy and cookies would be useful, if hunger became intolerable during the night. The nurse was still asleep when she crept back to her room. The candy was put under the mattress, the fruit in the closet, the money—fifteen hundred Swiss francs and twelve hundred marks—was hidden in the bottom of her tissue box, next to the bed. As she returned to bed, she hooked herself up to the I.V., only to discover that the needle had clotted. Pressing the vein, jiggling the needle and running hot water over her arm didn't help. Her adventure during the night would be discovered by Dr. Perlmutter; and, eventually, Dr. Weiss would ask questions. They would suspect that she had been foraging for food; they would make the link between the thefts and her wanderings. She would sleep through breakfast and wait.

An old lady, dressed in black, except for a white blouse, as lean as a beanpole, bony hands folded at her waist, as though holding herself in, was sitting on the terrace at the Hotel de Paris. She passed several lamb chops to her chauffeur who carried her Pekingese under his arm. The dog waited in earnest, for he knew that the omens were good today. It wasn't that clear for Susan. She had met Bill Wernicke in Geneva at the World Health Conference, where he, like herself, was looking for research collaborators for an infant malnutrition conjoint project. She had discussed her own proposal with Bill, who had said that he expected to be in Monaco and would join her for lunch today.

She sat there sipping a Kir. Groups of tourists weaved in and out of the casino across the street, hoping, like herself, for something effable and definite—always there and available. Susan knew her dark underside, still huge and irreducible from childhood, keeping her on the edge of either panic or boredom. She knew the essential struggle within herself to bind together her needs through the will-to-intelligence. She understood that she saw herself along a spectrum of images in a repertoire of fantasies.

Susan wondered why her mind kept running off wildly and ending up in cul-de-sacs. An odd and unexpected thought occurred to her: she might be pregnant and have a baby boy. She knew that she had always wanted a boy for her first child—a big, blond, sturdy lad who would be strong and adventuresome. Barbara would, like herself, always be penalized for her sex. In this respect, she agreed with Freud: "Anatomy is destiny." And Peter who, although always a good student, wasn't her destiny; he would be a scholar, never an aggressive businessman or statesman—never a Henry Ford or a Henry Kissinger.

Bill Wernicke wasn't coming. It was as if he had hit her in the stomach, as if a film had suddenly fallen from her eyes and she could see her world clearly for the first time. The bubbling fountain, the shadows across the terrace, and the faces of the people on the terrace were as sharp as a razor cut.

The dining room at the Negresco was almost empty, except for the corner by the window, overlooking the Promenade Anglaise. A young English couple stared at each other—not needing words in a marriage not yet quieted by everyday life. Susan and Don watched them carefully; they hoped to identify the couple's regional accents and place them in a class niche, which their London friends always tried to do with them. They would put Susan's roots in a working-class family; Don's, in a rabbi's with Don breaking away into medicine and making his ascent to the money-class. Their friends, who had spent time in the United States, especially New York, would tease Susan about her Bronx accent. They finally stopped when it was painfully apparent to everybody— blushingly apparent to a few—that these remarks hurt her and widened the gulf between Susan and Don. She shared the same sentiments about her humble origins, which made her attractive to Don, always a rescuer, who could only love a woman that needed nurturance and cultivation.

"I think she's from Hampshire," Susan said. Vainly she looked for a word to describe the woman. "She has that nasal twang, that rural mumbling you hear around the New Forest."

"I doubt it," Don said. He crinkled his neck to look at the man again. "He's from the Manchester area, probably owns a small textile firm, an ambitious Jew, red-brick university education, still hurts from not getting distinctions on his A levels . . . poor chap!"

"Probably, but why can't she be a country girl," Susan asked.

"Elementary, Watson," he responded. He laughed angrily, overcome by a desire to bait her. "She wouldn't fit in his society if that were so."

"Aren't you condescending, my love!" Susan said. She moved her eyes to his face and sneered. "Ever since your medical meeting in Paris, you've been angry with me. Picky, irritable and aloof."

"Breakfast? Madame," the waiter asked.

"Just orange juice, a brioche and black coffee for us," Don replied to the waiter, looking down, grinning horribly. "By the way, Barbara called last night."

"She did! When?"

"When you were in the shower," Don said. There was a note of "of course" in his tone. "I didn't tell you. I knew it would upset you, keep you awake all night."

"What did she say?" Susan asked. She leaned forward in her chair and pressed the palms of her hands against her thighs.

"Oh, just chit-chat." He decided against being cagey. There was no point in teasing her. "She's feeling fine and looks forward to our visit next week."

"Visit next week?" Susan snapped. She turned to Don and looked at him with alarm. "Look! Only your salary continues while you're on this European trip; you can't see patients. We must get back to the office soon." She felt stifled in the dining room with its high, dark ceilings, red plush wallpaper and ornate floral rugs. "Anyway, don't you realize inflation will eat us up?"

"For Christ sake, Susan," he said. He leaned forward, glaring and, for a moment, he couldn't speak. The room filled with the sound of voices and the clatter of dishes. He said at last, spitting the words out, "We can't go back to New York without seeing our daughter and talking to her doctor."

"But I have to be back in the office by Monday," Susan said. This is no time for fantasy, she thought. "The office called yesterday. They told me the meeting had been moved up a week."

"All right, Susan," he said, sighing, then closing his eyes. "A few days doesn't make a real difference to me." He sat motionless, the tips of his fingers white with the pressure he was exerting against the arms of his chair. "This vacation—this work vacation, to be exact—hasn't been much fun, but I've learned something. And you, too, I suspect."

"Start with yourself first," Susan said.

"Okay." He drew his head up erect, his mouth twisted, eyes wide open. "You and I don't have much going for us. You have your work, which you consume like peanuts. I come second, something I've known for the last year. You've made a choice, don't you think?" He sat there for what seemed like minutes, waiting for an answer.

"Yes, I guess I have," Susan said. She closed her eyes, listening, close to tears.

"Is the choice necessary?" he asked.

"Yes. One has to make a choice," Susan said. She said to herself, he'll never understand. "Otherwise, it's too late. I need to do something of value. Sure, raising the kids is worthwhile, even if one of them is a skeleton. But one has to have a meaningful purpose."

"Bullshit! You just revel in the attention you get from the academic world. I'm not enough, nor are your children," Don said, snorting, more angry. He shook his head and took a gulp of coffee.

"Jesus," Susan said, looking flustered. Her head was tipped down, her eyes like little beads. "And what's wrong with that? Aren't I supposed to enjoy myself? Do you expect me to get all my kicks out of you?" She looked up gracefully, as if inquiringly to him, trying to hide her blind rage.

"It would be nice," Don said.

"What are you implying?" she asked, with a trace of a distant smile which flitted across her rigid face. Her right hand, holding a cigarette, moved a fraction of an inch in an ever so slight sign of dismissal.

"You know what I mean," Don said. He bit his lip and checked an overpowering urge to scream.

"Oh, you'll never understand!" Susan threw her napkin on her plate and gulped down the rest of the coffee. "I'm late already for my appointment," Susan said. "Goodbye!" Abruptly, she walked out of the dining room, down the hallway, her high heels clicking like shots.

Don looked out of the window, watching people walking down the avenue in various directions, as though they knew where they were going. The English couple, hand in hand, left. He began to shake, with his fingers pressed to his eyes; and a sickness spread all through him now, like something green and stinkingly rotten. There were tears in his eyes; he had to grind his teeth to keep from breaking down altogether.

Bright sunshine almost touched Barbara's bed. She woke up stiff and miserable with the covers tangled around her knees; the rest of her body was exposed to the chill. She looked in the mirror: her eyes were dark rings, and her lips were white. Half-imagining, half-dreaming of getting up, she looked around the room and, except for Frau Kupernik, a middle-aged woman who wrung her hands all day while she accused herself of something Barbara couldn't hear, the other patients were still asleep. Footsteps approached from around the corridor, those of Nurse Müller, the head nurse at Einfurt.

"*Guten Morgen,* Fräulein Gordon," she said. "Did you sleep well?"

"Fine," Barbara said, smiling pertly at her.

"*Gut.* Dr. Pearlmutter has ordered a chest X-ray for you," she said. "Please come with me."

"But . . . there is nothing wrong with my chest," Barbara said. She turned away, frozen, trying to erase the nurse from her mind. Then she swung her feet over the side of the bed. Her limbs ached, and her mouth was parched. Panic, like the aftermath of nightmares, stirred in her chest.

"Let's hope not," the nurse said. "Your X-rays on admission didn't turn out well. I'll leave you in the waiting room. The technician will be with you soon." The nurse looked at her watch. "There's hot coffee over there and some newspapers on the rack."

The room, small and cold, was placed against the perpetual north winds at Klosters. Barbara walked around the room, trying to find a soft chair that would be kind to her bony derriere, where the skin was worn tissue-thin at two pressure points. Cold air seeped through the window; it made her nostrils smart. Although the rest of her body was reasonably warm, her hands, deep in the pockets of her robe, were icy and several fingers felt dead. She helped herself to some black coffee, ignored the black bread and cherry preserves next to the coffee-maker, and looked at her fingers. The nails, she discovered, were ridged and pitted. Several were broken off, and, on the right index finger, the nail was beginning to detach from its bed. The skin of both hands was reddish and mottled; the palms were burgundy-red and as rough as shark skin. She recalled this morning how purplish her toes were. She sipped steaming coffee and glanced at a copy of *Die Zeitung* and wondered whatever in their tribal beginnings ever made the Germans link words into such tongue-paralyzing monsters and then tack the verb on at the end of the sentence.

Barbara spun around to see who had entered the room. It was Fräulein Richter, who also was Dr. Weiss's patient. She was elegant as glass: tall and thin, fine-boned, eyes blazing and far apart like royalty. She spoke English in a clear voice, only a bit accented, the tone of which was not familiar to Barbara's ear. Several weeks before, the Austrian girl had fallen under Barbara's spell, ran errands for her, and did almost everything that Barbara asked, even dispose of food for her. Barbara couldn't trust the girl, because she knew that rivalry for Dr. Weiss might make the girl reveal how Barbara was exploiting her. She enjoyed talking to the girl about Dr. Weiss, especially hearing Fräulein Richter's praise for Dr. Weiss. She also wanted to believe in the doctor's goodness, and when Fräulein Richter suggested that Dr. Weiss go walking with them by the lake—help them make decisions about life— Barbara silently scorned the girl for saying things which she herself had briefly entertained. At first, Dr. Weiss had been seen by Barbara as a protector and defender against attackers. If afraid, Barbara could go to Dr. Weiss for comfort, get it without even having to acknowledge her fear. But Barbara's feelings toward Dr. Weiss had changed when she first allowed herself to say hateful things about her mother. Several times Barbara thought that Dr. Weiss had winced disapprovingly when she mentioned how she had thrown her mother's food packages from Nice into the garbage.

Fräulein Richter had barely acknowledged Barbara.

"Ja wohl, meine Fräulein," said the tall technician with small steel-frame glasses, riding his tiny nose. "We are ready."

Barbara nodded, as if immensely pleased with herself.

There was more activity than usual in downtown Nice. German tourists filled the restaurants and shops; American sailors on shore leave milled around the side streets. As Don drove by the town's harbor, he noticed several launches loaded with sailors. He put his car into low gear and started to climb the Grand Corniche. He had nothing to do that afternoon; he thought he would drive toward the Italian border. Ten years ago, Susan and he had been to the Italian Riviera. They had liked San Remo; they had even looked at a little villa by the sea. It was cheap by today's prices—$5,000—but Susan had thought the place would eventually be boring. As he climbed the road and passed Villefranche, he could see the USS Enterprise, anchored in deep water in the horseshoe harbor. The aircraft carrier reminded him of his naval reserve college training cruises in the summer. As a young man, he lived only for the day. No sense of responsibility. Those days were gone forever. Now that Susan didn't love him—or, at least, love him the way he wanted—the best thing for him to do was give up his dreams and go back to work. Idiot, he whispered to himself as he caught sight of his face in the rear-view mirror. Humiliated, he was hot from head to foot with anger, and, meeting his eyes in the mirror, he began to cry. And now, rational at last, he recognized the hollowness of his life and became aware of an image of himself, stark, fixed, as if burned into his mind: an impoverished middle-aged man. He knew that he had neglected his profession to some degree, but it wasn't too late. He could still go back to the main channel of academia.

He would always be needed as a doctor, and once he let the Board of Trustees at the medical center know that he wanted the chairmanship of the department, they would think that he was tired of research. At the top of the Grand Corniche, he noticed a hotel by the side of the road. It was perched at the top of a cliff, without any visible support, drawing its strength from a 180° view, from Menton to Monte Carlo. Half way down the face of the cliff was a swimming pool, carved out of rock, like a shrine. He would spend the afternoon there, catching up on some back issues of his journals. But before going to his room to change, he would call Switzerland to let Dr. Weiss know that they would arrive a week early at Einfurt. He sent off a telegram to Barbara:

ARRIVE EINFURT APRIL 6TH WEEK EARLY STOP STAY ONE DAY STOP MOTHER RETURNS NEW YORK NOW STOP WORK CALLS STOP LOVE DAD STOP

When Barbara returned to her room, she found her bed stripped and her clothes removed from the closet. Her presence on the ward was gone. Nurse Müller walked up to her.

"Fräulein Gordon," she said. Her face worked violently. "Your doctor has ordered that you be moved to a private room."

The nurse led her to a room on the other side of the sanatorium. It was a room that she had discovered on one of her walks—a large room that overlooked the lake. The furniture was relatively new, almost contemporary by German-Swiss standards, and the room faced south-east and embraced the sun for a large part of the day. But she knew that one of her neighbors down the hall was a college student, a Frederick Niedermann, from Cologne. An angular, muscular man, he spent most of his time in the gym, working out on the parallel bars. On the way back from dinner last week, he had walked next to her and insisted on being on the left because she was "a young lady."

Looking around the room, she saw a cache of fruit and candy bars on the bureau; behind her were the heavy steps of Dr. Perlmutter.

"Fräulein Gordon," he said, closing his hand for a moment around Barbara's arm. His anger made the room crackle like burning boards. "You've been discovered. We know you left your room last night, went to other rooms and took food and money. You also disconnected your I.V. when you're starving to death." He leaned forward, neck craned, motionless, studying her with beady, black eyes. "For these reasons, you will have to remain in this room with a special duty nurse around the clock." He walked toward the door. "Nurse Müller will start the I.V. now."

A ripping pain passed through Barbara's lower abdomen; a faint nausea reached toward her mouth. Suddenly, she feared that she would soil her nightgown. Brown-tinged water, flecked with particles that reminded her of the hot breakfast cereal Rose used to make for her, ran down her leg, like a fast leak from a rusted water tank. The leakage bewildered Barbara, for, at first, she couldn't be sure it wasn't simply urine. But the smell told her otherwise: the feces were the overflow of her constipation. Barbara couldn't understand it; she had hardly eaten a thing. And there was a smell of decay, reminding her of the nauseating air in a bathroom after an old person had moved his bowels.

One of Nurse Müller's assistants handed Barbara a towel and directed her to the shower.

"Dr. Weiss," she added, "will see you in your room after your shower. Here is a clean nightgown." The woman nodded and smiled one last time, funereal, and walked out of the room.

Barbara faced Dr. Weiss, who sat in the overstuffed chair by the bed; she was smoking, which she had seldom seen Dr. Weiss do before.

"Good morning, Barbara," Dr. Weiss said, scowling at her patient, irritated by her omnipresent smile.

"Hello, how are you?" Barbara asked, widening her smile.

"You have lost another pound," Dr. Weiss said. She bit her lip and checked an absurd urge to spank Barbara: she was the therapist, *not* the mother. "Dr. Perlmutter fears for your life. You not only didn't eat yesterday, but you also disconnected your I.V. and wandered around the hospital, exhausting yourself."

"And?" Barbara asked, challengingly. Her pale lips smiled.

"And, of course, you stole—food you wouldn't eat and money you don't need. You are desperate," Dr. Weiss said, suddenly feeling exhausted.

Barbara said nothing. She pretended not to hear. She needed something to fix on, steady herself, like the pattern on Dr. Weiss's dress. She would never submit to the doctor; she might just as well be given the injection, which she suspected was awaiting her. She would no longer talk to her therapist; she had the right to be self-determined. Dr. Weiss would destroy her principles, if treatment continued. She would fight to the end with the most powerful weapon available; silence. Dr. Weiss could never defeat her.

"What makes your desperation worse is that you can't talk about your feelings." The therapist fixed her gaze on Barbara's face, now frozen to a cheerful smile.

They both were silent to the end of the session. Dr. Weiss stood up to leave; she told Barbara that future sessions would be in this room at the usual time. Barbara turned away.

"Goodbye. *Auf Wiedersehen,*" Dr. Weiss said. She whispered something to Nurse Müller, as the nurse brought in another bottle of 5 percent dextrose and water for Barbara.

"A letter for you, Fräulein," Nurse Müller said, rather loud, not fondly, not with shock either, only as one might address a remote stranger, trying to touch the person's deeper senses.

Barbara tore the letter open with her teeth and held it in her left hand. The nurse, positioning her right arm, jabbed the I.V. needle into the vein punctured last night. The letter was from Rose, in short, choppy sentences. Angus had been killed by a taxicab on Park Avenue. Peter had been walking him and suddenly, according to the boy, the dog had lunged in pursuit of another dog on the island in Park Avenue. Rose had always been honest with Barbara: the accident wasn't Peter's fault. Peter felt badly that Angus had run from him, and Rose cautioned Barbara not to make him feel any guiltier. Barbara could imagine Rose putting her hand to her heart, shaking her head. She was trying to protect Barbara as she always did. She could hear Rose saying, " 'Course I'm worried about you. Anybody'd worry." Unpersuaded, she suspected that Peter had let Angus go. She knew that Peter was angry that his parents had been away so long and blamed her. She was familiar with his restless arrogance, his disgust for her. Angus would have been twelve years old next week; he was still in good shape, the veterinarian had recently told Rose. He only needed a high-protein dog food. She knew her mother would never get her another dog.

Barbara smiled, nodded, and with her left hand made an entry in her journal. It wasn't legible.

She bristled, then calmed herself. She drew in a deep breath, eyes blank for a moment, and looked at herself in a hand mirror.

The lake across from Einfurt was still frozen, although the surface of the ice looked soft under the blades of several skaters. The warmth of the April sun was beginning to penetrate the winter cover at Klosters. Already there was corn snow at the lower altitudes. A jay, perched on a pine bough, sang a song of spring by a stream, choked with buckling ice and melting snow.

"Is your winter pretty much over?" Susan asked the chauffeur, sent by the sanatorium to pick them up at the station. The sunlight had yellowed in the afternoon snow.

"One never knows, Frau Gordon, when the next storm will come." He laughed with the tone of resignation. "Not until May does winter forgive us for the pleasures of last summer."

"We should come sometime in August," Don said in a thin voice.

"You never know how Barbara's going to be," Susan said to Don. She was unaware of the shift in her thinking. She began to speak rapidly, smiling all the while with a look of pleasure on her face. "She's such an individualistic teenager—a real mind of her own."

"Do you really think that?" he asked, sarcastic.

"I'm glad we didn't raise Barbara on some book," Susan said. "She's not a Spock baby, and I wouldn't have raised her on Gesell, Montessori, Rousseau or John Locke." Her smile seemed ghostly, a bit mournful. "I never needed any advice on raising children."

"Mmm," Don said. "Let's find out what Dr. Weiss thinks Barbara needs," Don said.

"Where's Barbara?" Susan asked, concerned. "I expected her to be at the entrance to greet us."

"There's Dr. Weiss," Don said.

"Hello, Dr. and Mrs. Gordon. I'm glad you are here. Coming a week early is actually a relief for us." Dr. Weiss stopped for several seconds, bending to the Gordons, white; and Don's chest filled with a chill. "We're greatly concerned about Barbara's health. Come. We'll discuss the situation in my office over some coffee."

"I see winter is beginning to break in Klosters," Susan said. The room was full of sunlight around her. "Spring must be beautiful here."

"It was a bitter winter," Dr. Weiss said, "and, as always, it took its toll: blinding snowstorms, avalanches, and soon, I fear, floods . . . Well, to get to the center of things, Barbara's physical and mental condition is grave since her elopement last February." She cleared her throat. "She has continued to lose weight; in addition, she has drawn more into herself, to the point where she barely speaks to other patients—and rarely to me." She saw Barbara's mind vibrating to a different tone, certainly, not hers. "She now weighs 58 pounds. Her iron will has no chinks." She wanted Barbara's parents to understand: she wanted no responsibility for this case.

"What do you think can be done?" Don asked. He could not look at Dr. Weiss as he asked it.

"Because of her medical state, she should be transferred to a hospital, where they have had experience not only with anorexia nervosa but also starvation." She looked straight at Don and then, as if speaking to herself, she said, "I'm in favor of Frankfurt or perhaps London."

"What about psychological treatment?" Don asked, raising the palms of his hands as though treatment were a concrete object to be grasped.

"It's of secondary importance now, Dr. Gordon." She shook her head and rolled her eyes up. "As long as she is in a profound state of starvation," Dr. Weiss said, "treatment is stalemated."

"For God's sake," Susan said. Don felt his jaw go tense. "Can't you drive some sense into her head?"

"She feels she's been ordered around enough," Dr. Weiss said with caution in her voice.

"Well," Don said, "I think the best thing is to take Barbara back to New York." His face was drawn with fear and lack of sleep. "There we can be with her more, and I can have her cared for in a university hospital."

"I agree," Dr. Weiss said, "but the flight must be a direct one." Her voice was quieter than before. "Exposure to the cold, a long period off I.V. feedings, and the risk of her running away must be minimized."

"That should be no problem," Don said, nodding, indifferent.

"Hey, you two," Susan said. "How's Barbara going to feel about this?"

"How do you, Susan?" Don asked, objective as ice.

"It would be safer now," Susan said, "to transfer her to Frankfurt."

"Let's go to Barbara and ask her," Dr. Weiss said, stern, determined to give some direction to this case. "I suspect she'll prefer New York." She stopped talking, and her fists closed tight.

Barbara looked forward to seeing her parents. She knew—Dr. Weiss had pointed it out several times, too many times—that she was ambivalent about her mother. Perhaps love and hate alternated, like summer and winter; they certainly couldn't exist together, side by side. She had last seen her father in February, when he had come from his Paris conference to join her mother in Nice. He had spent the day in Klosters, part of it with her, shopping and cross-country skiing through the valley. Barbara had been disappointed because father was aloof, preoccupied with his work and detached from her. She doubted whether he was bored; it was more that he didn't know what to say to her. And he had told her that he was thinking of taking up the chairmanship at the medical school. He seemed more preoccupied with his work. She wondered whether she had influenced his decision in any way. Had she convinced her father of the importance of challenge and perfection?

At the sanatorium, she had kept to herself, totally living inside her mind. Through the winter, she hadn't had a head cold—not even a sore throat—unlike her mother, who always seemed to have colds from November until May. Even at the sanatorium, living close to groups of people, she had been free of all virus infections—even Hong Kong "flu," which had sent most patients to bed. It was as though immunizations had been given to her last fall. Her only illness in two years was a mild staphloccocal infection on her foot, and it had cleared up after some application of neomycin ointment. Never in her life had she been so healthy and fit. "May neither God nor man take this strength away from me," she whispered to herself, strong as a chunk of steel.

She looked at the odd color of her skin. At first, it seemed a dusky tan from skiing in the sun; but when she looked at her hands in the light of her bedside lamp, the color was yellow-orange, mostly concentrated in the creases of the palms, but also around her nose and chest; she looked like a carrot. Her ankles no longer showed any bony prominences. They had disappeared, as though during the night fat ankles had been substituted. She could only conclude one thing: water was accumulating in her body from the I.V.'s and filtering down to her feet. And the sharp, angular lines of her face had lost their sharpness. She would have to increase the dose of water pills, which she had stolen from her father's office before they had left New York.

In the first-class section of the train, Barbara felt alone. She sat in the corner by the door, diagonally opposite her parents. The train passed through Kusnacht, ignoring the few people on the platform. The snow, driving against the mountains, was agitated by the train, turned upward into funnels that seemed never to settle to the ground. Since early morning, three feet of snow had fallen. Dr. Weiss had warned them that April often turned bitter in Switzerland. On her advice, Barbara's stick legs and arms had been wrapped against frostbite.

"It's time to have a drink," Susan said to Barbara. High-protein drink, she meant to say.

With both hands, bony white, she took the plastic cup from her mother. Against her lips the cup was cold and seemed thick, almost too big for her mouth. She sipped at the bland drink; it reminded her of milk shakes that she used to have at a vegetarian restaurant in New York. Going back to New York meant going to vegetarian restaurants; never again would she eat heavy German food; never would she even look at pork and sausage; she would eat only vegetables.

"Zurich, zehn Minuten," the conductor announced, as he peered into the compartment.

Barbara put her head back and tried to sleep.

In what seemed like seconds, the train lurched to a stop and the compartment doors flew open with a snap, like a crack of nearby thunder, and people poured into the aisles and quickly pushed the outer doors open before the train came to a full stop. Twirling snows swept into the train and slowed the passengers' exit. Two uniformed men, both in black leather coats and peaked caps, emblematic to Barbara of Teutonic power, helped her off the train to a waiting wheelchair. The older of the two men walked ahead, acting as though he were clearing the way for Barbara and his younger colleague, as they pushed through the clutter of people who waited for trains delayed by snow. Finally, they reached a Mercedes limousine, its heater runing, and helped Barbara into the rear seat, where she waited, covered by fur robes, for her parents.

"Have you ever seen such a mob?" Don asked. "It's worse than Grand Central's rush hour."

"TWA," Susan said to the chauffeur, without troubling to look at him. "Please hurry. The plane leaves at 2:18."

The chauffeur frowned and pulled onto the road. He stole a quick look at Susan in the rear-view mirror. The limousine moved like a shadow through the snow. The chauffeur avoided Bahnhofstrasse, choked with shoppers and tourists, struggling through the snow, and took a labyrinth of dingy back streets to the airport.

In six hours, Barbara thought, they would be back in New York. Did Rose know that she was returning? Would she prepare something special? Telepathy had always fascinated her; she had experimented with her powers once in a restaurant in New York when she wished for the waiter to bring her a frozen cocoa sundae. She was relieved when grapefruit, which she had actually ordered, arrived. Perhaps thought and action weren't the same thing after all.

The windshield of the ambulance, as it moved along the Triborough Bridge, was covered with a dirty mist. Barbara had lost any sense of time since leaving JFK Airport; she tried to raise her head to look out the side windows, but her mother made her lie down. Since Barbara had eaten nothing on the plane—not even sipped her protein drink—both Don and Susan felt that Barbara shouldn't use any energy.

"Where are we going now?" Barbara asked.

"The hospital, Barbara," Don said.

"Yours?" she asked.

"Yes," Don said. It was probably wrong saying that, it came to him. But he had. "You are very weak and badly need physical care." He wondered whether he was talking to himself.

The ambulance, flashing its light to clear a path through the traffic, crying out *wha-ah, wha-ah,* sped along the East River Drive to the midtown area.

Barbara was moved from the ambulance; but, until she heard a page-operator calling for a Dr. Gillespie, she wasn't entirely certain where she was. She found it difficult to look at the young doctor who was examining her. Only the light over her bed was on; it created shadows about his face that hid his eyes. He didn't act like a psychiatrist, and this had disappointed her to some extent. She wanted to tell him about an inner inertia—something new to her experience—which made her feel heavy and tired. But before she could speak to him, he had completed the physical examination and had her hooked up to an I.V. bottle.

The medical resident went to the nurses' station at the other end of the hall. He lit a pipe and draped his white coat over the chair. There was excitement in his chest—queerly pleasurable—what he usually felt after he had worked up an unusual case and expected to present it that week at grand rounds. He wrote on the chart:

> The patient is an adolescent girl whose body resembles a skeleton. Weight is 57 pounds. She looks as though she might well be an Auschwitz victim. Her facial expression is blank, hiding a mournful quality; there is a sardonic smile on her lips. Her eyes are black-socketed. Her nose is etched by bones that show through thin skin. Her eyes are sunken and "fishy"; they move slowly, unpredictably, as though she is searching for something or somebody. Her hair is dry and lacks luster. Her thorax is a grill of bare bones, her abdomen deeply concave and her buttocks almost absent, mostly loose skin, a confluence of fine blue veins stretched over pelvic bones. Pubic and axillary hair are present, but baby-like, downy hair is present over her back, arms and sides of the face. Her skin, slightly orange-yellow, is cold and roughened with blotchy patches. Nails are brittle and cyanotic. Below the last joint, left fifth finger, there is a hairline scar from a traumatic amputation, reconnected successfully. A trace of edema is at the ankles. Her lungs are clear. The heart is small by percussion and the sounds are distant. Heart rate is 50. A grade one systolic murmur is at the base; it sounds functional. The liver and spleen are palpable but not enlarged. Gynecological examination was deferred. There is amenorrhea by history.

He continued his note after gulping down a cup of coffee, placed in front of him by the charge nurse:

> The patient moves and speaks slowly with no gesticulation. Although sullen-looking, she responds to my questions. She agrees that she is acting oddly, wasting her life and inflicting pain on her parents. She claims that she is not afraid of fatness and has no idea of why she can't eat. She denies any severe degree of emaciation—"I'm a little thin these days"—and acts suspicious of anybody who would suggest that she should

eat. Otherwise, she seems not deluded, nor is there any evidence of hallucinations or thought deprivation. Her affect is blunted and very controlled. She is highly intelligent, keenly alert, and well-oriented to time, place and person. Diagnoses: 1. Anorexia Nervosa—primary. 2. Starvation and dehydration, secondary to anorexia nervosa in a borderline psychotic adolescent. 3. Heart murmur, functional, probably secondary to anemia.

Before writing the medical orders for Barbara's care, the young doctor called the attending physician, Dr. James Pritchard. They agreed that I.V. 5 percent dextrose/water had to be continued with careful attention to potassium and sodium. A regular diet was to be enforced by the nursing staff, as well as protein supplements every four hours. Barbara's private doctor had already consulted with Dr. Kron, a psychiatrist. A program of behavioral modification was to be used: Barbara would be rewarded for eating her meals by being allowed to sit in a chair for a few hours each day. He would also start daily psychotherapy, as much as was possible now.

"What is he going to do about the parents?" the resident asked. It was more a statement than a question. "When they brought her in, they acted as though they were delivering a package to the United Parcel Service." He shook his head, partly wanting to deny his sarcasm, his anger toward the parents, the judgmental attitudes he couldn't keep to himself, much less understand.

"Well, yes. I know what you mean," Dr. Pritchard said. He studied the floor and mused for a moment. "They're splitting now and are gearing up for a big divorce battle." He wondered if he should be telling the young doctor the Gordon's family problem. It sounded like an apology for admitting such a pathetic patient, or an antidote to his impotence. But he had to teach the house staff, he reminded himself. That was the understanding for accepting admitting privileges. "They see psychiatric help for themselves as too dangerous; neither one of them wants a reconciliation. There's no way they'd let a family therapist into their lives."

"I guess it's all on Barbara," the resident said, sounding baffled.

"Yes," Dr. Pritchard said, quietly, after a moment. "I'm afraid that's the way it is." He shrugged, infinitely sad.

Dr. Gordon liked his new apartment. After he had decided to leave Susan, he had called his secretary from Nice and authorized her to get a one-bedroom apartment near the hospital. When he got back to New York, he asked an interior decorator at Bloomingdale's to help him on decoration and furnishings. The young girl, probably no more than twenty-five, had selected glass, stainless steel, and leather upholstery; she suggested that the walls be painted pure white enamel with China red trim and ceilings. It was different, very different, like all the rest of his life now. In the two weeks back from Europe, he had made many changes. He had cut his practice down to only a few office hours a week; this would give him more time for research and writing, as well as save on alimony for Susan. Life would not begin for Susan with bountiful alimony. He expected the chairmanship at the hospital; the search committee would offer it to him if they picked within the departmental staff. He was their logical choice. Hopefully, the "golden boy." If not, he would have to wait for a chairmanship at another medical center in New York. The only other town he would consider was San Francisco; but that wouldn't be practical since he wouldn't be able to see Barbara and Peter except on long vacations. He had already talked to his lawyer about visitations with the children and had started alternate weekends and weekly Wednesday nights with Peter. Last weekend, Peter had slept on the couch in his living room, and he enjoyed it. They had dinner together Saturday night at his apartment, and after Don had returned from visiting Barbara, they spent the rest of the night watching television. He wondered where he would put Barbara when she began to visit. Probably a pull-out cot in the living room would be satisfactory.

The phone rang. "Hello," Dr. Gordon said, looking at his watch. It was 8:21 a.m.

"This is Dr. Pritchard—Jim Pritchard," a voice at the other end said, dangerously serious.

"Yes, Jim, how are you?" Dr. Gordon said.

"Not so good, Don," he said. "The interns just paged me here at the hospital. They're worried about Barbara. They've had to transfer her to the Intensive Care Unit because of a strange heart rhythm she's developed." His voice faded as though he had stopped talking to concentrate on something before him. "These ventricular premature beats are what I don't like."

The phone seemed to go dead. Don waited, inhaled; the air was still.

Dr. Pritchard suddenly, boldly, seized a word with all the conviction he could find: "We've *digitilized* her and are following her electrolytes, especially potassium." It made sense to him—it would to any good internist—yet something, he couldn't put his finger on what, made him resist reason. "I think it would be best if you came by when you get to the hospital . . . I've just spoken to Susan."

"Oh . . . I'll be over shortly," Dr. Gordon said, looking out the window, half-ideas, vague sensations washing over his mind.

The charge nurse, stethoscope dangling from her neck, had come into Barbara's room, taken her pulse and blood pressure and listened to her heart. She mumbled to herself about someone being right and quickly left the room. Barbara's eyes closed again; a warm flush ascended her body, reducing her awareness, making her feel a little dizzy. The I.V. needle no longer seemed to be lodged in her arm. Inchoate images drifted by her; people rushed into the room; a man's face was several feet from hers, his eyes peering into hers, his breath upon her face. A bell was ringing in her dream—a telephone bell. She answered and heard her mother's voice: "I think you should know that your father died of a coronary last night."

The bed moved to the right and swung around. Shuffling feet were behind her. People whispered to one another a few feet ahead of her. Her bed swung around again and stopped, leaving her nauseated by a sweet sickness of bad perfume. Now the bed was moving again; it bumped twice, like a car crossing railroad tracks, as she passed over an unknown terrain. Her stomach moved up to her mouth, leaving a sour taste. Two more bumps and a wide swing to the left. She was flying out of her body. Endless motion. Beyond inertia. A loud metallic noise. The sound of wind, the babble of voices in a strange language—Finnish?— and the roar of a jet. The motion stopped; she was on her side; and, like a turtle trying to right itself, she turned to draw energy from a lamp behind her.

A taxi crossed the wide avenue and headed for the main entrance of the hospital. It was a warm, late April afternoon. Susan Gordon vaguely noticed the red azaleas almost in bloom in the gardens of the hospital; and, as the taxi turned into the tight circular entrance to the hospital, Susan observed that the red tulips were at their peak of bloom. She gave the driver several dollar bills and rushed through the hospital's revolving door into its stark, main lobby. She pushed past a large Puerto Rican family, screeching at one another, and went to the private elevator.

"Fourteen . . . please," Susan said, failing to see that the elevator was automated. She pressed the plastic disc—14; it turned white.

The elevator rose quickly into the private patient tower. She stared at the blank elevator door. An old couple glanced at her. The elevator stopped. She rushed ahead of the couple and went into the Intensive Care Unit. Two interns were at Barbara's bed. A third doctor stepped out of nowhere and stopped Susan.

"Hello, Susan," said Dr. Pritchard, straightening up and turning to look at her. "I thought you and Don should be with Barbara. Her physical condition has taken a bad turn." He said, leaning forward and touching her arm, "I reached Don; he will be over as soon as possible."

"What's gone wrong?" she asked, frowning, dizzily waiting.

"Barbara hasn't eaten a thing in two days. We've done everything possible," he said with the kindness of a priest. "We can't feed her by vein any more; they've clotted and collapsed. Tube feeding is useless; her gag-reflex throws the tube back at us. We have her on I.V.'s, but we can't keep up with her serum potassium. That's why I wanted you here. Her heart isn't responding to digitalis; I'm afraid she's in cardiac failure. And, with her potassium falling, her heart is increasingly irritable."

Several technicians pushed electronic equipment into the room.

"I've called in the intensive cardiac care team," Dr. Pritchard said. "We have a defibrillator standing by in case she gets into any real trouble."

"This is ridiculous," Susan said, her mind turning in on her and filling her with panic. "Can't anyone talk sense into her stubborn, little head?"

"Dr. Kron is with her now. He told me that he's not certain if she can relent and start eating. Oh, there he is now."

He took Dr. Pritchard aside for a moment. "I've been telling Barbara that she can't control death. It's as though she's in a state of ecstasy. She's so high I can't break through to her." He looked over at Susan Gordon. "You can't let Barbara see her mother," he said, wholeheartedly meaning every word of it, at least for the moment.

"I couldn't stop her if I wanted to," Dr. Pritchard said. He said, whirling, "I've known Susan for years."

He turned to Susan who was already heading for the cubicle where Barbara's bed had been pushed. It was no good stopping her from seeing her daughter, but just the same, he wanted to, probably to spare himself the pain more than Susan.

"Susan, Dr. Kron agrees that Barbara is gravely ill." He looked past her. "We feel your visit must be brief."

Susan and Dr. Pritchard went to Barbara's bedside together. The bedcovers were pulled down; Barbara's wasted, cadaverous body was stark naked. An intern was frantically trying to insert another I.V. needle into a collapsed vein. Another injected something into her upper arm. A technician adjusted an electrode to the cardiac monitor. Blips on the electrocardiographic screen danced crazily. One intern looked up to see if the irregularity was persisting. Susan touched Dr. Pritchard's arm. Barbara's hair lay on the side of her pillow and accentuated the gauntness and angularity of her face. Her breathing was now fast and shallow, and she seemed to be staring out the window, as though looking at the East River.

"Why are you doing this to me?" Susan asked. "Don't you know you can't win? Eat and we'll make everything good again."

Barbara glanced in her mother's direction. Her eyes, dull and glassy, focused on the mother's face. A faint smile appeared at the corners of Barbara's parched mouth, and she whispered: "Where is . . . Rose?"

Barbara's smile left, but her eyes remained on her mother's face.

Dr. Pritchard looked at the electrocardiogram and then at the interns. "She's arrested, shock her."

Dr. Pritchard took Susan to the door and asked her to wait in the hall. Don rushed up to Susan.

"What's happening in there?"

"Her heart has stopped," Susan said.

"What!" He pushed open the door. "Oh, my God!"

He went to the window, stared out for a moment and began to sob.

Dr. Pritchard turned to Don. "I'm sorry, Don. We couldn't get her going again."

Susan returned to Barbara's bedside. The technicians were removing the electrodes from Barbara's wrists and ankles. An intern, after wiping his forehead with the sleeve of his white jacket, pulled out the needle that he had struggled with a few minutes ago. Then he turned off the electronic instruments. Barbara's eyes were still looking where her mother's face had been.

Susan turned to Dr. Pritchard. "You have our permission for an autopsy." She hesitated. "Maybe something good can now come of her life." She left alone, moving slowly like a burned-out star.

A nurse covered Barbara's body with a sheet.

3

The History of the Anorexia Nervosa Syndrome

. . . Yes, yes, you want those tits, can't get enough of them. Breast-fed babies to the end of your days. But out in the world the future has started blazing trails. Nature is sick of being submitted to with womanish passivity; it wants to be mastered by men. Trace canals. Drain swamps. Fence in the land, plow it, take possession of it. Beget a son. Hand down property. Your suckling time has lasted two thousand years too long, two thousand years of waste and stagnation. My advice to you: away from the breast. Wean yourselves.

—Günter Grass, *The Flounder*

The history of anorexia nervosa proves that history does, indeed, repeat itself; it recapitulates the megalithic history of psychiatry. Contemporary controversies over nosogenesis and pathogenesis are reminiscent of those of the nineteenth century; and, like gales that rent trees and bend grass permanently, they leave their mark. Psychiatrists still struggle for meaning, looking for a language full of suggestion, indulging in polemics over issues of classification and a dialectic of organic-functional etiology. Often what is seen depends on what is known, ending in repetition.

Anorexia nervosa is one of the few subjects which Hippocrates did not write about; perhaps he overlooked it. No mention of anorexia nervosa is made in the Bible. But in the third century A.D. there is a record of the fasting Bodhisattva Lahore, a Buddha in search of enlightenment. He wanted to prove to the fakirs that self-denial leads to starvation. The next allusion to anorexia nervosa was in the eleventh century, when Avicenna, a Persian physician and philosopher, wrote about his treatment of a young prince who was suffering from melancholia and the symptoms of anorexia nervosa. Avicenna was able to communicate with the man, break into his delusional system and create an effective therapeutic situation. This case—a male anorectic—is the first well-described case, and it precedes those of Porta, Gull and Lasègue by over 800 years.

Phase One (1600–1910)

The first phase in the history of anorexia nervosa concentrated on the description of the syndrome. During the Middle Ages there were many anorectics whose symptomatology was hidden behind pseudomysticism, diabolic possession, and witchcraft (Stone 1973). Yet Medieval historians do not describe epidemics of anorectic behavior in towns and religious communities, like the sudden explosions of anorectic denial seen nowadays in girls at private schools and colleges. In the sixteenth century, Simone Porta, a Genovese, reported a case of anorexia nervosa. And in 1613 Pedro Mexio recorded the story of a French girl, Jane Balan, who fasted for three years. He doubted supernatural influences and, instead, suggested "hurtful humors" (Morgan 1977). But it was Richard Morton (1694), who in 1689 first presented two authentic, documented cases of anorexia nervosa, some 160 years before Freud's description of Dora. He called the disturbance "phthisis nervosa," a nervous atrophy, a consumption of mental origin, without fever or dyspepsia, with the symptomotology of food avoidance, amenorrhea, lack of appetite, constipation, extreme emaciation, and overactivity. He described an eighteen-year-old English girl, whom he had seen in 1664, a girl who had starved herself because of a "multitude of cares and passions of her mind." He suspected that the etiology was tuberculosis and was dismayed when, after a few months of treatment, she died during a fainting fit that "preceded from sadness and anxious cares." Morton later described another anorectic, a sad and anxious girl. He was impressed with the girl's indifference to her starvation. One of his other patients was an eighteen-year-old boy, who also displayed sadness and anxiety, wasted away to skin stretched over his skeleton, but who finally survived.

The next reported cases, in 1767, were by Whytt, an English physician, who believed that anorexia was related to disturbances of the gastric nerves. And in 1789, Naudeau described a case which ended in death, which he attributed to the pernicious influence of the anorectic's mother. Clinical descriptions of the disorder between those of Morton and later English and French physicians in the nineteenth century are no different from those of today: Relentless starvation to death, a sudden loss of control with compulsive binges and violent vomiting, and the unpredictable natural history of the disturbances, leading to recovery or death, were clearly recognized.

In the ensuing years, clinical emphasis was primarily on identifying anorexia nervosa as a clinical diagnostic group and understanding the disturbance from the standpoint of classification of mental disorders.

An effort was made to comprehend the distinctive morbid and pathogenic features of the disorder.

In 1868, Gull encountered several cases of anorexia nervosa in
London—cases which he published in *The Lancet*. He first called the
anorectic disturbance "apepsia hysteria"; and, much like Lasègue in
Paris, he related it to a gastric nervous malfunction, reflected by a
repugnance for food, which he thought was connected with "a perversion of age as a cause." When he later discovered, in 1874, that pepsin
was present in the stomach of anorectics and that the condition
occurred in males, he changed his formulation and, likewise, the name
of the disturbance to "anorexia nervosa" and searched for psychopathological factors. Gull described one patient who had died of
cachexia, profound emaciation of mad starvation. He realized that
death could result simply from starvation and depression of vital
physiological functions, and, when anorectics did recover, they were
usually compulsive overeaters. One of Gull's patients was a male: and in
his papers he repeatedly made the point that anorexia was not simply a
disturbance of young women. He also indicated the cohesive quality of
the anorectic family by pointing out that the relatives made "the worst
possible attendants." Gull knew that anorexia nervosa was predominantly a psychological disorder. Yet he was not optimistic about its
outcome.

In 1873, unbeknownst to Gull, Lasègue, across the English Channel,
also described the disorder and indicated that the etiology was hysterical, caused by a peculiar mental state, an intellectual perversion that
made them think that "they have never felt better; they complain of
nothing, do not realize they are ill and have no wish to be cured." He
believed that "hysterical anorexia" was related to a malfunction of the
gastrointestinal tract; he was impressed by the "stomach pains" of
anorectics and their "inability to eat." He thought that the term
anorexia should be replaced by "inanition." (In 1883 another French
physician, Huchard, noting that the usual accompaniments of hysteria—paralysis, anesthesis, and blindness—were absent from anorexia nervosa, advocated dropping Lasègue's "anorexia hysterique," and
substituting "anorexia mentale," by which term the disorder is known
today in France.) Following the French school of psychiatry, he was
convinced that hysteria was the etiology and advised that the physician's attitude to the patient was the most important part of the
therapeutic approach to the disturbance. In addition, he warned that

"both the patient and her family form a tightly knit whole, and we obtain a false picture if we limit our observations to the patient alone." Lasègue was relatively optimistic about his patients' recovery, more so than Charcot (1889), who recommended, like Gull, removal of his hysterical patients from their families.

At about the same time, Gilles de la Tourette (1895) tried to separate primary from secondary anorexia and gave primary anorexia the name "anorexia gastrique." He knew that the anorectic suffers not from a loss of appetite; instead, a blatant refusal to eat and a distorted perception of food and her body are the hallmarks of the condition. The fact that a rapid gain of weight ushered in recovery convinced Gilles de la Tourette that the disturbance was psychological. Treatment consisted of separating the patient from the family and kindly encouraging her to eat. And in Vienna, Freud (1887–1902), in an 1895 letter to Fliess, mentioned a patient who illustrated "melancholia of sexually undeveloped girls," which he considered a form of anorexia. Ten years later, in writing about an adolescent girl, he commented on anorexia as one of Dora's symptoms. In 1907 Ballet noted that amenorrhea could be the first symptom of anorexia nervosa; it could also continue after restoration of weight (Gee 1908).

Pierre Janet documented several cases of anorexia nervosa from 1903 to 1909. His attempt to distinguish two groups of anorectics was the first to be made. His most interesting case was "Nadia," a young girl who, dreading the fleshiness of the female body, refused to play a feminine sexual role. He thought that anorectics suffered from psychasthenia, an obsessive form of concern with one's own body. And he also wondered whether there were several varieties of anorexia nervosa: first, an obsessive type with refusal to eat because of an obsession and phobic anxiety about eating. This group, he felt, was always hungry and struggled constantly for control. Disgust for their bodies and appetites was overwhelming. Some feared their stomachs would explode or they might choke to death if they ate. There was a second type of anorectic who complained of a "queer" taste and experienced paresthesias, nausea, regurgitation, and vomiting to the point that they were unable to eat. Unlike the obsessional group, they vomited without conscious effort or nausea. He thought that those anorectics were hyperactive in order to suppress their feelings of fatigue. As a group, the hysterical anorectics had a worse prognosis and were resistant to treatment. But, some years later, Binswanger (1952), Jung, and E. Bleuler doubted whether these patients were anorectics; to these clinicians, they seemed schizophrenic. Dubois (1913) had warned earlier of a schizophrenic outcome.

A few years later, other French psychiatrists, Déjérine and Gauckler (1913), also identified eating disorders which they believed resulted from depression, psychasthenia, and psychotic states and were refractory to treatment. They also classified two types of anorexia mentale: primary, in which food intake is volitionally reduced by young women, and secondary, leading to loss of hunger after food reduction because of gastric disturbances. Secondary cases, both men and women, were not hyperactive; they soon weakened and became lethargic. Another French psychiatrist, André-Thomas, wrote in 1909 that anorexia nervosa was not a single disease but probably a syndrome of uncertain etiology. He widened the concept of anorexia nervosa, removing it from the simple formulation of hysteria. And Karl Jaspers (1910), a German psychiatrist and philosopher, demonstrated that anorexia nervosa could be mixed with a form of psychosis. More sophisticated concepts of anorexia nervosa were now being proposed, and at the same time, because anorexia of depression, phobic anxiety, and psychosis were being equated with anorexia nervosa, the disturbance could not be defined. The literature was contradictory, unclear, and confusing.

Phase Two (1910–1938)

There was soon, however, a turning point in the history of anorexia nervosa, but one that did nothing to dispel confusion. Medical thinking about anorexia nervosa went in another direction; the second phase in the history of anorexia nervosa commenced. In 1914, a Hamburg pathologist, Morris Simmonds, described a case of cachexia with atrophy of the anterior lobe of the pituitary gland. Gull and Lasègue's psychological stance, their conviction that anorexia nervosa was a psychological disturbance, was challenged—on erroneous evidence, we now know—for the first time. His subsequent anatomical and clinical description of these panhypopituitary patients strongly suggested that they were cases of anorexia nervosa, although on later scrutiny of records, many of his patients proved to have been, in fact, not poorly nourished, lethargic, or asthenic. In the following twenty years innumerable anorectics were diagnosed as suffering from panhypopituitarism and were treated with various extracts from the pituitary gland.

Panhypopituitarism, we now know, is clinically and pathologically different from anorexia nervosa. Simmonds's findings were misleading to clinicians and shifted the focus of research from the psychological to the physical. By 1916, the psychological view of anorexia nervosa was doubted by most clinicians. Anorexia nervosa was regarded for twenty years as pituitary marasmus, the result of hypophyseal insufficiency; this view offered a unitary physical explanation for all cases of pubertal and adolescent emaciation.

In the 1930s, several clinical observations were made that challenged the concept of Simmonds's disease. H. L. Sheehan (1937) questioned the theory that the destruction of the pituitary gland led to cachexia and finally refuted the concept of pituitary cachexia in 1939, and, along with Ryle (1936), H. B. Richardson (1939), Sheldon (1939a,b), and Decourt (1946), anorexia nervosa as a disturbance of psychological origin. Supporting Gull's opinion that anorexia nervosa is a psychological disorder, they strongly argued that the condition was not the same as Simmonds's disease. Sheehan (1937) demonstrated that postpartum amenorrhea and failure to lactate can occur when necrosis of the pituitary is a complication of pregnancy. In 1936, Ryle demonstrated that psychosexual trauma could lead to amenorrhea. His psycho-endocrine thesis was further elaborated by Reifenstein in 1946, when the latter described several cases of amenorrhea demonstrably due to psychophysiological causes. This research clearly established that developmental traumas and interferences, as well as psychosocial stress, can alter hormone patterns and secretions, and led to a burgeoning of interest in the psychobiology of anorexia nervosa.

Phase Three (1938–1960)

The third phase in the history of anorexia nervosa had started in the late 1930s, when psychoanalytic interest gained momentum. Psychosomatic medicine, beginning with Weiss and English (1957), Selye (1950), and H. G. Wolff (1948), became concerned with organ system vulnerability, conflict, and defense, and Grinker (1953) extended the focus to the social context of the psychosomatic disturbance. Oberholzer's concept of anorexia (1930), as a wish for a father-penis-baby, stimulated a depth psychology approach to anorexia, while on the continent Mayer-Gross (1954), from the standpoint of constitutional psychopathic states, continued his phenomenological approach to anorexia nervosa. Nicolle (1938a,b) suspected, as had Meng (1934a,b), that anorexia nervosa was allied to schizophrenia. Binswanger published his "Case of Ellen West" in 1944, showing how this starved young woman dealt with her sense of helplessness and hopelessness and finally allowed herself to die of starvation. Kuhn (1953) later published a case in which he emphasized the phenomenology of space and time in anorexia nervosa. And other studies in the phenomenological and existential area of psychiatry were done (Boss 1954, May, Angel, and Ellenberger 1958).

In 1939, Rahman, Richardson, and Ripley delineated the dynamic, compulsive feature of anorexia nervosa. A year later, Waller, Kaufman, and Deutsch (1940) suggested that anorexia was the result of rejection of a wish to be pregnant. Psychoanalytic investigators tried to clarify many issues in anorexia nervosa: some emphasized orality as an important component of anorexia nervosa; others viewed unconscious pregnancy fantasies as the sine qua non of the disorder. Impregnation fantasies resulted in anxiety and guilt, they indicated, as well as amenorrhea and constipation. In 1945, Berlin pointed out oral-sadistic tendencies in anorexia nervosa as well as reaction-formations against incorporation wishes found in severe cases of anorexia nervosa. Ansel Keys and his associates published, in 1950, a definitive study on the biology of starvation, defining the psychological effects of human starvation and establishing their existence independent of neurosis and psychosis. A few years later Falstein et al. (1956) reiterated what Morton and Gull had known quite well: Male anorectic patients present a dynamic pattern somewhat different from that of female patients. Falstein asserted that the male disturbance was mainly related to a feminine identification and the wish to remove fat, which was for the male anorectic linked with the feminine form. The psychodynamics of anorexia, Falstein also said, went beyond impregnation fantasies: The symbolism of food included part and whole objects, a parent, sibling, breast, feces, poison, and genitals. The specificity theory was then abandoned; pluralism had arrived.

In 1957, Meyer and Weinroth wrote that the anorectic defense was an attempt to reestablish the mother-child unity. Later, Jessner and Abse (1960) elaborated the regressive forces in anorexia nervosa. A few years later an extensive psychoanalytic study of anorexia nervosa was done in

Heidelburg by Thomä (1967). Focusing primarily on the drive disturbance in the disorder, he noted that sexual fears in anorectics were
displaced on the body. The anorectic fended off oral-receptive wishes;
she viewed food as an invader of the body, nourishment as an
impregnation.

Phase Four (1960–1980)

The fourth phase in the history of anorexia nervosa occurred in the last
two decades. Engle (1960), Mirsky (1957), and Grinker (1953) presented a more sophisticated concept of psychosomatic medicine; they
shifted their interest to positive and negative feedbacks, field theory,
and the need to consider pathology from the social to the molecular
level. Once again attempts were made to distinguish between primary
and secondary anorexia nervosa: primary patients who derive pleasure
for self-imposed starvation and secondary patients reluctant to eat
because of digestive concerns, depression, or psychosis (A. King 1963).
Similarly, Dally (1969) proposed a triadic classification: obsessional,
hysterical and mixed—or primary, atypical, and a hotch potch of many
disorders with anorexia as a symptom. The Göttingen Symposium
(Meyer and Feldman 1965) accented the need for a multidisciplinary
approach to anorexia nervosa. Several studies have attempted to
redefine the clinical description of anorexia nervosa (Bliss and Branch
1960, Schachter 1974, Beumont et al. 1976). The possibility of organic
etiology in anorexia nervosa has been further pursued by Boyar and
Katz in New York (1974), Russell in London (1965), Halmi in Iowa
City (1978), Dally and Gomez in London (1979). Using new subtle
research techniques, the investigative groups have emphasized that
there is no demonstrable pituitary dysfunction in anorexia nervosa, but
they have raised the question of a hypothalamic disturbance. Whether
the hormonal deviations are the cause or result of starvation or are
functional remain unclear. In 1976, there was a multidisciplinary
conference on anorexia nervosa at the National Institute of Mental
Health. The proceedings of this symposium, edited by R. Vigersky
(1977), stress the need for a more precise definition and diagnosis of
anorexia nervosa.

In the past ten to twenty years, except for Thomä's studies in 1967,
the dynamic formulations of anorexia nervosa have not been based on
drive theory. Contemporary theories of object relations, separation-

individuation, development of the self and gender identity are all part of recent explorations in ego psychology. Concepts of symbiotic fusion with the mother, incorporation of part objects, transitional objects, dual self-representation, vertical splits of the ego, and object relations by projective and introjective identification are used to describe the aberrant behavior.

M. Selvini Palazzoli (1965) bypasses the eating function in anorexia nervosa. She does not believe that the anorectic is truly afraid of food; instead, it is "the feeling that the nourished body is threatening, gnawing, and indestructible," which frightens the patient. This viewpoint is consonant with the thoughts of Fairbairn (1962), who noted that the goal of the libido is not pleasure but the object itself. "The body is regarded as a threatening entity; it must not be destroyed, but must merely be held in check." For Palazzoli, the central phenomenon of anorexia nervosa is the threatening body which distinguishes it from other forms of anorexia; she regards anorexia nervosa as a type of "intrapersonal paranoia": the body is invested with negative attributes of the primary maternal object. Because of this pathologic fusion of self- and object representations, the body is perceived as an intrusive and disparaging entity whose growth must be stopped. The mother, in Palazzoli's paradigm, is seen as overprotective and unable to perceive her daughter as separate. She controls the child and goes against the latter's efforts to derive pleasure separate from her. Compliance is rewarded. The child's learning experiences are inseparable from the mother's teaching of signals and operations, which give the girl a sense of ineffectiveness in thought and action. The anorectic, faced by tasks she cannot accomplish, develops a depression of the ego. It is the helplessness of the ego, rather than merely oral-aggressive needs, that is central to the depression. Furthermore, the patient views her body as a fully incorporated object that disparages her and forces a passive role on her. Palazzoli asserts that the anorectic patient distinguishes oral helplessness. The ego incorporates and represses the bad object. In latency, identification with the real mother is attained by compliant surrender: in puberty, there is a splitting between the incorporating ego and the identifying ego. For Palazzoli, the central pathogenic mechanism is concretization; the body is invested with primitive, negative identifications and becomes symbolically equated with discontent with the self.

Palazzoli's theoretical position is generally in agreement with

Klein's and Fairbairn's views (1941). Repression of the bad object is central to her theory. "The real mental anorectic, therefore, makes use of a formidable repressive mechanism that leads to a splitting of the ego." Splitting gives rise to "coenaesthetic diffidence" which, she feels, is akin to Bruch's concepts of conceptual and perceptual disturbances in anorexia nervosa. She also subscribes to a similar theory of the mother's unwillingness to allow her child to recognize her own signals and needs. Body-image disturbances, for the anorectic, are explained on the basis of two factors; namely, equation of the body with the bad object, and failure in recognition of body needs and signals. Likewise, she supports Bruch by subscribing to the position that the anorectic patient is burdened with a "special psychosis." Specifically, this psychosis is, for Palazzoli, "mid-way between the schizo-paranoid position and depression," whereas Bruch (1973b) views ego-disorganization along the lines of schizophrenic despair.

Because of her meager results with individual psychotherapy, Selvini Palazzoli (1974) has parted company with Bruch in the last few years by adopting a family therapy approach to anorexia nervosa. She has gone from a Kleinian approach to development to a family system approach, which is an offshoot of communication theory (1972), information theory, and family studies from the last several decades. Bruch (1973a,b), however, has continued to use individual treatment, as she sees family therapy, at best, as sometimes supplemental to the therapeutic relationship with the anorectic. Both Palazzoli (1974) and Salvadore Minuchin (1974) prefer a family therapy systemic approach to anorexia nervosa to the linear approach, which emphasizes life history and ignores the family system with its own checks and balances. Family therapists are not interested in explicating the past history of the anorectic or how she as an individual became ill; instead, through improvising various plays, strategems, and dramas, they try to shake the family system out of its maladaptive rut. This is sufficient, they believe, to give the anorectic separation and autonomy. Individual treatment is never needed, according to them.

Bruch's formulation of anorexia nervosa is well articulated (1973b). Over the last forty years, she has concentrated her research efforts on eating disorders. In recent years, she has turned to a study of conceptual and perceptual processes in patients with eating disorders and schizophrenic reactions. Her basic interest has been in the modes by which eating functions are transformed maladaptively in the service of nonnutritional needs. Thus, her focus has been altered from psycho-analytic libido theory to the neurophysiology and neuropsychology of entero-exteroceptive learning, the underpinnings of which, she believes, cannot be found in extant analytic theory. Instead, she has turned to neurophysiology and developmental psychology for her theory. She rejects, as do most analysts, the old notion of the utter helplessness of the infant: The infant is capable of emitting signals and cues to its caretaker, who may respond dutifully or negligently, inhibitively or permissively, appropriately or inappropriately. Infantile transactions are the precursors to later interpersonal relationships. The processes of emitted and elicited behavior, parts of respondent learning, and simulation and accommodation constitute the various levels of interaction between the environment and infant. Diffusion of body boundaries, faulty recognition and conceptualization of enteroceptive and affective experiences, and paralysis of volutional independence and self-effectiveness are the triadic dysfunctional ego processes central to anorexia nervosa.

In her synthetic, developmental theory, which starts with a Piagetian sequence of presymbolic conceptualization, Bruch has constructed a pathogenetic theory of "falsified learning experiences"—neuro-codifications of incorrect learning experiences attained at various levels of maturation. She has used Harlow's primate research data as evidence for her developmental learning theory. With this theoretical background and particular developmental viewpoint, she formulates a pathogenesis of anorexia nervosa, as well as schizophrenia and developmental obesity. Unless a child is taught by mother to recognize hunger as distinct from other internal needs and perceptions, the youngster is at a loss to respond specifically and appropriately to nutritional needs and internal signals. Bruch indicates that the perception of appetite and hunger is largely a matter of learning: from the infant dependent on its mother to the gourmet wedded to his or her *Larousse Gastronomique.*

Bruch maintains that there is a triune of disturbances in the anorexia nervosa syndrome; disturbances of body image, perception, and effectiveness. Pathognomonic of anorexia nervosa is the distortion of body image: denial of emaciation concomitant with a long-standing fear of ugliness and fatness, which is regarded by Bruch as tantamount to the delusional disturbance in body image and self-concept. Otherwise, reality testing is grossly intact until later in the illness, when, according to Bruch, disordered thinking and transient breaks in reality occur. Disturbances in perceptual and cognitive interpretation of body stimuli (both denial and nonrecognition) involve hunger and appetite, as well as fatigue, weakness, and cold. Laxatives, enemas, and self-induced vomiting, presumably for control of weight, express disturbances in awareness of integration and regulation. Absence of sexual feelings and responsiveness and inability to conceptualize emotional states, according to Bruch, can fall into the same categories of disturbances. The third disturbance, a sense of ineffectiveness, which is developmentally related to the other disturbances, may be shrouded by defiance and negativism.

It is Bruch's belief that these developmental disturbances and associated pathology are distinctive enough to warrant establishment of a specific, nosological entity, although she wants to avoid setting up many subgroups and, instead, employ concepts of deviant, adaptive patterns. She finds that her model of true anorexia nervosa closely resembles the model that has been described for schizophrenic development. Thus, anorexia nervosa, for Bruch, is a distinct form of schizophrenia. She believes the need for autonomy and effectiveness, maladaptively sought through control over the body, is a key diagnostic factor in true anorexia nervosa.

Never does Bruch restrict the diagnosis of anorexia nervosa to female patients. Other investigators, however, have excluded males by making amenorrhea the essential diagnostic criterion. Palazzoli does not believe that her male anorectics meet her diagnostic standards because of two atypical signs; namely, the desire for food and exhibitionistic behavior. Kay and Leigh (1954) do not exclude male patients; they attribute the low frequency in males to the importance of hysterical and phobic mechanisms which equate pregnancy with fat. In the study of four prepubescent, male anorectics, Falstein and his associates (1956) noted that male patients were inordinately tied to their mothers, with whom they identified and by whom they were overfed. Encouragement by the mother to diet, given to the latency son with a guilty exhortation to assume a more masculine role, pushes the boy into self-initiated starvation to which the mother responds by forcing him to eat. Struggle for mastery and control ensues between the mother and the son. Through starvation, the male anorectic attempts to kill the incorporated mother with whom he identified and reduce the fat which he associates with the female form.

In the last fifteen years, an explosion of both laboratory and clinical research in anorexia nervosa has recurred (Vigersky 1977). Sometimes the disorder is rediscovered, renamed; it can ruffle the mind. But Arthur Crisp and his colleagues at St. George's Hospital (1965–1980), London, have systematically studied anorexia nervosa, from its phenomenology, diagnosis, and treatment to its overall psychobiology. No apocalypses. On the basis of present evidence they question a functional hypothalamic disturbance in anorexia nervosa, related to anything other than biological and psychological immaturity. Epidemiological studies have finally been done, to some extent, as well as refined investigations of body perception, body image and dimensions. Approaches to treatment have multiplied, from chemotherapy to family therapy, with little inclination toward a multifaceted stance.

Never has there been so much lay, public interest in a psychological disturbance. A large popular literature has appeared in the last ten years.[1] Newspaper, magazine, radio and TV coverage of anorexia nervosa is unprecedented, usually macroviews and metaviews of the illness. Much of it is a warning to young women against the dangers of self-starvation and gorging-purging (a glimpse of the terrors) but, often enough, an affirmation of our cultural attitude that "thin is beautiful" and, for every woman, a touch of anorexia is advised. And feminists, riding full tilt, have helped make anorexia nervosa daily news by pointing to the disorder—most prominently the gorger-purgers ("bulimarexia," so named by Boskind-Lodahl [1976])—as examples of what happens to young women fearful of male rejection, as they face femininity and wifehood.

Instead, murmuring that "it was better when we were together in one body" (1971), Louise Glück, in her paleontological unconsciousness, in one stanza of her poem, "Dedication to Hunger," astonishes; she says so much (1979);

1. Susana Duncan's article, "When Dieting Goes Berserk," published in *The New York Magazine,* January 29, 1973, p. 44, covers many aspects of the anorexia nervosa syndrome. Likewise, *Newsweek Magazine,* September 9, 1974, p. 56, ran an article under "Medicine" entitled, "The Starvation Disease." On November 10, 1974, *The Sunday New York Times Magazine,* p. 63, published an article by Sam Blum on "Children Who Starve Themselves." On July 28, 1975, *Time Magazine,* p. 50, published "The Self-Starvers" in the "Behavior Section." In *Vogue,* November 1976, p. 236, Nonie Carol Murphy published "Portrait of an Anorexic" and "The Starving Disease." Arthur J. Snider (*The New York Post,* April 28, 1976, p. 24) wrote an article entitled, "Anorexia: A Deathly Fear of Gaining Weight." Barbara Coffey published "Are You Obsessed with Being Thin?" in *Glamour,* March 1977, p. 110. And in *Psychology Today* (March 1977, p. 50), Marlene Boskind-Lodahl and Joyce Sirlin described "The Gorging-Purging Syndrome." There are many more.

It begins quietly
in certain female children;
the fear of death, taking as its form
dedication to hunger,
because a woman's body
is a grave; it will accept
anything. I remember
lying in bed at night
touching the soft, aggressive breasts,
touching, at fifteen,
the interfering flesh
that I would sacrifice
until the limbs were free
of blossom and subterfuge: I felt
what I feel now, aligning these words—
it is the same need to perfect,
of which death is the mere by-product . . .

For many women, perfection is timeless, permanent, always twisting itself in pain.

4

The Anorexia
Nervosa Syndrome

Accuracy of observation is the equivalent of accuracy of thinking.

—Wallace Stevens, *Adagia*

Definition of Anorexia Nervosa

The names for the disorders of self-starvation, gorging, and vomiting—often terms which are the same but just multiplied, others which remind one of nothing but themselves—began with "nervous consumption"; but later, when it was apparent that tuberculosis had no relationship to the illness, the name was changed to "anorexia nervosa," soon to be followed by an exfoliation of other names, many of them ambiguous. They have settled into the literature like snow. The disorder is now called "the hunger disease," "the diet disease," "the affluent neurosis," "the feeding disorder of thin-fat people," "nervous malnutrition," "essential dieting," "pubertal starvation—amenorrhea," "Kylin's syndrome," "late pubertal cachexia," "adolescent weight-phobia," "dysorexia," "bulimarexia," the "baffling disorder," and the "gorging-purging syndrome." In Germany, it has been referred to as "compulsive pubertal emaciation" (Pubertätsmagersucht). In France and Italy, it is known as "anorexia mentale." Some clinicians have suggested that the term *anorexia* be dropped since it is not accurate; it is a misnomer, for there is no lack of hunger and desire for food—only the denial of hunger and appetite. Anorexia nervosa, however, remains well entrenched in the psychological literature; it seems best to retain it as a syndromic word, an umbrella term that includes a spectrum of eating disturbances.

In the *Diagnostic and Statistical Manual II* of the American Psychiatric Association (1968), anorexia nervosa is listed as a "feeding disturbance," whereas in the first manual it was categorized as a psychophysiological disturbance. And in the third manual (DSM III), published in 1977, anorexia nervosa is placed under "disorders usually arising in childhood and adolescence" in the company of bulimia, pica, ruminations, and other nonspecific eating disorders. Bulimia is descriptively separated from anorexia nervosa because of the lack of appreciable weight loss and denial in the former disturbance. The Group for the Advancement for Psychiatry (GAP) lists anorexia nervosa under Symptom List I: disturbances related to body function, (a) eating (1966).

Not all clinical investigators agree that a definition of anorexia nervosa is possible (Bliss and Branch 1960, Vigersky 1977, A. King 1963, Bruch 1965b). The one given by Dunton and Langford (1962), a definition descriptive of the self-starving anorectic, stresses the peculiar relationship of the anorectic to the environment: "Anorexia nervosa is a psychological disorder characterized by voluntary, self-initiated dieting which gradually exceeds the limit of conscious control and leads to marked weight loss, overactivity and a fear of eating. In addition, there is a compulsive preoccupation with food, weight and dieting, which is expressed in the never-ending coercive and manipulative struggle with the environment over eating." Although clinicians argue whether anorexia nervosa is prepsychotic, psychotic, or schizophrenic, they agree it is a disorder but argue whether it has definable boundaries (Kay and Leigh 1954, Eissler 1943, Crisp 1968, 1970b, 1970c).

In England, on the continent, and in the United States, countless attempts have been made to define anorexia nervosa as a specific nosological entity (Theander 1970, Gatti and Robutti 1970, Meyer 1971, Warren 1968, Galdston 1974). The disorder has been called hysteria, obsessional neurosis, a *forme fruste* of manic-depressive or schizophrenic psychosis, a special form of psychosis, halfway between depression and schizophrenia, or an obscure organic disease of appetite regulation (Sours 1969). Clinical evidence now strongly suggests that anorexia nervosa should be considered a developmental syndrome or a symptom-complex with its components—X_1, X_2, X_3, . . . X_n—not related to a specific reciprocal cause, Y, but, instead, to a behavioral-dynamic pattern of multiple, complex, and interacting factors (see also chapter 5). Anorexia nervosa can also be thought of as a maladaptive attempt, expressed within a range of nosological and classificatory clusters, for resolving developmental issues through symptomatic and characterological changes.

Anorexia nervosa, it is clear, is a developmental and psychosomatic syndrome (Nemiah 1972), which is associated with certain psychopathologies and characterological styles. The range of the eating disturbance extends from total food avoidance, on the one hand, to gorging, vomiting and purging, on the other. For the more typical case of self-starvation, as well as mixed cases of food refusal and periodic gorging and vomiting, there is a consensus about the constellation of signs and symptoms which one can expect to encounter. For instance, a relentless, self-imposed and enforced diet usually starts with avoidance of carbohydrates. The young, self-starving anorectic is obsessively preoccupied with her quest for thinness, which she may continue doggedly to the point of cachexia and even death. Her lack of initiative and autonomy is hidden in obstinacy and negativism. The constellation is usually found in female, pubertal, or late adolescent patients who inevitably become amenorrheic, either before or during starvation; sometimes they continue to be amenorrheic even after restoration of their normal body weight. Anorectic girls involve themselves in strenuous physical activity, usually antedating the dieting behavior. The exercise is solitary for the purpose of burning calories, warming up the body, denying fatigue, frustration, and anxiety, and demonstrating endurance. Jogging is increased in distance and speed; calisthenics are doubled and tripled. Anorectics show peculiarities in their self-perception; because of denial, often they do not seem to be aware of their cachexia. In addition, they reveal disturbances in autonomy and aggression. Their usual cultural background is middle- to upper-class. Matriarchal authoritarianism usually dominates the family, moreso for the self-starver than the regular gorger-purger. The anorectic family system, maladaptive and poorly coping, does not function well, as Mluachin (1978) points out, because of its extreme enmeshment, overprotection, conflict avoidance, rigidity, and other mechanisms and strategems for detouring conflict. But the anorectic family system and pathology are not pathognomonic for the disorder—only for psychosomatic families.

Since Morton's case report (1694) of a sixteen-year-old son of a minister, it has been recognized that anorexia nervosa occurs in males. This male anorectic, a dieter as well as a gorger and vomiter, is a reminder that anorexia nervosa also occurs in males—a fact repeatedly forgotten and rediscovered.

§A nineteen-year-old New England college student was referred for evaluation because of dieting, gorging and vomiting. Thin as a boy, with short, cropped hair and squinting eyes, David had begun this eating pattern about a year before and had lost fifty pounds. He felt that his present weight of 120 pounds was appropriate for his frame, and he sought help only because his eating frenzies interfered with his study habits and his sense of well-being. David was matriculating at a very competitive college, was a physics major, and hoped to pursue a career in astrophysics. He readily acknowledged that he regarded himself as an anxious, frightened person who avoided any kind of aggressive competitiveness, most notably, the wooing of women—whom he could not take his eyes off, especially their crotches. If caught gazing, he would gnaw at his lip, embarrassed, but go on imagining the woman's vagina anyway. In going to bed at night, he feared being drawn into his sexual fantasies and suddenly finding himself with a hypnocampal erection.

He saw his world as a very threatening and frightening place where combat between men occurs daily. He compulsively popped his knuckles and, much to his surprise, would find his fists clenched like weapons. Was he snakelike or sharklike? he would wonder. He would fancy himself as one of Vermont's Green Mountain Boys, while smiling sweetly, rehearsing murder in his mind. Aware of his aggressiveness, he found it necessary to withdraw from social contacts with his peers and to direct his aggressive energies to his studies. But his main regret was that his effort could not be sustained. He knew he was often idle; he hated himself for any trace of passivity and feared he might lose his will to live. In many respects, he knew that he was a man of unstoppable extremes, capable of sustained physical and mental exertion in his work and, at the same time, given to idleness and apathy, sinking toward nothingness like a stone. He saw his masculinity as "moth-eaten and despicable" and doubted that in any company, whether among women or men, he would be respected as a man. He felt like a fat lizard hiding behind a rock. He found the human body—his own as well as others—disgusting. He could not bear to see people hurt. Yet he was part of a world given to unthinkable cruelty and misery. On the other hand, the idea of kindness and physical intimacy was repulsive. Just thinking of his mother—her endless cooking, offerings of cakes and pies—made him go limp, feel overcome by an unnatural contentment. He favored abstract interests. Tense and restless, he would drive for hours along isolated country roads where he could think about his work: new frontiers in theoretical physics, alchemistical achievements, exhilarating at first, his joy but also his curse, a destiny he could never reach. Upset, David would gorge on junk food and vomit; then, he would not be able to study for a day or two; ashamed, he would stay secluded in his room.

The developmental disturbance in males is often misdiagnosed because physicians still do not expect the disorder to appear in this gender (Beumont 1970, Bruch 1971a, Hogan et al. 1974, Davidson 1976). As in female anorectics, pursuit of thinness is the strong force behind the developmental disturbance. Male anorectics, however, differ in some respects from their female counterparts. Usually their disturbance begins in prepuberty; dauntless dieters, they are fearful of fatness, femininity, and sexuality. A later onset, usually with gorging and vomiting, is toward the end of secondary school, prior to college. They plunge into rigid starvation, usually with bulimia and vomiting, are extremely hyperactive and often rapidly lose weight. In general, however, male anorectics are clinically similar to female patients. For the sake of simplicity, discussion of anorexia nervosa, unless otherwise indicated, is in terms of the female anorectic.

Primary Signs and Symptoms

Apt to change over its duration, the signs and symptoms of the anorexia nervosa syndrome, for the typical, primary self-starving anorectic, are characterized by a deliberate and increasingly adamant refusal of food, and elective restriction of eating with a desperate pursuit of thinness as the ultimate pleasure in itself. There is a frantic effort to lose weight and establish control over the body and its functions (an attempt to blame the body for any discomfort and to try to solve all emotional problems by changing the body, if not give it up, through starvation) as well as food avoidance and preoccupation with eating and the culinary environment. The anorectic's fierce ambition to succeed in self-starvation quickly leads to an escalation of the starvation state with physical and mental consequences. On the other hand, the gorging-vomiting anorectic, also determined to fix her weight at a self-prescribed level, from fashionably thin to ghastly wasted away, prevents, through vomiting and purging, absorption of ingested food. And other anorectics vacillate between self-starvation and gorging-vomiting, from the beginning of the illness or after some months of dieting.

Amenorrhea is a common finding. For women who had regular menstruation prior to the disorder, a three-month duration of amenorrhea supports the diagnosis; six months for those anorectics who have had irregular periods. Anorectics may not menstruate because they are prepubertal or because puberty has been delayed by self-starvation; or their menstrual periods stop before they begin dieting—the usual situation—or after they are well into the diet and their weight has begun to melt away. Loss of weight is not the cause *per se* of amenorrhea in the anorectic; for every woman there is a critical weight for menstruation, just as there is a critical weight for menarche. The weight loss of anorectic emaciation, however, interferes further in menstrual dysfunction (Russell 1972a,b, Holmberg and Nylander 1971).

Most patients manifest neuromuscular hyperactivity and a prodigious energy output. Hyperactivity usually appears early in the illness, but it often goes unnoticed since it is hidden in calisthenics and gymnastics. Once starvation sets in, overactivity and restlessness increase as a secondary feature of inanition, but eventually, with weight falling to 50 percent below the premorbid weight, the patient fatigues and relaxes her exercise regimen, increasing her anxiety, frustration, concern, and ever-present chilliness except during summer. Like amenorrhea, hyperactivity may be an early symptom in 25 to 50 percent, months to a year or so before the diet is begun, and it may persist after the anorectic returns to eating and regains her weight.

The body is seen as a thing to be controlled and not indulged. It is a despicable threat and not an object of pleasure or beauty. Yet, disordered functions of the body, like amenorrhea, are of little concern to the anorectic. The anorectic appears to be insensitive to pain and fatigue; she acts like a fakir who is able to ignore pain through supreme mind-control. Although the anorectic complains about being chilly indoors and may overdress for room temperature, it is not unusual for her to underdress for cold, snowy days. She delights in the attention this brings her.

She claims to have no hunger and appetite; yet she continues to be hungry, using any number of ways to deny the fact. Appetite may increase, heightening her preoccupation with food and, to some degree, indirect gratification. The anorectic may complain of abdominal discomfort, difficulty in swallowing, and constipation (taking large doses of laxatives in hope of ridding herself of food). Less frequently, she may complain of diarrhea, caused by excessive use of cathartics, hunger, eating too much on an empty stomach, or overly rich food after starving; or of severe constipation (sometimes long-standing encopresis), caused by frequent, strong laxatives and resulting in retention-overflow of feces. Weight loss may be slowly progressive, steady, increase stepwise, or alarmingly precipitous.

The typical, primary anorexia nervosa syndrome with remorseless self-starvation is illustrated by this adolescent girl.

§An attractive, sugary, physically mature fourteen-year-old girl, Kathy "decided one day," while in a swimming class, that she looked pale and lumpy, like unbaked dough. She resolved to limit her carbohydrate intake and restrict her eating entirely to organic, protein health foods. She engaged, determined, obdurate, the gears of her will. After the first week on this diet, she felt that she was still eating too much and further restricted her diet to under 600 calories a day. Concurrently she exercised more, seeking new feats of endurance in gymnastics and becoming much more daring on the trapeze and rings. Kathy then started to jog, first contented with a daily run of a mile and a half; but within a month, she had increased her jogging to three miles a day. She felt ecstatic during her jogging, as she watched the ground pass under her feet. In the mornings, her parents noticed that she was doing her ballet exercises, something her mother had unsuccessfully attempted a few years before.

When her parents first commented on her diet, her initial response was that she was trying to eliminate all junk foods from her diet. Kathy later, when pressed by her parents, claimed, ruminating, that her appetite had diminished because of her increased academic load. She now studied until 2:00 a.m. every morning. Her parents voiced concern about her late studying and her 5:30 a.m. risings to do her daily exercises and running in the park. Kathy's only reply was a malevolent leer, a lowered head and pursed lips.

It became apparent to everybody she knew that she was pursuing thinness as a pleasure in itself and that this pleasure far exceeded any pleasure she got from eating. She no longer dressed like a teenage model in *Seventeen.* Oddly preoccupied with catching glimpses of herself in the mirror, she even, in a tidy way, let her appearance go, allowing her long, golden hair to look like seaweed and be a torment to her immaculate mother. Her pleasure from exercising and seeing fat disappear was apparent even to her. She found that being able to control her body, especially her hunger, particularly her appetite for ice cream and cashew nuts, made her feel superior to everybody. Kathy believed that she was part of a new elite with unspeakable power. Her friends at school teased her because of the way she picked at the school lunches. They were annoyed with her because she would entice them into ice cream stores and recount to them with great pleasure the addition and substitutions made to the stores' many flavors. Then, she would order ice sherbet, and after several bites she would either discard it, or, more frequently, feed it to a passing dog, preferably a poodle. In fact, her craze in feeding others overwhelmed her family. She took back issues of *Gourmet* out of the family library and, much to the cook's annoyance, chose complicated and exotic menus. She spent weekends shopping in gourmet stores for unusual foods, preferably as light as puffballs. Her older brothers, although athletic boys with enormous appetites, were piqued with her because she insisted that they eat at least double portions. At dinner Kathy encouraged the maid to serve second and third portions to the family, hovering between outrage and escape, while she herself stubbornly refused to eat even half of her serving.

Her hyperactivity and extraordinary energy were soon noted by her teachers, who thought that she had now realized the importance of education and achievement. Although just beginning ninth grade, she attempted to raise her grades to A-pluses with a view of going to Stanford University, from which her mother had graduated. Before she had started her dieting, her menstrual periods had ceased. Since menarche at age eleven, she had had regular periods.

When Kathy was invited to Philadelphia by another young girl, she was quite upset on discovering that her control suddenly failed her. Friends of her family had taken them to a harborside restaurant where she had consumed two appetizers and several entrees along with a half-dozen popovers, three salads, and a variety of vegetables. After this gourmandizing, she decided to restrict her food intake even more.

In a few months, Kathy showed some of the secondary signs and symptoms of the primary, typical anorexia nervosa syndrome. Manipulation of her environment around food increased to the point that the mother, frustrated and defeated, had outbursts of murderous fantasies against her. She told Kathy to stop talking to the cook, feeding the family and shopping in the local gourmet stores. When she was finally hospitalized because of a starvation weight, at less than 50 percent of her normal weight, the staff recognized they would have to control her manipulative behavior on the ward. The very first day she attempted to feed all the children. Foiled, she put her fists on her hips, glanced at the staff, grinned, eyes narrowed: sheer will power. She was increasingly distrustful of the nurses and doctors; she knew that the world was conspiring to feed her and to make her fat. Although her weight had dropped to 60 pounds by the second month of her illness, she remained convinced that her "legs were heavy" and that within a few years she would have voluptuous breasts. At times she appeared sad to her family and the hospital staff; yet she never acted weighed-down in spirits. In fact, Kathy was often cheerful, obviously pleased that she was not gaining weight. She denied her cadaverous look for four months until she finally could trust her therapist.

Another starving, anorectic young girl exemplifies a more infantile tie to her mother, both ignorant of their will to hurt each other. She had not progressed to a pubescent level of sexual development.

§Stephanie, a thirteen-year-old girl, thoughtful-looking behind her steel-rimmed glasses, was in the tenth grade at her regional New Jersey high school when in January, two weeks after her parents went off on vacation with their younger children, she developed "flu" and stopped eating. The grandparents, with whom she was staying, could do nothing to comfort her. The parents, therefore, prematurely ended their vacation, and the mother, a fleshy, baggy-lidded eyed woman, attempted to "nurse her back to health." She prepared special foods and "squeezed dozens of oranges for her," but Stephanie refused to eat anything. She quickly lost ten pounds; and, even though she was still refusing to eat, the pediatrician felt that she was ready to go back to school: she would be "her old self" once she got back with her friends.

This was not the case. She continued to be a "poor eater," and her parents persisted in preparing special dishes for her. At school, Stephanie was in a play in which she had a leading role. Her younger sister, Debbie, then decided she wanted to join the play; Stephanie worried that Debbie might "steal her glory from her," and she finally told her parents that she did not want her sister to be in the play; they were annoyed and accused Stephanie of being egotistical and self-centered. They told her to change "her bad feelings toward her sister."

Stephanie continued to function fairly well in school and in extracurricular activities. Her behavior at home, however, was much more difficult to cope with. She ate very little and insisted, as firm as steel, that her mother be with her at all times; she had "temper tantrums over nothing." In April, she performed in a play; everybody was amazed that this withdrawn, emaciated girl was, on stage, "sexy, humorous and charming." She received a community award for her performance. When the play closed, Stephanie, however, "collapsed," was dejected, withdrawn, and even more determined to continue her weight loss.

A complete medical evaluation by her pediatrician was "entirely negative." Stephanie was referred to a local psychiatrist, whom she refused to see. She was then hospitalized in a local community hospital, where she weighed 93 pounds at the time of admission. Her behavior in the hospital was regressive: temper tantrums, baby talk, thumb in her mouth (particularly when her mother visited), and attempts to take over feeding all the children on the ward. Her mother brought special meals to Stephanie three times a day. Finally, mother's visits were restricted by the staff, and Stephanie gained weight to the point that she weighed 107 pounds and was discharged from the hospital. She talked and double-talked, convincing her therapist that she "was cured."

Arrangements were made for office psychotherapy, but after a few sessions she refused to return to the therapist. She was hunched over, depressed, and anxious, constantly seeking her mother's company and increasingly preoccupied with recipes, food preparation and feeding the entire family, including the two dogs. She was demanding, childish, and had "bad tempers" whenever around her family. Her mother responded by screaming and throwing things at the wall; but, on most occasions, the mother met all the demands made by Stephanie.

In September, she returned to school but was not interested in anything. She began to lose more weight, "was terribly depressed," and often wept. At times she would yell and scream at her family without apparent reason. Her psychiatrist then insisted that she be hospitalized, and she was admitted to a university hospital for treatment.

The mother was dismayed by her daughter's illness because Stephanie had always been a "perfect child," a voracious reader, lover of art, and had gotten the best from her "protective family atmosphere." She could recite on cue memorable prose and poetry; she had a keen insight into human nature. The father generally agreed with the mother; but, occasionally, he made fun of the mother in front of Stephanie by referring to her as "Portnoy's mother."

Stephanie was described by everybody as a "very good girl." The mother said: "She always as a child wanted to be with us all the time." Her mother recalled her own childhood, much in the same way, emphasizing that she was unable to cross the street until she was eleven years old because of her protective mother. Stephanie's early development was a blank to the mother, except that she was certain—crisply vague—that "everything had been just perfect." The father worked at two jobs in order to maintain a style of living which his father-in-law would think appropriate for his daughter.

When Stephanie first went to nursery school, she was frightened; and only after three weeks could she permit her mother to leave. When an attempt was made to send the girl to sleepaway camp, the parents worried that her homesickness would be "too severe." Her mother had prepared her for menarche but admitted quite openly that she felt sorry to see her daughter "now a young lady." She remarked that Stephanie had objected to puberty, fearing that "she would look like her fat grandmother." The mother was proud that her daughter devoted herself to her studies and was not "boy-crazy and never would be."

On hospitalization, Stephanie, restless eyes roving, frightened, was uncooperative the first two days. She had violent temper tantrums, objected to leaving her room; and, unwilling to talk, she refused to participate in ward activities. Her constant grin was insufferable to the staff. Several times she had to be placed in the "quiet room." She complained of constipation day and night, bent over at the waist with abdominal cramps, often flatulent. She refused to eat and squeezed-shut her eyes. In her therapy sessions, when not clenching her fists, she expressed fears of losing her mother and complained of the depression, which she had experienced during the parents' vacation.

Early in treatment, Stephanie began to cling to the therapist. With an eyebrow cocked, she asked questions about the future and sought reassurance. Soon she smiled wickedly, like a witch, at the staff. After a month, she suddenly handed her therapist a "sign-out letter," indicating that she was homesick, fed up with the "mumbo-jumbo," and wanted to go home immediately. She shook her head, screamed, yelled, and banged on the walls of her room to be taken home. Hot anger flushed her face. Her parents, however, responded negatively to her letter, saying at their next visit that she would have to stay in the hospital until "everybody decided it was time for her to return home." Stephanie became childish, always acting and talking like a taunting three-year-old. She asked her mother when she was going to be with her and be allowed to be "a baby once again." She wavered between self-pity and righteous indignation, lips compressed, furious, thinking about revenge, intent on defending the indefensible. Finally, Stephanie retracted her "sign-out letter" and went back into her infantile behavior, eyes swimming in tears, whining during sessions and, on occasions, even speaking baby talk and crossing her eyes.

After the therapist's vacation, several months later, the patient produced a second "sign-out letter," screaming and yelling that she wanted to see her parents immediately and, if necessary, her lawyer. A few days later, however, she retracted the letter. Her weight had dropped ten pounds in four days. She soon became aware that her "sign-out letters" were related to her anger at her therapist for having gone on vacation and abandoning her. For the first time, she could see the connection between her behavior and her feelings of being rejected; she recalled past examples of similar behavior in which, instead of expressing her anger, she had refused to eat, cried and had temper tantrums. "I would do anything, but express what I have inside. I figured if people knew what you're feeling, they could work you over. Now I know: I made mountains out of molehills."

Stephanie continued her hospital treatment for several more months and was then discharged to a local therapist to continue psychotherapy.

A distortion in body image, body concept, and body attitude is frequently found in all types of anorectics, from the self-starvers to the gorger-vomiters.[1] It is most marked in those primary anorectics—young adolescent self-starvers with massive denial and control—the group which Bruch has made the object of her research. Donning kaftans and flowing dresses, they hide their "fat and shapeless" bodies. Before their bedroom mirrors, they gaze at themselves by the hour; but,

1. Overestimation of body size in anorexia nervosa (Buvat and Buvat-Herbaut 1978, Garfinkle et al. 1978, Garner et al. 1976, Pierloot and Houben 1978, Slade and Russell 1970), although not unique to the syndrome, is associated with several aspects of the eating disorder: greater denial of illness, less weight gain during treatment, and other pretreatment indicators of poor outcome (Caspar et al. 1979). Button, Fransella, and Slade (1977) indicate that body perception disturbances are not specific to anorexia nervosa and, instead, reflect an exaggerated sensitivity about body size, change in weight, anxiety over weight, and preoccupation with slimness.

as the satisfaction and pleasure of weight loss wane with the eventual skin-and-bone reality of their bodies, revulsion at their ugliness may set in. If not, if the distortion of body image persists, then the likelihood of a chronic course is increased. The distortion can range from an uncomfortable feeling or fantasy about the body, to a bizarre psychotic view of the body. The distortion may manifest itself simply as over-estimation of body size and diminish as the anorectic regains weight. The body-image alteration may be commensurate to expectable adolescent discomfort, a result of denial of weight loss, or an expression of disordered body perceptions, such as found in severe borderline and psychotic patients. Whatever its nature and intensity, the distortion is only one of a number of signs and symptoms and should not be viewed as pathognomonic of anorexia nervosa—or any nosological category, for that matter. There is no diagnostic specificity to distortions in body image. Adolescent girls are prone to distortions of body and self-perceptions; their changing body contour throughout adolescence makes their body image unstable. Loss of weight, in itself, upsets the body image. Furthermore, pregnant women manifest a variety of such distortions (Slade 1977a). And it should not be ignored that there are many people—dancers, runners, weightlifters, models, jockeys, figure skaters, "body-beautiful" culturists, etc.—who harbor distorted views and feelings about their body.

In several ways, the anorectic differs from the thousands of teenage girls who are obsessed with dieting and food fads. The most striking difference between the two groups is that the diet-conscious teenager abhors the idea of dieting, takes no great pleasure in it, and derives little sense of superiority from the fact that she can lose weight. Furthermore, the willpower of the ordinary dieting teenage girl is a shadow of the anorectic will—the apotheosis of "the will to supremacy."

Once the anorexia becomes apparent to her parents, the young girl complains that she has lost her appetite; she loathes food in any form. She may complain of stomachaches and bloated feelings, indigestion, nausea, but her hypochondriasis is limited to eating and the gastrointestinal tract. Just watching another person eat can make the anorectic feel full, as though she has consumed a phantom meal. She may also complain of being constipated and try to obtain laxatives to rid herself of the last meal. Beneath the aversion to food, however, is a profound fascination with it, a preoccupation with culinary things: recipes, gourmet shops, cook books, and menus in restaurant windows. She will talk to her peers and adults for hours about the latest restaurants and their reviews by food critics.

At the time of referral, the anorectic complains of having lost her appetite, feeling bloated, and distressed by stomachaches, indigestion, and nausea. She talks about liking only a few foods, often exotic and complicated dishes, which she has read about in gourmet magazines and books. Usually she will not eat regular meals; and, if she condescends to have dinner with the family, she may simply pick at her food and act unpleasant. Primary anorectics—those who after a period of self-starvation break down in their self-control—will eat nothing at family meals, or, later in their illness, overeat with seeming pleasure, and then get up after everybody has gone to bed to forage in the kitchen and later vomit in the early hours of the morning.

The anorectic likes to discuss with the family—or anybody else, for that matter—what she has eaten, or not eaten, that day. Eating, for the anorectic, has a mystique, and she makes a metaphysic out of the cliché: you are what you eat. If she eats with the family, she may insist on standing up at her place at the table, or picking her plate up and walking around the dining room while she stabs at her food. Watching other people eat will put the anorectic off all food, for she may feel that she is uncertain whether she is eating for herself or for the other person. Wandering through the dining room and eating tidbits from her plate, as well as others, may be done to placate and tease her parents. At the same time, she exercises to burn off calories from her dinner. The anorectic can secrete food in her napkin and then nibble at it in her room in the early morning hours when she is less capable of denying her hunger. On the other hand, she may pretend to eat, let the food fall into her lap and then, with muted glee, feed her dog. Although she may want to eat absolutely nothing, the anorectic nevertheless wants to feel that she has free access to food and that it is always available in case she wants it.

Starving anorectics are extremely fussy about what they eat, even though it may be a miniscule amount; they abhor fatty and farinaceous foods. Sometimes the anorectic girl will ask a parent to go to a gourmet shop at midnight to buy a delicacy. When it is provided, she may be only mildly interested and simply nibble at it. The anorectic, on the other hand, may have a temper tantrum if food which she requests of her parent is not provided. Her fantasies about food are extensive and elaborate but are usually not disclosed in her everyday conversations.

Initially during treatment these fantasies, as well as others, are re-pressed and suppressed; only after layers of denial are broken through will she disclose them. Until then, she might act out the fantasies by cooking, taking over the kitchen from the mother, and trying to feed the family exotic, high-calorie foods in great quantity in the hopes of "fattening them up."

This anorectic college girl is a clinical example of how anorexia nervosa symptoms can be masked by a life-situation and deflecting complaints. Her family physician failed to make a diagnosis, partly because he believed true anorexia was essential for the diagnosis of anorexia nervosa.

§Mary Lou, a nineteen-year-old girl, frail-looking with large, strange eyes, steel-wool brown hair, a daughter of a very successful lawyer, was referred because of weight loss of forty pounds during the fall. After her graduation from high school, the parents noticed that Mary Lou was eating less, but they attributed her weight loss to "her swimming and running around with her friends." In September, Mary Lou went off to college in Boston. She discovered that many of her classmates went home each night; she came to view the school as a "commuter college." She found the students and faculty unfriendly, cold and distant and dreaded each night, as well as those weekends when she could not go home. Her life seemed reduced to nothing. One reason for choosing this college had been that her best friend was going there. The patient, always reluctant to leave home, latched onto this friend as a means of reducing her separation anxiety.

During the fall term, Mary Lou almost stopped eating because the school's food was "intolerable," but it was obvious that she had stopped eating in an angry protest against her parents, who had discouraged her from attending a local community college, which they felt "might be too soft for her." She returned home at Christmas, eyes red at the edges, and complained bitterly to her parents that she was depressed. They insisted that she return to school, but after three days she "packed her bag and took the earliest train home." For the next three months, Mary Lou lounged around the home, seldom going out, and refusing to see her old boyfriend from high school days. Her weight continued to fall, and she became more demanding of her father, tyrannizing him, insisting that he be with her as much as his schedule would permit. Yet when together with him, she spoke little, a reservoir of silence. In the evenings she demanded that he go out to delicatessens to buy various salads; he would spend hours, trying to find unusual salad combinations, returning home to observe that she would only whimper, pick at his selections, and later dump them into the garbage can. For no reason apparent to the parents, she would burst into tears, her pale hands trembling, wringing her fingers; and she would faint from exhaustion. Her parents finally realized that the dieting and starvation were not simply a matter of "homesickness." They agreed that she start treatment.

Gorging, Vomiting and Purging

The self-starving anorectic, fierce in her pursuit of thinness, unfleshliness, and uncorruptedness, may have disruptions in her denial of hunger and oral impulses. Losing self-control over eating, her eating style changes; binges may alternate with panicky efforts to reestablish dieting. Vomiting may be episodic or regular—binges may occur after every meal. She may fling herself into a bulimic frenzy, eat to the point of risking gastric rupture and then vomit, perhaps even purge with cathartics, for her redemption (Brusset and Jeammet 1971).

Because of the constellation of self-starvation and gorging-vomiting, these anorectics are more properly called mixed anorectics. Barbara Gordon, the protagonist of the novel (chapter 2), is a mixed anorectic, left to destroy herself.

The gorger-vomiter may be a former dieting anorectic who has lost control of her abstinence, now binges alternately with vain attempts to regain control, resulting eventually in weight gain—perhaps only to a normal weight or only a few pounds above it—which is fought off by vomiting and purging.

The anorectic who gorges and watches her weight by vomiting is another type of anorectic. Ironically, she may find periodic overeating and vomiting both enjoyable and continue this reinforcing behavior for years, frequently in clandestine circumstances. By vomiting, she may keep her weight at what she considers an ideal level, or her vomiting may become uncontrollably compulsive so that after each meal, even if she has not overeaten, she must vomit (Boskind-Lodahl 1976). In the latter case, weight loss may be considerable, to the point of cachexia and nutritional collapse.

Her feelings swollen like a stuffed stomach, an anorectic with dieting, gorging, vomiting—a teenage girl who held her silence like an empty vase—puts the focus of the clinical picture of anorexia nervosa into the foreground.

§Clarissa was a seventeen-year-old college freshman who one year ago joined a students' group for a summer vacation in the South of France. She returned home, having lost ten pounds, which was attributed by everybody in the family to the fact that Clarissa had bicycled a great deal during the summer. In the next six months, however, Clarissa lost twenty pounds more, for no apparent reason, although her father, an accountant, did wonder whether her eating habits during this freshman college year had deteriorated. It was later noticed that she had grown hard, a bit of a cowgirl in stance, was extremely hyperactive, ice skating every day, jogging three and a half miles daily, and studying until 2:00 a.m. On a weekend, home from college, Clarissa ate only rye crisps and honey, then vomited, behavior convincing her parents that consultation was now essential.

It soon became apparent, even to Clarissa, that her feelings had been mixed about leaving home to attend college. During the summer in France, she had felt some homesickness, perceived it even then as unnaturally strong, and had been upset because she had not been able to rendezvous with her older sister because of a breakdown in the travel plans. In addition, that September her older sister had announced her engagement with plans to marry in the spring. Clarissa, square-jawed, brooding, acknowledged bitter jealousy, memories that seemed like dreams, which she had been trying to choke off and keep "under wraps." Like the hunger always rousing her, her jealousy was aimed at her sister, not only because of the coming marriage but also because of the sister's long-standing special relationship with the mother. Their relationship had even increased since Clarissa's departure to college. Lips trembling, Clarissa wondered if, because of the resentment— images strongly rising up in her mind—she could even look at her sister; in fact, she doubted whether she would be able to go to the sister's wedding in the spring. She disclosed that her sister, also preoccupied with weight and perhaps also an anorectic, had warned her several years before that she would also have to watch her "carbohydrate eating" after she had matured as a woman.

Clarissa, usually a touch aloof, was quite open in acknowledging her dieting, gorging and vomiting, and even her weight loss. She was horrified and disgusted, going over and over it in great detail, peeking through weeping, almost closed eyes. She spoke freely of her jealousy of her sister, sometimes shaking her fists as though trying to work up a tantrum, and of the fact that she herself had longed to be a boy. She saw her mother as insecure and unsuccessful (this always filled her chest with pain); she viewed herself as superior to her mother as far as social life and affability were concerned. But her fantasies, the worst as well as the best, were all junk, mere foolishness. To think of them put her on the edge of another crying fit. Clarissa was also jealous of her three younger brothers, fleshy, sweaty kids who shared Father disproportionately to the sisters. She believed—giggling and blushing, her eyes wet—that her father, handsome as a king, did not encourage her to be athletic, for he had never invited her to play tennis, and seemed to avoid jogging with her. Her charms were unconvincing—or perhaps frightening to him because they were so convincing. Clarissa saw the father as a highly achieving, perfectionistic, successful boat designer, but also remote, aloof, and unable to fill the gap left by the mother. Her grief was frail and small.

During treatment, Clarissa realized that in her effort to please her parents she had forfeited her individuality and revealed her desire to be special to her mother. She found this wish humiliating and tried to counteract it by efforts to be a boy and, therefore, at least special in the eyes of the father. She feared that her identification with her mother would commit her to a lifelong pattern of humiliation, of not knowing when to stop eating. For Clarissa, gorging was tantamount to surrendering to her mother—an ineluctable existence. Because of the identification with the mother, she thought that she was disgusting. She pitched her voice higher up and said: "I hate my mother and because I hate my mother, I hate myself." She had turned her aggression upon herself. Her sexual feelings were in large part denied, and not until well into treatment was she able to consider dating young men.

The anorectic gorging and vomiting eating disturbance, with or without dieting and starvation in the past, is part of the anorexia nervosa syndrome. The following patient indicates some of the symptomatic and developmental differences of these patients.

§Jeannette, a sober-faced thirty-two-year-old married computer operator with shy, faded-looking eyes, was referred for consultation because of her therapist's alarm that she was vomiting between six and ten times a day after repeatedly gorging herself, to the extent that she was exhausting her savings and risking physical collapse. In consultation, the patient—limp, drained of feelings—immediately talked, in a quavering voice, about her bulimia and daily episodes of self-induced vomiting, which she attributed to her sensitivity to criticism and her persistently low self-esteem. An unsightly overbite had always plagued her, though she did nothing about it. She felt that her vomiting was uncontrollable, would get worse and eventually result in her self-destruction; not only was she running out of money but she feared that her work record would be jeopardized by exhaustion and absenteeism because of the emotional and physical strain from vomiting. In addition, she dreaded the prospect of the young man with whom she was living moving out; he was increasingly disgusted with her and wondered if he were "living with a maniac."

Jeannette said that in high school she had weighed almost 190 pounds, weight markedly in excess of her five-feet-two-inch frame. At the end of high school, she had decided to go to college on the West Coast in order to be free of her family and in "control of her destiny." Halfway through her freshman year, however, confusion and distress grew; she was more depressed, made a suicidal gesture, was unable to concentrate, and was preoccupied with her obesity and image of "fat, scowling Jeannette who is always hated." She failed all her subjects and felt ashamed of herself. Several weeks preceding the suicidal gesture, she had fantasies of being pregnant, which she preferred to her thoughts of being obese. On returning home, she worked as a clerk for a short time and took night courses at a community college. She was then in treatment with a lay therapist who gave her an increasing sense of self-confidence.

The following September she reentered college, now attending a small women's college in New England. After several months, she hated the school; nevertheless, even with thinking up justifications for leaving, she felt that she had to remain until the end of the year. During that time, she felt all alone in the universe. She returned home once again and matriculated in the local community college. Atempting to diet, she was unsuccessful; increasing anxiety interfered with her studies. On one occasion, after gorging herself all morning, she suddenly decided that she "would not allow food to get into her system." She went into the bathroom, vomited, and felt relieved. She experienced a sense of discovery and joy that she could eat anything that she wanted and never have to "pay the price of obesity." This discovery started her on a more regular diet and a cycle of gorging and vomiting. Within a few months she became alarmed that the cycle was controlling every aspect of her being; she was fearful that she might die because of her "discovery." Nevertheless, with increasing weight loss, she received congratulatory remarks and attention from young men. Although she had lost considerable weight, the image of herself as an obese woman continued.

At mid-year, she transferred to a university in the Northwest. There she was able to concentrate and attend to her studies, although she was aware of being withdrawn, felt threatened by her peers, and dated only on occasion—with considerable anxiety, always feeling that she was inadequate. It was there that she met Bourne, whom she viewed as antipodal to herself—fun-loving, outgoing, and committed—and she rejoiced in this relationship. She half-realized that other men now seemed less threatening to her. Bourne was an affirmation of her very "being and essence." In college, she and Bourne lived together and were eventually married shortly before her graduation. He enabled her to rouse herself from fear, rise to consciousness, struggle upwards from her darkened spirits. Her sexual relationship with him was orgastic and fulfilling, but they progressively spent less and less time together. Throughout the marriage, she would surreptitiously binge and vomit; he never did discover her eating disorder. She hid it even though they did a lot of partying. The marriage continued for four years with gradual, benign disengagement and eventually mutual agreement that they "no longer had much in common except good sex."

Jeannette returned home after her divorce. She began to date and was confident. Within a few months, another relationship rather quickly deteriorated, making her feel suddenly endangered, plunging her into frenzied gluttony and vomiting. She sought psychiatric consultation. She was found to have normal weight for her height and build. Spontaneous and rather anxious, she presented no evidence of any thought disorder and was judged by the consultant to be an obsessive-compulsive neurotic who gorged to satisfy "a feeling of being alone." He viewed her eating as a compulsion, an act of doing and undoing. He did not consider her anorectic since her weight was normal. He viewed the bulimia as multi-determined, "with food symbolically standing for her mother with a masochistic defense to her competition with women and fantasies of impregnation."

She started psychotherapy which continued for about a year. She found, however, that she was unable to relate to her male therapist and requested transfer to a woman therapist. For the first six months, Jeannette experienced most of her difficulty at night. Often she would act "manic," be up most of the night, unable to relax unless she was exhausted. During the evenings she would repeatedly gorge herself and vomit. She met a young man whom she found "fulfilling," moved in with him, but in subsequent weeks realized that her expectations were unrealistic and would have to be scaled down to his reality. She believed that this "new attitude" was the only way of viewing her lover; nevertheless, she felt disappointed that he offered no perfection, no hope of curing her damaged self-esteem and loathesome image.

In consultation, Jeannette plunged deep into conversation, blushing: Since the age of five, until age twenty, she had been markedly obese, especially during her high school years. Throughout her life her parents had been obsessed with her weight and tried in innumerable ways to control her eating. She recalled, smiling acidly, that when her brother was born she was three years old, obviously unhappy about the brother's intrusion, and experienced her mother as insouciant toward her. Now her mind raced almost as rapidly as her heart. She remembered that her mother often gave her cookies instead of attention, and was quite sharp with her if this placation were not successful. Later, the parents attempted to withdraw the cookies, as well as other carbohydrates. This led to a family game in which Jeannette would be deprived of cookies and cake; in the evening she would search for them, determined, usually finding them, and surreptitiously feasting before going to bed. This disclosure filled her with so much anxiety she could hardly catch her breath.

Her jaw stiffened and she described her mother as constantly depressed throughout her childhood. She talked incessantly, half with indignation, half with self-pity, saying that "life was not worth living." Her father, on the other hand, was an extremely successful executive who exuded self-confidence and initiative; he demanded the same of anybody in his life. He always criticized the patient for her lack of drive and self-reliance—or so she imagined all her life. Her brother, an asthmatic since childhood, moved from the family home several years ago and lived on the West Coast. He was a self-designated Marxist, who studiously attempted to stand for everything antithetical to the father's values.

In the course of the consultation, Jeannette was able to see a repeated pattern of either real or fantasized rejection by a man, leading to self-hatred and feelings of emptiness, attenuated somewhat by repeatedly gorging herself to the extent that she "would burst." The dread of permanently hurting herself, as well as the fear of growing fat, would then trigger vomiting. She would be unrelentingly enraged with herself, binge again, and continue the gorging-vomiting cycle through the night to the point that she was exhausted and "wrung-out." She was able to see that her view of herself was based on how she felt men regarded her. The only anodyne to her pain was "the perfect man" who would view her in the light of his own perfection, heal her "wounds," and fill her up with "joy and satisfaction." The patient was encouraged to continue her treatment, intensify its frequency as a means of experiencing the affective forces behind the bulimia-vomiting cycle, and finally reach the bedrock of her vast, primitive longings for her mother.

Gorging-vomiting is part of the anorexia nervosa syndrome, although some clinicians exclude it and think of it as atypical and secondary, or as a separate phenomenological and psychodynamic eating disorder. It is, however, more accurate to view the bulimic vomiter as part of the spectrum of anorexia nervosa (Beumont, George, and Smart 1976). On the left of the spectrum of the anorexia nervosa syndrome are the anorectics who diet, sometimes to profound cachexia, and do not lose control of their oral impulses. In the middle of the spectrum are the mixed anorectics, who are able to abstain from food and lose weight but periodically, especially in the overeating phase, lose control of their oral impulses. On the far right of the spectrum are the gorger-vomiters, who never seriously diet but, instead, regularly gorge and purge themselves in an effort to maintain an ideal weight.

The gorger stuffs herself to relieve emotional hurt and feelings of rejection. A rift in her life results when she feels rejected. She hears her hurts in quadraphonic. Her voice stirs within her, but her tongue shrivels, and she thinks her words, if utterable, will fall to the floor. Then, wishing she could turn to her mother, she can only hear the dogs barking at her. She wishes her father were in the next room, waiting for her; and she can see herself frantic, her head spinning with dizziness, her phallic fists pounding blindly at his door.

This vignette of a mid-adolescent girl demonstrates some facets of the bulimic vomiter, an increasing group of anorexia nervosa patients. Unlike the anorectic self-starver, she was not able to control her oral and recuperate for the rest of the spring; later he resumed his studies in impulses (Beumont 1977).

§A sixteen-year-old girl, with a face like a mask—she looked about ten—an eleventh grader at a local high school, Joanne lost weight after her brother's illness. Earlier that year, Paul had gone off to college and promised his parents that he would be "the success of the family." He had academic difficulties, however, and was observed by relatives, with whom he lived in a southern college town, to be thin, pale, overactive, and distractable. He was evaluated by a college physician, who diagnosed ulcerative colitis. The brother returned home to get treatment and recuperate for the rest of the spring; later he resumed his studies in a local college.

It was at this time that Joanne first started to binge and vomit. Five feet four inches tall, she lost weight, from 125 to 95 pounds, became insomniac, wickedly irritable and extremely critical of her mother. It was Joanne's gynecologist who made the diagnosis of anorexia nervosa. In consultation, Joanne stated that she "hated school, hard work, ambition, and her father's attitude of no fun." Speaking of these things seemed to make her stomach jerk in as though she would vomit the statement. Compulsively ambitious and monomaniacal about rising above his immigrant background, her father worked eighteen hours a day in his small business and insisted his children work for at least Ph.D.'s. It was soon obvious to Joanne that she was extremely resentful of the attention her parents gave the brother, not simply during the time of his illness but over the years, because of his academic promise. It was a cross she could scarcely bear. She was especially angry with the mother who, she felt, was "selfishly overprotective" but at the same time not sufficiently caring, sympathetic or understanding of her needs.

Onset often in late adolescence, or in the early twenties, with an earlier background of obesity, bulimic vomiters—those who do not ordinarily diet—eat regular, nutritious meals; but, like obese people, they turn compulsively to food. Yet they continue to work satisfactorily in school and on jobs, keenly feeling their burdens and responsibilities, and usually maintain a modicum of social life. Not infrequently, they have had sexual experiences, perhaps lived with a man or even married.

They may have used drugs. They look for personal growth and expansion in life. But lonely, depressed, they labor against a low self-esteem, plead for compliments and flattery, and long for love and devotion from a man, whom they want to please, while at the same time dreading passivity and surrender. A vast fear burns in them. Shame-faced by their eating and purging—not to mention stealing food like a rat in a grainery—they fantasize fitting into a glass slipper (or a variant of this grandiose fantasy)—a presentation by a prince, a derivative of her hero-father, whose main fault is that he failed to shield his daughter, with all her competitiveness, against a hostile, depressed mother. They run from the hollowness of their mother's life. Not as locked into their family, like the dieting or mixed anorectic, they move back and forth, from control to chaos, eating normally for a while and then, because of rejection and disappointment, plunging into gourmandizing, with shame and anxiety, then ridding themselves of food by vomiting and purging. Events like rejection by a man, defeat in a competition with a woman, or a work failure trigger binges, which, for the moment, not only relieve tension but also built up excitement—sometimes even to the point of alimentary orgasm—which then leads to redemptive vomiting, secrets they must live with in great fear. And their bodies do not show the effects of their eating behavior. Unlike the self-starvers, they have little to no lanugo hair, bradycardia and menstruation, if it stops, more quickly returns in their recovery.

Compare the regular gorger-vomiter with the dieting anorectic: The latter is younger—under mid-adolescence—shy, obviously insecure, often feels hopeless, and is painfully ambivalent. She lacks social skills, never has had sexual relationships, and cannot fall back upon social successes. For her, there is no place to flee, and her realtionship to her father, a vague image adumbrated by mother, offers no promise of support. She doubts if there is a self to speak of. Only if she is smart and good will she be taken care of.

§Marie, a twenty-five-year-old single woman with comic-book blue eyes, bold against her thin face, was referred by her mother because of a long-standing, hidden anorexia nervosa. To her family, she seemed healthy and "fairly happy." As a social worker, she did her work well and hoped to be a therapist. Her mother indicated that her daughter had always had a "magnificent figure," her weight had remained at 120 pounds in spite of eating large amounts of food. At five feet eight inches, she was a "strikingly attractive young woman."

Her mother recalled that over the years Marie constantly drank clear tea or diet cola. Eight years ago, they had sent their daughter to their internist because they wondered whether her metabolism "might be too high." But in the last year the parents had noticed that Marie was losing weight. When her weight fell to 96 pounds, they insisted that she see a therapist. Then she disclosed to the parents that, beginning in the last year of high school, she had vomited after every large meal.

A few years before, her mother had suspected vomiting on one occasion. (Marie had denied it to the mother.) At a restaurant, she had inadvertently followed her daughter to the bathroom and thought she heard vomiting from one of the stalls. Marie later admitted, laughing lamblike, that, although she had been in psychotherapy from time to time over the years, she had never disclosed her vomiting to any therapist. Professionally, she had seen a number of anorectics, all witnessed from a very safe psychological distance, as though they talked a different language. She revealed her "secret" because of the distress she felt about the loss of her boyfriend—a curious sense of being terribly alone, as if in space—and the need "to finally get help."

Marie is an example of the way the bulimic vomiter can maintain a constant weight over a long period of time without any obvious social or physical deterioration. It was only after her boyfriend had thrown her over that she abstained from food, lost weight, and made a full disclosure of her predicament, shaking her head in disbelief, falsely brave about starting analysis.

The gorging-vomiting group of anorexia nervosa patients makes up at least 25 percent of all cases of the disorder. This figure, however, does not include the many young women—college students, dancers, and models—who maintain their ideal weight, between dead weight and buoyancy, by vomiting after meals. The goring-purging group has significantly increased in recent years, particularly among college women. It is well known that numerous college women, many having learned this behavior from other gorging-vomiting women, regularly vomit after evening meals—and many do so for years—in their attempt to maintain an ideal weight. This type of anorexia nervosa is unusual in males, found mostly among jockeys and male dancers.

The gorger-vomiter, after her binge, is extremely uncomfortable, both physically and mentally, and must relieve herself by vomiting. This results in fatigue, shame, guilt and sometimes even actual physical collapse. Eyes buggy, face puffy, she is too tired to think. She has little time or energy left over from her food ritual-addiction, which makes her feel not only depressed but also guilty. She renews her compulsive resolution against overeating and resolves to maintain her weight at her ideal level. The compulsive eating is done either privately or publicly, but her vomiting is kept private, often even from a therapist with whom she is in treatment. (Bulimics have been known to be in treatment for years for another complaint without having revealed to the therapist their compulsive eating-vomiting cycle.) Gorging and vomiting usually take place at night, after everyone else in the house has gone to bed. Often the anorectic cannot sleep; she awakes and goes to the kitchen where she consumes enormous quantitites of food which are later vomited. Unlike the self-starving anorectic, who seldom steals except to take jewelry to adorn her uncertain femininity or a household item for symbolic reasons, the binger steals food, or cheats on expenses, to accumulate money for a future binge. During her illness the stealing is compulsive, but after full recovery it ceases to exist as a symptom just as before the onset of the disorder. She sees her gorging as an imperfect solution to weight control. She can eat whatever she wants, give in to her impulses and binges, and eliminate the food through vomiting and purgation.

If the young woman is a self-starver and periodic bulimic, the weight loss is apt to occur faster—and be more life-threatening—than for the self-starving anorectic. If she eats moderately, occasionally binges and vomits, then the weight loss may be minimal. Bulimic patients are keenly aware of gastric sensations and hunger and spend a large part of their time attempting to deny hunger. They can get themselves into toxic states by grossly overeating, vomiting, and inducing prolonged diarrhea. In some instances, violent vomiting can rupture the stomach with resulting peritonitis, but this is a rarity. Some bulimic vomiters are skilled in triggering the vomit reflex. Bending over a toilet bowl may be enough of a trigger to vomiting. Others may use simply their finger, stick a Q-tip or a spoon down the throat, swallow a cloth belt, almost drown themselves with salty water, or gulp down something nauseating, like castor oil. Others are repulsed by the thought of ritualistic vomiting. When they sense a binge may occur, they may call a friend for reassurance and companionship, much like an alcoholic calling an Alcoholics Anonymous member.

Fear of insufficient food for a binge and privacy for vomiting can induce in the bulimic a profound tension state. She may flee from her home and make the rounds of local coffee shops and restaurants, eating a meal at each, until she feels on the verge of bursting. If short of money, she may steal from parents or roommates, cash personal checks without sufficient funds, or recklessly charge food to her parents' credit cards. Her cruelty is rarely conscious. The combination of bulimia and vomiting becomes "habit-forming," taking on an autonomy which eventually seems independent from the original conflicts over food. As mixed anorectics who starve and gorge, bulimic patients tend also to have more distorted body images. They struggle with their body and feelings of disgust. They do not usually become amenorrheic unless their weight falls to the level where the hormonal changes associated with amenorrhea are triggered.

Secondary Signs and Symptoms

The secondary signs and symptoms of anorexia nervosa are both physical and mental. Signs of starvation appear quickly after a relentless diet; its secondary effects are exponential and escalate the starvation state. Other secondary phenomena are manifestations of the anorectic's manipulation of the environment around food and diet and her distrustful attitude toward important people in her life. Sadness and guilt sometimes are apparent. The secondary features of anorexia are variable, and they depend on the degree of self-starvation or gorging-vomiting, the pattern of the eating disturbance, the character structure of the patient, and the quality of relationships in the family. For instance, guilt and shame are much greater in bulimic patients because of breakdown of self-esteem and the loss of self-control. Guilt and shame in these patients can lead to a depressive reaction with suicidal gestures, relentless starvation, self-injury and mutilation, such as head-banging and wrist-scratching.

Depression may be a reflection of the anorectic's retroflexed anger on the self or represent her feelings of ego-depletion, helplessness, hopelessness, and the breakdown of the idealized self. For example, the depression of the primary self-starving anorectic is related to a discrepancy between the ego and ego-ideal; major affects are shame, humiliation, inadequacy, weakness, and inferiority—all part of fallen self-esteem—eventually leading to ego-depletion, hopelessness and helplessness. On the other hand, the gorger-vomiter, at the other end of the anorexia nervosa spectrum, is apt to experience a depression more oedipal in nature, with guilt and moral masochism, part of a stringent, punishing superego. Hostility is deflected back on the self, and death becomes the punishment for the wish to kill.

Diagnostic Considerations

Clinical Diagnosis

For the clinical diagnosis of anorexia nervosa, what criteria should be used? And should they differ from those used in research? Anorexia itself is not adequate, for the anorectic is actually hungry. Weight loss of 25 percent is not specific; it would include depressive and neurotic cases of failure to eat. Furthermore, such a criterion would exclude many gorger-vomiters who lose minimal, if any, weight. In addition, the clinician wants to make the diagnosis at a much earlier stage in the natural history of the self-starving and mixed anorectic. The dyad of refusal to eat and loss of weight excludes the bulimic vomiter, who often admits joy in eating and keeps her weight at her prescribed level. Distortion of body image, as it is seen in young primary self-starving anorectics, is not specific to the anorexia nervosa syndrome, nor is it a constant finding, even in this particular group. The anorectic complaint of inadequacy, impotence, and ineffectiveness, found to some degree even in neurotic character disturbances, is common to all borderline states and expresses the need for autonomy and individuation. Likewise, disturbances in enteroceptive perception and cognition are central to borderline pathology. And the same can be said for another criterion: the sense of the body as threatening, an intrusive and disparaging entity invested with primitive, negative identifications and equated with discontent for the self. Overwhelming wishes for passivity and resultant fears of surrender to and body-invasion by an aggressive object are pivotal to the panic of the anorectic's nightmare, as well as other types of borderline patients.

What is specific to anorexia nervosa, as well as pathognomonic of it, in all its forms, is the anorectic's frantic pursuit of thinness with pleasure, the disturbed and overdetermined attitude toward, and the enormous investment of energy in, food and eating. Unlike the ordinary teenager, she takes great pleasure from her dieting or her ability to control weight by vomiting after gorging. In addition, her preoccupation with food and obsessive culinary interests are manifestations of her attitude toward food and eating. Other findings, like amenorrhea, and hyperactivity, are neither specific to nor pathognomonic of anorexia nervosa.

Research Diagnosis

The criteria for the research diagnosis of anorexia nervosa are not necessarily the same as those for clinical diagnosis.

Feighner et al. (1972) have established research diagnostic criteria with the hope of using multivariate statistical techniques. They distinguish the signs and symptoms of the syndrome from those of physical disease, pointing out that the signs and symptoms of anorexia nervosa are not derived from physical disorders where pathological and biochemical delineation is possible, and one can understand tissue abnormality. On the contrary, the signs and symptoms of the anorexia nervosa syndrome are taken from clinical data and empirical investigation, not based on physical causative factors.

For Feighner, the criteria for the diagnosis of anorexia nervosa are part of the syndromic definition of the disturbance. In order to use a diagnosis reliable enough for gathering together cases for research study, two of six criteria, according to Feighner, must be present. They are: (1) age of onset under twenty-five years of age; (2) weight loss of at least 25 percent, or 10 percent below the normal body weight. (It is best that the diagnosis be made before this level of inanition is reached and its course has been established.) (3) A distorted attitude toward eating, food, and weight as evidenced by denial of illness, enjoyment in losing weight, refusing food, avoiding pleasurable indulgences, attaining a desired body image, and an unusual hoarding and culinary preparation of food; (4) the absence of any other psychiatric illness; and (5) at least two of the following: amenorrhea for at least three months (unless the disturbance occurs before menarche), lanugo hair, bradycardia (60 beats or less a minute), periods of overactivity, episodes of bulimia, self-induced vomiting, and the mood of the anorectic, which can vary between euphoria and depression depending on her success in curbing her appetite and her satisfaction with herself.

Feighner has also considered anorexia nervosa from the standpoint of categories of presentation and syndromic picture. He combines typical presentation and typical syndrome with atypical presentation and atypical syndrome in a set of four possibilities.

The first category is that of typical presentation and typical syndrome which is the classical and core anorectic picture. The second category consists of atypical presentation and typical syndrome. An example of this category is a patient who has an onset of a typical syndrome after the age of twenty-five, or a typical syndrome presenting after the birth of a first child. Once the syndrome has appeared, under both these categories the signs and symptoms are predictable and persistent. The third category is that of typical presentation and atypical syndrome. For this category, there are two subgroups. There are those cases which are quantitatively atypical, like a mild syndrome or an incomplete syndrome. An example of a mild syndrome is an anorectic whose weight loss is well below 25 percent of body weight. In this syndromic picture, the criteria of 25 percent of body weight loss can be ignored. Another example of a quantitatively atypical patient would be the anorectic with an incomplete syndromic picture. Anorectics with an incomplete syndrome are sometimes middle-aged; they can be regarded as examples of anorexia tardive. The second subgroup is the qualitative, atypical patient; namely, anorectics who differ qualitatively from the syndromic picture. An example would be a male teenager who sees himself as chubby and is fearful of developing fat arms and legs. His preoccupation is not weight loss per se as much as a desire to develop his muscles. The fourth category is atypical presentation and atypical syndrome. A clinical example is weight loss of unknown origin. Patients who evidence failure to thrive or neglect of appetite also fall under this category. In general, patients in this category go into a heterogenous group of disorders, many of which are clinically *formes frustes* of anorexia nervosa, cases which require a complete medical and psychiatric evaluation to rule out organicity.

Feighner's criteria, intended primarily for the research investigator, are valid and reliable criteria; they are useful for collecting discrete and reproducible groups of patients for further study; and, in addition, they encourage the pediatrician and internist to look for anorexia nervosa in his office and hospital practice.

Clinical Forms and Variants of Anorexia Nervosa and Its Differential Diagnosis

The anorexia nervosa syndrome is distinguishable from other mental disorders, like endogenous depression, schizophrenic psychosis, and hysteria, as well as organic states with anorexia, weight loss, and psychopathology.

The anorexia nervosa syndrome is not a schizophrenic psychosis with omnipotence and oral-sadistic impulses. The schizophrenic non-eater is not like the primary anorectic, if schizophrenic process diagnostic criteria, like Mayer-Gross (1954) and Schneider's first rank symptoms (1925) (auditory hallucinations, experiences of influence on the body, thought-withdrawal, thought-broadcasting, delusional perceptions, and outside influences on feelings, thoughts, and actions) are used. The distinction, however, becomes complicated, if not impossible, with anorectics in severe borderline states, when clinicians like Bruch (1973b) and Palazzoli (1965) refer to a schizophrenic core of anorexia nervosa. The schizophrenic is not generally fussy about food and does not have temper tantrums over food. She acknowledges hunger and weakness but misinterprets the process of eating. Apathetic and indifferent to emaciation, the schizophrenic usually has a delusion about swallowing food. Schizophrenic eating behavior is usually oddly ritualistic and bizarre, frequently indicating fantasies of cannibalistic incorporation and mutilation. The schizophrenic noneater tends to consider herself a victim and speaks about fantasies of being poisoned. She also harbors fantasies which reveal visions of great destruction and world calamity, if she gives vent to her desire to eat. Delusional mood *(Wahrstimmung)* and disturbances in symbolization are part of schizophrenic noneating.

The anorectic young woman described below, also a severe bulimic vomiter, functioned at a primitive, acting-out level. She was always gluttonously hungry, often unable to deny and control the impulse to eat. A psychotic, she displayed more severe pathology than the other patients presented in this chapter.

§A loud gum-chewer, Roberta, a nineteen-year-old single woman with tinted glasses, second of four children, was admitted to the hospital because of gorging and vomiting, repeatedly running away from home to make her father come and get her, stealing money for gorging sprees, gaps in her consciousness, bizarre promiscuity, excessive use of marijuana, and unwillingness to go to college or get a job. On some days it came to her that she had a transcendental purpose in Christendom: No glass should be empty; food should be in the stomach of the humble, she would say in her rasping voice. And then she would go out and steal food like a mouse in the pantry.

All through her childhood, she was moderately obese. At age twelve, her father bribed her to lose weight, agreeing to pay her twenty dollars per pound of weight-loss. She took up his bet by inducing vomiting after every meal. Because of frequent fights with her mother, Roberta increasingly spent less time at home and became very close to her older, rebellious, defiant, married sister. From ages twelve to seventeen, she was usually at this sister's home. There she was introduced to marijuana, alcohol, sedatives, and sex—activities which were kept secret from the parents until a year prior to admission, when Roberta confided in them. They believed Roberta's soul, long bent out of shape, had been lost—stolen by her devil-sister.

Throughout her childhood Roberta had been a thumb-sucker, until the age of twelve when she had come under her sister's influence, a move she made in an attempt to separate from her parents and negate "all her babyish feelings." At age thirteen, Roberta had sexual intercourse but was disappointed and disillusioned by it, and stayed away from boys for the next few years. After high school graduation, she went to college on the West Coast but was homesick, anorectic, depressed, made a suicidal attempt, was hospitalized and given a course of electroshock treatment, and returned home.

A few months before admission, her parents became concerned about her marijuana usage. Because her weight had fallen to 85 pounds—she was now so shrivelled her face was like a skull—they wondered whether she might be brain-damaged; they feared that she had ruined her health. A psychiatric consultant suggested family treatment, to which the patient responded by smoking more marijuana, stealing more often from her father, and running away from home. She had plunged into vast confusion, they believed. The father responded then by placing her in a juvenile detention center with the view that his daughter was psychopathic. She soon escaped from the detention center and fled out West, where she was picked up by local police and returned home. Another consultant recommended hospitalization.

Roberta remained in the hospital for two weeks until she was promptly discharged after she had destroyed her room. It was now apparent that the anorexia nervosa syndrome was a part of an undifferentiated schizophrenic psychosis with psychopathic features. During the hospitalization, the parents went off on holiday. Later, a few weeks after discharge, they again left. In order to get the parents to return, Roberta, tricked and befouled, drove the family car into a parked truck, was hospitalized for minor head injuries and facial lacerations. She was successful in retrieving her parents. They recoiled as though hit in the stomach; they grew less tolerant of Roberta's manipulative behavior and, at the same time, more denying of their own hostility toward her. Both parents insisted that they could no longer support her and had her admitted to a state hospital.

Inquiry some months later revealed Roberta had been discharged and had run away from home to live with friends in Maine, where she supported herself and was in treatment with a local psychiatrist. Her parents felt pleased with this outcome. It absolved them of responsibility and ostensibly provided their daughter with enough distance and local support to no longer seek their help.

The anorexia of psychotic depression must also be distinguished from that of primary anorexia nervosa. Depressed patients have a decreased physical vitality that clearly distinguishes them from the primary anorectic. Manic-depressive (bipolar) patients reveal histories of parallel cyclical mood and eating behavior. Fluctuations in mood and eating (depression and gluttony, elation and dieting) are part of manic-depressive illnesses; but, contrary to Kraepelin's view (1920), manic-depressive eating behavior does not suggest an equivalency between the two disorders. The combination does not warrant a diagnosis of anorexia nervosa. And cyclothymic mood changes in an anorectic do not justify a manic-depressive diagnosis (Porot, Couadau, and Collet 1970, Weinberg-Dagoni 1966, Cantwell et al. 1977, Mastrosimone and Pacini 1971, Berg et al. 1974, Dugas, Gueriot, and Jullien 1973). Agitated, depressive individuals complain bitterly of vegetative disturbances, including lack of hunger and continuing bowel difficulties. The melancholic, inert patient is oblivious to her lack of initiative. She does not have the perpetual motion of the hyperactive anorectic. Depressed pubertal boys, on the other hand, can present an atypical anorectic picture. Their anorexia may be an atonement for sexual feelings and be followed by withdrawal, indifference and apathy.

The hysterical noneater, a type of secondary anorexia, complains bitterly about her weight loss and thinness and does not attempt to deny hunger and asthenia. Her pathological rejection of food may have followed an upsetting sexual experience; unconscious fear of pregnancy may be a factor. The hysteric may simply lose weight in order to manipulate people. The eating disturbance is a symbolic expression of conflict; rarely does it lead to a full-fledged episode of bulimia. And it is easily distinguished from malingering. No Munchausen cases of anorexia nervosa are reported (Stern 1980).

Other types of atypical, secondary anorexia must be considered (Schachter 1974, Bruch 1973b). Phobic anxiety can be expressed in terms of psychogenic dysphagia, a sucking phobia, or a phobia of swallowing, and is often combined with diffuse anxiety and depressive affect in obsessional and hysterical character disorders. The typical anorectic with a "weight phobia" does not truly suffer from a phobia. The real phobic is aware intellectually that tension and fear are not justified and wants to be rid of the phobia. The typical anorectic sees nothing wrong with starvation and does not want relief from "phobic" anorectic behavior. In young women, secondary anorexia may be part of a psychasthenia, mixed with anxiety and hysteria in a borderline personality. A food fad can be part of a secondary anorexia; the fad expressed a disgust and avoidance of certain foods, usually connected with shape, smell, color, and consistency. Atypical, secondary anorexia usually is not associated with a distorted body image, although, as in any group of young, body-conscious and concerned people, a shifting, unstable body image may be found and made more prominent by increasing denial.

Vegetarianism can mask primary anorexia nervosa, be part of an atypical picture, or be simply a statement of separateness and autonomy from a world found not ideologically acceptable. It is not anorexia nervosa proper unless definite signs and symptoms are present and mixed with the food and eating ideology and behavior. Vegetarianism itself is a defense against regressive cannibalistic and sadistic fantasies, or against contradictory identifications and primal scene memories.

The following adolescent girl illustrates several differential diagnostic possibilities.

§Paula, a fourteen-year-old, sharp-nosed girl, was referred to a pediatric endocrinologist because of slow growth and delayed puberty. The endocrinologist found her short in stature, thin, and immature looking for her age. Gonadal dysgenesis (Turner's syndrome) was his first diagnosis, but buccal smear showed a normal female sex-chromatin pattern. Physical examinations were essentially negative. Her sexual development seemed immature. There were thirty to fifty pubic hairs and bilaterally ten to twenty axillary hairs. The labia minora were juvenile, but the vaginal mucosa was not dull in its appearance. Breast enlargement had not yet occurred, but the endocrinologist believed that small, glandular subareolor discs were beginning to develop.

Laboratory studies were not helpful in establishing the cause of the delayed growth. Growth hormone and gonadotropin studies were entirely normal. The endocrinologist finally concluded that the problem was simply a constitutional delay in growth and sexual maturation.

The psychiatric consultant, however, after seven interviews with this reticent, fawnlike girl, established a history of anorexia nervosa. When Paula was twelve years old, her father had suddenly died of a coronary occlusion. The mother refused to mourn, made every attempt to "go on with things," and discouraged Paula from thinking about her father. The mother returned to college at night in order to get a Masters of Business Administration degree, necessary for advancement at her bank. Then Paula became more involved with her school work, got straight A averages, and turned into the best athlete in her class. It was then that she started to lose weight.

At the time of consultation, she weighed 62 pounds; a pipe-cleaner figure, she was wasted to a skeleton, eyes huge and glassy. She clenched her teeth with a look of fury, while pulling at a strand of hair. In treatment, Paula finally revealed that her father had been greatly disappointed that she had not been born a boy. The father made every attempt to teach her how to "bat a ball, catch a high fly, throw a pass, and sink a basket." She had avoided athletics until her father's death, when she plunged into a fanatic athleticism and consciously attempted to "make her father's dream come true."

Smith and Hanson (1972) and Toms and Crisp (1972) have described several cases of anorexia nervosa with stunted growth.

A variety of intracranial lesions can produce panhypopituitarism with variable clinical pictures of anorexia and weight loss (Udvarhelyi, Adamkiewicz, and Cooke 1966, Heron and Johnston 1976, Mecklenburgh et al. 1974, Lewin 1972, White, Kelly, and Dorman 1977). The anorexia is a true loss of appetite and hunger.[1] Craniopharngioma, glioma, cranial injury, sarcoidosis, and granulomatous lesions (Hans-Schüller-Christian's disease) are possible causes of panhypopituitar-

---

1. True anorexia is also associated with carcinoma, high fevers, metabolic disorders, gastrointestinal disturbances, as well as depression and prolonged anxiety reactions.

ism. Pituitary insufficiency results in understimulation of the thyroid and adrenal cortex with secondary degeneration; myxedema and hypocorticordism also occurs with clinical signs and symptoms of asthenia, apathy, sexual frigidity, amenorrhea, and cold sensitivity. But there are no signs of malnutrition. The patient's face is characteristically swollen and pale; the skin is pale and lacks melanin. Axillary and pubic hair in panhypopituitarism is sparse or absent. The eyebrows are thin. There is no lanugo hair. The breast tissue is shrunken. The panhypopituitary patient has no desire to lose weight and is not opposed to treatment. A patient with the pituitary disturbance usually is apathetic and indifferent to the vicissitudes of daily family living, in contrast to the ambivalent and controlling ways of the anorectic. Both disorders are associated with secondary amenorrhea and decreased libido. In addition, hypotension, as well as constipation, is likely to be present in both disorders. Chemically, however, they are quite different. Plasma growth hormone response to insulin is normal in primary anorexia nervosa, although in cases of prolonged anorectic starvation there may be a degree of pituitary depletion. Furthermore, in panhypopituitarism there is no cachexia with lethargy and asthenia. Panhypopituitarism is usually caused by an eosinophilic tumor of the pituitary which leads to increased intracranial pressures, erosion of the sella turcica and a visual field defect, bitemporal homonymous hemianopsia, all of which are readily found on physical examination.

There are other organic disorders which superficially resemble anorexia nervosa (Turnbridge and Frazer 1972, Seaver and Binder 1972). Organic confusional states with true anorexia can be caused by cerebral tumors of the frontal lobe, diencephalon, and fourth ventricle. Bradycardia, low basal metabolic rate, and high serum cholesterol in a starving patient always raise the question of hypothyroidism. On the other hand, tremulousness, tachycardia, sweating, voracious appetite, and a racing pulse point to diagnosis of hyperthyroidism, but the patient may, instead, be a bulimic vomiter.

Several less common diseases have to be considered in the differential diagnosis of anorexia nervosa. Volvulus and sprue are among them. There are case reports of patients with granulomatous disease of the small bowel similar to ulcerative colitis and Crohn's disease; they present with severe anorexia—a genuine distaste for food—and profound weakness. Fever and constipation are prominent in the gastrointestinal disorder, and radiographic studies of the small and large intestines demonstrate a symmetric pattern of skipping and fistulization (Pasternack 1970). Among the findings are severe arterial and arteriolar thickening associated with normal blood pressure and high blood renin, indicating the possibility of Bartter's syndrome (Codaccioni et al. 1972, Tarm et al. 1973). There are also reported cases of anorexia in which there is an accompanying diarrhea. These patients vomit frequently and have electrolyte imbalance and secondary hyper-aldosteronism (Pasternack 1970, Herman, Goth, and Rado 1973, Stewart and Loewenthal 1974).

Pernicious anemia must also be differentiated from anorexia nervosa. About a third of the patients with pernicious anemia are anorectic, genuinely so, but megaloblastic anemia is unusual in anorexia nervosa. Another disturbance that must be considered in the differential diagnosis is periodic psychosis which has associated with it a disturbance in fluid balance, sudden weight gain, acne, and delusions of pregnancy, along with irritability and resentfulness. These patients are frequently polydypsic and bulimic, and have episodes of anorexia. The vomiting is frequently a defense against bulimia.

Another eating disorder is the night-eating syndrome. These patients are surreptitious, regular night-eaters. They eat during the night and early hours of the morning; their compulsive eating is hidden from their families and even from therapists with whom they may be in treatment for anxiety or depression.

An additional group of gorgers, mostly males, are the constant eaters, day and night, who derive no pleasure from food and feel helpless to control their eating. Histories reveal weight fluctuations; they lose weight during periods of oral control and then relapse into bulimia and superobesity. There is another group of compulsive eaters, the Levin syndrome, smaller in number and phenomenologically different in some respects. Their binges, ego-dystonic, are irregular, unpredictable, pleasureless, and personally loathsome. Their guilt and shame are monumental. During their "eating attacks," as they come to call their impulsive eating sprees, they feel unreal and out of touch with their environment. After the gluttony subsides, they have an irresistable urge to sleep. It is this last group that Green and Rau (1977) believe have neurophysiological disturbances. These patients tend to have disturbed electroencepholographic (EEG) tracings, as well as other evidence of out-of-control, compulsive behavior in areas other than simply eating. Green and Rau have found that the anticonvulsant, Dilantin, helps these patients, although the reasons are not clear.

Bulimia, with a ravenous, uncontrollable appetite, is also found in the Prader-Willi syndrome. Usually seen in mentally retarded children, the disorder is associated at times with diabetes mellitus, infantile limpness, poor sucking, and other stigmata which make it readily recognizable to the informed clinician.

A number of psychoneurotic disturbances should also be considered. Psychogenic vomiting (Nagaraja 1974, Sperling 1978) is a distinct group of disturbances. Its onset is usually abrupt, with violent vomiting leading to severe dehydration and acidosis. There is also a group of female psychogenic vomiters, who eat a bizarre diet, have secret episodes of bulimia, vomiting, and, at times, purgation. Patients complain of pain which is thought to be ovarian in origin. During the bulimic episodes, the pulse may race and the patients be feverish. Sometimes these patients are misdiagnosed as having acute appendicitis. There are also psychogenic vomiters with trichophagic trichotillomania; they eat the hair which they pull from their head or eyebrows.

Other psychogenic, atypical, secondary anorexias can be encountered (Lakoff and Feldman 1972). Neurotic abstinence from food can result from fear of swallowing, as well as mechanico-functional dysphagia, such as esophageal and pyloric spasm. There are also patients with chronic, secondary anorexia due to hypochondriacal dyspepsia. In general, secondary, neurotic anorexia often starts in early infancy and appears later in life, frequently after a humiliating or frustrating situation. The anorexia, however, can lead to chronic inanition and hypochondriacal gastrointestinal disturbances and psychasthenia. The secondary neurotic anorexias do not have the signs and symptoms of typical, primary anorexia nervosa.

In differentiating the amenorrhea of primary anorexia nervosa from other menstrual disturbances, there are several organic disturbances that should be considered. Gonadal dysgenesis (Turner's syndrome), polycystic ovaries (Stein-Leventhal syndrome), and galactosemia must be eliminated. The majority of amenorrheas, however, are psychogenic in origin.

There are variants of primary anorexia nervosa. Often seen in London is the "Twiggy" type of anorectic, a late adolescent or young woman who diets vigorously as part of her life as a fashion model. She does not avoid sexuality and, in fact, tends to be promiscuous, although without orgastic pleasure and sensual delight. Another variant is the mild to moderate chronic alcoholic, frequently a chain smoker, who hides her anorexia nervosa behind drinking and claims that she eats very well (Asbeck et al. 1972, Halmi and Loney 1973). She reduces her food intake in order to continue drinking without gaining weight, and eventually she encounters severe complications from chronic alcoholism. One other variant of primary anorexia nervosa is that of the young woman, socially busy and professionally ambitious, who pursues intense vocational, social, and sexual activity as a means of denying her hunger, avoiding eating, and losing oral control. She is found in the executive ranks where her eating habits are hidden by the style of her everyday life.

Dancers tend, to varying degrees, to be anorectic. A surprisingly large number are either dieting anorectics or regular binger-vomiters, who keep their weight at what they—and often their dance instructors—consider a "perfect dancing weight." In their quest for sublime thinness, some lose control of their eating, become cachectic, exhausted, and collapse. They do not usually succeed in their careers and return home to the mother whom they cannot escape. However, others do not lose control of eating and run the risk of cachexia, fatigue, and exhaustion. This group uses postprandial vomiting to remain thin. At an early age, they break with mother and join a ballet company. In doing so they join another family, governed by the ballet mistress, who is a demanding, all-purpose mother. With the bona fide, mixed anorectic, dancers have many things in common: food faddism, fasting, self-denial, self-induced vomiting, weight hovering at 100 pounds, distortion of body image, repetitive and ritualistic exercises every day of the week, the wish to desexualize and defeminize themselves to neuters, and a desire to achieve perfection. But, as Druss and Silverman (1979) have indicated in their study of ballerinas, the less primitive anorectics (the ones who can escape from an archaic tie with mother) have a greater sense of effectiveness, less overwhelming preoccupation with food, a feeling of accomplishment, and a place in the dance community. Like the dieting anorectic, as well as many professional swimmers, figure skaters, long distance runners, and musicians, they seek a transcendental perfection.

Many long-distance runners, mostly men, astoundingly resemble adolescents with typical anorexia nervosa. They are hyperactive, full of energy, and hardly ever tire. They restrict their food intake, go on food fasts to attain the ideal weight, and follow repetitive and routinized daily exercise programs with intense dedication. They annoy their lovers or spouses with their monomaniacal focus on running and fitness, often to the relative exclusion of instinctual interests. Women distance runners find that amenorrhea eventually occurs if body mass decreases below the critical point for menstrual function. In general, runners maximize pain and minimize pleasure in their ascent to control and mastery. The functional pleasure of thinness and fitness exceeds and substitutes for oral gratification. The fear of fat is constantly with them. They can only freely eat if they first run long distances, the reverse of the bulimic vomiter who eats first and then rids herself of food. And like the anorectic, they keep a record of calories, as well as miles. They know that running dulls the appetite and decreases hunger and they look forward to carbohydrate loading before a marathon. Yet they still fear weight gain. George Sheehan (1978) reminds runners of this "enemy": "The struggle against the slowly advancing glacier of lard begins before we attain our maturity. It never ends. In this war against fat, you have to be a career person."

Distance runners, much like anorectics, regard their bodies as complicated machines which must be regularly used and serviced. They sleep like anorectics, waking up early full of energy and ambition. They start their physical routine often before sunrise. Fat is abhorred—it must be reduced to 12 percent of body mass—and the body is never really thin. Runners often examine their bodies, palpating fascial planes for lumps of fat. The top runner who runs for perfection is the idealized hero for the distance runner. Body-image distortions are common. Even professional Boston marathoners marvel at their bodies when they see themselves reflected in Hansen's plate glass windows as they run through the Newtons. Many runners cannot believe that they are thin, for they tend to overestimate their body size. They distrust their body perceptions, unless they are photographed along the course. Also like anorectics, they do not trust their bodies to the medical profession, for they know an orthopedist will advise rest for an injury. As Fixx (1977) says, "Running is my doctor." At best, only a sports podiatrist, preferably one of their own, can be trusted.

Although Gull's patients were under age twenty-five, Lasègue, Berkman (1930), Ryle (1936), Carrier (1939), Bliss and Branch (1960), Kellett, Trimble, and Thorley (1976), and Dally and Gomez (1979) have described women with anorexia nervosa of late onset, past thirty years of age, the so-called "forme tardive" cases. Hyperactive, if not agitated, these women may be depressed, sleepless, aggressively resistant to eating in a frightened, phobic way, different from the simple, depressive anorectic. Antidepressants are not helpful. In addition, they vomit and purge, unlike a more common group of anorexia tardive women, who, sedentary, perhaps even bed-ridden, are passive-aggressive to any offer of food, seldom vomit or take carthartics.

Tardive anorectics, in general, often are locked into competitive situations with young daughters, with whom they share a contempt for the husband-father.

Although anorexia nervosa usually appears between ages ten to fifteen, the disorder may go undiagnosed for years, for the anorectic may not lose control of her eating until later in life.

§A middle-aged suburban housewife, cocksure and quick-witted, a life insurance salesperson, quite successful, requested consultation because of a marital problem. She complained bitterly that her two children were in college. Now she and her husband were again "flung together." Making depreciatory gestures, she was increasingly disenchanted with him and with the fact that he was "letting himself go." She gasped, hooted, guffawed, and howled that his earning capacity had plateaued. Now he cared less about his appearance, had gotten fat, never exercised anymore, and "seemed ready for the nursing home." She found living with "this kind of man intolerable." Now that the children were no longer significantly in her life, she thought that she could not continue in the marriage. Firm that she was exempt from fears, she prided herself on her ambitions and achievements, as well as the fact that she had always kept herself in fine physical condition. In elaborating on her fitness, she recalled that, at the time of her marriage, she weighed 109 pounds which, for a frame of five feet four inches, admittedly was "excessive." But she had been able to bring her weight down to 90 pounds in the last ten years and was now, with pride, able to say she weighed 84 pounds. It came to her mind how she maintained this weight on a diet of 1,500 calories a day which, although to her mind was "a bit heavy on calories," was nevertheless manageable because she ran four miles every day. In addition, she was getting a master's degree in economics at night, which she found not difficult to combine with a hectic life insurance career. In fact, with maniclike glee she asserted that she was the "top seller" in her community; she was proud she was a member of the "Hundred Thousand Dollar Club."

An extended consultation produced historical information, establishing the fact that her anorexia nervosa had first occurred at the time of her father's business failure and bankruptcy. Shamefaced, she had withdrawn from her friends, gone on a diet, and become a compulsive student. Throughout high school and college, she was occasionally amenorrheic when her weight dipped below the weight critical for menstruation. In the early years of the marriage, however, she had allowed her weight to increase and she got pregnant several times. During the babyhood of her children, she relaxed about her weight and dieting; but, when all the children were finally off to grade school, she resumed her anorectic course, as she prepared to push away from her devalued husband.

The thin spinster, emaciated for a lifetime and now in her fifth and sixth decade, is another example of anorexia tardive. There are two clinical reports of women, fifty-two and seventy-two years old, anorectic for many years (Carlberger et al. 1971, Bernstein 1972, Kellett et al. 1976, Lutzenkirchen and Boning 1976). Agitated depression with somatic and hypochondriacal delusions, delayed grief reactions, and chronic schizophrenia are part of this differential diagnosis. Over the years, these patients become increasingly emaciated. They do not consult a physician until significant medical problems arise from anorexia nervosa. Then there are also anorectic individuals who conceal lifelong starvation behind a feigned malabsorption syndrome, which they claim resists treatment.

An anorectic may be symptomatic for years and never see a physician because her family cannot emotionally afford her getting well.

§Dolly, a twenty-six-year-old single, unemployed woman, was first seen in consultation at the age of twenty-five, after having passed through a foggy, thirteen-year history of anorexia nevosa. At the age of twelve, when she weighed 140 pounds, she suddenly put herself on a diet because she felt her legs were "getting too fat." She believed that her obese parents were a sign of her "fated obesity," which she could never leave behind. At the same time, she was convinced that she could never leave her parents. After two years, she dropped out of high school because of separation anxiety. She could not leave her mother. Doomsday was not far off. She was hospitalized at a local hospital for "depression" and given two courses of electroshock treatment. She returned home, like a lost child, and continued her anorectic diet, keeping her weight between 75 to 80 pounds. Her parents made a number of attempts to arrange consultations. Each one was supposedly aborted by Dolly's negativism and temper tantrums, but her mother, a fat, fearful, hawk-eyed, chronically depressed woman, who never worked, wanted Dolly home as a phobic companion and buffer against her husband. The two enjoyed chatting with each other, when not quarreling; neither one ever said what she was really thinking.

About six months before consultation, she started to have angry dreams of hitting her mother, running out of the house, and dying alone in the woods. She also talked about her fear of pregnancy, a fear which seemed real to her even though she had never dated. She often called the family physician about constipation, a symptom she had at four and five years of age, when she was treated for encopresis and fecal incontinence.

In consultation, it was found that Dolly's mother had made her daughter her protector—a hushed knowledge at first. She could go nowhere without Dolly. Likewise, the father supported this unwholesome arrangement because of his reluctance to be with his wife and family. The patient found herself in a responsible position with her mother, from whom she thought she could never draw back. After several months of an extended consultation, with many cancelled appointments, the patient with strength of resolve agreed to enter individual treatment. The parents started conjoint therapy, and eventually the mother entered psychotherapy.

Young adolescent girls, subclinical anorectics, who begin to diet, lose a few pounds and are then sent by their parents to the family physician. The consultation ends in a fatherly discussion by the family doctor whose firm reassurance and long-standing trust allow the young girl to stop her dieting. Such abortive cases are not included in any epidemiological study and are not evaluated by psychiatrists. These are mild cases of typical, primary anorexia nervosa which do not progress beyond a few missed menstrual periods and a slight weight loss. They stop their dieting, for one reason or another, and their menses soon return. They are teenage girls who, in the first flush of puberty, experience an upsurge of sexual feelings and anxiety. They respond with transient regressions from which some are not able to emerge without a little therapeutic intervention.

This vignette, from the analysis of a young adolescent girl, illustrates a mild course of anorexia nervosa, which would have escaped psychiatric attention if she had not been in treatment.

§Emily, a panic-filled, wide-eyed teenager, started treatment when she was thirteen years old because she felt unattractive, stupid, awkward, lonely, and helpless. Psychological testing revealed a full scale IQ of 104, a lower than expected score, resulting in part from her panicky and disorganized approach to testing. Spelling and vocabulary were weak, but no learning disability was evident. There was no history of anorexia nervosa; her eating seemed free of conflict.

The themes in the opening phase of analysis had been her sense of deprivation, sibling rivalry with her younger brother, fear of body ugliness and damage, a wish to be a boy to gain the father's love and respect, and a fear of harsh criticism by the mother, who, when angry, was inclined to say that Emily was mean, stupid, and hateful. In school, Emily acted out her hostility in a manner her mother would never tolerate at home; her mother regarded Emily as gloomy-hearted, impulsive, attention-seeking, and rude to the maids. She often did not do her shool work; hard work, Emily concluded, never seemed to get results. It just turned her stomach.

In her analysis, she often talked about her ambivalent relationship with her rejecting mother. She could see herself in her mind as spunkless, bent double, hopping mad but scroonched away in a corner. A devil, she feared, dwelled under the surface of her frantic thoughts in a chaos of old and new feelings—a mythological creature as black as the bottom of a well. By the second year, her school work had improved. In the spring, her parents considered sending her to boarding school— part of the family tradition. When so informed, she smiled, head tilted, saying clearly and precisely that she was no slave; she refused, sitting as solid as a boulder, determined not to be driven away. Emily recalled a number of early baffling memories, including one at age six when, while watching a sports car rally with her parents, she was rescued by a bystander from an out-of-control car—an incident regarded by her parents as trifling.

She increasingly elaborated over the next few months her sense that her mother had really wanted a boy. Helpless, she was trapped inside a girl's body. At the same time, she sensed that her mother, a very attractive English woman, was competitive with her. This perception, whenever spoken of, made Emily's anger boil up. The mother spent hours every day keeping up her appearance. Ominously, she announced that she had gone on a diet to restrict carbohydrates. Like several school friends who had also decided to diet, she had eliminated lunch at school altogether. At about the same time, the mother was preparing to take a six-week trip to Scandinavia. Determined, Emily proceeded to lose ten pounds before spring recess. She was absurdly proud of her weight loss, as though she had tamed a monster, but complained, darkness sliding over her face, that she was feeling weak, dizzy, and "a little upset because her ribs were sticking out." She now weighed 96 pounds, rather low for five feet nine inches, she acknowledged, now always half hungry, half angry. Nevertheless, she maintained her willpower in keeping to a 500-calorie diet and was delighted that, for the first time, she was athletic at school. She had a sense of her mind crinkling open like an old wad of paper, long forgotten in a wastepaper basket. Cold sober, alert, she said, "I don't feel like a dead animal, bloated and ugly." Her school work was better, for which she received praise from the teachers, who at the same time feared that she was "withering away." With the mother away, she saw her father more. Now he was more than a form in a dream. (Ordinarily, he would have been out three to four times a week with the mother at dinner parties.)

At spring recess, her father took Emily to Utah for a skiing holiday. There she became the "pride and joy" of the skiing instructors, who appreciated her wit and spirit. She was the "belle of the ball." After she had returned from her ski holiday, she began to date boys in groups. Her social life increased enormously, and she resumed normal eating. She was able to talk about her hostility to Mother, the many separations in the past and her outrage at her mother's recent departure to Scandinavia, and the fact that her mother never seemed to accept her as a "young woman." She was also able to understand how the increased relationship with her father had sexually excited her and, at the same time, made her feel guilty about "spending so much time with the father while the mother was away."

This brief, anorectic episode during an analysis of a young adolescent girl is an illustration of a not unusual appearance of anorexia nervosa which remits often as quickly as it appears.

There are clinically unrecognizable anorectics who are able to stabilize their weight at a fixed two-digit number—often 98 or 99 pounds—

and keep it from exceeding 100 pounds. These anorectics refuse to eat as part of a sisterhood with a small group of dieting school peers. In these "near-epidemic" episodes, which usually occur in the spring of the year, there can be six to twelve girls who join together in this comraderie, lose from five to fifteen pounds, and become dedicated "sisters" for the purpose of shunning boys and demonstrating their supreme wilfulness. The group forms because the girls believe that they have found a mutual way to achieve weight control, as well as a means of gaining control over instinctual needs and propelling themselves toward separation from home. These girls are mostly abstainers, but occasionally they are bulimic with gorging, hoarding of food, vomiting and purgation. Their voices disappear inside them.

5

Phenomenological Aspects of Anorexia Nervosa

What we must do is use all our power. That is all the universe demands.

—Goethe

We asked the captain what course of action he proposed to take toward a beast so large, terrifying, and unpredictable. He hesitated to answer and then said judiciously: "I think I shall praise it."

—Robert Hass, *Praise*

It is time to examine in depth specific, descriptive aspects of the anorexia nervosa syndrome, mostly from a phenomenological point of view.[1] We will look at the anorectic more carefully, with occasional repetition, to see how her landscape assembles, and to establish a broader base of inquiry. We will follow her into her inanition and withdrawal to the point where she is unable to giggle, put joy in her words, be filled with life without caution—unable to become what she dreams of, but claiming to be unique, not knowing what it is that she sees. At this juncture, love has departed from her, leaving her with ghosts to face in a purgatorial future.

Onset

The exact onset of anorexia nervosa is often difficult to recognize (Crisp 1979, Beumont et al. 1978b, Theander 1970, Galdston 1974, Kay and Leigh 1954). Frequently, the anorectic socially isolates herself in the year preceding the illness, less commonly acts out by being difficult at home, argumentative, apt to shout defiantly at parents and be rude, or has difficulty in decision-making. Parents and teachers, however, often are not keenly aware of the changes until the patient begins to lose weight.

Anorexia nervosa is primarily a disturbance of adolescent girls with the usual onset in a trimodal age-span of ten to fourteen, fifteen to

1. Phenomenology, a presuppositionless inquiry in search of essences, not apparent by ordinary observation, is a technique for discovering what lies behind appearances by trying to experience them as the subject of the investigation.

eighteen, and nineteen to thirty. The younger patients are mainly self-starvers; the ones between fifteen and eighteen are self-starvers and mixed anorectics. Anorectics in the age range of nineteen to thirty tend to be largely gorger-vomiters, especially a subgroup between nineteen and twenty-five; and anorectics with onset after age thirty are atypical, often cases of anorexia tardive. Male patients have the same trimodal distribution; age of onset after thirty is also rare. The peak onset for the male is nine to twelve years of age (Wiener 1976, Bruch 1971a). Male anorectics, with onset after age fourteen, sometimes show a delayed puberty. Peak age of onset for females is fifteen to eighteen years. Anorectics under the age of eight have been reported, but their authenticity as primary anorectics is dubious (Sylvester 1945, Radford 1969). Childhood anorexia, distinguishable from anorexia nervosa on the basis of attitude to food and eating, expresses tensions and anxiety in both parents and child. Passive-regressive about eating, the child still is interested in food and wants to eat. In predisposed anorectic families, childhood anorexia may blossom forth as anorexia nervosa in adolescence. About 8 percent of the youngest cases occur slightly prior to age ten; they are exceptions to the rule that early onset augers well for an early recovery. If the disorder occurs after twenty-five years—certainly after age thirty—the more atypical the features, and the outcome is apt to be poor (Launer 1978, Anderson 1977, Kellett, Trimble, and Thorley 1976).

§An older woman with clinical anorexia tardive of two years' duration is a case in point. The husband of this anorectic requested consultation for his wife by letter, which revealed his anguish over the wife's eating disorder and his difficulty in getting help for her. He wrote in a small, cursive hand:

> I have reason to believe that my wife, Jennifer, who is thirty-four years old and the mother of three children, is suffering from anorexia nervosa. Her weight has declined from 100 pounds to 58 pounds over the last eighteen months. She had been to her general practitioner during that period, and he did not know what the problem was. Jennifer recently underwent a series of diagnostic tests at a local hospital, and nothing was found organically wrong with her. The physician thought that the problem might be anorexia nervosa, but he had little knowledge of the subject. He recommended that my wife see a psychiatrist, which she did. The doctor we visited said that the problem sounded like anorexia

nervosa; however, he had never treated a patient with this condition. For the last year and a half, I have been completely frustrated, because I have seen my wife dissipate to the point where her very life is in danger, and the doctors that I have seen were unable to help me. I was completely beside myself as to what to do, because I did not know what the problem was and was not able to get professional direction. I started to research anorexia nervosa and read with considerable interest articles which had been written on the subject in the last few years. The very substance of an article in a magazine clearly defined my wife's condition, and while I am not a doctor, there is no question in my mind that this is the problem. For the first time in a year and a half, I believe I know what the problem is, have an understanding of it, and know that unless I get professional help immediately, my wife will most probably die.

The wife was seen in consultation and referred to a psychiatrist in her community. Psychotherapy proved to be difficult, taking ten years, with little change in character structure.

Gender Distribution

For a variety of reasons, the prevalence of anorexia nervosa is much higher in girls. Girls are more apt to diet because of cultural pressures to be thin (Nylander 1971). More rapid and earlier biological growth of pubescence makes the young girl more aware of her body and blossoming femininity. Changing pubertal body contour, mostly breasts, hips, and thighs, makes the female body image less stable. Menstruation can be traumatic for the pubertal girl, as is the case for girls with an early onset of the anorectic disorder. Girls are more likely to inhibit wishes and feelings and cannot depend on a coterie of girlfriends or a gang to sanction affective expression. Girls also have more hysterical and phobic components to their character structure, are more self-conscious of burgeoning adolescent sexuality, and are uncomfortable with surfacing aggression. Pubertal girls feel vulnerable to intrusion and invasion, whether by maternal demands and criticisms, passionate embrace, sexual penetration, impregnation, voyeuristic male inspection, or the ubiquitous demands of infant care. They feel victimized by their passive-receptive wishes. In addition, growing plumpness, weight gain, and secondary sex-characteristics are equated by girls with pregnancy. Girls are more readily attached to their mother, with whom they identify. Boys, on the other hand, do not experience cultural pressure to be slim; instead, to be fit and strong. With puberty a boy's body does not add adipose tissue in the breasts, thighs, and hips; if concerned about obesity, it is his body in general that worries him. Fatness, to the boy, unless he labors with gender confusion, does not mean femininity and pregnancy—rather, it connotes weakness, passivity, and babyishness. It can also mean, decidedly so in adult men, strength, power, and dominance. Male puberty occurs later and less abruptly than it does in girls—when boys are more prepared for adolescence, are encouraged by their mother to detach, and are given more freedom, from the very beginning of infancy, to express aggression more openly. Their friends and gangs encourage them further. Likewise, pubertal changes for boys heighten self-assertion and aggression, direct the aggressive energy outward in the service of imposing force and control on others.

The incidence of anorexia nervosa is not the same for males; the frequency for males is one in ten cases. Although there is surprisingly a general agreement on the male incidence (Sreenivasan 1978, Beumont 1970, Hay and Leonard 1979, Davidson 1976, Halmi 1974b, Crisp and Toms 1972, Bruch 1971a), inaccuracy is likely. Female anorexia nervosa is widely recognized today; any teacher and physician can spot it in a girl. If there is any doubt, a change in the girl's menses over a three-month period confirms the diagnosis. Yet a boy can lose weight without getting any similar attention. The only comments made are whether the boy is getting enough rest and food.

Prognostically, males generally fare worse over time than female anorectics and are more heterogeneous in symptomatology. Their eating ranges from total abstention to bulimia and vomiting; they stop eating because of fear of generalized fatness, sometimes mixed with complaints of nausea, distaste for food, loss of appetite, and fatigue. They go through starvation with the same signs and symptoms as the female anorectics, but overall the males tend to be more schizoid and obsessive-compulsive. In a few other respects, they differ from female patients: they are not as uniformly good students, organized and driven, come from perhaps a slightly higher socioeconomic group, have less manifest sexual interests, and have a higher incidence, according to Crisp and Toms (1972), of affective-disturbed relatives. Frequently, anorectic boys display blatant paranoid trends; and, unlike their female counterparts, they acknowledge early on their longing for food. In general, their prognosis is worse than for the female cases in terms of fixed character pathology; and they are much more resistant to treatment, both crisis intervention, long-term psychotherapy, and analysis.

Food refusal and peculiar ideologies about eating, without overt psychosis, are found in males. Hypochondriacal anxieties and preoccupation are more often present. The prognosis for the male anorectic is also guarded in terms of a later exfoliation of symptoms with frank paranoid psychosis. Bruch (1971) agrees with this view, adding that overt schizophrenia is more apt to be masked by anorexia nervosa in the male patient. Dally and Gomez (1979), however, are more optimistic about the prognosis of male anorectics.

Social Class Distribution

The disorder is most common in social classes I and II: the professional and managerial segments of our society, where parental demands and responsibilities are high and readily imposed on children (Fenwick 1889). The earlier the onset of anorexia nervosa, the more apt is the patient's family to be social classes I and II. In this group, academic achievement takes precedence over social and sexual experiences. Many patients' fathers are teachers, doctors, lawyers, successful businessmen, bankers, stockbrokers, certified public accountants, and architects. Mothers often are dieticians, nurses, social workers, and physicians, who work for self-fulfillment, not a second income for the family. Also part of the higher socioeconomic groups are diet consciousness, aversion to carbohydrate foods, body care and concern, higher IQ, and early menarche.

When the disorder occurs in a wealthy family, the parents of the anorectic are particularly less apt to notice the disturbance. In rich families, anorectic behavior may be first apparent to the maids or cook, because they are more involved in the anorectic's dieting. (The anorectic will go with the maid or cook to the local grocery store to make sure all her delicacies are ordered.) In the middle-class family, where there is no cook, she may take over the cooking herself. In social classes IV and V, the so-called "blue collar" families, the incidence of anorexia nervosa is remarkably low. Crisp (1977b), however, has reported cases from social classes IV and V. When a case is found, it may well be an atypical or secondary anorexia nervosa; the psychopathology is more severe, usually starkly sexual. It is usually apparent that the anorectic girl from this background has extreme anxiety in her sexual relationships, usually having been traumatized by rape and other aggressive sexual encounters.

Once thought to be common in Jewish families, the disorder is not ethnically linked with any group, even though it seems more common in subcultures where food, eating, and family solidarity, especially at the dining room table, are important. The association of anorexia nervosa with the "Jewish mother" is disputed by the fact that the incidence of anorexia nervosa in Norway, which has a small Jewish population, is high. (Norway is also, like its Scandinavian and southern neighbors, experiencing an increase in the disorder.) The disturbance is widely found in "WASPdom." However, one is not likely to see patients with anorexia nervosa in a poor black or Hispanic population. In the ghetto, where food is not plentiful, the syndrome is probably replaced by pica and drug addiction.

Intelligence

High intelligence has always been linked with anorexia nervosa. Dally and Gomez (1979) found that in the age range of eleven to fourteen years, 90 percent of their patients had an IQ of 120-plus. Later age of onset, however, was associated with lower IQ's: fifteen to eighteen years, 78 percent; and 19 years or over, 73 percent.

Anorectic girls work hard in school. Examinations are terrifying to them. They drive themselves to academic achievement, but academic performance is much more based on their need to be perfect and pleasing than on sheer intellectual curiosity and the capacity for abstract understanding. Although anorectics get good grades, achievement and aptitude testing not infrequently reveals a disparity between achievement and capacity. Hard work and retentive memory sustain the anorectic well. In mathematics, for instance, the anorectic may learn by rote procedures and methods for solving mathematical problems.

Precipitating Factors

The precipitating factors in anorexia nervosa are only aleatory triggers to the surfacing of symptoms; they are not truly causative. Anorectics are sensitive to parental criticism and negative peer comments. They imagine insults. They cannot tolerate teasing, even with humor, and they take any critical remark in deadly earnest. A failure at school or at work sometimes appears to be a precipitant. Events that require decisions are difficult for anorectics. Menarche, sexual conflicts, and sexual confrontations in adolescence are powerful triggers, for they foster anxiety and regression. Comments about her face being "too fat" may have dire psychological consequences for the potential anorectic. Family snapshots of the anorectic, referring to her as a "cute, chubby baby," are upsetting. Death of a parent, loss through a divorce, or a move to a new neighborhood, with disruption from her close friends, can also be very upsetting to the anorectic. Physical illness of the mother, like a mastectomy with postoperative depression, can set off anorexia in a predisposed adolescent girl. A romantic rejection may plunge a young woman into gorging and vomiting.

Precipitants are apparent in well over 50 percent of anorectics. They are usually traumatic events—painful confrontations or humiliations which open old wounds and challenge her vulnerability to narcissistic injury, break down her resistance to regression, and make her inner dissatisfactions unbearable, inclining her to blame her body for her pain and self-dissatisfaction and forcing her to find a solution to the distress by way of changing both her relationships with her mother and her body through control, mastery, and self-starvation. She attempts to make time stand still with the idea of going back to childhood in size, feelings, and bodily function. She finds herself frozen in time with nowhere to go: no past, no future, and an abomination of the present.

There are anorectics who have experienced traumatic losses—usually of the mother—during adolescence. They rally around the family, like blackbirds making a quorum in a tree, and are disillusioned when they cannot recreate the original family.

§A twenty-five-year-old single woman, Claire, a brooding, redhead, rumpled from sleeplessness, sought treatment after moving from Seattle back home to live with her father and stepmother. Trying to suppress tears, she could not tell whether her tears were of sorrow, fear, shame, or what—perhaps all of them, part of the feelings surging through her like fire. Then she wept, half in fear, half in loss

Her move back to New York entailed leaving her therapist of five years, finishing school, and returning to what had been an unhappy family situation, initially caused by the death of her mother when she was seventeen and made worse by the father's remarriage four years later. From age eighteen, she was anorectic, avoiding all foods to the point that she required hospitalization for a metabolic crisis and intensive psychotherapy.

Claire, returning to her father's home in January, requested twice-weekly therapy, which was continued to the end of July. The content of the treatment was largely focused on anxiety about living with her father and stepmother and being constantly exposed to her hostile feelings toward the stepmother. She repeatedly dreamed of swimming in a tropical lagoon; she would anxiously watch for her father, for she was convinced that she could only escape from the lagoon if her father pulled her out. The treatment material revealed increasing resentment toward the stepmother, partly defensive; and, at the same time, in the transference a great deal of sexual feelings toward the father. Her eating improved. She had reached the weight of 100 pounds and "expected any day to have a menstrual period"; she had been amenor-rheic for eight years. But as July approached and she faced the prospects of her therapist's vacation in August, she became increasingly angry and depressed. Just before the summer vacation, she announced, pursing her lips with disapproval, that she would get in touch with the therapist in the fall after her return from a September vacation. Although feelings of being deserted by her father, as well as the loss of her mother, had been interpreted in July, a negative transference grew. In order to be in control, she had arranged to take her vacation in September; she consciously planned never to come back. When she finally revealed her intent, she rationalized the decision by saying that she wanted to move back to Seattle to her former therapist. Claire, uncomprehendingly, believed that living near her father and step-mother made it impossible for her to continue with the present therapist because her feelings had become "just too real." She was adamant: "I've never known a soul in my family to change his mind."

Clinical Stages in the Syndrome

There are three stages in the clinical evolution of the anorexia nervosa syndrome (Casper and Davis 1977).

It is unusual for anorexia to be the first symptom. Handwriting may turn small and closed in (Beumont 1971). Once compliant and sweet, the incipient anorectic, often plump during latency, now turns a little difficult, is less polite, less considerate, and even becomes argumenta-tive, if not outright abrasive to her parents. Some may show telltale signs of sexual interest, but usually, except for older anorectics, who may leave home, libido seems to disappear. Headaches may be mentioned more in the prodromal phase; eczema and other skin disorders may appear for the first time. Prior to dieting, abdominal discomfort, sometimes even pain, mimicking a surgical condition, may set the stage for dieting.

Prodromal hyperactivity and heightened energy output with no apparent fatigue may occur first but are seldom noticed in the early weeks since the anorectic hides her overactivity and her long hours of school work in ritualistic activities, like calisthenics, skating, or running. Not infrequently, amenorrhea and decreased libido also antedate the symptom of food-refusal and persist, like hyperactivity, beyond the nutritional problems. In the prodromal stage of anorexia, one may find in the patient's history that a year or so before the onset of the anorexia, there occurred a drifting away from peers and increasing isolation from the family. Other early manifestations are a sensitivity to criticism, direction, and suggestion, defended against by a diffuse stubbornness and insensitivity to the effect of their eating behavior and food attitudes on other people. Attitude toward menstruation can become one of horror and rejection (Fries and Nillius 1973). Anxiety and depression, before the progressive loss of appetite, can also be prodromal. Depressive mood is usually mild, but in the older anorectic, suicidal ideation, occasionally even a gesture, may occur. The depressed ego, faced by what seems like an impossible adolescent developmental task, reactivates a profound sense of helplessness, experienced in the past when the anorectic was incapable of providing for her essential needs. The early signs of ego depression are often transient and can be associated with a passing sense of unreality. She may feel bored or different from other teenagers, or she may complain to her parents that she is lonely. Feelings of helplessness and uselessness are common. In over half of anorectics, there is prodromally an increasing awareness of irritability. Premenstrually, they are often aware of aggressive, violent fantasies, making them fearful of impulsive acting out.

The second stage is basically that of self-starvation, with or without bulimia and vomiting, and regressive behavior. This stage commences before the patient sees a consultant. Dieting or gorging-vomiting is underway, and her peculiar attitude to food and eating, as well as the relentless pursuit of thinness (and an ideal weight)—the basic diagnostic features of anorexia nervosa—is ingrained in the anorectic's whole fabric of life and relationships. Untruthfulness about eating—really a kind of defensive self-deception formed by fear—and subterfuges, adroit methods of deceiving parents and physicians about caloric intake, are common. Food is hidden in handkerchiefs, paper bags, purses, pockets, pillow cases, lockers at school, fed to the dog, thrown out the window, and flushed down the toilet. Even if confined to a hospital bed, the anorectic can find a place to hide her postprandial vomitus. In the initial part of this stage, the anorectic claims that she feels fat; as the stage becomes more entrenched, she talks about being "not thin." She prepares larger and larger meals for her family as she herself eats less and less—or vomits more and more. Finally, a territorial battle with mother occurs. What she does eat now she dusts with condiments to dull taste and numb hunger, then cuts the food up into tiny pieces to prolong eating time. Cheese, fresh fruits, and vegetables become the mainstay of her diet, with occasional fish, bits of meat, nuts, and pickles. Food fads are common: salads, carrots, cabbage, radishes, lemon rinds—much like the fads of pregnant women.

The effects of starvation can overshadow the anorectic symptoms, even at this stage. Restlessness and hyperactivity may increase as subnutrition worsens. Paradoxically, the patient shows little concern over her cachectic appearance; but, as subnutrition becomes more severe, and the end stage of cachexia is approached, she may show some awareness of her gaunt appearance. Saliva may be retained with dribbling when she speaks, so as to arouse annoyance and disgust in her family, reduce hunger, and resist swallowing food. She may be weak, stumbling, and on the verge of physical collapse. No longer can she deny what is happening to her. At this time, she may be receptive to comments about her wasted body; she may even reach out to the hospital staff and therapist for help; or, as happens in a high percentage of patients, she may remain steadfast in her omnipotent belief that she can conquer and transcend death.

The third stage of anorexia nervosa is post-starvation, after nutrition has been restored. Hospitalization and medical care have usually been terminated; and the patient, for a variety of reasons, often does not continue therapy. The family may oppose further family and individual therapy, or the anorectic will use discharge from the hospital as a resistance against continuing treatment. She usually continues to be anorectic in attitude toward food, eating, thinness, and an ideal weight, finicky about relationships, and anxious about sexuality. She still cannot tolerate strong feelings. She may remain at a low weight, go through a painful stage of chubbiness, or maintain her weight at an appropriate level. Nevertheless, she continues to lack self-esteem, tends to be self-effacing, fearful of aggression, determined to be perfectionistic and controlling. She is timid in her social and work relationships and seeks situations where there is always a chance for escape. Her relationship with men, more often than not, is tenuous; and in about 50 percent there is a likelihood of marriage and sometimes children. Sexual gratification is disturbed by anxiety and depression. This stage of anorexia nervosa requires continued psychotherapy and, when indicated, psychoanalysis (see chapter six).

The need for treatment of anorexia nervosa through the third stage is evident in this brief vignette.

§Her head tipped back, determined, arrogant, Sally, a twenty-seven-year-old married computer science specialist, came for consultation because of her uncertainty over whether she should remain in New York with her husband or return to Texas where her family lived. Her cold, gray eyes made her hardness metallurgical. She paused, from time to time, but as she told her story, it seemed, whatever her inner question or doubt was, that she had already decided.

After graduating Phi Beta Kappa from college, Sally had gone home for two years in order to take care of her ailing mother. During the stay in Texas she met her husband, and after her mother's death decided to marry him. They moved to New York to pursue their respective careers. After two years in New York, she felt alienated from her husband, was disinterested in sex, and decided to lose weight by going on a diet. Determined, she saw herself as a kind of machine, needed by the world. She tried to achieve this goal, but she began to binge frequently, vomiting after every evening meal. She increasingly thought that she had "to do something."

Although Sally felt some love for her husband—she would pat him like a wet dog—she no longer cared for his presence. She found herself more aware of her mother's death, reminded by frequent memories of the last few years and of the good times she had spent with the mother during her childhood. At the same time, she was more in touch with her anger toward her father, "a vulgar, obese man," retired from his "blue-collar" job. He spent most of his time "just lounging around and eating everything." During the consultation, Sally, her face alight with hatred, revealed that she had been in treatment for two years, broken off therapy because of frightening, aggressive impulses toward the therapist and now was seeking consultation only to face the question of whether she would be lonelier in New York or Texas.

Looking down, face flushing, she disclosed that while caring for her terminally ill mother, she had found the latter's demands unending and her father's reluctance to help her inexcusable. It was at this time she became anorectic. In treatment then, her nutrition was restored, and she lost her concern about food and eating. She then stopped treatment, never believing half of what the therapist said, alarmed that she was feeling increasingly angry with her therapist, was giving him a good going-over every session, "for no reason at all."

When the therapist told her that he could not advise her on this question of where to live, she was incensed and refused to return. Her husband later called, saying that his wife had left him and the city and intended to stay in Texas. He had decided to "let her divorce him."

Incidence

Although there is a heightened diagnostic awareness of anorexia nervosa, an absolute increase in the incidence of the disorder has occurred in the United States, Great Britain, Japan, and continental Europe (Crisp, Palmer, and Kalucy 1976, Nishimura et al. 1979, Kendall et al. 1973, Duddle 1973). In Scandinavia, the increase is fivefold with similar figures for northeast Scotland and southeast London. The disorder seems to be more common in Puerto Rico in the upper middle-class. Although there is clinical consensus about the increases, statistical data to support these epidemiological impressions are limited. Incidence figures in one survey are in the order of 1.6 to 0.66 new cases per 100,000 population a year; 0.24 to 0.61 per 100,000 population in another study. Theander (1970), having evaluated ninety-four anorectic women hospitalized in Sweden over a thirty-year interval, found 3.1 new cases per year from a population of 1.3 million: an incidence of 0.24 per 100,000 population. From 1951–1960, he noted a rise of cases with an incidence of 0.45 cases per 100,000 population. These figures, of course, include only hospitalized cases. Nylander's study (1971), also done in Sweden but including mild cases not hospitalized, concluded with a prevalence figure of one in 150 adolescents. Figures for Scotland are 0.61 per 100,000 population. Prevalence figures in London are in the range of one severe case for every 200 school girls and one new severe case for every 250. Crisp, Palmer, and Kalucy

(1976) believe that the incidence of anorexia nervosa is higher. Among English school girls aged sixteen to eighteen, they found that the incidence in girls in private schools was 1 percent, in public schools one in 550. Dally and Gomez (1979) estimate that about 1 percent of bright girls, eighteen years of age or older in western countries, have mild forms of anorexia nervosa, lasting up to twelve months and then remitting spontaneously. It is doubtful whether any epidemiological study of anorexia nervosa has accurate statistics; the incidence is probably higher, especially if nonstarving gorger-vomiters are included (McAnarney and Hoekelman 1979).

The fact that anorexia nervosa is increasing is incontestable and baffling. Not only is it increasing in its incidence, but it also seems more common in social classes III and IV. In the United States, as well as parts of Europe, parent-patient organizations have formed, like the Anorexia Nervosa Aid Society[2] founded in England in 1974 and now organized in Ireland as well as parts of the United States. The reasons for the increased incidence of anorexia nervosa are not clear. Certainly, it is not simply due to an increased recognition of the disorder, a greater tendency to admit patients, better record-keeping, or improved statistical and computer methods for its detection and identification. It has been suggested that greater availability of food and better nutrition over the last fifteen years in the more affluent countries of the world are important factors. Food no longer is something a family directly works for; it is an assumed "given." No longer is hunger to be feared; now abundance and overeating are the dangers. An increasingly early onset of menarche in Western society is perhaps another factor. (The age of menarche in white girls in Western culture has decreased from 16.5 years to 12.5 years in the last 125 years. Mean weight, however, has remained constant.) Children reared in more affluent cultures are apt to be pushed more quickly into adulthood. Middle-class families make more parental and social demands on their children. Developmental issues of separation-individualism and autonomy are more difficult to negotiate in our society, where precocious growth, premature stimulation, repeated early separations, and increasing responsibility go hand in hand. It is clear that there are psychosocial forces in Western culture that favor the syndrome, as in Japan, where Westernization has apparently increased the incidence of anorexia nervosa.

2. Anorexia Nervosa Aid Society, Inc., 101 Cedar Lane, Teaneck, NJ 07666.

Increased Incidence: A Decadal Change

It is difficult to assess what factors are responsible for the increase in anorexia nervosa. The Western madness about slimness is good soil for food-phobic obsessional characters, and pressure on women to compete with men are important forces behind the increased incidence of anorexia nervosa. But Western societal emphasis on slimness and beauty, as well as the changing female role, cannot wholly explain the phenomenon. Nor can our society's increase in discretionary income.

The anorectic's situation is a mystery to people, a fascination to adults, just as is the adolescent's unhappiness, her enigmatic protest against the experiences of childhood. Being a teenager, for many, is as meaningful as winding one's watch. The media also identifies with the anorectic's Angst; it glorifies it in quasi-existential terms. For example, Anatole Broyard (1980), in reviewing Rebecca Joseph's novel, *Early Disorder* (1980), adds to the mystification of the anorectic's struggle: "She is sad without really knowing why" ... "the pathos of being" ... "a protest against the condition of childhood." It is chic—intellectual, sensitive—for a teenager, secure in the relative affluence of middle-class life, to feel uneasy, to wonder about the interface between herself and her family, to strive toward transcending the everydayness of her life and be a twenty-first century martyr. What adolescent worth her intellectual salt, caught in the struggles of a blossoming sexuality, dissonant, disparate parts of herself pushing for separation and autonomy, would not be tempted to hide her developmental disorder under the mask of profound ignorance, behind a wall of Satrean rhetorical questions?

It is apparent that our society and culture have changed in the last two decades. New forces now strongly operate. These changes have taken place in those parts of the Western world where anorexia nervosa is more common (Lasch 1978, Glick 1979). Whether these transformations in society and culture are directly related to the increase in the prevalence of anorexia is uncertain. But it is apparent that people, in general, feel these forces and respond to them. What are these forces?

People are no longer able to deny death and now are preoccupied with its eventuality; societal and cultural institutions are no longer trusted; societal and group ego-ideals do not mitigate a sense of insecurity; relationships are shallow and open to exploitation; narcissistic therapies have replaced religion in celebration of the self; and, believing that they and society have no future, parents ignore the needs of their children and struggle to find themselves in marriages that soon dissolve. These factors and others blur the boundaries of the self, make people feel vulnerable to passivity, loss of control, and liable to intrusion, invasion, and control by vague, outside forces. Anorectics dread obliteration by the outside world—a fear represented by food.

In many respects, anorexia nervosa has parallels with running and the recent explosion of interest in physical fitness and survival. Both have captured the interest of the media, which, one suspects, may be responsible for the increased numbers in both the eating disorder and the sport. The anorectic is glorified in newspapers, magazines, TV, movies, and books, just as is the long-distance runner. And both draw their energies from our society and culture (Branch and Eurman 1980).

The popularity of running and physical fitness is symptomatic of the changes in our society and the emergence of a prominent ego-style (Milvy 1977). In addition, some of the motives behind running and the behavior of runners are similar to those of anorectics (Sours 1979a). Everybody is running these days, perhaps 25 million, from Alice Cooper to Mayor Ed Koch, on streets, in parks, along motel hallways and airport runways. Some run for health benefits and physical and mental alertness, knowing very well that their life is really one of bedrest with bathroom privileges. Others run for companionship out of the need to relate to other people; and some run to be with the current fad—while at the same time merchants dash for the dollars. But many run for a sense of survival, self-realization, and autonomy (Morgan 1978).

The rhythm of strenuous, repetitive activity indicates for these runners a metaphoric journey to independence or a chance to "be born again" and overcome alienation. Rejection of this certified self-help nostrum, some say, shows a yearning for the grave, or an indication of intractable lassitude and terminal mental flabbiness. Like a teenager, the runner thinks that he is supposed to endure agony without asking himself why he should; and, furthermore, he believes that running must dominate his life. At any time, he may preach the running gospel with annoying hyperboles, stretch against a tree or wall, or prop up a building. If this runner is not gaunt—well under 150 pounds—he is out of shape, indeed fat, not moved by the drive for the "body-perfect" or the desire for unending strength and endurance. For him, running is part of life's survival course, a test of body, mind, and self. The run is essential to his sense of security and well-being, as well as an anodyne to his pain of everydayness and his feelings of futility and purposeless-ness. As a runner once put it, "Without the run, we become engulfed in an extreme sense of guilt and shame and exhibit tension and strange outbursts of tension because of excessive energies." We are told that running becomes a habit, a daily event that requires no planning. "Automatically, at a certain hour the body starts changing its clothes and tells the mind it's going running. I have no control over the process."

Although the "running high" is ill-defined, it is supposedly an experience of every runner who has gone beyond initial release of tensions (Greist et al. 1978, Morgan 1978, Milvy 1977). Skeptics call it hypoxia; those in the drug culture hope it is a release of morphinelike substances from the brain. Those more spiritual call it a mystical unity with the surroundings, a transcendental peak of great pleasure with feelings of boundless endurance and mental acuity. The body becomes the object of its own sensuality, and aggression forgets its object and is dissipated in solipsistic, repetitive activity. Others prefer to refer to the "high" as a Zen experience, in which visual perception changes, colors run together, and thought patterns shift into a fluid, more free-form, creative style resembling, they hope, the approach to primary process thinking and the promise of creativity. "It was like I'd just gotten a jolt of morphine, a warm rush all over," one runner reported. "I felt I could run forever."

A mystical self-awareness and heightened self-direction occur, ac-cording to many runners (Shainberg 1976, Altshul 1978, Bahrke and Morgan 1978). Some report a religious experience and view it as essential to the new life of the "new me." One runner described it: "For humanity to survive, it will have to invent a new religion. A religion has been invented. It is the religion of the runner." But for the more ambitious and self-directed, running is an indulgence of the self and what it can become. It can never, for them, be a religion, for religion implies a belief in a force bigger and better than any person can be. Nevertheless, for some, running is a cult that draws people together, but without the malignant magnetism of a cult leader.

For many runners, running is a kind of psychotherapy (Kostrubala 1976, G. Sheehan 1977), a cleansing experience through the psychic pores, or a cosmic laxative, a natural psychotherapy which "unjams the time locks on the past," heightens both inner and outer sensory experiences, evokes memory and plays out fantasy; it makes one more accessible to deeper emotions. The self is transformed into a new consciousness (Perry and Sacks 1978, Peretz 1978).

The popularity of running has astounded even professional runners. There has been an "Americanization" of running, with all the energy and drive the obsessional character can bring to an activity and purpose. We can also attribute the popularity to the self-centered mood of the nation, the unabashedly narcissistic attitudes that now permeate our culture and provide a life style for people. This contemporary narcissistic wave is attested to by self-help manuals, warnings against passive wishes, like *Looking Out for Number One* and *Pulling Your Own Strings,* documents obvious enough in their encouragement toward self-assertion, self-fulfillment, and sexual gratification without guilt or shame.

This spirit has bred a new elite, the long-distance runner and marathoner. These are runners who are interested in more than being simply fit (Little 1979). They want to be in competitive shape—and totally sure of body and mind. They search for perfection, try to project a physical self which fulfills an ego-ideal. They run to be at the top of the game, where everything perfect will fall into place. They long for days of perfection on the road. They must feel special. Passivity cannot be tolerated. As George Sheehan (1978) says, "We need that feeling if we are to go it alone. We need the support of self-esteem, of a positive self-image, of feeling ourselves worthy. We need some way of being special." If the runner can maintain a sense of being special, he has a secret to support him in societal isolation. As another runner said, "Without running, life has no meaning, no purpose, no way to supremacy." Long distance runners look to power and control, to be "a runner moving in a slow-motion universe in absolute control." Competitively, they want to increase their speed, do a sub-three marathon and perhaps someday the "perfect marathon." Their drive toward the inner goal of perfection is private, something people often cannot understand. Only professional dancers (Druss and Silverman 1979), figure skaters, Olympic swimmers—and anorectics—can understand this inner drive (Morgan et al. 1972).

The body must be perfect; it must be controlled and denied sensuous pleasures. Only by control and mastery can the runner get beyond pain and boredom to a transcendental state filled with the pleasure of closeness with an omnipotent ideal. These satisfactions take primacy over instinctual oral and genital pleasures and nullify the pain of intensive training, dieting, self-denial, and asceticism. These narcissistic satisfactions become habituating; the runner must strive for a better time before his pleasure begins to pall, just as the abstaining anorectic must repeatedly attempt to reduce calories. If the runner is forced to give up running, a sense of loss ensues with increasing tension and dissatisfaction with himself, like the anorectic who must relinquish her starvation and return to everyday eating and the threat of a fat body out of control. Like anyone aspiring to perfection—be it composer, figure skater, ballerina, or anorectic—the distance runner lives for his ego-ideal, for the moment when he might be "bathed in a column of white light," and when the sense of passage of time and distance is lost and he passes out of his body into timelessness.

Running, like fasting and starvation, narrows the distance between what the runner is and what he can be, between the ideal self and the actual self, between aspiration and reality. For some, running is a means to divine perfection, a way whereby a transformation of self can occur, a means that will enable one to be left alone with the self and experience the body and self as a separate, ultimate reality.

People must play out old childhood traumas and impairments in object relations around which they have over the years organized their character structure. Attempts at the realization of the "perfect image" is one "solution" for the anorectic, the runner, and many other individuals in our society, to childhood feelings of worthlessness and inadequacy. But regrettably a solution to an old trauma usually results in a repetition of the trauma—a frantic and abortive try at "getting it right this time." As Solzhenitsyn reminds us, he who is born to the cage returns to the cage. The long-distance runner cannot run it out. Perfection is no cure for pain—for either the runner, the anorectic, or anybody else. Narcissistic restitutive efforts are maladaptive; they do not correct distortions in the sense of physical and mental well-being, when distorting defects occurred early in the formation of the self.

Will and Power

The anorectic's determination is a caricature of will. She feels that she must control sensual enjoyment and delight, while at the same time, because of the heightened emotions of adolescence, she fears her secrets will be easily detected—her furtive glances, sensuous feelings and impulses—and her private self, on the edge of being, will be revealed with all its desires. In addition, she believes she must push away from the mother of her childhood and establish herself as independent, outgoing, resilient—able to put herself aside from the mother as a way of being-in-the-world. But, at the same time, faced with the glimmerings of sensuous, genital feelings, she finds herself longing to return to her mother for solace and guidance. She protests against the condition of childhood. Maybe her life was too good; maybe she is in the throes of her being. She will nourish the self on an expanded diet of will by becoming a virtuoso of power politics.

Usually the anorectic feels that there is little she can do in facing her uncertain adult future except to deny her needs, remove any suggestion of telltale plumpness and hints of burgeoning sexuality. She hopes to create a situation whereby her mother will continue to be responsible for her; and, at the same time, be challenged, as she has never been challenged before, by the starvation of her daughter and the possibility of her death.

The anorectic struggles against feeling enslaved, manipulated, and exploited. She believes that she has not been given a life of her own. She wants to establish a survival system. Her goal is power, expressed by a grand gesture which gets its energy from the fact that it is difficult to stop anyone from starving herself. She wants to avoid any kind of accommodation to the demands of others, contrary to the compliant, sweet, posture she maintained in her earlier childhood. She treats her body as though it were a threatening entity which, like a demon, needs to be controlled at all times. As her flesh falls away, her soul is revealed, made free again, given shape and nourished by a diet of primitive anger thinly disguised by a falsely appealing, chic narcissism masquerading as Puritanism.

§Brigette, a twenty-two-year-old, languorous French woman, called for a consultation two days after she had received her Bachelor of Arts degree from a university in Quebec. When she came to the consultation, she was dressed as though hiding from someone: a shapeless brown-checked dress, a stained down vest of several winters' vintage, old white wool socks, and L. L. Bean rubber boots well-worn at the heels—all of which, unsightly as her dress was, took little away from her beauty. She immediately commented, with a breathy voice and flaring nostrils, that, now out of college, she was alarmed at the prospect of an unstructured life and "being at the mercy of her mother," who lived in Paris. While at college, Brigette had been able to avoid the mother's scrutiny by spending one year abroad at Cambridge and her summers in Scandinavia, where she worked for an architect. Her relationship with her mother had always been tortured in that the mother "found nothing good at all about her," a tendency, which, in her memory, went back to the age of five when one day her mother looked at her and said that she was turning into a "barrel." Since that time, Brigette had been preoccupied with her weight, furious that she was not "tall and angular," like her mother, who was considered—among the "European beauties"—a fashion designer and "world-recognized authority on beauty and elegant living." The young woman's relationship with her mother throughout her life had been marked by numerous separations, unexpected disconnections, unsavory disputes, and painful interventions by third-party negotiators and go-betweens, who attempted to work out reconciliations.

There had been ten nannies for Brigette up until the age of five. At age eight, she was "sent off to Switzerland" where she remained until age eighteen at a Catholic boarding school. Now that she had graduated from college, her mother believed that she had the prerogative to arrange "the rest of her life." In the last two years, after having struggled all her life with trying to control her weight by avoiding carbohydrates, Brigette had taken to gorging and vomiting. These symptoms first occurred at the time when one of her mother's previous husbands contacted the patient at school. Over the next several months, he presented himself as a kindly, adopting father—not the distant, solitary, quasi-humanized person she once knew—but soon he let it be known that he wanted to have an affair with her. Brigette was very upset and felt disgusted; and, at the thought of her mother's anger, she felt guilty, even though she had rejected the man.

After the first consultation session, Brigette returned home to her mother's Boston apartment to find that her friend, whom she had asked to come over for the afternoon, was not there. She went into a panic, felt totally abandoned, got into bed and spent the rest of the day "hiding under the bedclothes." The following day, she was interviewed by a journalist because of her mother's notoriety. During the interview she referred to her mother as a "perfectionist," saying to herself at the same time how malicious and coy her mother was. After the interview,

Brigette met a friend who made an offhanded comment about the girl's remark to the journalist, suggesting that he might distort the comment and enrage her mother. She suddenly felt terror; her mother would see the remark as a "slur" against her. Vague thoughts of suicide were replaced by ones of an imminent catastrophe. She abruptly left her lunch companion, ran into the street to hail a taxicab, and rushed to look for her mother only to discover that she had left for the weekend. She went to the kitchen and then "ate her way through the refrigerator." She spent a half-hour in the bathroom, vomiting up "her insides" and thinking what a ghost of a monster she carried in her guts.

Another anorectic portrays the intensity of the adolescent daughter's flight from the controlling mother.

§A mother requested consultation for her sixteen-year-old daughter, Vicky, away at boarding school, because of her concern that the daughter was interested "only in fags, drugs and sex." Constantly preoccupied with such worries, the mother, a former singer now married to an investment banker, added that she had given her daughter "too much freedom" and now "wanted to reel her in."

With dignified disapproval, Vicky's mother claimed that her daughter hated to be a woman, loathed having hips and breasts, wanted to look like a linear mannequin, and made a point of not shaving her legs to deny her femininity. She had told her mother, with incautious words on more than one occasion, that she was afraid "men would rape her" and, for this reason, preferred the company of homosexuals who were "nice and sweet" to her. Vicky's biologic father, a jazz drummer, had died when she was twelve years old; and the mother had remarried to her present husband, a much older man who hardly spoke to Vicky. At boarding school, Vicky, always sensing the mother's presence—her sea-blue eyes, steady, unblinking, forever watching, scrutinizing, spying—made every attempt to be unpopular with the headmaster and teachers, except for her housemaster whom she "adopted" with the hope of being part of his family.

The mother was also concerned that Vicky had recently made friends with a young man at boarding school; and, although still presumably fearful of sexuality, she had "gone on the pill" and was having intercourse with him. Vicky had complained to her family doctor, matter-of-fact, that oral birth control pills were making her "feel more feminine"; and, in addition, they made her heavier. The thought had occurred to her that she might be pregnant, but she soon "forgot" it. She had put herself on a diet. In the last month, she had lost eighteen pounds, and, for the first time in her life, she appeared gaunt and angular—iron nerves. Her mother had read in *Vogue* an article on anorexia nervosa, concluded that Vicky was a "victim," and hoped to "nip it in the bud" as soon as possible.

Starvation

For the self-starving and mixed anorectic, dieting is a compulsive force which rules her life while at the same time giving her a false sense of pride and superiority. She is flattered to get attention, feels intoxicated by her bogus success, experiences heightened senses, sometimes hyper-acusis and hyperacuity, and is exhilarated by indefatigable hyperac-tivity. Her adamant pursuit of thinness produces a pleasurable affect, the "high of fasting"—comparable to the "high" of running—which intensifies denial by mitigating the pain of the struggle. Starvation, at least before physical collapse occurs, heightens mental alertness and concentration, reinforcing the anorectic's determination to diet. She may eat only baby food—and then only surreptitiously. And, if forced to eat with her family, she may furtively give it to the dog or hide the food in her napkin.

Much of the behavior of the self-starving anorectic is similar to that of people deprived of food in famines and concentration camps. Starving people toy with what food they have and make up bizarre and distasteful concoctions which they eat with seeming tolerance. They may use large amounts of spice and salt, add vinegar to their food, or put mustard on lettuce to make the food less appealing and longer-lasting. They hope to stretch out the remaining food they have. Anorectics, on the other hand, sprinkle condiments on their food or soak food, like meat and fish, in vinegar to make it less appealing and appetizing. They hope to dull taste and hunger. The prisoner of war, like the anorectic, fantasizes what he will eat when "it is all over." The anorectic ruminates over food, is narcissistically absorbed in her appearance and relationships, and acts infantile and selfish, in much the same way as a laboratory-induced starvation subject.

There is some variation in an individual's vulnerability to subnutri-tion and starvation. The psychological effects of starvation depend upon the individual's intrinsic personality structure, the susceptibility to increasing isolation, past traumatic experiences, and the extent and duration of starvation. Starved people experience a temporal distortion, most notably in terms of the future. The anorectic, like the starving person, knows only a vague passage of day and night. Time moves fast for the self-starving anorectic, but her days seem endless if her denial of hunger falters. Hunger can make her feel that she is under the influence of a drug. Wooziness, dizziness, and syncope of starvation heighten narcissistic oceanic and fusional feelings; space and time are altered. The anorectic is unaware that many of her emotional reactions and affective states stem from her hunger and starvation. Depersonalization, splitting of the ego, gross overestimation of body size, and defects in ego-functioning in the self-starving, borderline anorectic are exaggerated by starvation. In fact, often the pathology of the severe anorectic cannot be fully assessed, particularly ego-disorganization, until starvation is corrected. If the starvation has persisted over a period of years, its overall effects are hard to separate from the patient's basic personality disorder.

The biological effects of starvation are mainly known from naturalistic and clinical studies of victims of war, famine, concentration camps, survivors of the Leningrad siege, and sufferers from protein-calorie malnutrition (Silverstone 1975, Brozek, Wells, and Keys 1946). The experimental studies of Ansel Keys and his associates, in 1950, also provide a great deal of information. Starvation leads to apathy, fatigue, depression, loss of libido, withdrawal, ruminations and preoccupation with food, as well as fantasies and dreams about food and eating. But in profound starvation dreams and fantasies seem to wane. Starving people continue to be hungry; hunger is rarely lost even at the time of death. Their need for food may lead to dishonesty and violence. In starvation, there is a coarsening of human feeling, with indifference to the moods and sentiments of others. Irritability and labile moods—even occasional psychotic, confusional states are superimposed on fatigue, weakness, and apathy. Indecision about trivial matters occurs with loss of drive and spontaneity. The starving person is sluggish, lethargic, manifestly depressed, and weak.

Metabolic adaptation occurs in starvation: the metabolism of the body changes to cope with starvation by conserving energy. Blood pressure, cardiac output, and body temperature fall (Freyschuss, Fohlin, and Thoren 1978, Davies, Fohlin, and Thoren 1977). All metabolic pathways unessential to the maintenance of life are closed down. Fat stores are called on with the appearance of ketone bodies in the urine. Famine edema, mostly in the lower legs, a reflection of an increase of extracellular fluid, occurs for reasons not clear.

When starvation persists for long periods—whether it is protein or carbohydrate depletion—functional changes occur, as part of a conservation-survival adaptation. Starving people, like anorectics, experience constipation because of slowdown of the gastrointestinal tract. This starvation effect on the bowel-conscious anorectic may panic the patient into taking increasingly large doses of laxatives; compulsively, she may even turn to digital removal of feces. Anorectics can also be besieged by hunger and diarrhea, the latter caused by the intestines being unable to compensate for demands of normal digestive work. Nocturia may also occur in starvation. Not only are the clinical features of starvation similar to those of anorectic self-starvation but also similar are the central and peripheral endocrine changes. There are, however, some differences in protein-calorie malnutrition; growth hormone secretion is increased, not suppressed by glucose, and is inversely correlated with levels of serum albumin and alanine (Isaacs 1979). Functional failure of the hypothalamic-pituitary-gonadal axis results in amenorrhea. Luteinizing hormone (LH) and follicle stimulating hormone (FSH) responses to luteinizing hormone releasing hormone (LHRH) are poor and variable (Isaacs 1979). This finding, however, is not fully explained by the malnutrition. Amenorrhea may persist from six months to six years after starvation. In severe, prolonged starvation congestive heart failure can occur. Circulation time is prolonged, and cardiac output is decreased. Tachycardia takes place in the terminal stage of starvation. Death may occur from congestive heart failure. Cardiac arrhythmias have also been reported in starvation, as well as cardiac arrests; but these anorectics are largely bulimic vomiters of long-standing. And excessive use of cathartics further complicates their electrolyte imbalance, increasing the likelihood of disturbances in cardiac rhythm.

There are some differences between the starvation of anorexia nervosa and that of concentration camp victims and laboratory subjects (Casper and Davis 1977). The starving anorectic continues to be active, restlessly hyperactive, until near the end of her life. Anorectics can suppress hunger more readily than can victims of starvation. In anorexia there is less muscular weakness and atrophy, whereas in simple starvation there is considerable atrophy of the muscles as protein is broken down. Shrinkage of the breasts is severe in starvation. A high incidence of severe infections and vitamin deficiencies is found in starvation states. Vitamin deficiencies and infections are rare in anorexia nervosa. Delayed return of menstruation and disturbances of fat and carbohydrate metabolism in anorexia nervosa reflect, according to Crisp (1978a), "the more constitutional aspects of the disorder such as premorbid obesity." On the other hand, anorectics with binging and vomiting have a higher level of metabolic and endocrine function than the self-starvers; their menses and fertility return at a lower than usual body weight.

Hunger and Its Vicissitudes

Hunger of the anorectic is present at most times, even increased on occasions (Mayer 1972, Ceaser 1979, Garfinkel 1974, Mawson 1974, Kestemberg and Kestemberg 1972). If she did not worry about weight gain, she would eat with unqualified pleasure; abdominal discomfort would not be a complaint to the extent it is. She feels all the possible components of hunger: gastric contractions, a sense of emptiness, weakness, fatigue, cold, and sometimes nausea and headache, if severely hungry. In her desperate need to become thinner, she tries to deny her hunger. Her appetite also must be held in check at all times. Appetite also persists; it is increased by hunger and gratified, in part, by reading about food and cooking for others. Often, the anorectic's preoccupation with food makes it difficult for her to separate her food and eating preoccupations from appetite and hunger. Severe borderline anorectics complain of a sense of fullness when they eat with others, as though eating their food as well, or when simply thinking of a fat person. They fear that other people's eating will result in weight gain for them; they will be invaded as though by a mass of fat. Although they know intellectually that the fears are irrational, these thoughts nevertheless preoccupy them.

Appetite stimulants do not help in anorexia nervosa. Anorectic patients report that marijuana increases hunger and appetite; and partly for that reason, they avoid marijuana or hashish. Except for alcoholic anorectics (Halmi and Loney 1973), they tend not to be smokers, even though one might expect that they would smoke to decrease hunger and satisfy oral cravings. But, again, they dread invasion and control.

The anorectic is truly hungry but tries to displace her hunger. She plunges into anorexogenic activities. She may direct her attention to feeding others in the hope of diminishing her hunger. Any cook is aware that hunger wanes when a person spends a lot of time in the kitchen. The self-starving anorectic also assuages hunger by drinking large quantities of fluids, especially diet soda. Or her hunger can be relieved by gorging, followed quickly by vomiting. Hyperactivity can also reduce hunger. After extreme physical activity hunger tends to diminish, as any long-distance runner, swimmer, or cross-country skier knows. Affective states influence hunger. Depression and apathy minimize it, though for some individuals, like the bulimics, depression and anxiety may maximize hunger and appetite. Anxiety over sexual feelings and yearnings can decrease hunger and lead to nausea. This is why anorectics, after a while, may claim with some conviction that their hunger has diminished or ceased. Many anorectics deny their hunger during the day, only to experience it acutely at night. Self-starving anorectics continue their denial during the night, but the bulimics often lose their control. After abstainers have continued their starvation for months or years, their stomach becomes atonic and contracted (Crisp 1967). Hunger is not diminished by these gastric changes, although the capacity of the stomach and its emptying time are reduced (Dubois et al. 1979). Then anorectics use the complaint of "bloating" and "fullness" as an excuse for not eating.

It has been said that anorectics do not experience satiety at the end of a meal. This is true for only some bingers. Anorectics, in general, do not use satiety as a signal to stop eating; they stop when still hungry, knowing, by trial and error and routine and ritual, how much to eat. By eating pretty much the same foods and quantity each day, the anorectic is less influenced by external cues, which, unlike her internal cues to eating and satiety, she feels less capable of controlling.

In anorexia nervosa there is no biological disturbance in appetite regulation, no known neuropsychological or neurophysiological mechanism, singly or in combination, which is disturbed. There is no evidence to support the possibility of a disturbance in the glucostatic mechanism, or a lesion of the ventromedial hypothalmic glucoreceptors. Nothing at this time supports a theory that glucose utilization is impaired, glucagon released in response to a meal altered, or thermogenesis disturbed. Mawson's postulations (1974)—that noradrenaline and dopamine depletion occurs subcortically and results in acetylcholine predominance leading to stimulation of the satiety center of the ventromedial hypothalamus and understimulation of the eating center—have no empirical support. Studying the relationship between taste and eating habits in anorectics, Lacey et al. (1977) found that anorectics do not have a specific abnormality in sucrose sensitivity. Likewise, there is nothing to suggest that the anorectic has a primary disturbance in gastric contractility or emptying time (Silverstone and Russell 1967, Stunkard 1971). There is, in general, a low correlation between gastric activity and the subjective sense of hunger. Balloonkymographic, radiographic, and endoscopic techniques, as well as telemetering capsules and synchronized fluorocinematography, have all been used, with various degrees of success, for research in affectivity and gastric physiology (Barbara et al. 1970). The electrogastrogram (EGG) is another physiological instrument which has been employed in the study of gastric activity, as well as self-perception of body image and function in both obesity and anorexia nervosa. EGG studies have demonstrated that electrogastric activity takes place in either localized areas or throughout the stomach (Coddington, Sours, and Bruch 1964, Coddington and Bruch 1970). Sudden changes in the EGG tracing are seen when the subject experiences anxiety, anger, or pain. It is well known that alteration in gastric secretion, motility, and vascularity is found with anxiety, anger, and resentment. Electrogastrographic research also indicates that electrical, as well as mechanical activity, is altered by affective states. But EGG studies of gastric functions in anorectic patients have not demonstrated a physiological connection between anorexia and gastric function. In general, gastrointestinal research buttresses the clinical conclusion that the anorectic does not truly lose appetite and hunger but merely denies their presence. She convinces herself that she is above basic physical needs, must remain plugged into her body, and ride the fullness of her power.

Physical Findings

The physical findings in anorexia nervosa are the direct result of chronic starvation; like loss of weight, the result of cachexia, they include decreased vascular volume and dehydration and are corrected by refeeding. Physical findings encompass hypothermia, hypotension, bradycardia, bradyphea, secondary amenorrhea, decreased libido, acrocyanosis, skin changes, diminished secretion of sweat and sebum, paronychia, cold intolerance, chilblains, peripheral and facial edema, dehydration, Raynaud's phenomenon, and even gangrene of the finger-tips. Starving patients bitterly resent cold weather; they bundle them-selves in winter like Eskimos, partly to hide their fleshless bones, and move around constantly to generate body heat (Davies, Fohlin, and Thoren 1979). Cold intolerance also ceases after nutritional recovery. (Gorger-vomiters, on the other hand, complain of sweating, breathlessness, tachycardia, "hot flushes and flashes"—an overall sense of heat exhaustion from an extreme binge.) Severe weight loss gives the anorectic a cadaverous appearance, like that of a walking skeleton, a concentration camp victim. Slow pulse is a result of emaciation. Tachycardia, however, may occur with the gorger-vomiters and termi-nal self-starvers, as well as patients on Thorazine. Hypotension is a consequence of starvation, and, although severe, may not be associated with signs and symptoms of orthostatic hypotension. The anorectic loses subcutaneous tissue; and, because her fatty tissue layers disappear, she soon looks vertical, angular, and bony. Yet, breast tissue is pre-served; there is no atrophy of the external and internal genitalia, although in severe chronic cases of anorexia nervosa there can be atrophy, along with endometrial fibrosis and atrophy of the vagina, because of reduced levels of estrogen (Moulton 1942b). Amenorrhea often occurs (Crisp 1978a).

Anorectic skin changes are among the commonest findings. The skin looks dirty, rough, like sandpaper; and it is frequently covered with long, silky lanugo hair, extensively covering the trunk, extremities, face and back. The skin may be blotchy, sallow and dehydrated, thin, scaly, desquamated; sometimes it has a peculiar yellow-orange hue from carotenemia, a result of vitamin A deficiency. The carotenemia pro-duces an orange-yellow hue around the nose, in the folds of axillary skin and on the soles and palms. A brownish pigmentation of the skin and nails may form with severe starvation. Those who eat great quantities of Brazil nuts develop a yellow pigmentation. And sometimes the skin of bulimic patients is hot and clammy, and they develop bounding peripheral circulation, peripheral edema, and abdominal pain. Through vomiting and laxative-induced diarrhea, severe dehydration can occur with life-threatening hypokalemia, even more likely if diuretics have been used. (Profound asthemia and toxic-infusional states can also occur, largely from electrolyte depletion and fluid balance disturbances.) There may be a loss of scalp hair, but the scalp is not glabrous.

Often, the teeth have numerous cavities and show gingival deterioration. The dental deterioration includes enamel dissolution in cases of gorging-vomiting or when there is compulsive consumption of citrus fruits, as well as severe caries due to excessive carbohydrate consumption (Hurst, Lacey, and Crisp 1977, Reinhardt and Reinhardt 1977). Vomiting patients also suffer from lingual-occlusal erosion (perimylolysis); buccal erosions from vomiting and drinking of acid fruits and beverages to relieve dehydration thirst or medication-induced xerostomia are also encountered (Hellstrom 1977).

The hands and the feet look bluish; the nails are brittle. Subcutaneous edema is rare at the time of malnutrition, unless the starvation is extreme and long-lasting with resultant famine edema; but as protein intake increases with the restoration of nutrition, the feet and calves become edematous; there may be evidence of periorbital edema. This is treatment edema. Rarely is ascites found. The anorectic is often hypoproteinemic; and blood studies show an anemia, either iron-deficient or megaloplastic, and a leukopenia with relative lymphocytosis (Amrein et al. 1979). Yet there is no increased infection propensity with leukopenia (Bowers and Eckert 1978, Armstrong et al. 1978, Amrein et al. 1979). Bone marrow studies reveal varying hypocellularity with slight neutropenia to severe pancytopenia (Kubanek et al. 1977, Lampert and Lau 1976). The bone marrow of the cachectic anorectic patient, according to Cornbleet, Moir, and Worf (1977), has an increase in bone marrow and mucopolysaccharide, which may represent a serous fat atrophy rather than an increase in ground substance. Blood coagulation tests in anorexia nervosa are normal, perhaps explaining the low incidence of hemorrhage (Cravetto et al. 1977). But intravascular coagulopathy has been reported (Sutor et al. 1977), and ESR and fibrinogen changes have been noted (Anyan 1974). Signs and symptoms of pancreatitis (Schoettle 1979, Keane et al. 1973) and hepatic and pancreatic dysfunctions (Nordgren and Von Scheele 1977) are found in some patients. There are reports of pneumomediastinum (Donley and Kemple 1978, Brooks and Martyn 1979), subcutaneous emphysema, and pneumomediastinum and pneumoretroperitoneum (Al-Mufty and Bevan 1977). Foot drop from peroneal nerve palsy has been found in anorexia nervosa (Schott 1979, Fowler, Banim, and Ikram 1972). Urogenital malformations in anorexia nervosa have been noted (Halmi and Rigas 1973). Finger clubbing is found in severe purgers (Silk, Gibson, and Murray 1975).

Anorectic physical findings, however, are not always typical.

§A twenty-five-year-old single, unemployed, anorectic woman entered treatment with the complaint that she felt total disgust for her body. The thought of sex could make her wince, sometimes even shake her head as if to drive out painful thoughts. A year previously, because of "a flat chest," Yvonne had gone to a plastic surgeon who had inserted "plastic breasts." She later complained that she seemed to have less pubic hair than other women and also indicated that she was not pleased with the silicone breast implantations.

Physical evaluation by an internist indicated somewhat atypical physical findings for anorexia nervosa. The patient did not have lanugo. Her nipples and areolas were prepubertal. Skull X-rays of the sella turcica, visual fields, and endocrine values were all normal.

Laboratory Findings

The basal metabolic rate (BMR) is 20 to 40 percent reduced. Fasting blood sugar (FBS), extremely low in starvation, is often in the range of 60 to 80 milligrams per 100 cubic centimeters. (Hypoglycemic coma is rare.) FBS rises and falls less sharply in anorexia nervosa. There is a sensitivity to insulin but not to the degree found in pituitary deficiency. The BUN may be somewhat elevated because of increased protein metabolism from starvation or severe dehydration. Polyuria from polydipsia is found (Sundstrom 1977). Oliguria is often present, but the kidneys are usually responsive to water. Nocturia may occur when there is serious starvation. Capacity to excrete a water load is diminished, due to a reduction in glomerular filtration rate (Russell and Bruce 1966). Impaired concentration power is reduced in anorexia nervosa according to Mecklenburg et al. (1974), who found patterns of partial diabetes insipidus in some patients. Vigersky and Loriaux (1977) noted a partial defect of antidiuretic hormone secretion; this suggests a hypothalamic disturbance. Likewise, Aperia, Broberger, and Fohlin (1978) found a concentrating defect, which they relate to a reduced water permeability of the glomerular capillary.

Urinary ketone bodies are found with cachexia. Serum cholesterol levels are elevated for those patients who try to starve themselves to death. Hypothyroidism is not related; high cholesterol food, like cheese, may be responsible (Crisp 1977c) to some degree, as well as biochemical mechanisms not properly understood (Halmi and Fry 1974). Protein fractions are not significantly altered. The gastrointestinal tract shows a slowing of stomach and duodenal activity. Skull X-rays of anorectics reveal a normal sella turcica. X-ray studies of bone growth show that skeletal development is delayed when body weight has fallen enough to stop menstruation (Lacey et al. 1979). Otherwise, X-rays demonstrate absence of subcutaneous fat and reduced muscle mass (Haller et al. 1977). Abnormalities of heart size and rhythm are found in anorexia nervosa, but cardiac dimensions, particularly left ventricular mass, may increase after refeeding, along with an increase in heart rate and blood pressure (Gottdiener et al. 1978). The electrocardiogram shows bradycardia, low voltage QRS complex and T-waves inversed or flattened with ST segment depression, all in the absence of ischemic symptoms. Impaired myocardial contractility has been found (Kalager, Brubakk, and Bassoe 1978, Palossy and Oo 1977, Thurston and Marks 1974).

Water balance also returns to normal after refeeding, although starvation edema may persist for several months. After a few weeks, metabolic disturbances from starvation may become profound with symptomatic epilepsy, a confusional organic brain syndrome, general collapse, chloride-responsive metabolic alkalosis (Warren and Steinberg 1979), potassium depletion, and cardiac arrest. Heart congestion and failure can also occur. (On X-ray, the heart is small and displaced vertically because of the emaciation.)

Abnormal electroencephalographic changes may be found in over half of the cases, especially in gorger-vomiters, even in the absence of epileptic symptoms. Crisp, Fenton, and Scotton (1968) found that 10 percent of their patients had one or more fits, usually following severe vomiting and purging, excessive intake of alcohol, treatment with large amounts of Thorazine, or severe water retention during the first two weeks of treatment for cachexia. The fits were of the grand mal variety. The EEG findings are nonspecific, although some electroencephalographers believe that they may reflect a "neurological dysregulation," correctable by anticonvulsive medication. Anorectic sleep is often disorganized with sleep-time reduced to three hours a night. With loss of weight there is a reduction in both slow-wave sleep and REM sleep, correctable, as is sleep-time, with weight restoration (Lacey et al. 1977). Nevertheless, they claim anorectics wake up alert and cheerful. Hypnotics do not help the disturbed sleep. Sleep EEG studies reveal a gross reduction in slow-wave sleep and REM sleep with a reduction in total sleep time. Awakenings occur without descending REM phases; stages III and IV tend to be diminished.

Endocrine and Metabolic Findings

Biochemical and endocrinological research in anorexia nervosa has continued since Simmonds's endocrine studies in 1914. Chemical techniques in the first half of this century were confined to bioassays of limited sensitivity and specificity. But, nowadays, radioimmunoassays allow fine quantification of hormones; and the synthesis of hypothalamic releasing hormones has furthered refined research methods. Neuroendocrine research now suggests control dysfunctions at the hypothalamic level. Abnormalities in pituitary secretions have been discovered, related to functional impairment of release and release-inhibiting hormones, as well as of feedback mechanisms which control synthesis and hormone release of anterior pituitary hormones. They include follicle stimulating hormone (FSH), luteinizing hormone (LH), luteinizing hormone release hormone (LHRH), plasma growth hormone (PGH), and prolactin.

An abnormally sustained insulin response to intravenous injection of glucose is found in some anorectic patients. Delta-glucose values usually return to normal after refeeding, as does glucose tolerance. For reasons not entirely clear, insulin response can continue at an abnormal level, even after refeeding (Wachslicht-Rodbard et al. 1979, Stephan et al. 1977).

Hypothalamo-pituitary-adrenal function is altered in anorexia nervosa. ACTH secretion is essentially unimpaired. Peripheral metabolism of cortisol is decreased with an increase in plasma concentrations, possibly an effect of reduced T3 levels because of starvation. Hypothalamic control is sometimes abnormal with altered responsiveness to insulin-induced hypoglycemia and changes in the diurnal variations of plasma cortisol—impairments reversed with refeeding and weight gain (Isaacs 1979). The adrenals produce an increased amount of cortisol during sleep (Crisp 1968). Catecholamine metabolism, according to Halmi et al. (1978), is altered in anorexia nervosa. Urinary 3-methoxy-hydroxyphenylglycol (MHPG) concentrations are lower in depressed anorectics and increase with relief of depression. Thyroid functions, including thyroid-stimulating hormone (TSH) and protein-bound iodine (PPI), are unreliable. Thyroid hormone deficiency, mostly T3, is detectable in anorexia nervosa (Croxson and Ibbertson 1977). Refeeding may cause a self-limiting overshoot of T3 levels, producing a clinical picture of mild hyperthyroidism (Moore and Mills 1979). Affected by both dieting and psychological stress, TSH control may be defective, leading to a reduction of T4 secretion. And peripheral conversion of T4 can be changed in anorexia nervosa, but it is reversible with restoration of nutrition and weight (Isaacs 1979).

With starvation, FSH, LH, and gonadal steroid levels are low, and the secretory pattern of LH is prepubertal in type. Pituitary response to LHRH is altered, most markedly, LH levels. Total estrogen, progesterone, LH, and FSH output usually approaches normal after refeeding and weight gain. In some instances, estrogen output, FSH secretion, and LH remain low. Baranowska and Zgliczynski (1979) noted in a young woman with anorexia nervosa dramatic elevations of serum testosterone and estriol concentrations, whereas LH, progesterone, estrone, and estradiol were decreased. Low levels of testosterone have been found in male anorectics (Crisp 1978a). With weight restoration, FSH responds to LHRH, as does LH, initially more slowly, but then, as in puberty, it surpasses FSH (Isaacs 1979). Pituitary gonadotropin, however, shows no consistent rise to normal after refeeding, which once suggested that there was a pituitary involvement in anorexia nervosa. Circadian LH secretory pattern in anorexia nervosa is immature (Katz et al. 1978). It is not apparent to investigators, however, whether decreased gonadotropin levels are caused by continuing poor nutrition, long-sustained effects of weight loss, a defect in the responsiveness of the pituitary gland to hypothalamic releasing hormones, or an impairment in regulation and secretion of gonadotropin-releasing hormones (Jeuniewic et al. 1978, Halmi 1978, Boyar 1978, Vigersky et al. 1976). According to Crisp (1978a,b), continued absence of gonadotropins is found after "target weight" is regained for those anorectics premorbidly obese. Having had a menarchal weight greater than their treatment target weight, having grown fast as obese children, they initially stopped menstruating at a weight greater than the target weight chosen for refeeding. After awhile, these anorectics also regain their menses once proper nutrition has been stabilized over a period of time.

It is clear that anorexia nervosa is not a variant of panhypopituitarism, for the pituitary gland is functionally intact even when the anorectic is extremely cachexic. Clinical findings, however, have raised questions about hypothalamic disturbances in anorexia nervosa (Mecklenburg et al. 1974, Wakeling and Russell 1970). They include disturbances in temperature regulation, abnormal cycling of adrenocortical hormones, faulty water conservation, decreased thyroid stimulating hormone (TSH), partial diabetes insipidus, insulin sensitivity, depressed gonadotropins, decreased gonadosteroid levels, and occasional increase in plasma growth hormone (PGH) and prolactin. Plasma growth hormone secretion is impaired in anorexia nervosa, particularly when starvation is severe. Then high levels of growth hormone occur perhaps because of stimuli affecting the hypothalamus. Elevations of PGH fall with refeeding and weight gain. The fate of prolactin in anorexia nervosa is less certain, although there is some evidence of impaired nocturnal secretion. High levels of prolactin are associated with premorbid obesity and delayed menstruation, falling— with return to a normal body weight (Crisp 1978a).

It is difficult to ascribe a structural defect to these hypothalamic disturbances in anorexia nervosa. These findings, however, are reminiscent of idiopathic hypopituitarism, a disturbance of emotionally deprived children who fail to grow and display symptoms of polyphagia and polydepsia: gorging, vomiting, stealing food, and eating from garbage cans, which was originally thought to be due to a hypothalamic disturbance. These children do not respond to insulin-induced hypoglycemia and have increased gowth hormone levels. Removal of the children to total hospital care eliminates the eating behavior, brings about growth, and a normal growth hormone response to insulin-induced hypoglycemia (Powell et al. 1967, Powell, Brasel, and Blizzard 1976, Neufeld 1979).

Aside from disturbances of water conservation, insulin sensitivity, TSH and gonadotropin release, temperature control, and cyclicity of adrenocorticotropic hormones—all attributed by some workers to a disordered hypothalamic function in anorexia nervosa—other anorectic symptomatic accompaniments are also viewed along organic lines (Katz and Walsh 1978). The stereotypic, rigid, obsessive-compulsive behavior of the anorectic patient suggests, to some investigators, the speculative hypothesis of Parkinson's disease with central dopamine dysfunction (Barry and Klawans 1976, Mawson 1974, Johanson and Knorr 1974). In general, all the physical signs and symptoms of anorexia nervosa have come under investigatory scrutiny, using refined neuroendocrinological and neuropharmacological techniques. Vigersky presents a spectrum of this research in his anthology on anorexia nervosa (1977).

The usual evidence for organicity, however, is lacking in anorexia nervosa: family incidence, frequency of organic stigmata, organic signs on psychological tests, soft neurological signs, or frequent EEG abnormalities. Furthermore, the low incidence of anorexia nervosa in the population, its apparent increase because of cultural-societal factors, the lack of success in the treatment of anorexia nervosa by antipsychotic drugs (strong dopamine blockers), the high female to male sex-ratio, and the occurrence of symptom-substitution after symptom-removal are against an organic etiology.

But in the last few years, the endocrine literature on anorexia nervosa suggests a functional defect in the anterior hypothalamus. The hypothalamic abnormality is, according to some investigators, shown by a defect in the hypothalamic servomechanism in the acutely starving anorectics and by the lack of ordinary cycling in LH secretion essential for menstruation in the nutritionally recovered patients. Deficient secretions of LH, FSH—perhaps subtle defects in connection with TSH and prolactin—have been demonstrated and are thought to be related to deficient hypothalamic secretion of releasing and release-inhibiting hormones and mechanisms controlling synthesis and release of anterior lobe pituitary hormones. It is unlikely, however, that anorexia nervosa is a primary hypothalamic disease; vegetative and endocrine evidence of hypothalamic disturbance is related to starvation and weight loss (Vigersky and Anderson 1977, p. 383). Isaacs (1979) concludes his review of the endocrinology of anorexia nervosa: "The probability then remains that the hypothalamic dysfunction is secondary to a primary psychiatric disorder, either directly or indirectly as a consequence of starvation" (p. 200). Psychic stress, both acute and chronic, affects the subtle and delicate reproductive mechanisms involving hypothalamic control of anterior pituitary function. In addition, starvation causes many of the clinical features of anorexia nervosa, as well as hypothalamic function and hormone metabolism (Hurd, Palumbo, and Gharib 1977, Russell 1977).

A psychobiological developmental theory of anorexia nervosa suggests an updated psychosomatic model (Katz 1975). The proponents of the hypothalamic hypothesis point to the fact that anorexia nervosa is predominantly a disorder of adolescent girls and is, of course, connected with amenorrhea. They acknowledge that nutritional deficiencies and weight loss cause endocrine dysfunction. But it is possible, they think, that a hypothalamic disturbance may be created in the neonatal-infant stage by a mother who, because of her own oral conflicts, is poorly responsive to the child's hunger cues and insensitive to the child's need for food. Perhaps with the onset of puberty, increasing estrogen levels activate a dormant hypothalamic pattern laid down in the early years of the anorectic's life. Estrogen may, in turn, affect the anorectic's eating behavior through its effect on the satiety system of the hypothalamus. The hypothalamic abnormality may also affect the gonadotropin-releasing servomechanism. The supporters of this psychobiological theory believe that the family constellation, intrapsychic conflicts, external stresses of adolescence, hypothalamic disturbance, endocrine dysfunction, and peculiar eating habits may all be part of a new psychosomatic model for anorexia nervosa.

Genetics

There are no clear-cut genetic factors, even among multiple cases of anorexia nervosa in the same family (Halmi and Brodland 1973, Werman and Katz 1975, Debow 1975, Liston and Shershow 1973). No genetic pattern has been found. There are reports of monozygotic twins with anorexia nervosa, but the disorder in these cases seems to be an outcome of family life and developmental deviation (Wiener 1976, Simmons and Kessler 1979, Neki, Mohan, and Sood 1977, Bruch 1969, Nemeth 1977). Twin and adoption studies of anorexia nervosa patients do not indicate any chromosomal genetic pattern; it appears that psychogenetic family experiences are largely, if not totally, responsible for multiple cases within a family (Shafi, Salugeuro, and Finch 1973). Sibling rivalry is often an important factor, as is the passive-assertive fight against parental control and suppression.

The clinical narrative of a monozygotic twin with bulimia and vomiting speaks to these issues.

§Julie, a thirty-year-old divorced advertising executive, first man-ifested the syndrome of anorexia nervosa with vomiting and bulimia at the age of twenty-seven, when her husband left her after seven years of marriage. Markedly ambivalent about her mother and hostile to her identical twin-sister, who always teased her about her adolescent "fat face," she had married, immediately after college, a man who she thought would take care of her. The marriage suddenly broke up after five years, leaving her with a burning loneliness. Two years after the divorce, she began living with a man who indicated intentions of marriage. Gorging and vomiting, present since the time of her divorce, ceased, but returned when he later left her. Early in treatment, she became aware that she dreaded the prospect of her "father dying some day" and feared that she would never be able to hold on to a substitute for him. She felt an odd mixture of youthfulness and decrepitude. Her anxiety, often rising to an intolerable agitation, was relieved by eating, but then she would panic at the thought of being fat "like her mother and sister."

Endocrine speculations on the etiology of anorexia nervosa also arise from studies of gonadal dysgenesis (Turner's syndrome), a genetic abnormality with XO type and XO/XX mosaicism (Walinder and Mellbin 1977, Kron et al. 1977, Halmi and Debault 1974, Theilgaard and Philip 1975). These patients may be at risk for anorexia nervosa in that a few cases of XO gonadal dysgenesis have been found coincident with anorexia nervosa.

Brain Damage and Encephalopathy

There are anorectic patients who continue their self-starvation beyond the third decade because of inadequate psychiatric treatment, or the marked severity of their psychopathology. In their late thirties and forties, these patients are still locked into an engulfing relationship with a parent and look as though they have suffered brain damage.

§An example is that of a lawyer-father, who ensconced his thirty-five-year-old daughter in an apartment near their family home. He visited her daily, often unknown to the mother, to bring her food she might like. She would bite her lips a little, hiding from her feelings—whatever they were at that point—refuse the food presents and press a crumpled handkerchief to her mouth. Over the course of twenty years, Betty had seen a number of therapists, but no treatment was ever pursued beyond a year, usually because the father would not permit it. By the time the patient was thirty-five years old, starvation and anorexia nervosa behavior were fixed; her behavior and mental status indicated an early organic brain syndrome. Often incontinent and confused, Betty was unable to recall recent events, do simple arithmetic, or, in general, manage everyday details of her life. She eventually required custodial hospitalization after her father's death.

Brain damage and encephalopathy from chronic anorexia nervosa remain an unanswered question. Evidence from starvation reports and studies is inconclusive. There are some reports of World War II Norwegian concentration camp internees who appeared to have an organic brain syndrome after their nutrition was restored. British prisoners, however, interned in the "behind the bamboo" prisoner-of-war camps along the River Kwai and in Singapore, were often beaten by their Korean guards, who themselves had been humiliated by Japanese military superiors. For this reason, in studies of Japanese concentration camp victims, it is difficult to distinguish signs of organic brain syndrome secondary to malnutrition from those of head trauma.

Computerized tomography of several anorectics with clinically diagnosed cerebral atrophy confirmed the diagnosis, but follow-up CT studies after correction of starvation showed total return to normal (Heinz, Martinez, and Haenggeli 1977).

Suicide

Suicide is rare in anorexia nervosa; and, when it does occur, it is the refractory and atypical cases who suicide, mostly those who binge and become very depressed. Suicidal gestures and attempts occur mostly in older patients, either as their defense against bulimia fails and they become depressed over the prospects of surrender to mother, or after horrendous bouts of gorging and vomiting. Dally and Gomez (1979) reported that in their series 11 percent of patients fifteen to eighteen years of age and 20 percent of those over nineteen made gestures, mostly overdosages and some wrist-slashings. And suicide following psychosurgery is reported by Crisp and Kalucy (1973) and Russell (1979). But, in general, anorectic patients have no conscious desire to die. In fact, they either believe in an omnipotence so completely that death does not seem possible, or they voice the universal fantasy of rebirth by indicating the certainty of reincarnation—into a perfect body.

§A nineteen-year-old college girl, Janet, noted amenorrhea at the time she left for college. In the last year of high school, she had grown a little heavy, having surrendered to gnawing hunger, which made her wish someone would give her "a good spanking on her bare buttocks." During her first year at college, she dieted and later became a resolute vegetarian. Janet avoided all meat dishes and dreaded thinking about "animals being killed." She continued, however, to eat, about 1500 calories a day, until the following summer when she stopped eating altogether after making a trip to her father's grave. She then became obsessed with her need to eat small amounts of food, sometimes barely an egg for dinner. Her weight was then 106 pounds, but in the next few months it fell to 96 pounds. She dressed in "junior miss" sizes, colorful "mod" outfits which gave her the appearance of a sprightly "will-of-the wisp" little girl. Janet stayed at this weight in spite of pressure from her family; and, six months into treatment, she made several suicidal gestures, which she revealed only to the therapist. About the same time, she started having fantasies about members of her family being killed, daydreams which were at first foreign to her, associated with anxiety and feelings of being abandoned. But later, at about the time of her suicidal gestures, she regarded herself as "murderous" and "not fit to live."

Death

Although death does occur in starvation, the anorectic seldom seems aware of her precarious situation. Until she is engaged in treatment, she does not speak about death. And when treatment is a failure and the anorectic returns home to a hating, rejecting parent, death from starvation becomes a real possibility (Dettmering 1977). From 1 to 10 percent die (Sours 1968, Crisp 1979, Asbeck et al. 1972).

The anorectic sees her body as proof that she is winning the fight against passive surrender to oral needs. To varying degrees, she denies cachexia. Like a child, she may play with the idea of death, pretending that she can disappear from her family through death and then return in some mystical way. The story of Ellen West is an example. Binswanger (1944), an existential phenomenologist, believed that Ellen West saw death as a mystical personification of salvation, a flight from an imprisoned existence, and a justified move toward making an authentic choice. He regarded her anorexia as an attempt to preserve her existence.

The anorectic denial of death is illustrated by the protagonist in Franz Kafka's short story, *A Hunger Artist*. This is a story, set in medieval times, about an anorectic man who traveled from town to town, forcing himself to starve in the town's square. During his periods of starvation, the townspeople would make contributions to him. He would save them for the day when he could end his starvation. Just before physical collapse, he would triumphantly stop starvation, enjoy his rewards, and move on to the next town for another starvation performance. His career, however, was jeopardized by the fact that circuses became popular; he was displaced by the circus lion. Given a job in the circus, he was relegated to a side show where he would starve himself in a cage, usually unnoticed by both management and the public. The latter preferred the lion. As Kafka writes: "They poked into the straw with sticks and found him in it. 'Are you still fasting?' asked the overseer.... 'Because,' said the hunger artist ... 'because I couldn't find the food I liked. If I had found it, believe me, I should have made no fuss and stuffed myself like you or anybody else.' These were his last words, but in his dimming eyes remained the firm though no longer proud persuasion that he was still continuing to fast."

The anorectic may pursue her fast until she goes into a metabolic-electrolyte crisis with a hypokalemic syndrome, resulting in cardiac arrest. Her fast may also end with congestive heart failure or circulatory collapse. The dying anorectic takes on the appearance of "passing out of her body"; her eyes look distant, searching but never making contact, and eventually her eyes are "fishlike," announcing the approach of her death.

§Hilda, an eleven-year-old eighth grader, was referred for consultation because of a marked loss of weight in the last three months. The parents realized that Hilda now weighed 54 pounds, compared to 65 pounds a few weeks before. At camp, she had been discontented with the counselors and unhappy with the food. When she joined her parents at the end of August for a family vacation in Maine, they noticed that she looked thin and pale; yet she maintained her usual impeccable composure. During the family vacation, however, they paid very little attention to her weight because of their marital discord which, during this time, erupted into shouts and accusations of mutual disinterest and neglect of their child. The mother bitterly felt that the father, a professor of sociology, was only interested in his work. The mother, on the other hand, a paleontologist, was at this point in her life devoting only part-time to her career because of her three children.

The parents were not clear initially about Hilda's weight loss. They thought that her weight loss had occurred only in the last few months, but it was apparent that Hilda, a small girl, only four feet ten inches, had been thin all her life and looked undernourished. In October of the preceding year, Hilda had lost her lifelong nanny, a very loving, affectionate black woman who had retired and returned to her home in Detroit. At that time, Hilda was clinically depressed, but her parents thought that it would pass. They recognized that she had lost weight over the summer, but they attributed the weight loss then primarily to her unhappiness at camp and their own marital problems, as well as increased arguing among Hilda and her brothers. She had become more competitive with her older brother, who was her father's favorite.

The parents insisted that she was functioning in everyday life, was a "model" student with prospects of top college performance. She would soon blossom into a rose. They were particularly happy that she had kept up her outside reading and was, in fact, currently reading *Sons and Lovers* as well as *Lolita*. In the second consultation with the parents, they revealed their increasing fear that Hilda's anorexia would intensify family discord. No longer would she hold the family together with her illness. Hilda now was reluctant to eat more than 200 calories a day. Her father frankly admitted his frustration and defeat; he was quite happy to remain at the university into the evenings to avoid the unpleasantness of dinner at home—on any night an impending calamity.

Over the next three weeks, Hilda was seen in an extended consultation. A sleepy cast of her eyes became apparent. Her face grew more downy, her eyes buggy and seemingly more nearsighted, her lips chapped and a little swollen, her hands adolescently clammy and coarse. She moved languidly, disincarnate, muttering almost inaudible fragments, breaking intolerable silences by clucking her tongue. Her condition seemed irremediable and was excruciating to watch. Increasing fights, now stylized, occurred between Hilda and her mother with her sons looking at her askance, and on weekends, refusing to join the parents for Sunday dinner at a restaurant. They were embarrassed that their sister would pick at her meal for hours. They were also angered that Hilda would sit interminably at the dinner table, fighting with her mother about food and surreptitiously handing the dog bits of her meal. She would only complain of being cold to the point of nausea.

Hilda's weight continued to fall, and in the consultation sessions she drew back into herself and was reluctant to discuss even the most neutral topics out of fear that the therapist would tell her parents. She feared the whole wall of her life was crumbling. It became evident that what had been discussed with the parents in their own sessions was told to Hilda by the mother. And the mother wheedled out of Hilda what was discussed in her sessions; she was sabotaging treatment and trying to ward off any intrusion into her relationship with her daughter. She spied, she betrayed, she lured. At this point, Hilda's weight had fallen to 50 pounds. Looking wretched, a shivering, wizened skeleton of a girl, she was the apotheosis of suffering, frozen like a fresco. The consultation was ended with a recommendation that she be hospitalized to prevent death. The parents opposed hospitalization, objecting that Hilda would not be able to finish the school year. (They had been assured that she would be tutored in the hospital and be able to graduate from her grammar school.) The parents feared that her high intellectual performance (Full Scale WICS 154) would be blunted. Several days after admission to the hospital, her weight fell five pounds. She immediately required continuous intravenous feedings and remained on the critical list for several days.

Another danger for the severe cachectic is exposure to cold, which can lead to profound hypothermia and death. For the bulimic patient, death is also a possibility if the bulimic gorges herself to the point of rupturing her stomach and developing acute peritonitis (Scobie 1973, Evans 1968, Jennings and Klidjian 1974). Paralytic ilens, acute dilation, and spontaneous rupture of the stomach occur quite rapidly after gorging with antecedent starvation. For this reason, refeeding of severely cachectic patients should be begun slowly, with small amounts of milk, about 1500 calories the first few days, in intervals of two hours. Death from a ruptured gastric ulcer has been reported in the literature (Kline 1979). Another danger is gastric infarction, mostly along the lesser curvature of the stomach, which leads to hemorrhage and necrosis of the stomach. Cardiac and pyloric portions of the stomach can also be vascularly occluded due to distension. Intragastric pressure builds up after muscular contractions; vascular impairment occurs and infarction results. Another gastrointestinal threat to life for the anorectic is the superior mesenteric artery syndrome (Sours and Vorhaus, in press), presenting as abdominal discomfort, pain, and vomiting of bilious fluids, caused by partial or complete obstruction of the third part of the duodenum. With loss of omental fat, anatomico-mechanical pressure is put on the transverse duodenum (Kaiser, McKain, and Schumacker 1960, Rabinovitch, Pines, and Felton 1962). In anorexia nervosa, the superior mesenteric artery syndrome can be mistaken for psychogenic vomiting, obscuring both diagnoses and risking a surgical emergency (Friese, Szmuilowicz, and Bailey 1978).

Naturalistic History and Prognosis

The parameters usually used in follow-up studies of anorexia nervosa include weight, psychosexual development, attitudes to eating, restoration of menses, social adaptation, achieved degrees of independence from parents, education, work, and the mental status at the time treatment is terminated. Adjustment in adulthood is thought by Goetz et al. (1977) to be largely related to personality type. The nature of the population, sociocultural factors, duration of illness before hospitalization, length of hospitalization, nature of the treatment, and frequency of psychotherapy will influence the outcome of anorexia nervosa. The lack of consistent diagnostic criteria still plagues researchers in this area (Seidensticker and Tzagournis 1968, Halmi, Broadland, and Loney 1973, Crisp 1977a). Length of hospitalization and recovery are not correlated, but certainly duration of illness, attitude to food and eating, and initial weight on admission are relevant to outcome. Relapse after refeeding and discharge is common, to be expected if the patient is not at least followed after discharge and is still pathologically tied to her family, like a chain to an anchor. In the Dally and Gomez series of anorectics (1979) half of their patients were hospitalized more than once, two-thirds three or more times. They assume that after five years of unrelenting symptoms the prognosis is bleak.

Factors that predict whether anorexia nervosa may reappear under the psychological stress of menarche, engagement, marriage, childbirth, and menopause are not entirely clear. Often the outcome of treatment depends on factors which brought about the referral, rather than the nature of treatment. Retrospective studies on anorexia nervosa do not supply sufficient information necessary for prediction. Many cases of anorexia nervosa are seen early by family doctors who are comfortable enough to treat these young girls to the point of remission and knowledgeable enough to refer the more difficult cases to the psychiatrist. In reading a follow-up study of anorexia nervosa, one must remember that only a specialist in anorexia nervosa can accumulate a sufficient number of cases for publication. He has been referred the more difficult patients by other psychiatrists. Consequently, his results are skewed in the direction of borderline pathology, emaciation, and chronicity.

It is generally assumed, but not always correct, that early age of onset implies a good outcome. These between eleven and fourteen years of age regain weight most quickly; those in the middle years of adolescence are the slowest in weight recovery. In addition, history of a neurotic childhood with symptomatology suggests a better prognosis; it implies a more optimistic prognosis than a history in which the anorectic is superficially comfortable and deeply attached to mother without any obvious behavioral difficulty outside of eating (Halmi et al. 1979). A great amount of overactivity before treatment is a good sign. The presence of depression in anorexia nervosa is also considered a good sign (Farquharson and Hyland 1966). It signifies pain and a desire for help. A mild degree of overwight before the onset of anorexia is regarded as a good sign. Admission of her suffering, weight loss, presence of hunger and appetite, and a desire to stop her flat denial of her condition are favorable signs. And, of course, return of regular menstruation is a verification of a good prognosis.

Poor outcome for anorexia nervosa is sometimes predictable. Pleasure from a relentless diet and a monomaniacal attitude to food and eating, the diagnostic hallmarks of the syndrome, if they remain fixed during treatment, are against a speedy recovery and an uneventful treatment. A necessary condition for recovery is the achievement of biological maturity (Ziolko 1978). Male gender (Galletly and James 1979, Hsu, Crisp, and Harding 1979) and social classes IV and V are considered signs of a difficult treatment and a generally poor outcome. Unsuccessful outcome is also related to: late onset, previous hospitalization, gross denial of illness, severe appetite disturbance, history of past obesity which defied weight control for a long time, perinatal history of delivery complications, overestimation of body size, preoccupation with body size and shape, psychosexual immaturity, marriage to an anorectic, long duration of illness, extraordinary compliance and passive behavior during childhood, external family locus of control, numerous and shifting somatic complaints, clinical depression of parents at the time of referral of the patient, obsessionality in the mother with somatic complaints, acting-out behavior of the father, low motivation for treatment, parental rejection of the patient, severe derealization and depersonalization, and agitation (Halmi et al. 1979, Davy, Andersson, and Poilpre 1976, Garfinkel, Moldofsky, and Garner 1977). Excessive use of alcohol is also considered a poor prognostic sign.

In looking over follow-up studies, one sees a diversity of prognostic opinions. Gull's statement about anorexia nervosa, made in the nineteenth century, is still true: "For the most part the outcome is favorable." Full recovery is possible but usually slow, requiring up to five or more years (Cremerius 1978, Willi and Hagemann 1976). But this is only true for certain anorectic groups. The syndrome may be a short-lived, single episode in adolescence to a chronic illness with acute exacerbations throughout the life cycle. In general, follow-up studies (Theander 1970, Dally 1969, Crisp 1977b, Thomä 1967, Bruch 1974, Russell 1977) suggest a recovery rate of 50 percent at two years, going up to 70 percent after five years.

A naturalistic study of patients with anorexia nervosa admitted to the Columbia-Presbyterian Medical Center, New York City (Ziegler and Sours 1968), demonstrated that, during a period from 1932 to 1964, 115 patients were diagnosed as falling within the primary anorexia nervosa syndrome. The peak age of onset was between ten to fifteen years; the mean weight loss was 35.9 pounds, with the weight at hospitalization ranging from 67 to 81 pounds. Over 75 percent of the patients were single females who had been ill for less than two years. A sample of thirty-five patients, whose records were sufficiently complete for clinical analysis and symptom review, showed a symptomatic picture consistent with the clinical and psychodynamic data reported in other studies. A follow-up study of 21 percent of the patients revealed a significant shift back to health and maintenance of weight. About 50 percent had married; most of them had children. Another 50 percent were still students, at least partly dependent on their parents for support. Only one-third reported health problems, none of which appeared to be of any clinical significance. Four patients (3 percent of the original 115 patients) had died during or shortly after their admission to Presbyterian Hospital; while two patients were reported dead by their families. The clinical histories of those patients who had died indicated that in each instance the parent or the spouse denied the patient's emotional problem, covertly undermined treatment, and refused to take part in conjoint therapy. The followup studies also suggested that the patients who reported that they were alive and well were, in the main, still struggling to control their weight and, in addition, had not reached genital psychosexual maturity sufficient to enjoy the sexual part of their marriage.

Several investigators have referred to anorexia nervosa as incurable. Others have just reported no cures; and one investigator has asserted that the more accurate the follow-up study, the fewer the cures, and most likely none will be found. Still other investigators have said that between 25 and 50 percent have a poor prognosis, after four years there is a 40 percent recovery rate; two-thirds recover, under one-third are incapacitated, and 5 percent die, either by suicide or intercurrent medical illness (Kay and Leigh 1954, Beck and Brockner-Mortensen 1954). Most reports suggest that the outcome ranges from a short-term, single illness to a persistent disorder, often with acute recurrences, resulting usually in death (Lesser et al. 1960, Bliss and Branch 1960).

It is popularly stated that outcome depends on the nature of the conflict and the type of personality. For instance, a predominant hysterical personality has a better prognosis than a predominantly schizoid or obsessive personality organization (Lesser et al. 1960). Another study indicates two-thirds of the patients recover or improve; one-quarter relapse and 7 percent die. Neurotic symptoms and personality defects are found at follow-up in a large percentage of anorectics in another study, which points to the possibility that social and sexual adjustment was still impaired in the anorectics who had returned to normal weight and everyday function (Kay and Schapira 1965b). The same report concludes that schizophrenia is an uncommon occurrence unless characteristic symptomatology is present at an earlier stage in the illness. Most follow-up studies agree that the development of the anorectic symptomatology after eighteen years is atypical; there is, therefore, a less optimistic prognosis (Thomä 1967). A number of reports emphasize a high frequency of relapses and the high rate of partial recoveries. Sexual adjustment and pleasure are seldom achieved by nutritionally recovered anorectics unless they continue in treatment. Many reports indicate a mortality rate of 10 to 15 percent, but these patients are usually untreated even during their starvation. Minuchin presents the most optimistic results: 86 percent of his cases "recovered from both the anorexia and its psychosocial components" (Minuchin, Rosman, and Baker 1978). They acknowledge the fact that their successes may be, in part, due to young age and recent onset of the disturbance.

Chronicity in terms of character pathology is the usual sequela to inadequately treated anorexia nervosa. Geraldine's struggle for autonomy probably would have been settled if she had been able to work out her conflicts and characterological strain when she first went into treatment.

§Geraldine, a twenty-nine-year-old single woman, was anorectic from age fourteen to eighteen, dropping from 120 to 90 pounds, where her weight remained for three years, despite hospitalization for inpatient treatment and several haphazard courses of therapy with different therapists. Once a plump, buoyant, cow-eyed girl, with red apples for cheeks, slender ankles and a graceful gait, she had exuded a genuine warmth. She now had the habit of clearing her throat into her fist before she spoke, giving the impression she wished to arrest all her movements. Nevertheless, she would at times rub her hands together as though she were about to deliver a speech.

A thumb-sucker until age thirteen, Geraldine, a borderline character disorder, first showed signs of anorexia when the family moved from Westchester back to New York City. She protested that her mother continually manipulated her, selected her friends, clothes, schools, social life, and jobs—a litany of a foul life, which continued even though, like a somnambulist, she had barely left her bedroom in her family apartment in the last year, since the day her mother criticized her for not taking enough credit hours after she had decided to go back to school. Deep into her phantasmata, now she only talked to her father, who believed she was physically ill. Smiling usually in the wrong place of her conversations, grimacing, she complained bitterly of constant fatigue, muscle pains, and "people trying to tell her what to do"—all of which was recorded in an epistolary diary in jottings no one could read. Although concerned that she got little exercise, she was not overly aware of her weight. Menstrual periods and an odd friskiness had returned, and, perfectly platonic, she fantasized marrying an older man, a widower with several children, in a few years after her "exhaustion" had ceased.

Her anorectic need for control had a different pattern: she totally controlled her father, whom she manipulated against the mother in her struggle to remain a child, "too sick to go to school" and avoid what she feared would be a "total emotional collapse," if she had to work.

There are no studies of anorectic patients whose treatment commenced at the time of the starvation, continued through the nutritional crisis, the return of physical health, and then throughout therapy with a thorough working-through of conflict, analysis of transference and, finally, termination. Longitudinal studies of treatment are possible; this research is not like starting from zero and going to an imaginary number. It is not a knot that unties itself. It is more a matter of commitment, by both therapist and patient, to the long-term treatment of anorexia nervosa, to the point where the character structure behind anorexia nervosa can be changed.

6

Families of
Anorexia Nervosa
Patients

The hard, inescapable phenomenon to be faced is that we are living and dying at once. My commitment is to report that dialogue.
   —Stanley Kunitz, *A Kind of Order, A Kind of Folly*

Over my head, I see the bronze butterfly,
Asleep on the black trunk,
Blowing like a leaf in green shadow.
Down the ravine behind the empty house,
The cowbells follow one another
Into the distances of the afternoon.
To my right,
In a field of sunlight between two pines,
The droppings of last year's horses
Blaze up into golden stone.
I lean back, as the evening darkens and comes on.
A chicken hawk floats over, looking for home.
I have wasted my life.

                    —James Wright, "Lying In a Hammock at
        William Duffy's Farm In Pine Island, Minnesota"

It is characteristic of the anorexia nervosa family that it superficially functions well and is a polite family. But unlike the well-functioning family that interacts within its system, confronts conflicts, allows interpersonal differentiation, and permits separation and autonomy as the child gets older, the anorectic family enmeshes its members, is overprotective, rigid, lacks the ability for conflict-resolution, and involves the child in parental conflicts. Family stresses and strains— sudden absences that leave sudden holes, uncomprehended inclemencies, furtive glimpses at the terrors and dangers of the world, dogs howling everywhere, smoke bellowing out of the ground, suffocating loneliness—are ignored. Difficulties confronting the anorectic family may lie everywhere, like water after a long rain, but the atmosphere is as still as the woods after a downpour. There is an aversion to disorder. The family possesses a blueprint for happiness against their dog-eat-dog world. Their minds, full of words saying nothing, are blinded by averting eyes. They scribble over anxiety with a dead language, a dialect more apt to create misunderstanding than a foreign language. Their flat world allows no clues, leaving the teenager of the anorectic family to the refuge of garrulity and rhetorical questions.

The anorectic family has been well described by Bruch (1973b), Palazzoli (1974), and Minuchin et al. (1978), by both psychoanalytic and family system investigators (Jeammet et al. 1973, Malone 1979, Conrad 1977, Caille et al. 1977, Foster and Kupfer 1975). Their findings largely describe self-starving and mixed anorectics, but the structural and functional characteristics of the families of gorging-vomiting anorectics, as well as many families of male anorectics (Leger, Blanchinet, and

Vallat 1969), differ in that the fathers, rather than the mothers, tend to be the potent force in the parent-child subsystem (Boskind-Lodahl 1976).

The self-starving and mixed anorectics come generally from families with a rhythm of life sustained through generations. There is no mutual respect, no egalitarian relationship in these families. The anorectic-to-be is used to obfuscate the family conflicts in a smokescreen of joy and keep the parents united in their protective concern over their children. The preanorectic daughter, still as a leaf barely clinging, lives in a state of fear, expecting punishment and wishing that she could tell what her parents are thinking, which further blurs the family subsystem boundaries. The gentlest breeze makes their windows rattle, and the house grows shadows around the family. The anorectic must mediate parental conflict. Each family member says what the other means; no one speaks about his own feelings; the windows are nailed and boarded. These transactional family patterns encourage somatization, because they impound affect, discourage verbalization, and block affective discharge. They live in a subpolar ambiance that freezes their insides. The books they read they buy for one another, trying to read each other's minds.

No matter how successful and highly functioning anorectic families are, no matter how gracious their living, they do not convey an adequate sense of competence and self-value to their child. They preach an undifferentiated conformity, enmeshed in the family system. Nor do they provide the anorectic child a sufficient feeling of independence and a clear view of the body and its management. The family owns the anorectic's body. The parents, not well-stocked with ebullience, hold back; too vague are their images to merge into totemic creatures. In their minds, castaways of middle life, the parents, older than the usual parents of a teenager, are like two clouds, growing dark, between which burns the pale glow of a teenagers's anger (Hall 1904). Preordained to swim in her mother's wake forever, the anorectic seeks unnavigated waters, unclimbed mountains—the pursuit of perfection—to overcome a frazzled sense of self. But, half-excited, half-frightened, like a wasp sleeping in the eaves of her house, she perceives fears filtering into her bones. It is a dangerous world, her family recites to her every night; it is a world that must be placated; kept at bay, satisfied by pleasantness and smiles, while at the same time, as weak as wet leaves, she must draw her strength and gather speed for the last run. Obsessive perfection becomes her defense against parental criticism, entrapment and enmeshment.

The Anorectic Family Process and Somatization

Two hundred years ago Naudeau (1789) and Lasègue (1873) commented on the pathogenic influences of the family on the anorectic child. Minuchin and his associates (1978), after reviewing the history of the psychosomatic concept—at first, a linear, causal psychodynamic model of organ system vulnerability and patterns of conflict and defense and, later, a gradual shift to social context and system organization—have extended the theory of family psychogenic influences through the use of the systems model: the anorectic's behavior is no longer seen as triggered by others; it is not the sum-total response to introjects; instead, the behavior is determined by the degree and type of controlled interaction between the anorectic and her parents. Along these lines, Minuchin's system paradigm allows another way of viewing the anorectic as part of an open system, with its circularity of parts affecting one another.

The anorectic family, according to Minuchin and his associates (1975), is a psychosomatic family, in caricature, to the extent that the anorectic's diagnosis can be verified by study of the family, whose structure and function are typical, if not stereotypic. By way of stark contrast, the functioning quotidian family in the West (the so-called "normal family") fosters separation-individuation and autonomy while maintaining protection and security. The family subsystems (spouse, parents and children) are differentiated, have their own defining boundaries, which are roles identifying who participates in its transactions—rules flexible enough to allow differences of opinion, arguing, and, in general, aggression in response to internal and external familial change. In the middle of the continuum, with enmeshment and disengagement at opposite ends, is the functional family with more or less core boundaries, variable from subsystem to subsystem over space and time. For instance, the mother-child subsystem, when the child is a preschooler, is transactionally often enmeshed with the exclusion of the father, but, as a child approaches adulthood, the parental subsystem shifts from an enmeshed to a disengaged style. In the functional family, a family member at the moment of stress can appropriately cross boundaries for support without disturbing the other subsystems and upsetting autonomy. For example, if a latency child plays hooky once to go off to a baseball game with a friend, the family is not greatly upset or is insouciant. Developmental stages in the children are acknowledged, tolerated, and sanctioned: the teenage daughter's request to drive the family car from the suburbs to the city is approved and supported, if developmentally earned.

However, life is not flexible and happy for the anorectic family which is the archetypally enmeshed family, overprotected, painfully sensitive to conflict, and rigidly determined to maintain the family status quo. Like most families, the parents of the anorectic family carry over unresolved conflicts, disappointments, losses from their own nuclear families, identifications and roles from their families, and organizing images of self and objects—all of which coalesce into collusive interdependent systems in the family, reciprocal role expectations and projective identifications in which a hated element of one parent is projected onto and identified in a child or spouse whose image and behavior then develops to complement the projection. Symbiotic and dependent attachments, at various levels of pathology, are recapitulated and established. Projection, introjection, and splitting mechanisms abound in the anorectic family.

The anorectic family is vigilant to distress, wants to damp painful anxiety and to obfuscate conflict; the child is sheltered even from herself. Her body is not her own. Anxiety and tensions are somaticized. Developmental lines—those of dependency, autonomy, confidence, body care, nutrition, and affect-awareness—are stunted. Defenses and coping mechanisms of the anorectic remain infantile. Age-appropriate developmental changes in the child are frowned upon, often viewed as disloyal and destructive to the family. In addition, the anorectic family functions with triangulation and parent-child coalitions against the spouse coalition. And to confuse the family culture even more, the spouse subsystem is pseudomutual and united, deflecting the conflict onto the ill child. The anorectic, hypersensitive to herself, intolerant of any failures in her character, and convinced of her incompetence, cannot evaluate herself. Her defenses against enmeshment and criticism are denial, negativism, and the pursuit of perfection; her strategy against intrusion is countercontrol. And beyond this immediate struggle is the family struggle with cultural forces that represent discontinuity, transformation, and dissolution (Keniston 1977)—dynamic external factors which may be responsible for the increased incidence of anorexia nervosa. Their metaphors, for the anorectic family, are everywhere gnawing at their bowels; they cannot be denied so readily. If only barriers can be erected against these forces, then, perhaps, their rainbows will not disassemble.

Anorectic families, even though well over half are social classes I and II, professional and executive, envy their more affluent friends and neighbors and resent them for the images these people convey—the attainment of perfection. Jealousies and rivalries are not limited to siblings in the anorectic families; often the parents are choked by envy and jealousy. In the sibling subsystem intense competitions exist. Some studies (Theander 1970, Dally and Gomez 1979, Morgan and Russell 1975) reveal that 6 to 10 percent of anorectic's siblings displayed signs and symptoms of anorexia nervosa. It is usually the younger sister—rather than the younger brother—who becomes anorectic; she joins the diet frenzy and vies with her sister to isolate her mother for herself. But these jealousies and rivalries can involve multiple siblings of both genders and any grouping, further hindering subsystem differentiation. These families seldom engage in any rough play or overt aggressiveness. They are not disobedient citizens; they usually do not scream at one another or other people. The mothers are known for their cleanliness, orderliness, and sense of propriety; but some of the fathers are also obsessive, fussy, and petulant. Crying is frowned upon in these families. Tears are shed behind closed doors, but the anorectic is not allowed to keep her bedroom door shut; she is watched over by hypervigilant parents. Nor are the parents and children apt to show affection for one another. The giving of gifts is modest; members of the family do not believe they deserve gifts since they have not lived up to their ego-ideal. The anorectic child does not realize that she has a right to ask for something from the family. She attempts to guess what the parents want of her, what the parents plan to give her, and how to accept whatever she is given with enthusiasm. She fears her gratitude and thinly disguises her resentment and deceitful feelings.

The mother of the anorectic child provides well for her as far as basic needs are concerned. She is usually protective and solicitous, dominating as well, even though often chronically depressed. But rarely does she enjoy genuine pleasure from and mutual gratification with her family, whom she views as her responsibility and obligation. This type of mother is most common in the families of the young patient. The mother of the older patient, on the other hand, is less caretaking, more openly ambivalent, blatantly dominant and competitive. Her depression tends to be more on the surface, more severe, if not acute.

Just as there is no "schizophrenogenic mother," likewise there is no anorexogenic mother. There is no universal parental personality, marital pattern or configuration; family psychopathology is not uniform. Wold (1973) noted maternal depression in the background of the anorectic's childhood, with the fathers, angry, violent, rigid men, still idealizing their mother with the displacements to daughters. King (1963) and Wall (1956) both found, as did many other clinicians, abnormal dependency on mother with resultant resentment. In fact, Nemiah (1950) observed that the anorectic was uniformly resentful of a parent; his patients had both a good and bad parental object. But clinical generalizations are difficult to interpret; the age of onset of anorexia nervosa and the character structure of the parents are most revealing of the family dynamics and structure.

Clinical surveys and epidemiological studies do not provide an adequate picture of the anorectic family. There is no significant relationship between the weight of the anorectic and her parents (Halmi et al. 1978) One clinical study reveals only 20–30 percent incidence of prominent dominance–submission behavior in parents (Dally and Gomez 1979). The same study indicated that anorectics come from rather stable homes, low in divorce and breakups. In fact, divorce, separation, and parental death figures, under 20 percent in most reports (Theander 1970, Thomä 1967, Kay and Leigh 1954, Morgan and Russell 1975), do not reveal the structural and functional aspects of these families. Only by working with the anorectic and her family can the clinician come to an appreciation of their complex system, its manifestations and variations—its mysteries promulgated by the parents.

Mothers of anorectic daughters with younger age of onset show a number of characterological and behavioral similarities. They are attentive to the children and scrupulous about form; they fancy themselves gourmet cooks, and abhor any gourmand inclinations. They do not enjoy food and despise gluttons. The executive managers of the family, their domestic work habits are often demanding and arduous; they view themselves as martyrs. Meals must be on a fixed schedule. Everybody is expected to the dinner table on time; often a dress code is imposed. The family meal is not a time of joy. Dinner conversation is directed by the mother in an atmosphere of didacticism. She is frequently in bad humor over peccadillos of family members. While the family eats, there is an unspeakable tension among them. This is blatantly true of the parents; they say very little of all that can be said between a man and a woman. Sometimes disgust hangs over the dining room, the same quality of silent disgust expressed by the mother years before during breast-feeding and toilet training. Vomiting from any cause, whether from illness or anxiety, is attributed by the mother to the child having overeaten. But even though the mothers feel disgust with food and eating, they talk about food, often read *Gourmet* and *Bon Appetite,* and take cooking classes. They are greedy, sick with desire, but they refuse greed, wanting to weigh, like their daughter, no more than ashes.

Going back to school and pursuing a career, they believe, are good for them, just as the mothers are convinced that lessons and projects are good for their child. They are annoyed when their offers of tutors and lessons to their children are rejected. They make image relationships to their child and expect the latter to actualize image-derived expectations. In their social lives, the mothers do not risk social disappointment; the right parties should be attended. They do not condone signs of aggressive rebelliousness or radical individualism in the community. They are pacifists, quietly aligning themselves with the proper and socially appropriate issues. No social risks are taken. While being guardians of the home, the mothers never really accept the roles of wife and mother with pleasure. They see their lives as disappointing and themselves as failures vis-à-vis their narcissistic ambitions and expectations. Depression with low self-esteem, hopelessness, and anxiety is more or less always present. Dally and Gomez (1979) found 75 percent of these mothers depressed. Prolonged bereavement may be the substance of the mother's depression (Crisp et al. 1974). For their children, they encourage ambition and achievement, while at the same time they are bitterly disappointed that their husbands have not been able to provide what they sought from him early in the marriage. As the anorectic daughter retreats from life, the mother falls into despair, further displacing her anger onto the father; she withdraws from the family. The mothers harbor a not always secret disgust for sex and lovemaking, just as they do for eating and pleasure in general. Oral sex is unthinkable.

The parents of anorectics are conspicuously concerned with external appearances. They fight the temptation to make careers of pain. They are puritanical and are often bigoted about people and things unfamiliar to them. Nevertheless, even in their insecurity, they seldom give vent to argumentative comments or unpleasant squabbles. One can feel empathy for these families, as John Cheever (1978) does for the suburban characters in his short stories. They live in a constant state of tension, often bad-tempered, but usually controlled, although they can engage in low-key interminable arguments over trivial issues—indications of their latent aggression. Once the anorectic daughter improves, aggression may spring to the surface. They slavishly accept traditional rules, pretend to be the traditional American family, and to be devoted to their children. The Minnesota Multiphasic Inventory (MMPI) scores of the anorectic family support the clinical impression that they must always look perfect. The MMPI results demonstrate that the anorectic family stimulates normality, indeed, strives to present a caricature of normality—perfection—while at the same time the family shows signs of withdrawal and isolation (Sours 1979a). The family wants to think of the unit as happy and harmonious.

The parents are pretenders who go through life defending against low self-esteem and unacceptable feelings. Mothers usually attribute their tension and resentment to the belief that they have relinquished careers and creative interests for their children. The mothers, following a thread of grief, are concerned, at the time their children reach adolescence, about finding a new career in their mid-life transition. The fathers are boastful of their fitness, good health, and attractiveness. They let it be known that their fitness is indisputable; they insist that their present weight is the same as it was during college.

The father of the self-starving and mixed anorectics—and some male anorectics—usually feels "second best" to the mother. He is passive, frightened, and distant from the family (Palazzoli 1965). This is characteristically true in families where the daughter had an early onset of anorexia nervosa. But it is not always the case—usually not when the anorexia nervosa occurs in late adolescence or when the clinical pattern is one of bingeing and vomiting. Then the father may not simply be as dominant and powerful as the mother, or the roles are simply reversed. He may be the perfectionist, subordinating his wife and daughter to his will; he may clash with his wife—a battle of two wills—and attempt a split between mother and daughter by encouraging the daughter to diet in protest to mother. Less secure fathers may be very blustery in denying their passivity and submission to a wife by openly having affairs and getting drunk. Not infrequently, the mother of the anorectic encourages the child to displace her hostility onto the father in order to avoid aggression. The effect of the displacement is deleterious if the father were raised by a domineering, demeaning mother or older sister of similar character. In that case, the father is apt to identify the patient with mother or sibling and direct to his daughter the impounded hostility he had never been able to express directly to other women in his life. The hostile undercurrents in the father-daughter relationship are a further deterrent to the daughter's hetero-sexual development. The mother feels this hostility to the father, because he does not foster her narcissistic ambitions, goes his separate way in his career, and achieves successes which the mother fears are proof of the husband's superiority. The father's interests and successes are regarded by the mother as a challenge to family "togetherness." It is not unusual for the mother of the anorectic to complain to the daughter that father does not support family closeness and solidarity. She cites the father's career as the reason. The daughter, then, is apt to see the father as disloyal and running away from the family.

The father of the anorectic child finds it difficult to compensate for the mother. He is a master of the two-line letter. He wants his daughter to regard him as a fortress, seen from a distance, the self a gothic landscape. He may be aware that the mother discourages eating at the time of the daughter's puberty. He may know that the mother did not support the daughter in her pubertal anxieties, just as her own mother failed her and maintains a cross-generational coalition (Taipale, Tuomi, and Aukee 1971). But he believes that there is little he can do about the situation, short of confronting the mother.

An anorectic daughter may turn and become quite attached to the father in her attempt to move away from the mother during adolescence.

§India, a twenty-three-year-old single woman, through the intervention of her primary care doctor, called for consultation because of anorexia nervosa of one-year's duration. She presented a manlike, childish image, a hand-wrought image of Levis and Freye boots, a young woman in flight from emotions, yet wanting to be rooted like a tall cypress. After India had stopped smoking, she decided to go on a diet of health foods, and in the next year her weight fell from 137 to 94 pounds. Three years previously, she had dropped out of college because she no longer found her courses satisfying; but, over and above the lack of pleasure in her college work, she broke off her relationship with her boyfriend, whom she had dated for two years and sexually enjoyed. She had found herself dancing in her skull, sensing her roots beginning to tear loose inside her body. India decided to work for her father, a surgeon, and took a paramedical course for a year. She found the training at first "repulsive and difficult," but later she was unaware of any upsetting feelings about the "blood and gore." She was proud that she could join her father in the office. In her view, her father was getting old and tired, and the practice would flounder without her good management and direction. She devoted most of her time to the practice, staying home at night to do the office paperwork. A bride-image of the father, she wanted to possess him, know him thoroughly—open up her father's head and take out his thoughts. She refused all dates and complained that she had no sexual feelings. A storehouse of fire, she increasingly took over the management of the father's practice, regarded her mother as less competent than ever, and took to running the kitchen and managing all the household matters. Everything mattered because everything died. She had always been very close to her parents: rolled in protective layers, she was unable to go away to either day or sleepaway camp, reluctant to go to kindergarten, and unhappy during her first grade experience. But throughout grammar school, she had enjoyed horseback riding and became a devoted student of her riding teacher, a much older man, whom she admired.

As India got into treatment, her intense oedipal attachment to her father became evident to her, as well as the marked ambivalence to her mother. She responded quickly to treatment, as far as anorectic symptoms were concerned, but made slow progress in freeing herself from the inordinate attachment to her father and his life and in facing her primitive tie to her mother.

The father of the anorectic is sometimes seductive with his daughter. She is always a child, so he can touch her if he wants to. The end result is that the girl identifies with the seductive father against the aggressive, bitter mother. This kinship only augments her hostility to the mother and the daughter's perception of the mother as a dangerous, meddling person. Likewise, the father's hostility to the mother is increased because of his tie to the daughter; he resents even more his wife's lack of affection. With his cool, guttural voice, the father, his awed daughter believes, is a monster who leads an interesting life: vital, moving about at will, blasting down every wall with his name. There are times when the father's anger to the mother becomes violent, with outbursts of aggression and brutality, usually during a crisis in the daughter's anorexia nervosa.

At times, a father may attempt to possess his daughter by destroying the mother and strengthening a narcissistic tie to the girl.

§A physician-father called frantically for consultation for his eighteen-year-old daughter, a college freshman, who, because of weight loss and anorexia, was in psychotherapy with a "lay therapist." Jeannette, who was four feet nine and a half inches and weighed 60 pounds—more than twenty pounds down from her usual weight—resisted her father's intervention, feeling that he was uncomfortable with her treatment, not simply because the therapist was not a physician, but because the latter refused to see father and accept any of his medical recommendations. The patient had chosen a "tough woman" therapist, who would help her "escape from the father's medical influences." Jeanette needed a backup for her mother, who was long depressed, withdrawn, and immobile. And, one of two sisters, she was always the watcher, never sure of herself. For the same reason, she was also reluctant to see the family physician. On her visits home, she disliked talking to her father because of his own preoccupation with eating and weight. In an attempt to break the patient's anorectic diet, he would also suggest diets of his own which over the years had "been extremely successful in maintaining his youth." The patient continued with her therapist, and the father was referred to a psychiatrist.

Pseudorationality rules the anorectic family. The parents discuss rather than shout, think rather than feel, and debate calmly and logically their points of view. They dominate the anorectic by being more articulate and aggressively direct in the family debates. She keeps her tears in check by acting pleasant and agreeable. Family discussions invariably make the parents feel superior, because they have proven their intellectual acumen and taught the child the correct way to view life and negotiate with people. As "reason" and "insight" prevail in the family, helplessness, impotent protest, and inner turmoil lie dormant in the child and force her to simulate a docile disguise. Yet, the parents believe that they have given the daughter the instruments by which she can develop independent thinking and initiative. And they are shocked when she becomes negativistic, when, full of hunger and turmoil, she dances the tarantella backwards.

The anorectic family is a dysfunctional family, dependent on the mental and behavioral deviations of their anorectic offspring as a means of preventing disintegration. It is a psychosomatic family in that body function and metaphor are employed; an anorectic family in that food, dieting, weight control, and pursuit of perfection are their leitmotif. But aside from its food preoccupation, the anorectic family is not a unique family system; many of its structural and functional qualities can be seen in other nonfunctional families.

7

Developmental Patterns in the Anorexia Nervosa Syndrome

Actually, I was trying all that time to understand you . . . for you never really know a person unless you've known his childhood.

—Georges Simenon, *Letter To My Mother*

Puberty and Adolescence

A number of growth-maturational and psychobiological changes and events take place during puberty and adolescence (Frank and Cohen 1979, Blos 1962), physical and psychological, as well as social, educational, political, and economic. They include: a height spurt in girls a year or so before menarche with decreasing long bone growth as the epiphyses close—bone growth stimulated by the growth hormone, unlike sexual organ growth, stimulated by estrogen and androgen, which occurs earlier in girls with attainment of menarche after the adolescent growth spurt has passed its peak. Deposition of fat occurs in girls over hips, breasts, and thighs, after uneven accelerating physical growth has produced perplexing unevenness in size of feet, hands, limbs, neck and face, as well as sebaceous overactivity and acne of the skin. There is a shift in cognitive function, from concrete thinking to conceptualization and higher-order abstractions; heightened intellectual and emotional sensitivity and empathy; transformations in concepts of self and conscience; an augmented tension between dependence and independence, and an increasingly strong push toward the extrafamilial world.

Since adolescent development occurs over a decade, it can best be understood by its phases and immediate antecedents. Likewise, the psychopathology and developmental deviations of anorexia nervosa must also be viewed from this perspective. The phases of adolescence, preadolescence, early adolescence, adolescence proper, late adolescence, and postadolescence (Blos 1962), are negotiated in numerous ways, with individual variations, ending after differentiations and transformations in a complicated and subtle characterological structure, secured by a unified, continuous ego supporting a stable sense of self (Blos 1979).

In latency years, ages six to ten, no new instinctual aim appears. The ego functions of learning, memory, perception and thinking are consolidated in the conflict-free sphere of ego; instinctual pressure is less threatening to the ego. A shift from outer to inner objects occur with increasing stability of identifications. Self-esteem regulation takes the place of parental reassurances with an amelioration of the harshness of the superego. But in preadolescence—ages ten to twelve for girls, eleven to thirteen for boys—as the psychobiological effects of emerging puberty are felt, instinctual pressure increases with no apparent new love object or aim. Sap rises in the tree long before the leafing. This marked quantitative increase in sexual and aggressive drives marks the end of latency and ushers in the resurgence of pregenitality. She fears that she will suck on the hollow of her spoon, be as naked as the clear sky on a cool autumn morning. With pubertal maturation, early adolescence becomes apparent in the turn to libidinal extrafamilial objects and the overwhelming need to separate from early objects. The young adolescent girl, now wanting to float free, begins to give up her adamantly held "tomboy" image, which protected her against regression to the preoedipal mother. Now the girl, as well as the boy, must decathect incestuous love objects with the result that object libido looks for new directions, leaving the adolescent feeling empty and upset. Further and further away from the mother, who is the whole world to her, the adolescent girl must go, exploding in a fit of pointless energy, fearing annihilation, weeping when a leaf falls from a tree, meeting her new world with a handshake of disarticulated bones. Half-asleep, half-awake, she reads travel books at night, while sipping milk in bed. She promises herself that in the morning, like a bird, she will fly, altering the light.

During early adolescence the bisexual tendency of the girl is strong, expressed in her body image as well as interests and activities. Through shifts of narcissistic libido in heterosexual love and identificatory trial actions the bisexual position weakens as the girl passes into adolescence proper. The ego cannot depend on the superego, now weakened as an authority structure because of concurrent decathexis of early object relationships. The ego is now relatively impoverished by withdrawal of object cathexis, which leads to isolation, loneliness, and depressive affect of the young adolescent. There is an upsurge of intense idealizing friendships with the same sex, a shift from quantitative drive increase to the burgeoning, distinct new drive quality. Transformation of the ego-ideal occurs with idealization of new friends. This is a period of multiple attempts at separation from primary love objects, slipping from her like parts of herself, at abandonment of the preadolescent regressive position, with frequent transient identifications. During this phase hunger plagues the young adolescent with resultant food preoccupation and overeating, especially during transient regressions. Soon she will be stumpy and heavy, like poured lead—a flesh heap, fallen into the shape of a pot. Narcissistic libido, receding from life, withdrawn also from internalized parental objects, shifts to the ego at this time in the service of maintaining self-esteem during heterosexual object-finding. Development, however, is hindered if narcissism is used defensively, as a holding operation against disengagement. Her eyes will look in, instead of out, fearing the world can penetrate her mind. The tug of narcissistic regressive forces, the fear that she, like a bulb in a lamp, is likely to fail suddenly, lie down and slumber, is countered by object-focused ideation through a rich fantasy life which allows trial actions. The special sensory organs, particularly vision, hearing, and touch, are heightened. Sensory pulsations are translated into images. The hyperactivity facilitates object finding and holding as the adolescent struggles with object giving-up and object-finding.

In adolescence proper, there is movement toward heterosexual drive organization with relegation of pregenitality to foreplay pleasures. Object libido is turned out toward nonincestuous heterosexual objects, with a concomitant decline in narcissism. This shift to new objects reactivates positive and negative oedipal fixations, as well as issues in masculinity and femininity. At the same time, the ego musters up defensive and adoptive measures and processes, new psychic membranes and ego boundaries, as part of its evolving hierarchical organization. Now the adolescent is well into what Blos (1967) calls the second separation-individuation phase, when infantile inner objects must be given up. The defenses of intellectualization and asceticism become especially prominent, used individually and idiosyncratically by each adolescent. A stable arrangement of ego functions begins to be more apparent in late adolescence when consolidation of structures occurs: formation of irreversible identifications, sexual and personal identity, widening of the conflict-free sphere of the ego, investment of object and self-representations, and stability of self-esteem. Ego endurance has come from enduring adolescence. By the time postadolescence is reached, drive organization has more permanence, although ego development lags behind, to some degree, for most older adolescents, still to complete their development during adulthood. The tasks of postadolescence are to make intrapsychic conflict more specific, focus it on the real world through confrontation with life situations and tasks, as well as enduring relationships and roles (Blos 1979). Yet further growth and differentiation are possible, for the young adult is not a peg tapped by some mallet into the earth.

Adolescence and the Anorexia Nervosa Syndrome

It is well known that girls reach puberty at least two years earlier than boys, and experience radical, abrupt changes in their secondary sex-characteristics. Breast development, commencing at age nine, continues under the influence of gonadotropins, growth hormone, estrogen and prolactin, for five to eight years. Pubic hair, also an early sign of puberty, precedes growth of the vagina and uterus. All these changes are even more upsetting to the young anorectic girl. There promptly results a loss of angularity, with fat laid down over hips, thighs, and abdomen—the appearance of a curved belly and the advent of fuller hips, changed by widening of the pelvic outlet and angle of the ileum. Menstruation occurs sooner or later, anywhere from age nine to seventeen, usually between eleven and thirteen nowadays. It is more upsetting than the male pubertal counterpart, ejaculation, because menstruation seems mysterious and dirty to the young girl; it is frightening and humiliating to the youth who is apt to perceive menstrual blood and clots in terms of not only body damage and defect but also anal loss of control with soiling. The pubescent girl views sexuality, more often than not, as dangerous, because she is threatened by her passive, receptive self and fears, now so strongly vulnerable to surging libidinal and aggressive drives, that she will have less control over her body. She defends against the regressive pull to the preoedipal mother by turning to heterosexuality, becoming the aggressor and seducer in her strident games of love. She becomes increasingly aware of the sexual curiosity, if not lewd looks, of boys who insensitively joke about breasts, menstrual blood, and sexual penetration. She wonders if her new adolescent world is worth the pain, exposed as she is.

For boys, puberty is connected with strong wishes for self-assertion and desires for distancing oneself from childhood and parents. Charged with sexual feelings, pubertal boys want to impose force and control. Their energies are usually directed outward. But a resurgence of pregenitality marks the end of latency for the boy; a regression to the pregenital level as a defense against castration anxiety ushers in male preadolescence (Blos 1979).

A premenstrual, pubescent girl is subjected to many new feelings. She is apt to be restless, hyperactive, and surprisingly aggressive; at times, she fears being violent and even on the verge of criminal violence. Her moods vacillate during the menstrual cycle. In the estrogenic phase, she may feel assertive while later, during the luteal (progesterone) phase, she may sense passivity and vulnerability. God does not preside over her body; it is flesh that casts out wastes.

For the anorectic girl, puberty is an exquisitely difficult crisis; she draws back, wishing she could pass out of her body because of anxiety and disgust over bodily functions, feelings, and impulses. Perfection of the fleshy body: If she could only shrink to the size of a child, have a small, intelligent body, be elflike, or live in the body of a sparrow. She experiences her body concretely as an object of dread and worry. Puberty, for the anorectic, is a time when her secret wish to be a boy hits a stone wall. Her face and nostrils widen; muscles under her chin seem to thicken. Her voice, half-bird, half-boy, offends her. Bullets are in her words. She lives in dread of missing something. At the same time, she fears not being able to meet other adolescent girls on equal and fair terms; she wonders whether they will view her as infantile and dependent. She is apt to do heroic things, like traveling alone across the country, or backpacking to Europe, as a way of asserting autonomy and independence. In addition, puberty, for the anorectic, is another time for facing passivity and feelings of weakness, obstacles already struggled with through the latency years.

The anorectic young adolescent sees her body as a passive, helpless object which is easily invaded or taken over by outside forces, intrusions from the unknown. She sees food and her mother as potential instruments of control. Her mother is her Gulag. With fists clenched, she believes that she lacks willpower, perceiving herself as passive-receptive, like burdocks clinging, anxious and powerless. Her body is not authentic; it is not hers; it is vulnerable to invasion and parental misuses. She can return to a feeling of quintessential power only by separating flesh from her body through an act of will-to-intelligence. The anorectic adolescent sees herself only through images which she projects into the world. She is condemned to a repertoire of distortions, which she must manipulate in order to maintain self-esteem and fearlessness. Otherwise, fear will seep into her like a stain; parts of her will drift in and out; nothing will remain but the same old question: Does she exist?

The anorectic is unable to surmount new developmental problems of adolescence, phase by phase, much less control the old ones of pre-adolescence. Nonetheless, she pretends to accept the mores and style of adolescent culture. In fact, late adolescent anorectics may plunge into heterosexuality without pleasure in order to assuage impotence and inadequacy, as well as give themselves a feeling of membership in the youth culture. She is aware of appetite and eroticism, just as she is of hunger and sexuality. But seldom can she combine hunger and appetite, lust and romance.

Developmental Patterns in the Anorexia Nervosa Syndrome

Anorexia nervosa patients display quantitative and qualitative differences which suggest several clinical and dynamic groupings (Eissler 1943, Falstein et al. 1956, Sours 1979a). Anorectic symptomatology is clinically evident on many levels of psychopathology, from everyday cultural and societal manifestations, to severe psychosis (Sours 1979). There are essentially four developmental patterns connected with the anorectic syndrome. These are presented as abstracted paradigms, road maps of development gone wrong: fixation, regression, digression, progression in endless variations, defensive and adaptive mechanisms which have failed to evolve or have turned to stone, ego functions prone to regression or disintegration rather than dependable for synthetic functions and the formation of character structure.

Group I

In the first configuration, the disturbance appears usually in a young, adolescent girl who is skittish of her pubescent, instinctual life. (Occasionally, young, adult, anorectic, psychosexually immature women at the time of marriage and pregnancy are members of this group.) Her character, although far from consolidated, is predominantly hysterical with obsessional features which come to the fore in clinical regressions. (Rorschachs often show conversion hysteria with repressed orality [Wagner and Wagner 1978].) She senses that she is fleshy and heavy; she wants to be thin and ethereal (the fear of fatness masks the fear of total loss of impulse control and severe regression). She perceives her body as "too sexy" and decides to limit her food intake in order to turn down pubertal, metabolic processes and reduce libido. She thinks of sex as "dirty," "sickening," and "icky." More than a passing aversion, menstruation may disgust her, making her use toilet paper to hide the fact that she needs sanitary napkins—all with feigned nonchalance. The sexuality of her parents baffles her; how can they sleep together, she asks like an innocent child, after having decided never to have any more children. No longer can she eat with her parents; her lecherous father, eating "like a pig," is equated with lusty sexuality. (Older anorectics of the same character structure may develop anorexia with nausea and weight loss at the time of marriage. Severe dysmenorrhea may occur and during pregnancy disabling hyperemesis gravidarum.)

The young girl develops a fear of eating and becoming fat; she pursues a Spartan diet; she is hyperactive as a defense against bulimia and passive wishes. Now, even at rest, she blinks faster; her hands move in her lap like pigeons. The wish for thinness reflects the anorectic's preoedipal and oedipal body-phallus identifications. These anorectic girls want to side-step sexual impulses and fantasies; they regress to pregenitality, to an oral-aggressive position, where incorporative forces can give rise to a fear of merging with, destroying or being annihilated by, the infantile inner object. Oral conflict brings into focus the gastrointestinal track as the organ choice for symptoms. The fear of being fat defends against the unconscious incorporation of the ambivalently loved object and reflects an identification with a mother who similarly fears gaining weight. This identification is further strengthened by secondary identifications with both women and men in the fear-of-fat culture. A good object representation of the mother and of the self founders. The anorectic is not able to enter the second separation-individuation phase (Blos 1967), unless she can relinquish infantile inner objects and move comfortably toward external and extrafamilial ambivalent objects. Isolation, hyperactivity, and food-refusal guard against object closeness. Withdrawal of object cathexis leads to increased self-perception, self-absorption, and self-perception.

Anorectic patients in this first group are arrested in the late phase of separation-individuation (Mahler 1972), "on the way to libidinal object constancy," to use Hartmann's terminology. They are developmentally at the early phallic-oedipal phase. Their regression is not the normative, nondefensive regression of adolescent development (Blos 1979). They regress to an analized mode of ego-functioning, where self-object representations are not separate and full, but are still split into good and bad. Defense mechanisms, however, are high-level, with repression, reaction-formation, and sublimation available. Asceticism and intellectualization are available defenses for anorectics at the phase of adolescence proper. Fear of fatness is expressed by the defenses of repression and displacement of sexual conflicts. Ambivalent attitudes toward passive wishes and bad objects foster fantasies of oral impregnation which also arise, in regressive states, from fears of being controlled, invaded, and distended by the primary object. Such fears and fantasies are both oedipal and preoedipal; later, under pressure of regression, these anorectics fear the heightening of pregenital fantasies.

A college girl illustrates some facets of this group of anorectics:

§Betty Ann is a nineteen-year-old college sophomore from a northeast metropolitan community, who, during her first year at a southern college, began to lose weight. She first attributed the weight loss to the fact that the dining hall food did not appeal to her; she spent what extra money she had eating in local restaurants and often buying "junk food." At about the same time, she realized, in retrospect, she had increased her energy output, throwing herself into her studies, a gymnastic program, and weekend dating. It was in this setting that she lost ten pounds. During the spring when she returned home, she made plans to get a summer job, but because of an employment slump in her community, she was not able to obtain the job that had been promised her. As a result, she spent the first part of her vacation at home, reading and spending time with her former high school friends.

Her mother became concerned about her weight loss, even though it was only a ten-pound decrease. She started to monitor her daughter's eating, commented on her athleticism, and made snide remarks about the fact that she had broken off with her boyfriend. Betty Ann was perplexed; she did not understand why her mother was so critical and kept her under surveillance. The mother finally revealed that she had recently read Hilde Bruch's *A Golden Cage* (1978) and now knew that "Betty Ann was anorexia nervosa."

Her mother indicated that she was guilty about her daughter's "illness"; she wanted to do everything possible to "bring them together." The mother tried to take over her daughter's nutrition, telling her what were the best foods. She also, for the first time, became "confidential" about sexual matters, attempting to help her daughter overcome her "frigidity," which she assumed had been responsible for the breakup in Betty Ann's relationship during the summer.

Midway through the summer, the patient got a job and managed to remain away from home as much as possible. In returning to school, she tried to avoid speaking with her mother. All her phone calls were made to her father at his office. Because of increasing concern about the aloofness of her daughter, the mother demanded that she be seen in consultation for an evaluation. There was mild evidence of anorexia nervosa, none of a borderline character structure.

Young adolescent girls in the first developmental group of anorectics often have an early onset of puberty and an accompanying early reactivation of oedipal wishes with genital force. An early breakthrough of instinctual drives is apt to have occurred in late latency when the superego failed to give adequate protection against increased drive energy during preadolescence when there is no new love object or instinctual aim. An intensification of prelatency strivings is apt to occur with the appearance of infantile behavior. These patients show less severe adolescent disturbances in separation-individuation, with less dedifferentiation of ego function. Their early histories indicate that they are not consistently tied to mother; they have been given more freedom in certain respects. As toddlers and preschool children, they enjoy transitional objects and play with dolls and toys, unlike the more borderline or psychotic anorectics. As preschoolers they experience separations from their parents, who feel confident enough to leave them with responsible people and deserving of their own freedom and pressure during a vacation. But because of anxiety connected with the onset of puberty, regression occurs, but without disintegration. Aggression toward the mother is expressed to some degree; but, nevertheless, they remain rather compliant adolescents, but not the "perfect children" described by mothers of the borderline anorectics.

Anorectic girls in this first group are taught by the mother to conform to her rules and mode of behavior: joyless performance, achievement with minimal sublimation, strict morality, and the wish for the attainment of perfection. The anorectic's mother stands behind her camera, watching her daughter constantly. She is an oasis toward which all paths lead, and she becomes the maternal ego-ideal that encourages dependency and scorns aggression and homicidal fantasies. This negative oedipus complex, the main oedipal work of adolescence (Blos 1979), cannot readily be resolved by the anorectic. Because of their deep passivity, compliance, and desire to achieve, these girls are a joy to their teachers. The fathers are very proud of their daughter's attractiveness, spirit, and the high performance in schoolwork. But it is apparent that these young teenagers are fearful of life, in general, and, in particular, falling short of parental expectations and doing the wrong thing. They are also cautious with other teenagers and, as young children, they are fearful of their peers. Social maturation is impeded during latency; the group is not used for shared or projected guilt. In early adolescence, friends are not as readily available in the shift to libidinal extrafamilial objects, especially idealized friends of the same sex.

In their oedipal years, they show some attachment to the father and enjoy his attention into latency years. Later, during latency when the bisexual identification is more evident, they manifest a disinterest in and dislike for boys; they are dedicated "tomboys." They become "horse-crazy" or, as we increasingly see nowadays, addicted to running. Ego functions maintain a synthesizing function, are not easily susceptible to regression, and are able to hold to a demarcation between primary and secondary process thinking.

These patients find adolescence risky when final separation and individuation overtake their immaturity like a flush of blood to the brain. They want to feel dead from the torso down; seeking the heterosexual position in adolescence proper reactivates oedipal fixations. At the same time, the mother often feels left out of her teenager's life. She senses that something is happening to her in the middle of her life. Her own aspirations now seem pale and she tries to refurbish the closeness with her daughter. The regression that the anorectic of this group experiences in pubescence does not lead to deep activation of an archaic inner object, where self-object differentiation is lost. Throughout childhood, these anorectics display signs of mastery. There are attempts at extrafamilial identifications during the latency years—

identifications with teachers and popular figures outside of the family—and there is some degree of peer relationships, although rather cautious and critical. In peer relationships, the anorectic emphasizes academics, concerts and museum activities, often being didactic with her friends, sometimes alienating them with her sophistication and pretentiousness. Social integration, stability of self-esteem, and regulation of emotions do not occur as they should in the process of late adolescent consolidation.

Group II

The second group of anorectics, the largest group, is made up, for the most part, of middle to late adolescent girls and women. (Occasionally, some late latency and pubescent girls fall into this category.) In addition to the anorexia nervosa signs and symptoms, like other borderline patients (Stone 1980) this group shows serious defects in ego structure and organization, along with strong pregenital fixation and infantile object-dependency. Food substitutes for object relationships. Their primary disturbance is the perception of the self, not simply that of the body. The sense of self is not integrated, and when the self becomes regressively unstable, body symptoms become prominent and reflect the disharmony of the self. There is a breakdown of self-object, internal-external, and conceptual boundary distinctions. The level of differentiation of the self is below that of the first group of anorectic adolescents. These disturbances are distinctively the hallmark of the various borderline disorders, as well as a broad range of adolescent psychosomatic illnesses. Borderline anorectics are greatly threatened, because of their profound passive wishes, by engulfment during ego and id dedifferentiation. Fear of genital sexuality and heightened aggression forces them toward even more primitive object relations and pregenital drive discharge. They fear merger of self with an infantile inner object, and they turn to magical devices to save the self from passivity and merger. By falling back on the mother's magic, the anorectic masochistically falls victim to the mother's own falsification of reality. Disturbances of body image, false perceptual and conceptual interpretations of body stimuli, and an overall sense of ineffectiveness are clearly demonstrable in this group of anorectics. Looking for narcissistic, transitional phenomena to provide continuity, they live in a narcissistic state of consciousness, in a haze of frenetic activity which is only disorganizing, counterproductive, and which limits spontaneity of will, attention, action, and perception. They live with mood swings and struggle with defects in reflective awareness.

This is the core group of patients in the anorexia nervosa syndrome that Bruch (1966) and Palazzoli (1965, 1974) have studied for so many years. These patients have developmental arrests at the phases of symbiosis and separation-individuation. Kept passive by the mother, anorectic-to-be children are given, they do not take; they are made to be receptive and, unlike obese patients, food becomes the parents' weapon.[1] In order to feel good about themselves, borderline anorectics must rely on external supporting objects to maintain a narcissistic equilibrium. Their characters are vigorously obsessive-compulsive, schizoid, but, once well along in therapy, hysterical features may be apparent. When this support is threatened (for internal or external reasons) anorectics are apt to feel ineffective, helpless, incomplete, or overwhelmed. Their life is now boring, routine, and mechanical— feelings rooted in their deep sense of passivity.

They do not feel capable or worthy of respect. They sense no support for any spontaneous activity. Until the onset of the anorexia, they are passive and compliant in their everyday life and feel unable to influence people in the slightest matter. They want to be autonomous adults, often feeling impatient to grow up, yet wanting to hide from independent responsibility. With the onset of adolescence, there is an upsurge of aggression and sexuality. Their lack of individuation is now no longer hidden behind compliance.

Acutely sensitive to the inner and outer world, like her parents, the anorectic is never sure of what to make out of enteroreceptive cues; she cannot easily initiate cues any more than she can readily identify them. Having not achieved self- and object constancy and stable self-object differentiation, she is ill-prepared for separation and individuation. She has not been able to internalize, from parents and important adult figures in latency, the means to maintain self-cohesion, self-esteem, and neutralization of tension. Decathecting from parental representations is apt to bring about fragmentation of the self, first expressed in

1. Anorexia nervosa and obesity are two sides of the same coin: The anorectic denies oral impulses, while the obese surrenders. The anorectic superego is punitive, cruel, and perfectionistic; the obese individual's superego is punishing but uncontrolling; it does not know perfection. Both disorders express disturbances in separation and individuation.

preoccupation with eating, weight, and the body, and later with ways of logically controlling both the internal and external environment.

With regression in ego and drives, there is a regressive increase in oral aggression and anal ambivalence. Self-determination in action and thought becomes more intense and seemingly hopeless. Consequently, the adolescent begins to fear symbolic engulfment by the maternal object and fears abandonment by the object from which she feels so much aggression. On a defensive level, there occur splitting, projection, acting out, clinging, avoiding, and denying—all part of the overall failure in development of defense organization. The ego splits to foster denial of reality and distortion of the body image. She wants to disown the body, fight its demands, and stop being lulled into a false sense of security.

The long-standing ego weakness is complicated by the increased instinctual pressure of adolescence. Failure of the synthetic function of the ego makes for the tenacity of anorectic symptoms. Renewal of oedipal strivings, which cannot be denied, leads to regression of drives and dedifferentiation of ego function and analization of behavior. Conceptual and perceptual disturbances occur, as well as a compensatory drive for cognitive and perceptual control of the body and self, by focusing her instinctual life onto food and eating, and by using starvation as a means of gaining absolute power over the body, self, parents, and other significant people in her world.

For the borderline group, puberty sometimes has a later emotional onset than for the first group of anorectics. These anorectics show a marked denial of adolescent oedipal feelings; this is related to the fact that powerful oral pathology had prematurely heightened oedipal strivings. The genital strivings for the uxorious father now defensively substitute for frustrated oral-dependent needs toward the mother; positive oedipal strivings cannot continue because of pregenital aggression deflected from the mother to the father. Furthermore, oral rage and envy had intensified penis envy during earlier development, and, now in adolescence, the envy becomes more difficult to control.

The histories of the core anorectic and her mother reveal that the mother of the anorectic is herself a frightened, lonely, fragile woman, who has struggled to maintain her own sense of self. She remains dependent upon and ambivalently attached to her own mother (the anorectic's grandmother). An enduring but unhappy matriarchate, she struggles against her own mother's criticism and aloofness and the attempts of her mother to control her daughter and family. For these reasons, depressive symptoms are common in the mothers of anorectics. Cantwell et al. (1977) and Winokur, March, and Mendels (1980) believe the depression represents an affective disorder. The struggle between mother and daughter intensifies at the time the latter starts a family. Then, because of her mother's lack of maternal support and never-ending criticism, the daughter is ill-prepared to be a mother, understand the child's needs, differentiate herself from her infant daughter and, in general, enjoy her own daughter. Unsupportively, she holds her daughter close to her during infancy and does everything possible to control the daughter, just as she herself was controlled. But a crisis occurs between the mother and child at the time of separation-individuation, especially during the rapprochement subphase, when the mother cannot tolerate the toddler's ambivalence, assertiveness, and curiosity. She does not supply a teddy bear or other kind of transitional object, and so does not permit the toddler to express a full range of aggression and ambivalence. The mother makes herself available only if the child clings and acts regressive, and withdraws if the child separates from her and tries to individuate. The anorectic's mother, however, is not one to withdraw for long, and she tries to control the toddler even more in hopes of subduing aggression and minimizing separation. In the anorectic's preadolescence, the mother fosters the daughter's passivity and compliance and reinforces emulation of her by the daughter, who wants to be helpful and attentive in every way, especially with preparation of food. The daughter identifies with the mother in the latter's mechanisms of control and soon begins to dominate herself, not her mother, until the onset of the anorectic disorder and failure of adaptation. Both the daughter and mother reject each other while feeling indispensable to each other, each insatiable for endless love (Seligman 1976).

Denial of affect, feeling states and bodily experiences makes it difficult for the anorectic to feel separate and whole. The anorectic adolescent readily denies primitive impulses, probably more so than other adolescents with severe emotional disturbances. She projects sexual and aggressive images stripped of affect, much in the way as anorectic parents, who by model, attitude, and interaction inhibit affect in the family. The anorectic manifests distortions of the body and displays fluid dedifferentiation and the tendency to fuse with the primary infantile object. (Those mixed anorectics who vomit with the breakdown of the defense against bulimia have more bizarre notions about eating, food and body processes. They see their impulses taking over their world.) Premature, oedipal manifestations with condensations between pregenital and genital occur. Preoedipal fears and fantasies of pregnancy increase anxiety. Internalizations of oedipal demands and prohibitions—realistic parental images—falter on the shaky foundations of a poorly integrated superego. In latency, attempts at mastery are made but are superficial, empty, and not sublimatory. There is no real interest or pleasure in school work. The daughter's spontaneous expression is not recognized by the mother, and there is no encouragement free of maternal possessiveness. Compliant surrender is encouraged through the latency years. Idealized self- and object representations are played out in the anorectic's behavior. Seldom are they expressed otherwise until the patient is well into the opening phase of treatment. The fantasies are sadomasochistic and narcissistic, regressively acted out to repeat and relive old narcissistic hurts with the illusion of perfection. There are no "hero world" and family romance fantasies in the latency years.

In adolescence, a search for identity founders on disidentification with the mother. In addition, her biologic drive toward motherhood is challenged by the contemporary societal devaluation of motherhood. Her mere existence is the critical issue, forcing her to rely more on mechanisms of self-control, which she learned from her mother. Now she must strive for more psychological distance between herself and her mother. To deny her dependency to her mother, she attacks her for the latter's dominance and control over her. Her adaptation becomes tenuous. Defeat and control by the mother tighten the anorectic's tie to the maternal object and confront the anorectic with her aggression and resultant separation anxiety, as well as depression and fear of maternal abandonment. The combination of aggression to the mother and new challenges increases her separation anxiety. Infantalized, the anorectic is unable to make decisions. Stemming from weakness in self- and object constancies, cohesive self-other and inner-outer boundaries, transient unreality feelings may occur with the sense of being amorphously different, an obscure sense of helplessness, uselessness and ineffectuality, mixed with boredom and emptiness. Transient unreality feelings are expressive of a reactivation of feelings of oral helplessness, threatening an already weak sense of self.

Group III

A third group are male anorectics, who are usually prepubertal, passive, chubby boys, who fear phallic aggressive feelings; they are frightened by sexual feelings toward the mother (Hasan and Tibbetts 1977, Swann 1971). They fear male aggression.[2] They are only concerned about the shape of their bodies if they are extremely obese or struggle with gender identity. Those boys who reach puberty early fear their "puppy fat," which oddly contrasts with their quantitatively increased, instinctual drives (Crisp 1977a). Multiply symptomatic, they often complain of depersonalization and depression. In the wake of their regressive shift, they are fearful of castration and merger with the inner infantile object. Pregenital aggression reinforces old fears of the father. The boys view their chubbiness as an indication of profound passivity, femininity, weakness and homosexuality. A strong negative oedipal phase with passive wishes may predominate along with an unconscious feminine identification and feminine role in the family. Overt or latent homosexual conflicts are often evident beneath the fear of being fat. Otherwise, anorectic males are genetically and structurally similar to the female borderline anorectics but tend to be even more difficult to treat. If treatment is successful for the acute phase and starvation is given up, they transfer control and mastery to work and generally excel in academics, which leads them to an extremely isolated life. It is not unusual for male anorectics to choose the physical or statistical sciences, which will allow them to retreat even more from people into an abstract way of life.

The male patients, in some respects, are clinically different from the female patients. They tend to be much more obsessional, hypochondriachal, more suspicious of people, and are boastful of their fasting. They fear fatness but not weight gain itself. Males usually do not deny hunger; on the Eating Attitudes Test (Garner and Garfunkel 1979), they score with female obese and recovered anorectics. Otherwise their psychopathology is similar. Sinus bradycardia is a good prognostic sign. Often the mother and especially the father are over-

2. Breuer, in 1893, described a twelve-year-old boy who had been urged by a man to perform fellatio. Fleeing from the scene, the boy developed hysterical symptoms of anorexia and vomiting which persisted for some weeks until he confessed the incident to his mother. Breuer explained that the sexual trauma had excited passive-feminine wishes in the boy (Breuer and Freud 1893–1895).

weight, preoccupied with food (Sreenivasan 1978). Mutual hostility between father and anorectic son exists. After the age of fourteen, after pubescence has occurred and androgen levels are steadily increasing, their preoccupation with fat and eating usually lessens. Nevertheless, their fear of passive wishes and their need to control objects remains extremely strong.

Group IV

There is a fourth group of anorectics—those who do not starve themselves but, instead, regularly binge and vomit (Boskind-Lodahl 1976). Vomiting and purging become a habit for weight control. The developmental histories of the gorger-vomiters are somewhat different from the starving and mixed anorectics at the other end of the spectrum. First of all, their developmental histories do not show an unusually early onset of puberty with a marked reactivation of the oedipal wishes. Their early development does indicate a disturbance in separation-individuation, manifested principally in terms of separation anxiety and a clinging attachment to the mother. But, unlike the anorectic abstainers or mixed group, they are not deeply or consistently tied to their mothers. They are less dominated by passive wishes. During the toddler years, they have more independence and assertiveness and a better relationship with peers than do the borderline or psychotic anorectic abstainers. With puberty, there is an increase in aggression toward the mother; historically, however, there is early evidence of aggressive behavior. As Beumont, George, and Smart (1976), and Dally and Gomez (1979) point out, the gorgers and vomiters function at a higher level of psychosexuality, compared to the self-starvers. Many of the former regularly have intercourse, although often with limited pleasure. The outstanding feature of the bulimic vomiter is that the mother tends not to be the seeker of absolute perfection, found so often in the other groups of anorexia nervosa. In fact, the mothers, often manifestly depressed throughout their girl's childhood, are sometimes conspicuously nonachievers. They fear abandonment and are threatened by fragmentation and damaged self-esteem.

The bulimic vomiter vacillates between compulsive eating and vomiting. Only by vomiting—and exhausting herself—can she finally reduce tensions that threaten fragmentation of the self. Bulimia, with

its addictive force, brings the gorger-purger anorectic closer to recreat-
ing the fantasy of union with an idealized mother; no longer is she
helpless. Now the bulimia takes on, in some patients, a perverse
quality: eating brings about increasing erotic excitement with eventual
orgastic buildup in the abdomen and pelvis—the so-called alimentary
orgasm. Because of her overidentification with her concept of femininity, she becomes obsessed with pleasing men and in finding ways to
establish not only a gender-self but also an identity. Their pursuit of
thinness is part of their frantic search for the feminine ideal. Addiction-
prone, they come to depend on laxatives and diuretics (Davidson and
Silverstone 1972). Men are compared to her father, a kind of hero, if not
a god, who can be distant, preoccupied with work and achievement, and
invariably rejecting of her as well as other women. The father is usually
seen as a man of great mystique, a man filled with dark spaces which she
would like to invade and explore. Like other anorectics, the gorger
wants to be an achiever; but, unlike other anorectics, her achievement
has often faltered, partly because of the time and energy taken up by her
ritualistic eating behavior. Whatever achievement she has accomplished gives her no intrinsic reward. She usually dislikes the physical
aspects of her feminine appearance and thinks about plastic surgery for
correcting facial imperfections and disappointments in breast development. She wonders about her father's love for her. She spends hours
thinking about the father, wondering about his relationship to the
mother, puzzling over whether the mother is satisfying to the father
and trying to suppress any thought of his dying.

With her sense of unfulfillment and pessimism about men, she
believes there is no choice but to eat, fill up, and be complete. Losing
control of eating, at first, gives her some pleasure and allows her to
disassociate from her painful affect. Within a matter of minutes,
however, shame, guilt, and disgust ensue with renewed fears of fatness
and depressing memories of past binges. She feels, more and more, a
loss of perfection, past, present and future; she swears that she will
regain control. She purges to rid herself of the hated food and what it
symbolically means to her.

Etiologic Background

The etiological factors in anorexia nervosa are multiple (Beumont et al.
1978b): older age of the parents, their instability, the increased inci-

dence of both physical and psychiatric illness in the parents, high socioeconomic class, issues of dependence and independence, sexual challenge, concern over obesity, onset of "puppy fat" in female pubertal girls reaching preadolescence early (the weight/fat threshold for puberty), and psychosocial significances of body weight and shape. Constitutional and chromosomal elements in the etiology of anorexia nervosa are not convincing.

No single psychological hypothesis is presently supportable (Halmi 1978). The anorectic fear of being fat results from psychodynamic causes, heightened and reinforced by catalyzing forces now strongly entrenched in our culture. Each anorectic, for a lucid view of etiology of the disorder, must be evaluated in terms of the patient's developmental history and the genetic structural findings during assessment and treatment.

Ego Organization and Style

In general, the developmental histories of anorexia nervosa patients are regularly replete with evidence of parental emphasis on delay and control of pleasure, an exaggerated mode of ego functioning developmentally associated with anal phase-appropriate ego activity. Oral gratifications are tolerated and at times overindulged until the toddler stage when the child is prematurely encouraged to conform to a parental style of compliance and socially acceptable behavior. The care of these children is basically pleasureless but adequate, except that the parents do not encourage separateness and autonomy, most notably at the time when the first separation-individuation phase is taking place. At that point, muscular exploratory behavior, oppositional attitudes, and negativism are conspicuously absent. Her active wishes are discouraged. The child must suppress and deny wishes for separation-individuation in order to insure maternal supplies. The child becomes a pretender and denier.

The anorectic's mother attempts to anticipate the child's every need. She is overcareful and overcautious—defending herself against fantasies of starvation and incorporative and cannibalistic wishes by reaction formation—and does little to foster, for the child, a sense of self and any interest in the outside world. The child invests in the maternal object—not in the self—with fears of losing the object; she is left clinging to the mother, feeling even more helpless.

The mother sets a pleasureless, formal, and controlling tone to the family atmosphere and transactions, and the patient's individual needs are subordinated to mother's strict moral codes and rigid, ambitious, and narcissistic ego-ideals. For the anorectic, "all bad" object representations, the earliest superego precursors, strongly influencing superego formation, arise from archaic, sadistic pregenital images. They are reprojected as external bad objects. Ideal self-images and overidentified object images foster ego-ideals of greatness and perfection and prevent superego integration and modulation. Primitive fusions of the ideal-self and ideal-object images force harsh demands on the anorectic self. Primitive idealization of the mother creates an all-powerful object image for the anorectic, leading to omnipotent identification and projection of aggression. Thus, sadistic and idealized precursors of the superego press for satisfaction from the self under the guise of seeking perfection.

The anorectic displays, as part of her passive wishes, a chameleonic, adaptive quality until adolescence. But she eventually resorts to negativism as an expression of her rage at her mother's rules and demands that she remain tied to her to insure libidinal supplies. Negativism is a defense against oral surrender and invasion, just as hyperactivity is an escape from food, the object, and an attempt to contact the ideal self. As a consequence, the mutual cuing and communicative interplay, necessary for individuation, do not occur.

Because of conflict and anxiety around sexuality and separation, the anorectic patient experiences both drive and ego regressions. The need to relinquish the self to the object, to give into profound passivity, in order to guarantee maternal supplies makes the borderline anorectic very vulnerable to regression. Bulimic loss of control challenges the ego; eating and gorging threaten oral surrender, invasion, and re-instatement with the original oneness of the mother-child unit. In the ensuing regression, the ego falls back on its defenses, analized ego functions that promote withdrawal, contrariness, aggressive self-assertiveness, and autonomy. The functional regression of the ego overshadows oral mastery, which was learned during the anal-muscular stage. The ego turns against drive satisfaction to control the body: its movement as well as sensations and perceptions of bodily and affective states. Femininity and receptive passivity are rejected. The body as a passive vessel is denigrated. Passivity and surrender to the maternal object, the principal anorectic vulnerability, is activated. Hunger, the psychic representation of the stomach, is equated with fullness, pregnancy, and mother. Emaciation for the anorectic means security and power against inadequacy and weakness. Starvation promotes states of dizziness and wooziness, narcissistic states of consciousness, leading to oceanic and fusional experiences. The anorectic suppresses oral needs for the sake of security and power. Highly analized ego functions are clearly discernible in the perceptual and cognitive area. Magico-omnipotent thinking is prominent. Cognitive and perceptual control becomes a leitmotif of the anorectic patient. The ego pleasure of control and mastery now outweighs oral drive gratification.

Many of the signs and symptoms of anorexia nervosa are best understood in these terms. The conceptual and perceptual attainment of absolute power and control of the body, self, parents, and other significant object relations is central to the snydrome. Thus, conceptual and perceptual discrimination is compromised through denial and suppression of individuative feelings and actions. The narcissistic pleasure of attaining supreme thinness obscures, for the anorectic, both the realistic ugliness of cachexia and the painful craving for food. Control of pleasure dissociates body and affective feelings from perceptual impressions and mental representations. The pleasure of limitless energy and hyperactivity nullifies a sense of ineffectiveness, denies fatigue and attenuates both aggressive and libidinal excitement. The pleasure of perfect performance and perfect ego-ideal challenges the exalted ego-ideal of the parents. To prevent a further narcissistic challenge to the parents, which might bring about a painful crisis of conscience for the patient, the anorectic takes a masochistic delight in suffering, which modifies the strain of her archaic, primitive superego.

Anorectic patients often have a defect in conceptualization, although they are usually above-average students, if not brilliant. But they obtain in high-school scholastic aptitude and achievement tests scores lower than one might expect from their school performance and records. Their uneven cognitive development is apparent on closer scrutiny. Conceptual function is arrested at an early level with variable distortion of body image and body concept. Condensation and combinative thinking with blending and juxtaposing separate objects take place. Arbitrary and autistic symbolism is found; the boundaries between separately perceived images fuse into one idea. And demarcations between external perception and affective states are fluid. The anorectic overestimates body-size and body-width. Borderline anorectics are arrested in the phase of preconceptual or concrete operations (Piaget 1968), the period of egocentricity which is characterized by an exalted sense of magical effectiveness in thinking. The severe anorectic is not only arrested in this phase of conceptual development but also is blocked from moving into the adolescent phase of formal operations, which allows independent evaluation and abstract thinking to be exercised.

§Martina, a sixteen-year-old Roman Catholic girl with glaucous eyes, a senior at a boarding school in New Hampshire, was an object of concern to her headmaster and teachers. Her parents were asked by the headmaster to take her home for a complete medical evaluation. An anorectic adolescent, she had lost more weight and was now at 70 pounds, having fallen in a period of three years from a weight of 110 pounds. The school was worried about cold exposure (frostbite) and the possibility of hypothermia and circulatory collapse. They insisted that she have a medical evaluation before returning to finish her senior year.

When Martina was thirteen years old, her mother remarried. Martina became amenorrheic, began to starve herself, flew into angry outbursts against her mother, and started working long hours at school, hoping to dazzle her mother with academic achievements. She threw herself into a storm of schoolwork, was unrealistically ambitious with the hope of going to the California Institute of Technology for a Ph.D. in mathematics. But her Scholastic Aptitude Test (SAT) mathematics score was in the 500's, too low for such a collegiate choice. A nonvomiter, Martina lived on dietetic dairy products, mostly cheese, yogurt, and iced Alba. She drank huge quantities of diet soda and ate frozen yogurt, to the point of having frequent diarrhea.

The medical evaluation established that she was not on the verge of any medical collapse, as long as she did not lose more weight. She was followed for the remainder of the year by a local internist. In the fall, she went to a small college, a more realistic choice, where she went into therapy.

Neurotic and borderline anorectics, as indicated, vary considerably in regard to ego function and ego structure. What is common, however, to the entire anorectic group, as well as to their families, is an exaggerated mode of ego function, typical of the anal-muscular phase of development. During toddlerhood, these patients are taught to conform to parental models of behavior which emphasize joyless performance, achievement, fitness, strict morality, and perfection. At the time of pubescence, heightened oedipal strivings, a drive regression, and a parallel ego functional regression result in analization of defenses and behavioral modes. Cognitive and perceptual processes are then geared to control and mastery, which, in turn, are more pleasurable than drive gratification.

Administering the Minnesota Multiphasic Inventory (MMPI) (Hathaway and McKinley 1951) to borderline anorectics and their families shows an interesting profile; namely, a low F-K score and a high Sc score. The former score indicates a tendency "to fake good health"; the latter, a sign of schizoid tendencies. These results are in keeping with the parents' attitude of hiding feelings of self-doubt and insecurity and stressing status and recognition for good and acceptable behavior. Crisp et al. (1979) found an abnormally high "lie" score, as well as "introversion" and "emotional" scores in testing anorectics with the Eysenck Personality Inventory. The anorectic view of normality is a caricature (Story 1976). The Witkin Embedded Figure Test (Witkin 1950, 1960) reveals that anorectics, as well as their parents, tend to be field-dependent, which suggests a low level of body concept, identity, and separateness. Likewise, on the Object Sorting Test (Lovibond 1954), anorectics, as well as the parents, demonstrate a degree of cognitive impairment; they have difficulty in categorizing objects under universals. Both the Witkin Embedded Figure Test and the Object Sorting Test, however, are nonspecific, found in a variety of borderline patients.

Developmental and family studies demonstrate aberrant mothering and difficulties in mutual cueing in the early toddler stage. Early histories indicate that anorectics project a primitive aggression onto the mother, with the result that they form an archaic, cruel superego. This aggression intensifies the harshness of the hostile component of their ambivalence and invites them to believe they can destroy with their aggression.

Perhaps the marked preponderance of female borderline anorectics is due to difficulties which toddler girls have in the rapprochement subphase of separation-individuation; they have a more suppressed ambivalent relationship with their mothers. The normal increase in aggression, concomitant with locomotion development, does not seem to occur in the histories of anorectics. Instead, there is a decrease. This may be related to a sex difference in aggression, a diminution or inhibition of the aggressive drive in anorectic girls. The hypoaggressive behavior of the anorectic works against attainment of separateness. Later, these children turn regressively to pathologic defenses, like denial, projection, rationalization, magic control, externalization, and displacement. The marked preponderance of female patients is due to the mother's tendency to restrict and inhibit the activity of the female toddler during the practicing subphase that precedes rapprochement. Constitutional factors may also contribute to the gender preponderance. Fixation points, the style of regression, the strength and vicissitudes of the drives, and the health of the object relations are all important in understanding the development of anorectic children.

Anamnesis from parents and anorectics is not sufficient in etching developmental histories. Mothers of anorectics tend to be unrevealing historians. Their histories exude reports of absolute perfection on their part and celebrate the perfection of their children. It is only through transference and analytic reconstruction that one can learn more about anorectic developmental material and suggest to research psychologists possible genetic factors in anorexia nervosa. The interplay of developmental deviations and ego deficits with neuroendocrine, pschodynamic, and familial factors warrants further explication and validation.

8

Theory and Technique In the Treatment of Anorexia Nervosa

Remember one thing only: that it's you—nobody else—who determines your destiny and decides your fate. Nobody else can be alive for you, nor can you be alive for anyone else.

—e. e. cummings, *Six Nonlectures*

Psychotherapy errs not in being wrong but in being rudimentary.

—A. R. Ammons, *Sphere: The Form of a Motion*

Just as there is no one anorexia, there is no one treatment for anorexia nervosa; a variety of possible, disparate therapies must be considered for each patient in terms of the basic psychopathology and stage of the disorder.

The treatment approach to anorexia nervosa must be divided into two phases.

The first phase is the treatment of the acute disturbance, which threatens life and is a crisis to the patient and to the family—a medical and psychiatric emergency. This phase may range from an abruptly acute, short-lived state of adolescent turmoil to an unremitting disorder which leads to profound cachexia and toxicity, requiring medical and psychiatric hospitalization with hyperalimentation in order to sustain and restore life. In this phase, medical and psychological effects of starvation present obstacles to psychological treatment in that inanition makes the patient less receptive to help. Mental and physical fatigue, apathy, mental agitation, inattentive concentration, shallow affect, and object distancing work against therapeutic alliance and intervention.

The second phase of treatment commences with the patient returning to a more normal nutritional state (stage three of the disturbance—see chapter 7). This is the phase for the long-term treatment of the anorectic's pathological character. This second phase is often not reached by the anorectic. She chooses to leave treatment, or her parents will not support treatment. Her therapist may think that restoring her nutrition is sufficient for the anorectic to return to a normal life (Pillay and Crisp 1977), or believe that changing the family structure and function is sufficient to alter the anorectic's ego style.

Then there are a few anorectics who absolutely refuse treatment. Elizabeth's attitude and situation are not unusual.

§In the summer of her thirteenth year, Elizabeth, a horsey, onyx-eyed girl with yellow parchment skin and an erect posture, stiff as a tree, went on a severe diet, to the extent that by the beginning of fall she looked like a denuded skeleton. Each day at the family's country house, she performed her daily rituals of violent exercise in total silence, practically nonstop, starting with fifty to a hundred laps a day in the pool, then calisthenics and, finally, long-distance running. The neighbors would stare at her, wondering how she could relentlessly expend so much energy day after day on legs like a grasshopper's without collapsing. She complained matter-of-factly of fatigue every afternoon, but fatigue did not daunt her; she only smiled vaguely through clenched teeth. She skipped her lunch during the summer months. Close-mouthed, she often kept her arms crossed.

On returning home in the fall and being examined by her pediatrician for the new school year, she was found to have severe anemia and was given a large dosage of iron. For a while, she seemed to pick up a bit in spirits, although she did not go back to a normal diet. The world remained blue. She had shared her body long enough with her mother; now she would reduce her body to a thread of existence.

In the ensuing seven years, she remained fanatically weight-conscious, "storming and fuming" whenever she looked into the full-length mirror and saw her "heavy thighs." She was repeatedly told by the family physician that, although her thighs were "a bit heavy," she was certainly not overweight and should not destroy the rest of her body just because of her legs. She resisted medical efforts to get her into psychotherapy but relented enough to undergo an endocrinological workup, which was entirely negative. At age eighteen she went to college, where she continued her diet and, moving too rapidly, had no friends. She would become quite upset at college if she could not run twelve miles a day; or, if the weather were bad, swim a hundred laps in the pool. She refused the idea of consultation; a friend urged her to see the college psychiatrist. He attempted to arrange treatment for her through her university health service. She absolutely declined, insisting that she would do anything to prevent "getting fat." The world could lay siege to her solitude, to no avail. A year later, after a half-marathon, she collapsed from exhaustion and dehydration and was admitted to the hospital. Her choice was gone.

Treatments for Anorexia Nervosa

There are a number of specific treatments for anorexia nervosa, from coercive feeding to approaches focusing on dynamic issues (Van Buskirk 1977, Lucas, Duncan, and Piens 1976, Tolstrup 1975, Goodsitt 1969). Treatments vary from traditional psychoanalysis to psychosurgery, from education to behavioral modification, from simple observation and therapeutic indifference—allowing the natural history to run its course—to an intense family treatment (Russell 1977). The dream of every honest therapy is to enter the treatment of anorexia nervosa. The treatment recommended is usually determined by the clinician's experience with anorexia nervosa and, in general, by his own theoretical and personal orientation and ideology. Sometimes the treatments for anorexia nervosa bring to mind the image of a blind man moving pins on a map.

Some therapists take a predominantly organic stance to treatment, based on the belief that anorexia nervosa is primarily a hypothalamic disturbance (Katz and Walsh 1978). Forced feeding, confinement to bed, and psychotropic drugs may be their treatment of choice. Electroconvulsive therapy (ECT), contary to Laboucarié and Barres's report (1954), has no place in the treatment of anorexia nervosa—even for a grossly psychotic anorectic who rips out I.V.'s and nasogastric tubes. Psychotropic drugs can be used and the patient saved what she will see and experience as sadistic punishment. Leucotomy is still used in England (Sargant 1951, Williams 1958, Kelly 1973, Mitchell-Heggs, Kelly, and Richardson 1976), but now it is reserved mainly for chronic, intractable, severely obsessive-compulsive anorectic patients, who would have to be tube-fed indefinitely in order to live. The physician must be willing to follow the postleucotomy patient for a long period of time (Nemiah 1950). After neurosurgery, the anorectic usually cannot resist bulimic impulses; she experiences depression and guilt when she gorges and gains weight. If no psychotherapy is given in the postoperative phase, the anorectic may become a secretive vomiter, despair, and finally suicide (Crisp and Kalucy 1973, Russell 1979).

Pharmacotherapy

Chlorpromazine is still the drug of choice in anorexia nervosa for reduction of anxiety and the fear of eating, although it has probably been used less for anorexia nervosa in the last few years, and then largely for the older patients, such as anxious, middle-aged women who, because of extreme anxiety, resist refeeding. The dose range for its anxiolytic effect is 25 to 100 mg. three to four times a day. A suspension or syrup is available.

For older patients, depressed over their stalemated lives and unable to slough off their suffering, antidepressant medications may be helpful, especially if compulsive rituals appear around food and eating (White and Schnaultz 1977). The tricyclics, also possessing hypnotic and anxiolytic effects, are generally the preferred antidepressants. But most therapists dispense with antidepressants, as well as stimulants, because supportive-evocative psychotherapy is more helpful and to the point. It should be added that, since anorexia nervosa, with its tension-relieving hyperactivity, diminished sleep, and delayed insomnia, is viewed by some clinicians as evidence of hypomania (Cantwell et al. 1977, Winokur, March, and Mendels 1980)—instead of as signs of starvation—lithium (Barcai 1977) is a dangerous drug to give an anorectic, especially a binger-vomiter who excessively uses cathartics and diuretics (Davidson and Silverstone 1972). In the last few years, pharmacotherapy has been increasingly used for the treatment of anorexia nervosa. New drugs have been investigated because chlor-promazine was found to have complicating side effects: it leads to dyskinetic reactions, akathisia, and fluid retention, and is associated in some clinical situations with a 10 percent incidence of epileptic seizures. The newer drugs, often evaluated by uncontrolled studies, have been used only for a short time, and their effectiveness and side effects cannot yet be properly assessed (Johanson and Knorr 1977). Cyprohep-tadine, an antiserotoninergic drug, does not seem to produce weight gain in anorexia nervosa, even though it has been found to do so in the irritable bowel syndrome (Vigersky and Loriaux 1977). Amitriptyline, a tricyclic antidepressant, can bring about lightening of motor retarda-tion and reduction of sadness (Needleman and Waber 1979). A few anorectic patients given this medication experienced an increase in appetite and weight gain (Kendler 1978), as well as improvement in temperative regulation and motor behavior. Some investigators have wondered whether the drug acts at the level of hypothalamic catecholamines; others speculate that it blocks uptake of 5-hydroxytryptamine. Metoclopramide, an antiemetic, has not shown particular promise for the treatment of anorexia nervosa (Moldofsky and Garfinkle 1974). Diphenylhydantoin apparently inhibits the appetite center and facilitates a discharge response (Green and Rau 1977). Excitation of the central nervous system is depressed by this drug. Its overall effectiveness is questionable.

Treatment During the Acute Phase

A popular medical regimen is hospitalization (Maxmen, Siberfarb, and Ferrell 1974, Rollins and Blackwell 1968) with a program of chlorpromazine. Insulin usage, based on the rationale that modified insulin therapy brings about sweating, anxiety, dizziness and hunger, is seldom used now that most therapists realize that anorectics never really lose their hunger. Furthermore, insulin is dangerous for an emaciated patient with no glycogen reserve.

The hospital regimen is accompanied by a controlled high carbohydrate, protein diet, and, if indicated, intravenous hyperalimentation (Akamatsu et al. 1972), which avoids forcing the anorectic to take food by mouth or nasogastric tube and allows considerable weight gain without coercive confrontations over eating.[1] The goals of treatment are simply the stimulation of appetite, reduction of anxiety, and acceleration of positive metabolic processes. In this medical program, psychotherapy, if used at all, may range from supportive to supportive-expressive therapy, with possible emphasis on family therapy, conjoint marital therapy, or behavioral modification (Parker, Blazer, and Wyrick 1977, Silverman 1977). The acutely starving anorectic is told that she is toxic and cannot do adequate psychological work until her nutrition is at least partly restored. If she will not eat, intravenous hyperalimentation can be used; it is effective in restoring weight rapidly, avoids the struggle over coerced eating and the threat of tube feeding. Although still popular in some quarters (Brown et al. 1931, Hurst 1936, Williams 1958), tube feeding, which makes the anorectic feel she has been defeated, should be avoided if at all possible. Nevertheless, a degree of judicious coercion to eat is necessary if the self-starving anorectic is going to start eating and reverse the hormonal inactivity of the hypothalamo-pituitary axis and correct the psychological effects of starvation. In her early sessions, the therapist makes it

1. Total parenteral nutrition (TPN), by way of a catheter in the superior vena cava, may be necessary for the near-death anorectic; if so, complications, due to mechanical and chemical factors, should be guarded against.

known to the patient that he understands anorexia nervosa and is not puzzled by the mystique of the disorder. He may tell the anorectic, if appropriate, that she is one of a number of patients he has treated, a fact that she may not enjoy hearing in that it shatters her sense of uniqueness and entitlement. But he must be careful not to appear omniscient and stimulate the anorectic's own omnipotence.

A second approach emphasizes either hospital outpatient or office treatment of the anorectic (Ryle 1936, Reinhart, Kenna, and Succop 1972). Part of this approach is the avoidance of all coercive efforts to get the patient to eat (Palmer and Jones 1939), a tactic which can prolong the treatment and even endanger the patient's life by collaborating with her in her struggle with her family and her regressive wishes to maintain infantile dependency. Proponents of this method view the hospitals as contraindicated, even for the most severely cachectic patients. In this program, the therapist dissociates himself from the feeding problem and overall medical management, not simply working collaboratively with an internist or pediatrician in the medical management, but totally divorcing himself from medical knowledge of her physical status.

Treatment Program

Both approaches are paradigmatic and ignore the particular needs of the individual patient. A treatment program for the abstainer and binger-vomiter clearly must be based on a sound diagnostic and dynamic-structural formulation of the patient's disturbance, along with a careful assessment of the patient's medical and metabolic status (Silverman 1977). It should be communicated to the patient that the therapist and hospital staff are quite aware of her sense of helplessness and that a well-formulated regimen for her has been drawn up and coordinated. The immediate critical question the therapist must decide is whether hospitalization is indicated for the self-starving anorectic. Immediate hospitalization is indicated when starvation is relentless and has continued over a year, the patient adamantly blocking efforts to gain an agreed weekly weight, with a rapid or progressive loss to below 50 percent of the total body weight, urinary ketone bodies are absent, overt psychosis is present or imminent, and there is a persistent refusal by the parents to draw back from direct confrontation with the patient. The same criteria are relevant to the gorger-vomiter. Those patients who control their weight by vomiting and the use of laxatives—young adults often with electrolyte disturbances (Russell 1979)—need careful metabolic and nursing management. Historically, hospitalization of the anorectic with isolation from her family has always been favored (Gull 1874, Charcot 1889, Gasne 1900, Dubois 1909, Weir Mitchell 1907, Souques 1925, Gillespie 1931, Straus 1948). Physical separation from the parents, it must be remembered, can only assuage a crisis at home; it will not change the family system or alter her relationships with psychic representations of the parents. Unless she has psychological treatment, she will always find someone with whom to act out a negative mother-transference.

The patient should be admitted only to a medical unit which has had experience with anorectic patients and understands their pathology (Pierloot, Wellens, and Houben 1975, Moldofsky and Garfinkle 1974). The parents are allowed to visit during the regular hospital visiting hours. Totally shutting them out of the anorectic's life, as some therapists do (Dally and Gomez 1979), can negate their acceptance of treatment, either family therapy or individual treatment for themselves. The primary therapist need not directly take part in the medical regime and management. But he must keep in mind that, because of the pediatrician's or internist's management of the anorectic, split and institutional transferences are apt to occur (Cohen 1978). In this unit, cohesive, devoted teamwork is essential. The nurses do a major part of the work in seeing that the patients have a regular, bulky diet with small caloric increments (Butler, Duke, and Stovel 1977, D. A. King 1971, Masuda, Sehata, and Imai 1972). Anorexia nervosa, however, must be explained to the nurses, especially the younger women, themselves often preoccupied with weight and diet, so that they do not identify with the patients or treat them coercively. In the ward management of the mixed anorectics and the gorger-vomiters, the nurses watch for concealment and secret disposal of food by feeding others or self-induced vomiting. Laxatives and diuretics, delivered in the mail from friends or supplied by other patients and their families, must be watched for. Some patients simulate weight gain by the consumption of huge quantities of water, voluntary urine retention before weighing, and hiding weights in their hospital clothes. Nurses must also dissuade the patients from exercise, take responsibility for eating behavior and decisions on the ward, and discourage the patient from a preoccupation with a precise daily weight, although the team notes weight variations as communications from the patient and looks for a more or less progressive gain in weight. They encourage anorectics to take a healthy interest in the body. A dietary regimen helps the patient develop inner controls. Families are instructed to discard the clothes that the anorectic wore to the hospital, as well as those at home, which she had altered to conform to her emaciated body. The anorectic is told that the team is aware that her illness makes her do curious things, like hide food and feed other people. She soon learns that the team knows her full repertoire of anorectic tricks and strategies. The medical team informs the anorectic that she must select a target weight, appropriate to her frame and safe for her health, and both reach and maintain it before being discharged from the hospital. The target weight, usually about 90 percent of the weight appropriate for her age, gender, and height, is decided immediately without negotiation. Hospitalization will continue, she is told, until both she and the therapist are certain that she can maintain an ideal weight outside of the hospital. Enduring patience and understanding must be the rule for the therapist. Threats and cajolery cancel any rapport and convince the anorectic that the therapist not only does not understand her but also disrespects her.

The anorectic begins to be aware that she has ego defenses which interfere with her interpersonal relationships and autonomy. She is also made aware of her ambivalent struggle against anybody who she believes intrudes into her life. Exercise is discouraged. Bed rest for one hour after meals is part of her schedule. If a proper diet (Marshall 1978) is refused, supplements like Metrecal, Carnation Instant Breakfast, and other high-protein supplements can be given. The hospital team insists on one litre of milk a day with at least 2500 calories a day provided in the overall diet. Gorger-vomiters present a somewhat different challenge during hospitalization. They will eat what is given them—and even more—but little if any of it will remain in the stomach.

Behavioral modification, because of its simplicity and potential for rapid weight-gain, is often employed in the treatment of anorexia nervosa (Poole, Sanson-Fisher, and Young 1978, Perkin and Surtees 1976, Hauserman and Lavin 1977, Peake and Borduin 1977, Stunkard 1972, Agras and Werne 1977). The approach may vary, from neurodynamic and reflexological, to more sophisticated techniques involving feedback with contingent, positive and negative reinforcement. Behavioral therapy is a very effective approach to a severely cachectic patient who refuses to eat during hospitalization. Operant conditioning techniques can rapidly restore weight at the time of nutritional crisis. The therapist intervenes directly and prescribes interactional "tasks." The aim is weight-gain and symptom-removal with improvement of health, reduction in family preoccupation with the anorectic illness, and relief to the adolescent from the burden of symptom-bearer for the family. The hospitalized anorectic is rewarded in the behavioral approach, either by permission to engage in physical activity, once a prescribed weight is reached, or by being allowed visitors if she continues to eat the hospital diet. During the hospitalization, feedback techniques can be varied; they are markedly useful when they are combined with contingent, positive and negative reinforcement. Reliance on this single treatment, however, can be disastrous in that it potentially allows the patient to eat her way out of the hospital and then relapse again into a severe starvation crisis and even death without returning to her physician or behavioral therapist (Whipple and Manning 1978). In addition, the anorectic may be alarmed by the rapid change in body image, increasing the likelihood of depression, psychotic dedifferentiation, and even suicidal acting out. Furthermore, behavioral modification can upset the anorectic's hope of attaining self-determination and autonomy.

Family Therapy

Family therapy can be initially useful in delineating the disturbed, structured interactions that occur in these enmeshed families. It is most effective with young anorectics soon after the clinical onset of the disturbance. The more entrenched anorectic family, imbued with the mythic idea of superhuman performance and appearance (Bruch 1971c), is less responsive. Its members are loathe to reveal any family disturbance and pain. Their language is full of suggestions; it is a structure, a dialect called body metaphor, a dialect that has to be translated through treatment. Only family meetings bring to the surface the basic family system, its structure, function, communications, myths, metaphors, and pathology. Family therapy is drastic enough, in confrontations with family members, to bring the family system and pathology into bold relief, to lift up the anorectic to the point of buoyancy. The mother's narcissistic use of the anorectic child is immediately apparent, as is the inability of the family members to directly

verbalize their own aggression. In cases where the anorectic disturbance is more oedipally colored, one can see the seductiveness of the
hysterical father in the family sessions. In general, treating a young
hospitalized patient without involving the family leads to a relapse
when the family system is rejoined.

Family therapists suggest that family treatment breaks up the family
conspiracy to avoid all conflicts and teaches the family how to negotiate
their conflicts and restructure their operations (Palazzoli 1974, 1978,
Boszormenyi-Nagy 1965, Beels and Ferber 1969, Bowen 1966, Haley
1976, Caille et al. 1977, Rosman et al. 1977, Conrad 1977). Many think
that change occurs without understanding, without the awareness of
the person being changed. Insight is a by-product of change resulting
from the exploration of the interpersonal mix of the family. The
pathology of mother-father-child is played out in reality; only by
reenactments and paradoxical directives can patterns of behavior be
changed. For their purposes, family therapists do not believe that
unconscious content needs to be changed—only family patterns that
support certain kinds of behavior. Learning will occur later. This
approach, they acknowledge, ignores the intrapsychic structure of the
anorectic patient.

Minuchin (1974), a child psychiatrist, speaking most adamantly the
language of his world, believes that the only treatment for the anorectic
patient and family (psychosomatic families, in general—Minuchin et
al. [1975]) is family therapy; it brings about a transformation of the
family system and provides more workable alternatives to maladaptive
and inadequate coping mechanisms in the family mix. In his strategies,
he enters the family through the child and encourages the patient to
give up the psychosomatic system; then he moves into the family
interaction. The family therapist, Minuchin asserts, starts treatment
first by making himself the system's leader, who "joins, provokes,
clarifies, mystifies and pushes." Through strategic interventions and
enactment, he ushers the family problems into the treatment situation
(Liebman, Minuchin, and Baker 1974). He challenges the family relations, particularly enmeshment, overprotection, conflict avoidance,
rigidity, and conflict-detouring; he adopts the family's language and
explores its metaphors and myths—but never its fantasies, collective or
individual. Then he tries to arrange a new sequence for the family. The
anorectic is admitted to the hospital for several weeks. A lunch with the
patient starts off the family sessions (Rosman, Minuchin, and Liebman

1975), and a daily reward system, based on a prescribed daily weight gain, is instituted. No diagnostic evaluation is made; no diagnosis is made. A few family therapists, however, are uneasy about the adynamic and adiagnostic attitudes of family-system theorists (Malone 1979, Tseng and McDermott 1979, Sander 1979).

Minuchin's family approach to the acute, young, adolescent anorectic is largely accepted by therapists and found to be useful, particularly in the early, acute phase of the disorder. Anorectics are notoriously difficult in the early phase of any treatment; until the therapist is trusted; no early therapeutic alliance occurs. In the prodromal and acute phase, the anorectic must be helped to see herself in the family structure. Family therapy is effective at this stage of anorexia nervosa, particularly if the patient is a young, adolescent anorectic, only recently ill and not a casualty of inadequate or inept psychological, physical treatments or profound chronicity. Because of her iron-bound resistances to treatment and her starvation state, the anorectic at this stage is not amenable to an evocative therapy relying on symbolic representations and repetitive, affective reenactments. Family therapy, at this stage of the disorder, focuses on interpersonal conflict through iconic, enactive modes of cognition.

According to Minuchin, there is no other treatment beyond family treatment. He asserts that his treatment is effective in 86 percent of the cases, regardless of age, symptomatology, and character structure. With system treatment, anorectic symptomatology, Minuchin claims, ceases in two to eight weeks; hospitalization is seldom necessary, and rarely does treatment last more than ten monthly sessions. He does not mention whether characterological changes occur, nor does he comment on the fate of the anorectic's psychosexual conflicts and inhibitions. Understanding in treatment is said to come after change, the result of the interpersonal context of the family exploration (instead of self-awareness), but the degree and level of understanding obtained through family treatment are not clarified. But anyone who has done treatment with an anorectic knows that after changes in the family system are achieved, even profound alterations in the family structure and functions, the anorectic still feels the need to continue treatment and often requests "her own therapist" (individual therapy). One is reminded of the anorectic in Janet Malcolm's article on family treatment in the *New Yorker* (1978). When the writer asked Yvonne, the anorectic teenager, who was then weighing out her dinner on a Weight-

Watcher's scale because she was trying to lose ten pounds, how things now were at home, she replied: "Yes, they treat me better. . . . They don't come into my room anymore, and they don't beat me anymore, like they used to" (p. 113). Minuchin infers that psychodynamic therapy—which he calls linear and causal—is not only unnecessary but is ineffective at *any* stage of anorexia nervosa. One only has to remove the anorectic symptomatology through family therapy (Rosman et al. 1977).

It is unfortunate that Minuchin's presentation of this useful technique is weakened by his hyperbolas, rampant enthusiasm, and Nabokovian displays. Minuchin chides behavioral and analytic therapists and preaches family therapy, which he sees as the root to any approach to family pathology. He views anorexia nervosa as a unitary concept and diagnostically ignores the heterogeneity of the syndrome: the differences between the self-starvers, on the one hand, and the gorger-vomiters on the other, between pubescent girls and young, adult women, between male and female patients. But just as there is no unitary concept of anorexia nervosa, there is no unitary treatment for anorexia nervosa. The therapeutic approach to the anorectic depends on a genetic-structural assessment, the level of her fixation and regression, the primitiveness of her defenses, the extent of the family's pathology, and her ego assets which auger well for a therapeutic response.

The indication of family therapy is increased if the anorectic is under sixteen years old and has had anorexia for only a few months. Prepubertal onset, duration beyond five years, persistence of the disorder through adolescence, and a long-standing, unsuccessful treatment are grave prognostic indicators. Like chronic bed-wetting and obesity, chronic anorexia nervosa is extremely difficult to treat because the eating disturbance becomes autonomous of the original conflicts and, therefore, is refractory to psychotherapeutic intervention. But even in chronic cases, family treatment can give the anorectic a feeling of establishing a degree of autonomy. It provides the patient with the feeling that her parents are participating in the treatment; she is encouraged to free herself from the family system. Anorectics, symptomatic longer than one year, offer more obstacles to treatment. Their psychic disturbances require individual treatment. For this reason, it is important for the therapist to intervene as quickly as possible.

Conjoint marital therapy (Sager 1976, Paolino and McGrady 1978) for the parents is advisable, especially after the anorectic has made a solid alliance in individual treatment. The parents usually need therapy beyond what family systemic therapy can provide. Some may decide in conjoint treatment to enter individual therapy.

Treatment of the Gorger-Vomiter

Boskind-Lodahl (1976) has brought together a synthetic, therapeutic program for patients in the gorging-vomiting cycle. She combines group therapy and existential-behavior modification with a Gestalt approach to immediate experience. This strategy challenges the bulimic's fantasy that her life will become perfect if she attains the penultimate state of thinness and oral control. These patients are encouraged to increase assertiveness, overcome feelings of helplessness and dependency; they are also exhorted to heighten their awareness of feelings in general, expand their interests, and face their sense of incompetence. Role-playing of feared situations and feelings and assertiveness training are emphasized, as well as sensory-awareness and guided-fantasy exercises. In this short-term treatment, the therapist focuses on the bulimic's awareness of the physical and sexual aspects of her body. The approach does not encourage individual evocative treatment and, in fact, discourages psychoanalytic exploration of any sort. The patient is left still looking for the key to the kingdom. After this short-term treatment, patients are then directed to enter support groups, such as a women's consciousness raising group and Over-Eaters Anonymous. To understand this treatment program is to try to put together the pieces from three different jigsaw puzzles; not everything fits.

The binger-vomiter, usually older than the abstainer or mixed anorectic (Russell 1979), is admitted to the hospital for electrolyte imbalance and a relentless, devious cycle of gorging and vomiting. (The milder cases can usually be treated out of the hospital.) In the hospital, the severe vomiters and laxative abusers are told they must eat whatever they discard and in whatever form. An even harsher behavioral modification is apomorphine aversion (Slade 1977b) and Faradic stimulation (Kenny and Solyom 1971). Dally and Gomez (1979), on the other hand, employ videotape feedback techniques of eating and vomiting to break up the habit. But central to the treatment of these patients, contrary to the initial approach to the starving anorectic, is the immediate use of psychotherapy.

Violette's clinical history points out many aspects of the treatment of
the bulimic vomiter. A behavioral-Gestalt approach was not sufficient
for this patient.

§Violette was a twenty-five-year-old, divorced woman with a pale
face, framed by blond, flaxen hair, dressed in yellow like a marigold,
referred by her internist because of gorging, purgative abuse and
vomiting. She felt like a bird gorging herself on caterpillars. She spoke
in cartoon balloons, between sighs pouring from her mouth. The
symptoms had started two years ago, after the announcement by her
husband that he was now in love with a woman whom he had been
seeing for about six months. Violette had no inkling of his discontent,
although, in retrospect, she was aware that her husband's charismatic
qualities, so important to her during their engagement and first year of
marriage, had lost their appeal for her.

Although throughout her adolescence she had been weight-
conscious, she had no actual weight problem. Shortly after her marriage, she decided that she did not want to have children since
pregnancies would irrepairably distort her body and eventually ruin her
"good figure." In middle childhood, she had been obese for several
years, eating from fear, but at the time of onset of pubescence her
weight "seemed to melt away." She was prepared for menarche and
experienced it with minimal anxiety. In fact, Violette delighted at the
prospects of her wild sexual bloom; she believed that her attractiveness
stood her in good stead for the future. Throughout adolescence, she
kept seeing in her mind fantasies of marrying "the most perfect man."
This seemed to materialize when she met Jay during her freshman year
at college. She found him fascinating in a mysterious way. The qualities
that drew her to Jay were ill-defined and vague enough to allow her to
embellish them with her fantasies. She was also attracted to Jay because
he came from a Wasp family—a new silhouette, financially and socially
superior to her own. He had great promise in the family jewelry
business, which provided her prospective in-laws with everything that
Violette had ever imagined.

After the husband's announcement of his intended divorce, she
never left anything on her plate; she began gorging at night—
especially worse when she could not convince any of her friends to be
with her in the evenings. In the mornings she would stuff herself with
laxatives and have abdominal cramps for the rest of the day. The

gorging increased to three or four times a night, to the point that eating dominated her life and drained her of energy. Fantasies of trays of Napoleons and cherry tarts filled her mind. Increasingly, she was lacking in confidence, depressed, and experienced waves of helplessness and hopelessness. Her penitential eating pattern became an endless source of humiliation and guilt.

The patient hoped that she had done everything possible to avoid resembling her mother, whom she viewed as unappeasably tormenting and badgering, demanding and controlling—a hedonistic woman, voice cracked and raspy, who had four closets "stuffed with clothes and shoes," a woman of great vanity who, by age forty, had had several cosmetic surgical procedures and still complained of a pendant chin and stomach folds. Violette recalled as a young girl feeling inferior to the mother, dominated and subdued by her, in full knowledge of the oppressor. As she grew into preadolescence, Violette was increasingly aware of the mother's lack of confidence and feelings of insufficiency. Less vivid now was her mother in the shape of a monster. And no longer did Violette feel the simple silence of adolescence. It also became apparent that her mother was frequently depressed, felt deprived, and was silently enraged with her husband, whom she regarded as ungiving. Violette sensed that her mother "used her as a Cinderella," kept her in the kitchen and tied her to household chores, while her older sister, a more outgoing but less attractive girl, was favored and indulged, like a tern with one wing.

Violette was convinced, however, that her father deeply loved her and tried to support her to the best of his ability. She always found her father—a dark, handsome man with razor-notched sideburns—a mysterious and "deep" person, as smooth as wrist skin, and suspected that he had other women, since she could never imagine her mother satisfying him. As a little girl, she incessantly followed her father around, savoring his hurried kisses, hoping, in a blur of love and longing, that he would read to her or take her on his Saturday errands, which always seemed to keep him out of the house for the entire day. When her father traveled for business reasons, she longed to be with him; and, when he returned, she would monopolize him. She aggravated her mother by frequently coming into the parents' bedroom. Violette saw her father as the apotheosis of "all good things" and a paragon of gentle masculinity. She remembered her heart swelling like a stomach. She vowed that she would one day please him by being "the most beautiful woman alive." After the divorce, she frequently called her father at the office and, at times, even arranged lunch dates with him under the pretext of needing advice. The father attempted to discourage Violette's reliance upon him, but it was only when she contracted infectious mononucleosis and became depressed that she was able to seek psychiatric help. She expected the consultant would "charm her" and immediately provide her with paradisaic "solutions for all her problems" and make her feelings fall away to nothing, thoughts forgotton at once. With reluctance, she accepted hospitalization. She was found to have hypokalemia. Devious in her way of eating all her meals and then vomiting and purging, Violette, once she could trust her male therapist and face her immeasurable emptiness, began an evocative therapy.

Individual Therapy

The question of individual psychotherapy for the anorectic remains controversial (Szyrynski 1973, Thomä 1977). Some clinicians claim that no psychological treatment is superior to simply a good nursing regimen. Others are of the opinion that there is no effective long-term treatment, only crisis intervention; the illness must run its course. Even behavioral modification is questioned, because there is as yet no longitudinal study of its effect for even symptom-removal.

Psychoanalytic treatment, first used for anorexia nervosa back in the 1930s (Grote and Meng 1934, Weizecker 1937, Waller, Kaufman, and Deutsch 1940, Masserman 1941, Thomä 1967, Wilson 1979, Cohen 1980) was initially id analysis of the anorectic's wishes: fantasies of parthenogenesis, pregnancy, impregnation, and castration. Later, defense analysis evolved (Bornstein 1949), along with modifications for analytic treatments of borderline character disorders (Giovacchini 1972, Kohut 1977, Searles 1959). Still, some regard analytic treatments for anorexia nervosa as providing, at best, mystic comfort.

Bruch (1970b, 1974, 1977a) believes that psychoanalytic therapy is ineffective because it interpretively "force-feeds" the patient and provides no opportunity for self-exploration and development of an effective sense of self. She points to the so-called classical model of psychoanalysis which aims at analysis of resistances and transference. It would seem that, for Bruch, psychoanalytic treatment is either a long novel of associations leading to memory, or a duet of two deaf singers.

The analysand lies on the couch, cow-eyeing the ceiling. She ignores the fact that analytic techniques have changed over the last two decades. Techniques, modified for patients like anorectics, include active elaboration of the negative transference and interpretation of pathological defensive operations (Kernberg 1975, 1976). Bruch remonstrates that psychoanalytic treatment does not allow the anorectic to participate in the therapeutic exchange, leaving her unable to recognize her appropriate feelings and reactions. Furthermore, she asserts that psychotherapy should be goal-oriented, a psychic synthesis, giving the patient a more effective way of handling her loneliness. It is essential, she thinks, that the therapist distinguish between genuine and facade performance for the anorectic and help her gain trust in herself without resorting to her false sense of superiority. The anorectic should be helped, according to Bruch (1970b), to understand that she does not need the artificial superstructure of a "perfect life." She believes that nondirective, expressive psychotherapy, besides being passive in attitude, enhances the patient's denial, negativism, and distrust and does not help her to understand her body and perceptual disturbances.

A contrasting view of individual therapy is that the patient should be immediately confronted with the abnormality of her dieting behavior by telling her that dieting is her metabolic device for reducing her frightening sexual feelings and increasing her attachment to her mother. This is the St. George's approach (Crisp 1977b) which views anorexia nervosa as entangled in psychobiological mechanisms within individual and family psychopathology. Combining medical nursing skills with a behavioral approach, a psychotherapy is undertaken, with direct confrontation, like an agoraphobic brought to the feared situation (Crisp 1977b). This is an attempt to strengthen the ego, but it may simply enhance the patient's feeling of ineffectiveness and helplessness, and send the patient back to those to whom she thinks she belongs. Such a direct approach, unless carefully timed, confronts the ego and enhances resistance.

Whatever the individual therapeutic approach, no interpretive activity can be effective until resistances are recognized by the patient, and the focus is pulled to the foreground. The anorectic does not like, in a paradoxical way, not knowing. The main barriers to a therapeutic alliance are denial, negation, disavowal, splitting, and omnipotence. Before these defenses can be dealt with, the anorectic must experience and identify her denied and split-off affects. It is imperative that she recognize her abject feelings of helplessness and loneliness. Early in treatment the anorectic feels that the therapist wants to take her independence away; she is suspicious and defensive, expecting the therapist to feed her symbolically. Interpretations and clarifications are warded off; the analytic process is controlled and limited by the anorectic who finds any therapeutic intervention annoying and intrusive. The early therapeutic alliance is delicate because the anorectic firmly believes that anyone who participates in her freedom takes away from it (Tustin 1958). Once the therapeutic alliance is achieved, the anorectic, much like a young symbiotic child, seeks in treatment a new object once she feels less a part of the maladaptive family system. The desire for a new object provides the anorectic with the opportunity for further separating and individuation. Concrete interpretations about internalized objects are often necessary to put the patient in touch with feelings. Matters which cease to matter fall among the detritus. The anorectic begins to find her way back, accept her good and bad parts, and have a sense of identity. Idealized self- and object representations are played out in the anorectic's behavior. Seldom are they expressed otherwise until the patient is well into the opening phase of treatment. The fantasies are sadomasochistic and narcissistic, regressively acted out to repeat and relive old narcissistic injuries hidden by the illusion of perfection. Well into the middle phase of treatment, oedipal material is usually abundant, along with ideational and affect representations.

Analysis is, in fact, possible for many of the less severe borderline anorectics—after correction of the starvation state and, in the case of the young adolescent, some amelioration of her paralyzing family system. The prognosis is good for characterological change if the disorder is recognized early; if the patient is not a fragile borderline and not regressively headed toward dangerous cachexia; if the parents are willing to remain in conjoint treatment and the patient wants and is allowed to continue individual therapy after symptom-removal and restoration of nutrition. The poststarvation phase of treatment is essential in order to work out the anorectic preoedipal and oedipal psychopathology and to guard against relapse and recurrence of a nutritional crisis. Ego-strengthening techniques often must be used. Along with her blurred view of reality, she must be helped in changing her body image as she becomes aware of body structure and function and draws closer to an appreciation of an image appropriate to the structure of her own body. Likewise, she must be helped in recognizing her internal body sensations and forming a new body-concept.

The anorectic is apt to approach this phase of treatment with a fear that analytic therapy is seductive and will make her fat. Initially, the anorectic's free associations are limited. She is reluctant to reveal her dreams and fantasies—replete with naked aggression—and care must be taken in directing interpretive comments at defenses. Denial and projection are the first defense usually explored. On-couch analytic techniques are best postponed in the beginning of this phase in that the anorectic may be frightened by the passivity of the situation and view the couch as too seductive.

Once a solid therapeutic alliance is established, treatment of the character disorder through defense analysis can begin (Sours 1979b). The transference usually turns the analyst into a mother who is viewed ambivalently and distrustfully. Through analysis of the transference, she gains insight into her ambivalence toward the maternal object and then attempts to separate the analyst, as well as other objects, from the mother. First analyzing superficial defenses and resistances, the therapist is eventually able to approach content interpretation, even sexual material, once a more positive transference is established. At some point, the anorectic's masochism must be worked through, as well as mourning associated with separation from the mother. Through internalization and identification, new intrapsychic structures form related to whole object relations. The borderline transference is composed of split self-object representations, both positive and negative. These split-objects are brought to the patient's awareness, worked through and repaired, to varying degrees, as the separation-individuation phase in the transference is repeated.

All this takes time.

Medical Glossary

Adrenocortical function: The function of the cortex of the adrenal gland. The cortex principally produces hydrocortisone, cortisone, and desoxycorticosterone acetate (DCA).

Amitriptyline: A tricyclic antidepressant drug.

Asthenia: Absence of physical strength, weakness.

Bitemporal homonymous hemianopsia: Blindness in one half of the visual fields produced by a tumor invading the optic chiasma, the hypothamus and pituitary gland.

Bradycardia: Slowness of the heartbeat.

Bulimia: Excessive, morbid hunger leading to gorging.

Cachexia: Extreme emaciation due to a serious disease, as in tuberculosis, carcinoma, syphilis, and anorexia nervosa.

Catecholamines: Hormones of the medulla of the adrenal gland; namely, norepinephrin and epinephrin.

Clomiphene citrate: A chemical that blocks the action of estrogen on the hypothalamic receptor cells; the blockage leads to the production of increased plasma luteinizing hormones (LH) due to an outpouring of gonadotropin from the anterior hypothalamus.

Corticosteroids: The group of adrenocortical hormones.

Craniopharyngiona: An intracranial tumor of congenital origin, developing from the pars tuberculis of the pituitary gland and expanding into the suprasellar region, optic chiasma, and eventually the frontal lobes, third ventricle, and hypothalamus.

Cyproheptadine: An antiserotoninergic drug used to promote weight gain.

Diabetes insipidus: A chronic disease characterized by the passage of a large quantity of normal urine of low specific gravity; associated with intense thirst.

Diencephalon: Part of the brain between the prosencephalon and the mesencephalon; it includes the thalami and the third ventricle.

Diphenylhydantoin: An anticonvulsant medication, also known as Dilantin. It reduces the excitability of the nervous system and may inhibit the appetite center and prevent discharge in the hypothalamus.

Dizygotic twins: Double birth; arising from two eggs.

Electrolyte imbalance: Imbalance of fluids and minerals in extracellular-intracellular spaces, often leading to renal, central nervous system, and cardiovascular disturbances.

Encopresis: Extreme constipation often with incontinence of feces, usually due to emotional reasons.

Fistulization: The act or process whereby a tract is formed from an internal organ to the skin.

Follicle stimulating hormone (FSH): A hormone produced by the pituitary gland. If failure of FSH takes place in the girl's prepubertal period, there results a lack of sexual development at puberty; if after, a diminution of secondary sex characteristics.

Fourth ventricle: The space between the oblongata and the pons in front and the cerebellum behind.

Galactosemia: An inborn error of metabolism with a defect in the enzyme concerned with utilization of galactose. It can lead to brain damage, if not detected early.

Glioma: A tumor composed of neurologia cells and occuring in the brain, spinal cord, retina, and nerves.

Gonadotropin: Substances which facilitate the development of the gonads. These include FSH, LH, and ICSH.

Granulomatous disease: A disease which shows a destructive, inflammatory histiocytosis and repeated episodes of necrosis and fibrosis. Regional ileitis is an example of this type of disease.

Hand-Schüller-Christian-disease: A metabolic disturbance with exophthalmus, diabetes insipidus and defects in the membraneous bones.

Hyperaldosteronism: Excessive production of an adrenal medullary hormone causing hypertension.

Hyperalimentation: Supplemental nutrition, usually by way of intravenous feedings, for profound starvation.

Hyperemesis gravidarum: Nausea and vomiting of pregnancy reaching pernicious proportions and endangering the woman.

Hypokalemic syndrome: Low serum potassium produces cardiac and skeletal muscle fatigue. Cardiac rhythm irregularities and arrest can occur.

Hypothalamus: A group of prominences and aggregation of ganglia lying on the ventral side beneath the thalamus.

Infarction: A wedge-shaped area, either of hemorrhage into an organ or of necrosis in an organ produced by an obstruction of a terminal blood vessel.

Lanugo hair: Downy growth of hair often seen on the face of women and on the back and extremities of young women with anorexia nervosa.

Luteinizing hormone (LH): A hormone produced by the pituitary gland. If insufficient, it causes the persistent action of the graafian follicle and is associated with functional uterine bleeding and the failure to ovulate.

Megaloblastic anemia: An anemia due to defect of nucleo-protein synthesis; found in pernicious anemia and sometimes in anorexia nervosa.

Menarche: The onset of menstruation at puberty.

Metoclopramide: A potent antiemetic used for flatulent dyspepsia with delayed gastric emptying.

Monozygotic twins: Identical twins, coming from one egg.

Myxedema: A condition caused by thyroid underactivity.

Oliguria: Diminution in the quantity of urine output.

Pathognomonic: Characteristic of a disease, distinguishing it from other diseases.

Polycystic ovaries (Stein-Leventhal syndrome): Enlarged, encapsulated ovaries producing pain, anorexia, menstrual irregularities, excessive body hair, and acne.

Polydypsia: Excessive thirst.

Prolactin: A lactogenic hormone or luteotrophin, concerned with the maintenance of secretory function in the follicle, corpus luteum, and breasts.

Pyrexia: Elevation of the temperature above the normal, as in fever.

Sarcoidosis: A chronic disease of unknown origin which involves the skin, lymph nodes, eyes, salivary glands, lungs, and bones. It produces granulomas.

Sella turcica: Pituitary fossa of the sphenoid bone lodging the pituitary body.

Tachycardia: Rapidity of the heart beat.

XO and XX-XX: Mosaicism, chromosomal abnormality with phenotypical expression, as in the condition known as gonadal dysgenesis (Turner's syndrome).

Bibliography

Ackerman, N. (1966). *Treating the Troubled Family.* New York: Basic Books.

Adam, A., and Bauduin, A. (1973). Failure of the neurotic defense mechanisms in a preadolescent girl. *Acta Psychiatrica Belgica* 73:568–580.

Adams, J. (1888). Letter to editor. *Lancet* 1:597.

Aggeler, M., Lucia, S. P., and Fishbon, H. M. (1942). Purpura due to vitamin K deficiency in anorexia nervosa. *American Journal of Digestive Diseases* 9:227–234.

Agras, S., and Werne, J. (1977). Behavior modification of anorexia nervosa: research foundations. In *Anorexia Nervosa,* ed. R. Vigersky. New York: Raven Press.

Akamatsu, K., Nishizaki, T., Endo, H., and Taketa, K. (1972). A case of anorexia nervosa: improvement following intraveneous administration of fat emulsion (intralipid) combined with tube feeding. *Journal of the Japanese Society of Internal Medicine* 61:274–281.

Albeaux-Fernet, M. (1968). *La Maigreur.* Paris: Libraire Maloine.

Allbut, C., and Rolleston, H. D. (1910). *A System of Medicine.* London: Macmillan.

Al-Mufty N. S., and Bevan D. H. (1977). A case of subcutaneous emphysema, pneumomediastinum and pneumoretroperitoneum associated with functional anorexia. *British Journal of Clinical Practice* 31:160–161.

Altshul, V. (1978). The ego-integrative (and disintegrative) effects of long-distance running. *Current Concepts in Psychiatry* (July–August) Presented at the Medical Joggers Association, Boston, Mass.

American Psychiatric Association (1968). *Diagnostic and Statistical Manual of Mental Disorders* (DSM II). Washington, D.C.: American Psychiatric Association.

Amdur, M. J., Tucked, G. J., Detre, T., and Markhus, K. (1969). Anorexia nervosa: an international study. *Journal of Nervous and Mental Disease* 148:559–566.

Amrein, P. C., Friedman, R., Kosinski, K., and Ellman, L. (1979). Hematologic changes in anorexia nervosa. *Journal of the American Medical Association* 241:2190–2191.

Anderson, A. E. (1977). A typical anorexia nervosa. In *Anorexia Nervosa,* ed. R. Vigersky. New York: Raven Press.

André-Thomas, C. (1909). Anorexie mentale. *La Clinique* 4:33.

Anthony. E. J. (1970). Two contrasting types of adolescent depression and treatment. *Journal of the American Psychoanalytic Association* 18:841–859.

——— (1978). Operational thinking in adolescence in relation to psychosomatic disorder. *Journal of Youth and Adolescence* 7:307–317.

Anthony, E. J., and Benedik, T. (eds.) (1975). *Depression and Human Existence.* Boston: Little, Brown.

Anyan, W. R. (1974). Changes in erythrocyte sedimentation rate and fibrinogen during anorexia nervosa. *Journal of Pediatrics* 85:525–527.

Aperia, A., Broberger, O., and Fohlin, L. (1978). Renal function in anorexia nervosa. *Acta Paediatrica Scandinavia* 67:219–224.

Aries, P. (1962). *Centuries of Childhood: A Social History of Family Life.* New York: Random House.

Armstrong, E. C. A., Lacey, J. H., Crisp, A. H., and Bryant, T. N. (1978). An investigation of the immune response of patients suffering from anorexia nervosa. *Postgraduate Medicine* 54:95–99.

Asbeck, F., Hirschmann, W. D., Deck, K., and Castrup, H. J. (1972). Lethal course of anorexia nervosa: alcohol and laxative abuse in a female patient. *Internist* (Berlin) 13:63–65.

Askevold, F. (1975). Measuring body image. *Psychotherapy and Psychosomatics* 26:71–80.

Baba, H. (1973). Radioimmunoassay of serum testosterone: results of the study of normal subjects and patients with endocrine disorders. *Folia Endocrinologica Japanica* 49:60–79.

Bach, S. (1977). On the narcissistic state of consciousness. *International Journal of Psycho-Analysis* 58:209–233.

Bachrach, A. J., Erwin, W. J., and Mahr, J. P. (1965). The control of eating behavior of an anorexic by operant conditioning techniques. In *Case Studies in Behavior Modification,* eds. L. P. Ullman and L. Kramer. New York: Holt, Rinehart and Winston.

Bahrke, M. S., and Morgan, W. P. (1978). Anxiety reduction following exercise and meditation. *Cognitive Therapy and Research* 2:323–333.

Ballet, G. (1907). Anorexia mentale. *Rev. gên de chir. et de therap* 21:293–296.

Banting, W. (1864). *Letter on Corpulence, Addressed to the Public,* 4th ed. New York: Mohun, Ebbs, and Hough.

Baranowska, B., and Zgliczynski, S. (1979). Enhanced testosterone in female patients with anorexia nervosa: its normalization after weight gain. *Acta Endocrinologica* 90:328–335.

Barbara, L., Lanfranchi, G. A., Ferrari, G., and Rebecchi, E. (1970). Study of duodenal electric activity in mental anorexia: preliminary findings. *Rivista Sperimentale di Freniatria* 94:345–350.

Barcai, C. (1977). Lithium in adult anorexia nervosa. A pilot report on two patients. *Acta Psychiatrica Scandinavica* 55:97–101.

Barnett, J. (1966). On cognitive disorders in the obsessional. *Contemporary Psychoanalysis* 2:121–126.

Barry, V. C., and Klawans, H. L. (1976). On the role of dopamine in the pathophysiology of anorexia nervosa. *Journal of Neural Transmission* 38:107–122.

Bartlett, W. M. (1928). An analysis of anorexia. *American Journal of Diseases of Children* 35:26–31.

Beck, J. C., and K. Brockner-Mortensen (1954). Observations on the prognosis in anorexia nervosa. *Acta Medica Scandinavica* 149:409–420.

Bedoret, J. M., Destombes, A., and Warot, P. (1973). Psychotic episode in an anorexia nervosa: the role of isolation. *Acta Psychiatric Belgica* 73:437–447.

Beels, C. C., and Ferber, A. (1969). Family therapy: a view. *Family Process* 8:280–318.

Bell, M. (1971). Homage to the runner. In *The Escape Into You.* New York: Atheneum.

Bell, R. R. (ed.) (1968). *Studies in Marriage and the Family,* New York: Thomas Y. Crowell.

Benedek, T. (1936). Dominant ideas and their relation to morbid cravings. *International Journal of Psycho-Analysis* 17:40–56.

Benedek, T., and Rubenstein, B. B. (1939). The correlations between ovarian activity and psychodynamic processes. *Psychosomatic Medicine* 1:245–270, 461–485.

Benson, H. (1975). *The Relaxation Response.* New York: William Morrow.

Ben-Tovim, D. I., Hunter, M., and Crisp, A. H. (1977). Discrimination and evaluation of shape and size in anorexia nervosa: an exploratory study. *Research Communications in Psychology, Psychiatry & Behavior* 5:241–257.

Berg, I., Hullin, R., Allsopp, M., O'Brien, P., and MacDonald, R. (1974). Bipolar manic-depressive psychosis in early adolescence: a case report. *British Journal of Psychiatry* 125:416–419.

Bergen, L. van (1961). Anorexia nervosa: A study of 38 patients. *Nederlands Tijdschrift voor Geneeskunde* 105:464–471.

Bergmann, G. von (1948). Sheehan's disease. *Postgraduate Medical Journal* 3:327–340.

Berkman, J. M. (1930). Anorexia nervosa, anorexia, inanition and low basal metabolic rate. *American Journal of Medical Science* 180:411–420.

—— (1939). Functional anorexia and functional vomiting: their relation to anorexia nervosa. *Medical Clinics of North America* 23:901–910.

—— (1943). Some clinical observations in cases of anorexia nervosa. *Proceedings of the Mayo Clinic* 18:81.

—— (1945). Anorexia nervosa: the diagnosis and treatment of inanition resulting from functional disorders. *Annals of Internal Medicine* 22:679–691.

—— (1948). Anorexia nervosa, anterior pituitary insufficiency, Simmonds' cachexia and Sheehan's disease. *Postgraduate Medicine Journal* 3:237–245.

Berkman, J. M., Owen, C. A., and Magath, T. B. (1952). Physiological aspects of anorexia nervosa. *Postgraduate Medicine Journal* 12:407–415.

Berlin, I. N., Boatman, M. J., Sheimo, S. L., and Szurek, S. A. (1945). Adolescent alternation of anorexia and obesity. *American Journal of Orthopsychiatry* 21:387–419.

Bernstein, I. C. (1972). Anorexia nervosa: a 94-year-old woman treated with electroshock. *Minnesota Medicine* 55:552–557.

Bessingham, D. (1977). Acute gastric dilation in anorexia nervosa: letter. *British Medical Journal* 2:959.

Besterman, H. S., Sarson, D. L., Hsu, G., Crisp, A. H., and Bloom S. R. (1979). Gut hormones in thyrotoxicosis and anorexia nervosa proceedings. *Journal of Endocrinology* 81:143.

Beumont, P. J. V. (1970). Anorexia nervosa in male subjects. *Psychotherapy and Psychosomatics* 18:365–371.

—— (1971). Small handwriting in some patients with anorexia nervosa. *British Journal of Psychiatry* 119:349–351.

—— (1977). Further categorization of patients with anorexia nervosa. *Australian and New Zealand Journal of Psychiatry* 11:223–226.

—— (1978). The onset of anorexia nervosa. *Australian and New Zealand Journal of Psychiatry* 12:145–151.

Beumont, P. J. V., Abraham, S. F., Argall, W. J., George, C. W., and Glaun, D. E. (1978a). The onset of anorexia nervosa. *Australian and New Zealand Journal of Psychiatry* 12:145–149.

Beumont, P. J. V., Abraham, S. F., Argall, W. J., and Turtle, J. R. (1978b). Plasma gonadotropins and IHRH infusions in anorexia nervosa. *Australian and New Zealand Journal of Medicine* 8:509–514.

Beumont, P. J. V., Beardwood, C. J., and Russell, G. F. M. (1972). The occurrence of the syndrome of anorexia nervosa in male subjects. *Psychological Medicine* 2:216–231.

Beumont, P. J. V., Carr, P. J., and Gelder, M. G. (1973). Plasma levels of luteinizing hormone and of immunoreactive oestrogens (oestradiol) in anorexia nervosa: response to clomiphene citrate. *Psychological Medicine* 4:219–221.

Beumont, P. J. V., George, G. C. W., Pimstone, B. L., and Vinik, A. I. (1976). Body weight and the pituitary response to hypothalamic releasing hormones in patients with anorexia nervosa. *Journal of Clinical Endocrinology and Metabolism* 43:487–496.

Beumont, P. J. V., George, G. C. W., and Smart, D. E. (1976). 'Dieters' and 'vomiters and purgers' in anorexia nervosa. *Psychological Medicine* 6:617–622.

Bhanji, S. (1979). Anorexia nervosa: physicians' and psychiatrists' opinions and practice. *Journal of Psychosomatic Research* 23:7–11.

Binswanger, H. (1952). Psychiatric aspects of mental anorexia. *Z. Kinder psychiat.* 19:141–173.

Binswanger, L. (1944). The case of Ellen West. In *Existence,* eds. R. May, E. Angel, and H. Ellenberger. New York: Basic Books, 1958.

Bittker, T. (1977). Runner's gluttony. *Runner's World* 12:10–11.

Black, M. M. (1965). Anorexia nervosa in Cushing's syndrome. *Journal of Clinical Endocrinology and Metabolism* 25:1030–1040.

Blackwell, A., and Rollins, N. (1968). Treatment problems in adolescents with anorexia nervosa. *Acta Paedopsychiatrica* 35:294–301.

Bliss, E. L., and Branch, C. H. H. (1960). *Anorexia Nervosa: Its History, Psychology and Biology.* New York: Hoeber.

Bliss, E. L., and Migeon, C. J. (1957). Endocrinology of anorexia nervosa. *Journal of Clinical Endocrinology and Metabolism* 17:766–776.

Blitzer, J. R., Rollins, N., and Blackwell, A. (1961). Children who starve themselves: anorexia nervosa. *Psychosomatic Medicine* 23:269–274.

Blos, P. (1962). *On Adolescence.* New York: Free Press.

——— (1967). The second individuation process of adolescence. *Psychoanalytic Study of the Child* 22:162–186.

——— (1979). *The Adolescent Passage.* New York: International Universities Press.

Bornstein, B. (1949). The analysis of a phobic child: some problems of theory and technique in child analysis. *Psychoanalytic Study of the Child* 314:181–226.

Boskind-Lodahl, M. (1976). Cinderella's stepsisters: a feminist perspective on anorexia nervosa and bulimia. *Signs* 2:342–356.

Boss, M. (1954). *Einführung in die psychosomatische Medizin.* Bern and Stuttgart: Hans Huber.

——— (1957). *Psychoanalyse und Daseinsanalytik.* Berne and Stuttgart: Hans Huber.

Boszormenyi-Nagy, I. (1965). A theory of relationships, experience, and transaction. In *Intensive Family Therapy,* ed. I. Boszormenyi-Nagy and J. Framo. New York: Harper & Row.

Boucharlat, J., Maitre, A., and Wolf, R. (1970). Role of early oral fixations in the psychopathology of anorexia nervosa. *Annales Medico-Psychologiques* 2:577–582.

Bowen, M. (1966). The use of family theory in clinical practice. *Comprehensive Psychiatry* 7:345–374.

Bowers, T. K., and Eckert, E. (1978). Leukopenia in anorexia nervosa: lack of increased risk of infection. *Archives of Internal Medicine* 138:1520–1523.

Boyar, R. M. (1978). Endocrine changes in anorexia nervosa. *Medical Clinics of North America* 62:297–303.

Boyar, R. M., Katz, J., Finkelstein, J. W., Kapen, S., Weiner, H., Weitzman, E. D., and Hellman, L. (1974). Anorexia nervosa. Immaturity of the 24-hour luteinizing hormone secretory pattern. *New England Journal of Medicine* 291:861–865.

Branch, C. H., and Eurman, L. J. (1980). Social attitudes toward patients with anorexia nervosa. *American Journal of Psychiatry* 137:631–632.

Breuer, J., and Freud, S. (1893–1895). Studies on Hysteria. *Standard Edition* 2:1–305.

Brook, G. (1977). Acute gastric dilation in anorexia nervosa: letter. *British Medical Journal* 2:1153–1154.

Brooks, A. P., and Martyn, C. (1979). Pneumonediastinum in anorexia nervosa: letter. *British Medical Journal* 1:125–129.

Brown, R. (1978). The prescription of exercise for depression. *Physician Sports Medicine* 6:34–49.

Brown, W. L., Crookshank, F. G., Young, J. C., Gordon, G., and Bevan-Brown, C. H. (1931). *Anorexia Nervosa.* London: C. W. Daniel.

Browning, C. H. (1977). Anorexia nervosa: complications of somatic therapy. *Comprehensive Psychiatry* 18:399–403.

Broyard, A. (1980). Review of *Early Disorder* by Rebecca Joseph. *New York Times,* May 9, p. C25.

Brozek, J., Wells, S., and Keys, A. (1946). Medical aspects of semi-starvation in Leningrad. *American Review of Soviet Medicine* 4:70–79.

Bruch, H. (1955). Effects of starvation after World War II and its relationships to obesity. *Annuals of New York Academy of Science* 63:68–75.

——— (1956). Psychopathology of hunger and appetite. In *Changing Concepts of Psychoanalytic Medicine*, eds. G. E. Daniels and S. Rado. New York: Grune & Stratton.

——— (1961). Transformation of oral impulses in eating disorders. *Psychiatry Quarterly* 35:458–469.

——— (1962a). Falsification of bodily needs and body concepts in schizophrenia. *Archives of General Psychiatry* 6:18–30.

——— (1962b). Perceptual and conceptual disturbances in anorexia nervosa. *Psychosomatic Medicine* 24:187–199.

——— (1965a). Anorexia nervosa and its differential diagnosis. *Journal of Nervous and Mental Disease* 141:555–566.

—— (1965b). The psychiatric differential diagnosis of anorexia nervosa. In *Anorexia Nervosa,* eds. J. E. Meyer and H. Feldmann. Stuttgart: Georg Thieme Verlag.

—— (1969). The insignificant difference: discordant incidence of anorexia nervosa in monozygotic twins. *American Journal of Psychiatry* 126:85–90.

—— (1970a). Changing approaches to anorexia nervosa. *International Psychiatry Clinics* 7:3–24.

—— (1970b). Psychotherapy in primary anorexia nervosa. *Journal of Nervous and Mental Disease* 150:51–67.

—— (1971a). Anorexia nervosa in the male. *Psychosomatic Medicine* 33:31–47.

—— (1971b). Death in anorexia nervosa. *Psychosomatic Medicine* 33:135–144.

—— (1971c). Family transactions in eating disorders. *Comprehensive Psychiatry* 12:238–248.

—— (1973a). Thin fat people. *Journal of the American Medical Woman's Association* 28:187–188.

—— (1973b). *Eating Disorders: Obesity, Anorexia Nervosa and the Person Within.* New York: Basic Books.

—— (1974). Perils of behavior modification in treatment of anorexia nervosa. *Journal of the American Medical Association* 230:1419–1422.

—— (1975). Anorexia nervosa. In *American Handbook of Psychiatry,* vol. 4, ed. S. Arieti. New York: Basic Books.

—— (1977a). Anorexia nervosa and its treatment. *Journal of Pediatric Psychology* 2:110–112.

—— (1977b). Psychotherapy in eating disorders. *Canadian Psychiatric Association Journal* 22:102–108.

—— (1978). *The Golden Cage.* London: Open Books.

—— (1979a). Psychological antecedents of anorexia nervosa. In *Anorexia Nervosa,* ed. R. Vigersky. New York: Raven Press.

—— (1979b). Developmental deviations in anorexia nervosa. *Israel Annuals on Psychiatry* 17:255–261.

Brugger, M. (1943). Fresstrieb als hypothalamisches Symptom. *Helv. physiol. pharmacol. Acta* 1:183–200.

Brusset, B., and Jeammet, P. (1971). Episodes of bulimia in the development of anorexia nervosa in the adolescent. *Revue de neuropsychiatrie infantile et d'hygiene mentale de l'enfance* 19:661–690.

Butler, B., Duke, M. J., and Stovel, T. (1977). Anorexia nervosa: a nursing approach. *Canadian Nurse* 73:22–24.

Button, E. J., Fransella, F., and Slade, P. A. D. (1977). A reappraisal of body perceptions disturbance in anorexia nervosa. *Psychological Medicine* 7:235–243.

Buvat, J., and Buvat-Herbaut, M. (1978). Dysperception of body image and dysmorphophobias in mental anorexia. Apropos of 115 cases involving both sexes. II. Dysmorphophobias in mental anorexia. *Annales Medico-Psychologiques* 136:563–580.

Byrd, O. E. (1963). The relief of tension by exercise: a survey of medical viewpoints and practices. *Journal of School Health* 42:238–239.

Caille, P., Abrahamsen, P., Girolami, C., and Sorbye, B. (1977). A systems theory approach to a case of anorexia nervosa. *Family Process* 16:455–465.

Cantarini, A. (1970). Effect of cyproheptadine on appetite and body weight. *Minerva Pediatrica* 22:2404–2408.

Cantwell, D. P., Sturzenberger, S., Burroughs, J., Salkin, B., and Green, J. K. (1977). Anorexia nervosa: an effective disorder. *Archives of General Psychiatry* 34:1087–1091.

Caplan, G., and Lebovici, S. (eds.) (1966). *Psychiatric Approaches to Adolescence.* Amsterdam: Excerpta Medica.

Carrier, J. (1939). *L'Anorexie Mentale.* Paris: Libraire E. Le François.

Carlberger, G., Einarsson, K., Felig, P., Hellstrom, K., Wahren, J., Wengle, B., and Zetterstrom, J. (1971). Severe malnutrition in a middle-aged man with anorexia nervosa. *Nutrition and Medicine* 13:100–113.

Carryer, H. M., Berkmann, J. M., and Mason, H. L. (1959). Relative lymphocytosis in anorexia nervosa. *Proceedings of Staff Meeting of the Mayo Clinic* 34:425–429.

Carter, J. N., Eastman, C. J., Corcoran, J. M., and Lazarus, L. (1974). Effect of severe chronic illness on thyroid function. *Lancet* 2:971–974.

Casper, R. C., Chatterton, R. T., and Davis, J. M. (1979). Alterations in serum cortisol and its binding characteristics in anorexia nervosa. *Journal of Clinical Endocrinology and Metabolism* 49:406–411.

Casper, R. C., and Davis, J. M. (1977). On the course of anorexia nervosa. *American Journal of Psychiatry* 134:574–578.

Casper, R. C., Halmi, K. A., Goldberg, S. C., Eckert, E. D. and Davis, J. M. (1979). Disturbances in body image estimation as related to other characteristics and outcome in anorexia nervosa. *British Journal of Psychiatry* 134:60–66.

Casper, R. C., Kirschner, B., and Jacob, R. A. (1978). Zinc and copper status in anorexia nervosa proceedings. *Psychopharmacology Bulletin* 14:53–55.

Ceaser, M. (1979). Hunger in primary anorexia nervosa. *American Journal of Psychiatry* 136:979–980.

Charcot, J. M. (1889). *Diseases of the Nervous System.* London: New Sydenham Society.

——— (1892). *Poliklinische Vortrage,* vol. 1, transl. S. Freud. Vienna and Leipzig: Hans Deuticker.

Cheever, J. (1978). *The Stories of John Cheever.* New York: Alfred A. Knopf.

Codaccioni, J. L., Boyer, J., Jubelin, J., Conte-Devolx, B., and Hebreard, J. (1972). Hypokalemic alkalosis with hyperplasia of the juxtanglomerular apparatus (Bartter's syndrome). *Annales D'endocrinologie* (Paris) 33:281–284.

Coddington, R. D., and Bruch, H. (1970). Gastric perceptivity in normal, obese and schizophrenic subjects. *Psychosomatics* 11:571–599.

Coddington, R. D., Bruch, H., and Keller, J. (1963). Gastric perceptivity in normal, obese and schizophrenic subjects. Paper presented at the Annual Meeting of the American Psychosomatic Society.

Coddington, R. D., and Kohler, W. (1966). The relation between maternal affect and gastric secretion in twin infants. Paper presented at the Annual Meeting of the American Psychosomatic Society, 1966.

Coddington, R. D., Sours, J. A., and Bruch, H. (1964). Electrogastrographic findings associated with effective changes. *American Journal of Psychiatry* 121:41–45.

Cohen, P. (1980). An eating disorder in adolescence: a preliminary report. *Bulletin of the Hampstead Clinic* 3:49–56.

Cohen, S. I. (1978). Hostile interaction in a general hospital ward leading to disturbed behaviour and bulimia in anorexia nervosa: its successful management. *Postgraduate Medical Journal* 54:361–363.

Coles, R. (1978). *Walker Percy: An American Search.* Boston: Atlantic Monthly Press.

Collins, W. J. (1894). Anorexia nervosa. *Lancet* 1:202–206.

Collomb, H., and Valantin, S. (1974). A note on kwashiorkor as anorexia nervosa in infancy. In *The Child in his Family: Children at Psychiatric Risk: III,* eds. E. J. Anthony and C. Koupernik. New York: John Wiley & Sons.

Conrad, D. E. (1977). A starving family: an interactional view of anorexia nervosa. *Bulletin of the Menninger Clinic* 41:487–495.

Cornbleet, P. J., Moir, R. C., and Worf, P. L. (1977). A histochemical study of bone marrow hypoplasia in anorexia nervosa. *Virchows Archives of Pathological Anatomy* 374:239–247.

Cramer, B., and Bovet du Bois, N. (1973). Psychotic regression and representation of the body in a boy with anorexia nervosa. *Revue de neuropsychiatrie infantile et d'hygiene mentale de l'enfance* 21:767–773.

Cravario, A., Cravetto, C. A., and Autino, R. (1974). Study of liver function in anorexia nervosa. *Minerva Medica* 65:2990–2995.

Cravetto, C. A., Nejrotti, M., and Curtaz, G. (1977). Hematological findings and blood coagulation tests in anorexia nervosa. *Archivio perle Scienze Mediche* (Torino) 134:205–209.

Cremerius, J. (1978). Prognosis of anorexia nervosa (11, 26 to 29 year follow-up studies of psychotherapeutically untreated cases). *Zeitschrift für Psycho-Somatische Medizin und Psychoanalisis* 24:56–69.

Crisp, A. H. (1965). Some aspects of the evolution, presentation and follow-up of anorexia nervosa. *Proceedings of the Royal Society of Medicine* 58:814–820.

—— (1967). The possible significance of some behaviour correlates of weight and carbohydrate intake. *Journal of Psychosomatic Research* 11:117–131.

—— (1968). Primary anorexia nervosa. *Gut* 6:370–372.

—— (1969a). Some skeletal measurements in patients with primary anorexia nervosa. *Journal of Psychosomatic Research* 13:125–142.

—— (1969b). Psychological aspects of breast-feeding with particular reference to anorexia nervosa. *British Journal of Medical Psychology* 42:119–132.

—— (1970a). Premorbid factors in adult disorders of weight, with particular reference to primary anorexia nervosa (weight phobia): a literature review. *Journal of Psychosomatic Research* 14:1–22.

—— (1970b). Anorexia nervosa: Feeding disorder, 'nervous malnutrition' or 'weight phobia'? *World Review of Nutrition and Dietetics* 12:452–504.

—— (1970c). Reported birth weights and growth rates in a group of patients with primary anorexia nervosa (weight phobia). *Journal of Psychosomatic Research* 14:23–50.

—— (1973). The aetiology of anorexia nervosa. In *Anorexia Nervosa and Obesity*, ed. R. F. Roberton. Edinburgh: Royal College of Physicians.

—— (1974). Primary anorexia nervosa or adolescent weight phobia. *The Practitioner* 212:525–535.

—— (1977a). The differential diagnosis of anorexia nervosa. *Proceedings of the Royal Society of Medicine* 70:686–688.

—— (1977b). Diagnosis and outcome of anorexia nervosa: the St. George's view. *Proceedings of the Royal Society of Medicine* 70:464–470.

—— (1977c). The differential diagnosis of anorexia nervosa. *Proceedings of the Royal Society of Medicine* 70:686–690.

—— (1977d). Some psychobiological aspects of adolescent growth and their relevance for the fat/thin syndrome (anorexia nervosa). *International Journal of Obesity* 1:231–238.

—— (1978a). Psychopathology of weight-related amenorrhea. In *Advances in Gynaecological Endocrinology,* ed. H. S. Jacobs. London: Royal College of Obstetricians and Gynaecologists.

—— (1978b). Some aspects of the relationship between body weight and sexual behaviour with particular reference to massive obesity and anorexia nervosa. *International Journal of Obesity* 2:17–32.

—— (1979). Early recognition and prevention of anorexia nervosa. *Developmental medicine and Child Neurology* 21:393–395.

Crisp, A. H., Fenton, G. W., and Scotton, L. (1967). The EEG society and the electrophysiological and technological association: the electroencephalogram in anorexia nervosa. *Electroencephalography and Clinical Neurophysiology* 23:490.

——— (1968). A controlled study of the EEG in anorexia nervosa. *British Journal of Psychiatry* 114:1149–1160.

Crisp, A. H., and Fransella, F. (1972). Conceptual changes during recovery from anorexia nervosa. *British Journal of Medical Psychology* 45:395–405.

Crisp, A. H., Harding, B., and McGuinness, B. (1974). Anorexia nervosa: psychoneurotic characteristics of parents: relationship to prognosis: a quantitative study. *Journal of Psychosomatic Research* 18:167–173.

Crisp, A. H., Hsu, L. K., and Stonehill, E. (1979). Personality, body weight and ultimate outcome of anorexia nervosa. *Journal of Clinical Psychiatry* 40:332–335.

Crisp, A. H., and Kalucy, R. S. (1973). The effect of leucotomy in interactable adolescent weight phobia (primary anorexia nervosa). *Postgraduate Medical Journal* 49:883–893.

——— (1974). Aspects of the perceptual disorder in anorexia nervosa. *British Journal of Medical Psychology* 47:349–361.

Crisp, A. H., Kalucy, R. S., Lacey, J. H., and Harding, B. (1977). The long-term prognosis in anorexia nervosa: some factors predictive of outcome. In *Anorexia Nervosa,* ed. R. Vigersky. New York: Raven Press.

Crisp, A. H., Palmer, R. L., and Kalucy, R. S. (1976). How common is anorexia nervosa? A prevalence study. *British Journal of Psychiatry* 128:549–554.

Crisp, A. H., Stonehill, E., and Fenton, G. W. (1970). An aspect of the biological basis of the mind-body apparatus: the relationship between sleep, nutritional state and mood in disorders of weight. *Psychotherapy and Psychosomatics* 18:161–175.

Crisp, A. H., and Toms, D. A. (1972). Primary anorexia nervosa or weight phobia in the male—report on 13 cases. *British Medical Journal* 1:334–338.

Croxson, M. S., and Ibbertson, H. K. (1977). Low serum triiodothyronine (T3) and hypothyroidism in anorexia nervosa. *Journal of Clinical Endocrinology and Metabolism* 44:167–174.

Curran, W. (1880). The pathology of starvation. *Medical Practice* 29:210–229.

Czerwenka-Wenkstetten, H. (1969). Psychologic and psychopathological motivation in sport. *Z. Nervenheilk* 27:162–170.

Dalbiez, R. (1941). *The Psychoanalytic Method and the Doctrine of Freud.,* vols. I and II. London: Longmans, Green.

Dally, P. J. (1959). Carotenaemia occurring in a case of anorexia nervosa. *British Medical Journal* 1:1333.

——— (1969). *Anorexia Nervosa.* London: Heinemann.

——— (1977). Anorexia nervosa: Do we need a scapegoat? *Proceedings of the Royal Society of Medicine* 70:470–480.

Dally, P., and Gomez, J. (1979). *Anorexia Nervosa*. London: Heinemann.

Dally, P. J., and Sargant, W. (1960). A new treatment of anorexia nervosa. *British Medical Journal* 1:1770-1773.

—— (1966). Treatment and outcome of anorexia nervosa. *British Medical Journal* 2:793-799.

Davidson, C., and Silverstone, T. (1972). Diuretic dependence. *British Medical Journal* 1:505.

Davidson, D. M. (1976). Anorexia nervosa in a serviceman: a case report. *Military Medicine* 141:617-619.

Davies, C. T., Fohlin, L., and Thoren, C. (1977). Temperature regulation in anorexia nervosa proceedings. *Journal of Physiology* (London) 268:8P-9P.

—— (1979). Temperature regulation in anorexia nervosa patients during prolonged exercise. *Acta Medica Scandinavica* 205:257-262.

Davies, C. T., von Dobeln W., Fohlin, L., Freyschuss, U., and Thoren, C. (1978). Total body potassium fat free weight and maximal aerobic power in children with anorexia nervosa. *Acta Paediatrica Scandinavica* 67:229-234.

Davy, J. P., Andersson, J. C., and Poilpre, E. (1976). Development and prognostic factors in mental anorexia: 44 observations. *Annales Medico-Psychologiques* 2:464-480.

Debow, S. L. (1975). Identical twins concordant for anorexia nervosa: a preliminary case report. *Canadian Psychiatric Association Journal* 20:215-217.

DeBurger, J. E. (ed.) (1977). *Marriage Today: Problems, Issues and Alternatives*. New York: John Wiley and Sons.

Decourt, J. (1946). Anorexie mentale et cachexie dite hypophysaire. *Paris Med.* 23:249-255.

—— (1951). Nosolgie de l'anerexie mentale. *Presse Med.* 59:797-805.

Deegener, G. (1977). On the diagnosis of anorexia nervosa in children and adolescents [author's transl.]. *Monatsschr. Kinderheilkd.* 125:687-693.

Degraeff, J., Kassenaar, J., and Schuurs, M. A. M. (1960). Balance studies during refeeding in anorexia nervosa. *Metabolism* 9:814-820.

Déjèrine, J., and Gauckler, E. (1913). *The Psychoneuroses and Their Treatment*, 2nd ed., transl. S. E. Jelliffe. Philadelphia and London: J. D. Lippincott.

Demaret, A. (1971). Ethological perspective of anorexia nervosa in young women. *Acta Psychiatrica Belgica* 71:5-23.

Demos, J., and Demos, V. (1969). Adolescence in historical perspective. *Journal of Marriage and Family* 31:62-71.

Deniau, L. (1883). *De l'hysterie gastrique*. Thesis. Paris.

Derogatis, L., Rickels, K., and Rock, A. (1976). The SCL-90 and the MMPI: A step in the validation of a new self-report scale. *British Journal of Psychiatry* 128:280-289.

DesLaurier, A. M. (1962). *The Experience of Reality in Childhood Schizophrenia.* New York: International Universities Press.

Dettmering, P. (1977). An atypical case of anorexia nervosa. *Praxis der kinderpsychologie und kinderpsychiatrie* 26:165–169.

Dickens, G., and Trethowan, W. H. (1971). Cravings and aversions in pregnancy. *Journal of Psychosomatic Research* 15:259–265.

Dickens, J. A. (1970). Concurrence of Turner's syndrome and anorexia nervosa. *British Journal of Psychiatry* 117:237–240.

Dinnage, R. (1977). The starved self. *New York Review of Books,* February 22, pp. 6–9.

Dole, V. P. (1954). Treatment of obesity with a low protein calorically unrestricted diet. *American Journal of Clinical Nutrition* 2:381–383.

Donley, A. J., and Kemple, T. J. (1978). Spontaneous pneumomediastinum complicating anorexia nervosa. *British Medical Journal* 2:1604–1605.

Dowse, T. S. (1881). Anorexia nervosa. *Lancet* 1:827–830.

Druss, R. G. and Silverman, J. A. (1979). Body image and perfectionism of ballerinas. *General Hospital Psychiatry* 1:115–121.

Dubois, A., Gross, H. A., Ebert, M. H., and Castell, D. O. (1979). Altered gastric emptying and secretion in primary anorexia nervosa. *Gastroenterology* 77:319–323.

Dubois, F. A. (1949). Compulsion neurosis with cachexia (anorexia nervosa). *American Journal of Psychiatry* 106:107–110.

Dubois, R. (1909). *The Psychic Treatment of Nervous Disorders.* New York: Funk and Wagnalls.

———— (1913). De l'anorexie mentale comme prodrome de le dámence pràcoce. *Annales Medico-Psychologiques* 10:431–441.

Duddle, M. (1973). An increase of anorexia nervosa in a university population. *British Journal of Psychiatry* 123:711–712.

Dugas, M., Gueriot, C., and Jullien, P. (1973). Depressive periods in mental anorexia. *Ann. Med. Interne* (Paris) 124:637–640.

Dunn, C. W. (1936). Report of a case of Simmonds' disease with recovery. *Journal of Nervous and Mental Disease* 83:166–172.

Dunton, H. D., and Langford, W. S. (1962). Psychodynamic studies of pubescent girls with anorexia nervosa. *Bulletin of the Association of Psychoanalytic Medicine* 1:51 56.

Eckert-Ecke, D. (1979). Behaviour therapy in anorexia nervosa. *British Journal of Psychiatry* 134:55–59.

Edel, L. (1975). The madness of art. *American Journal of Psychiatry* 132:1005–1012.

Edge, A. M. (1880). A case of anorexia nervosa. *Lancet* 1:818–820.

Egart, F. M., and Glushchenko, S. K. (1972). Diagnosis and treatment of

Kylin's syndrome (late pubertal cachexia). *Problemy Endokrinologii I Gormonoterapii* (Moskow) 18:33–36.

Ehrensing, R. H., and Weitzman, E. L. The mother-daughter relationship in anorexia nervosa. *Psychosomatic Medicine* 32:201–211.

Eischens, R., Greist, J. H., and McInvaille, T. (1976). *Run to Reality.* Madison, Wis.: Madison Running Press.

Eissler, K. R. (1943). Some psychiatric aspects of anorexia nervosa. *Psychoanalytic Review* 30:121–145.

——— (1958). Notes on problems of technique in the psychoanalytic treatment of adolescents: with some remarks on perversions. *Psychoanalytic Study of the Child* 13:223–254.

——— (1959). On isolation. *Psychoanalytic Study of the Child* 14:29–60.

Eitinger, L. (1951). Anorexia nervosa. *Nordisk Medicin* 45:915–919.

Emanuel, R. W. (1954). *Some Physical Aspects of Anorexia Nervosa.* Oxford: Thesis.

Engle, G. L. (1960). A unified concept of health and disease. *Perspectives in Biology and Medicine* 3:459–469.

Erikson, E. H. (1968). *Identity: Youth and Crisis.* New York: Norton.

———. Epidemiology of anorexia nervosa. *British Medical Journal* 3:556–561.

Esman, A. H. (1979). On evidence and inference, or the Babel of tongues. *Psychoanalytic Quarterly* 43:628–630.

Evans, D. S. (1968). Acute dilation and spontaneous rupture of the stomach. *British Journal of Surgery* 55:940–942.

Eysenck, H. J., and Eysenck, S. B. (1968). *Eysenck Personality Inventory.* San Diego, Calif: Educational and Industrial Testing Service.

Fairbairn, W. R. D. (1941). A revised psychopathology of the psychoses and psychoneuroses. *International Journal of Psycho-Analysis* 22:250–257.

Falstein, E. I., Sherman, D., Feinstein, S. C., and Judas, I. (1956). Anorexia nervosa in the male child. *American Journal of Orthopsychiatry* 26:751–772.

Farquharson, R. F. (1941). Anorexia nervosa. *Illinois Medical Journal* 80:193–200.

Farquharson, R. F., and Hyland, H. H. (1938a). Anorexia nervosa: a metabolic disorder of psychological origin. In *Evolution of Psychosomatic Concepts,* ed. M. R. Kaufman and M. Heiman. New York: International Universities Press, 1964

——— (1938)b). Anorexia nervosa. *Journal of the American Medical Association* 111:1085–1091.

——— (1966). Anorexia nervosa. The course of fifteen patients treated from twenty to thirty years previously. *Canadian Medical Association Journal* 94:411–418.

Fedida, P. A non-receptive hunger. *Annual of Nutrition and Alimentation* 30:389–394.

Feighner, J. P., Robins, E., Guze, S. B., and Munoz, R. (1972). Diagnostic criteria for use in psychiatric research. *Archives of General Psychiatry* 26:57-73

Fenichel, O. (1945). Anorexia. In *Collected Papers of Otto Fenichel,*vol. II. New York: Norton.

Fenton, J. W., and Elphicke, T. M. (1969). Sleep disturbances in malnutrition. *Electroencephalography and Clinical Neurophysiology* 27:681-685.

Fenwick, S. (1889). *On Atrophy of the Stomach and of the Nervous Affections of the Digestive Organs.* London: J. and A. Churchill.

Ferrara, A., and Fontana, V. J. (1966). Celiac disease and anorexia nervosa. *New York State Journal of Medicine* 66:1000-1009.

Fiedler, L. (1978). *Freaks, Myths and Images of the Secret Self.* New York: Simon & Schuster.

Finkelstein, B. A. (1972). Parenteral hyperalimentation in anorexia nervosa. *Journal of the American Medical Association* 219:217-219.

Fiorillo, A., and Pellettieri, L. (1977). Anorexia nervosa in a patient with a clivus tumor. Case report. *Acta Neurologica* (Napoli) 32:427-431.

Fisher, S. (1970). *Body Experience in Fantasy and Behavior.* New York: Appelton-Century-Crofts.

Fixx, J. (1977). *The Complete Book of Running.* New York: Random House.

——— (1980). *Second Book of Running.* New York: Random House.

Fohlin, L. (1978). Exercise performance and body dimensions in anorexia nervosa before and after rehabilitation. *Acta Medica Scandinavica* 204:61-65.

Fohlin, L., Freyschuss, U., Bjarke, B., Davies, C. T., and Thoren, C. (1978). Function and dimensions of the circulatory system in anorexia nervosa. *Scandinavica* 67:11-16.

Forchheimer, F. (1907). Anorexia nervosa in children. *Archives of Pediatrics* 24:801-812.

Forssman, H., Mellbin, G., and Walinder, J. (1970). Concurrence of Turner's syndrome and anorexia nervosa. *British Journal of Psychiatry* 116:221-223.

Foster, F. G., and Kupfer, D. J. (1975). Anorexia nervosa: telemetric assessment of family interaction and hospital events. *Journal of Psychiatric Research* 12:19-35.

Fowler, P. B., Bahn, S. O., and Ikram, H (1972). Prolonged ankle reflex in anorexia nervosa. *Lancet* 2:307-308.

Fox, K. C., and James, N. M. (1976). Anorexia nervosa: A study of 44 strictly defined cases. *New Zealand Medical Journal* 84:309-312.

Frank, N., and Frank, M. J. (1973). Pulseless disease producing abdominal angina and stimulating anorexia nervosa. *Journal of the Medical Society of New Jersey* 70:830-833.

Frank, R. A., and Cohen, D. J. (1979). Psychosocial concomitants of biological maturation in preadolescence. *American Journal of Psychiatry* 136:1518–1524.

Franklin, J. C., Schiele, B. C., Brozek, J., and Keys, A. (1948). Observations of human behavior in experimental semistarvation and rehabilitation. *Journal of Clinical Psychology* 4:28–35.

Fransella, F., and Crisp, A. H. (1979). Comparisons of weight concepts in groups of neurotic, normal and anorexic females. *British Journal of Psychiatry* 134:79–81

Frazier, S. H., Faubion, M. H., Griffin, M. E., and Johnson, A. M. (1955). A specific factor in symptom choice. *Proceedings of the Mayo Clinic* 30:227–229.

Freud, A. (1946). The psychoanalytic study of infantile feeding disturbances. *Psychoanalytic Study of the Child* 2:119–132.

——— (1952). A connection between states of negativism and of emotional surrender. *International Journal of Psycho-Analysis* 33:265–271.

——— (1958). Adolescence. *Psychoanalytic Study of the Child* 13:225–287.

——— (1965). *Normality and Pathology in Childhood: Assessments of Development.* New York: International Universities Press.

Freud, S. (1887–1902). *The Origins of Psychoanalysis. Letters to Wilhelm Fliess, Drafts and Notes: 1887–1902.* New York: Basic Books, 1954.

——— (1905a). Fragment of an analysis of a case of hysteria. *Standard Edition* 7:7–122.

——— (1905b). Three essays on the theory of sexuality. *Standard Edition* 7:125–245.

——— (1912). Types of onset of neurosis. *Standard Edition* 12:229–238.

Freyschuss, U., Fohlin, L., and Thoren C. (1978). Limb circulation in anorexia nervosa. *Acta Paediatrica Scandanavica* 67:225–228.

Fries, H. (1974). Secondary amenorrhoea, self-induced weight loss and anorexia nervosa. *Acta Psychiatrica Scandinavica* (Supplement 248).

Fries, H., and Nillius S. J. (1973a). Psychological factors, psychiatric illness and amenorrhoea after oral contraceptive treatment. *Acta Psychiatrica Scandinavica* 49:653–668.

——— (1973b). Dieting, anorexia nervosa and amenorrhoea after oral contraceptive treatment. *Acta Psychiatrica Scandinavica* 49:669–679.

Friese, A. P., Szmuilowicz, J., and Bailey, J. D. (1978). The superior mesenteric artery syndrome: cause or complication of anorexia nervosa. *Canadian Psychiatric Association Journal* 23:325–327.

Frisch, R. E., and Macarthur, J. W. (1974). Menstrual cycles: fatness as a determinant of minimum weight for height necessary for their maintenance or onset. *Science* 185:949–951.

Frisch, R. E., and Revelle, R. (1970). Height and weight at menarche and a hypothesis of critical body weights and adolescent events. *Science* 169:397–398.

Frisch, R. E., Wyshak, G., and Vincent, L. (1980). Delayed menarche and amenorrhea in ballet dancers. *New England Journal of Medicine* 303:17–19.

Frosch, J. (1959). Transference derivatives of the family romance. *Journal of the American Psychoanalytic Association* 7:503–522.

Galdston, R. (1974). Mind over matter: observations on fifty patients hospitalized for anorexia nervosa. *Journal of the American Academy of Child Psychiatry* 13:246–263.

Galletly, C., and James, B. (1979). Anorexia nervosa in a male: comment and illustration. *New Zealand Medical Journal* 89:171–173.

Gallinek, A. (1954). Syndrome of episodes of hypersomnia, bulaemia and abnormal mental states. *Journal of the American Medical Association* 154:1081–1084.

Garfinkel, P. E. (1974). Perception of hunger and satiety in anorexia nervosa. *Psychological Medicine* 4:309–315.

Garfinkel, P. E., Garner, D. M., and Moldofsky, H. (1977). The role of behavior modification in the treatment of anorexia nervosa. *Journal of Pediatric Psychology* 2:113–121.

Garfinkel, P. E., Moldofsky, H., and Garner, D. M. (1977). Prognosis in anorexia nervosa as influenced by clinical features, treatment and self-perception. *Canadian Medical Association Journal* 117:1041–1045.

Garfinkel, P. E., Moldofsky, H., Garner, D. M., Stancer, H. C., and Coscina, D. V. (1978). Body awareness in anorexia nervosa: disturbances in "body image" and satiety. *Psychosomatic Medicine* 40:487–498.

Garner, D. M. (1977). Measurement of body image. In *Anorexia Nervosa*, ed. R. A. Vigersky. New York: Raven Press.

Garner, D. M., and Garfinkel, P. E. (1979). The eating attitudes test: an index of the symptoms of anorexia nervosa. *Psychological Medicine* 9:273–279.

Garner, D. M., Garfinkel, P. E., and Moldofsky, H. (1978). Perceptual experiences in anorexia nervosa and obesity. *Canadian Psychiatric Association Journal* 23:249–263.

Garner, D. M., Garfinkel, P. E., Stancer, H. C., and Moldofsky, H. (1976). Body image disturbances in anorexia nervosa and obesity. *Psychosomatic Medicine* 38:327–336.

Gasne, G. (1900). Un cas d' anorexie hysterique *Revue neurologique* 8:574–578.

Gatti, B., and Robutti, A. (1970). Anorexia nervosa: nosographical and clinical studies. *Rivista Sperimentale di Freniatria* 94:833–863.

Gee, S. (1908). *Medical Lectures and Clinical Aphorisms*, 2nd ed. London: Oxford University Press.

Gero, G. (1943). The idea of psychogenesis in modern psychiatry and in psychoanalysis. *Psychoanalytic Review* 30:187–211.

———— (1952–1953). Ein Äquivalent der Depression: Anorexie. *Psyche* (Stuttgart) 5:641–652.

Gifford, S., Murawski, B. J., and Pilot, M. L. (1970). Anorexia nervosa in one of
identical twins. *International Psychiatry Clinics* 7:139–228.

Gill, M. M., and Holzman, P. S. (1976). Psychology versus metapsychology:
psychoanalytic essays in memory of George S. Klein. *Psychological Issues,*
Vol. 9, No. 4, Monograph 36. New York: International Universities Press.

Gillespie, R. D. (1931). Treatment of functional anorexia. *Lancet* 1:995–998.

Giovacchini, P. L. (ed.) (1972). *Tactics and Techniques in Psychoanalytic
Therapy.* New York: Jason Aronson.

Girard-Doumic, A. (1971). Psychotherapy of anorexia in the child under the
age of three. *Revue de neuropsychiatrie infantile et d'hygiene mentale de
l'enfance* 19:625–633.

Glasser, W. (1967). *Positive Addiction.* New York: Harper & Row.

Glick, R. A. (1979). Individualism in our time—a report on the interdisciplin-
ary symposium on narcissism. *Bulletin Association of Psychoanalytic Medicine* 18:33–40.

Glück, L. (1979). Dedication to hunger. *Antaeus* 36:94–95.

Glucksman, M. L., and Hirsch, J. (1968). The response of obese patients to
weight reduction: a clinical evaluation of behavior. *Psychosomatic Medicine*
30:1–2.

Glucksman, M. L., Hirsch, J., McCully, R. S., Barron, B. A., and Knittle, J. L.
(1967). The response of obese patients to weight reduction: a quantitative
evaluation of behavior. *Psychosomatic Medicine* 29:323–330.

Goetz, P. L., Succop, R. A., Reinhart, J. B., and Miller, A. (1977). Anorexia
nervosa in children: a follow-up study. *American Journal of Orthopsychiatry*
47:597–603.

Gold, M. S., Pottash, A. L. C., Sweeny, D. R., Martin, D. M., and Davies, R. K.
(1980). Further evidence of hypothalamic-pituitary dysfunction in anorexia
nervosa. *American Journal of Psychiatry* 137:101–102.

Goldberg, S. C., Halmi, K. A., Casper, R., Eckert, E., and Davis, J. M. (1977).
Pretreatment predictors of weight change in anorexia nervosa. In *Anorexia
Nervosa,* ed. R. A. Vigersky. New York: The Raven Press.

Goldberg, S. C., Halmi, K. A., Eckert, E. D., Casper, R. C., and Davis, J. M.
(1979). Cyproheptadine in anorexia nervosa. *British Journal of Psychiatry*
134:67–70.

Goldney, R. D. (1978). Craniopharyngioma simulating anorexia nervosa.
Journal of Nervous and Mental Disease 166:135–138.

Goode, W. J. (1971). *The Contemporary American Family.* Chicago, Quad-
rangle.

Gooding, G. T. (1968). The delayed relaxation of the ankle jerk in anorexia
nervosa. *British Journal of Clinical Practice* 223:40–44.

Goodman, J. D., and Sours, J. A. (1967). *The Mental Status Examination.* New York: Basic Books.

Goodsitt, A. (1969). Anorexia nervosa. *British Journal of Medical Psychology* 42:109–118.

——— (1977). Narcissistic disturbances in anorexia nervosa. In *Adolescent Psychiatry,* vol. 5, ed. S. C. Feinstein and P. L. Giovacchini, New York: Jason Aronson.

Gosling, P. H. (1971). Migraine, anorexia nervosa and schizophrenia. *British Journal of Psychiatry* 119:228–229.

Gotch, F. M., Spry, C. J., Mowat, A. G., Beeson, P. B., and MacLennan, I. C. (1975). Reversible granulocyte killing defect in anorexia nervosa. *Clinical and Experimental Medicine* 21:244–249.

Gottdiener, J. S., Gross, H. A., Henry, W. L., Borer, J. S., and Ebert, M. H. (1978). Effects of self-induced starvation on cardiac size and function in anorexia nervosa. *Circulation* 58:425–433.

Gottesfeld, B. H., and Novaes, A. C. (1945). Narcoanalysis and subshock insulin in treatment of anorexia nervosa. *Digest of Neurology and Psychiatry* 13:486–490.

Grass, G. (1977). *The Flounder.* New York: Harcourt, Brace and Jovanovich.

Green, E., Miller, D. S., and Wynn, V. (1975). Oxygen consumption of obese and anorectic patients. *Proceedings of the Nutrition Society* 34:14A–15A.

Green, R. S. and Rau, J. (1977). The use of diphenylhydantion in compulsive eating disorders: further studies. In *Anorexia Nervosa,* ed. R. Vigersky. New York: Raven Press.

Greist, J. H., Klein, M. H., Eischens, R. R., and Faris, J. W. (1978). Antidepressant running. *Behavioral Medicine,* June, pp. 19–24.

Greist, J. H., Klein, M. H., Eischens, R. R., Faris, J. W., Gurman, A. S., and Morgan, W. P. Running as treatment for depression. *Comprehensive Psychiatry* [in press].

Grinker, R. R. (1953). *Psychosomatic Research.* New York: Norton.

Grote, L. R., and Meng, H. (1934). Medical and psychotherapeutic treatment of endogenetic magersucht. *Schweiz. med. Wochenschrift.* 64:137–139.

Group for the Advancement of Psychiatry [GAP] (1966). *Psychopathological Disorders in Childhood,* Vol. 6, No. 62.

Gryboski, J. D., Katz, J., Sangree, M. H., and Herskovic, T. (1968). Eleven adolescent girls with severe anorexia. Intestinal disease or anorexia nervosa? *Clinical Pediatrics* 7:684–690.

Guile, L., Horne, M., and Dunston, R. (1978). Anorexia nervosa, sexual behavior modification as an adjunct to an integrated treatment programme: a case report. *Australian and New Zealand Journal of Psychiatry* 12:165–167.

Gull, W. W. (1868). The address in medicine. In *Evolution of Psychosomatic Concepts,* ed. M. R. Kaufman and M. Heiman. New York: International Universities Press, 1964.

———— (1873). Meeting of the clinical society. *Medical Times and Gazette* 2:534.

———— (1874). Anorexia nervosa (apepsia hysterica, anorexia hysterica). In *Evolution of Psychosomatic Concepts,* ed. M. R. Kaufman and M. Heiman. New York: International Universities Press, 1964.

Guntrip, H. (1952). A study of Fairbairn's theory of schizoid reactions. *British Journal of Medicine and Psychology* 25:86–89.

Hafner, R. J., Crisp, A. H., and McNeilly, A. S. (1976). Prolactin and gonadotropin activity in females treated for anorexia nervosa. *Postgraduate Medical Journal* 52:76–79.

Hall, A. (1978). Family structure and relationships of 50 female anorexia nervosa patients. *Australian and New Zealand Journal of Psychiatry* 12:263–268.

Hall, G. S. (1904). *Adolescence.* New York: Appleton.

Haller, J. O., Slovis, T. L., Baker, D. H., Berdon, W. E., and Silverman, J. A. (1977). Anorexia nervosa: The paucity of radiologic findings in more than fifty patients. *Pediatric Radiology* 5:145–147.

Halmi, K. A. (1974a). Comparison of demographic and clinical features in patient groups with different ages and weights at onset of anorexia nervosa. *Journal of Nervous and Mental Disease* 158:222–225.

———— (1974b). Anorexia nervosa: Demographic and clinical features in 94 cases. *Psychosomatic Medicine* 36:18–26.

———— (1978). Anorexia nervosa: recent investigations. *Annual Review of Medicine* 29:137–148.

Halmi, K. A., and Broadland, O. (1973). Monozygotic twins concordant and discordant for anorexia nervosa. *Psychological Medicine* 3:521–524.

Halmi, K., Broadland, O., and Loney, J. (1973). Prognosis in anorexia nervosa. *Annals of Internal Medicine* 78:907–909.

Halmi, K. A., and Debault, L. E. (1974). Gonosomal aneuploidy in anorexia nervosa. *American Journal of Human Genetics* 26:195–198.

Halmi, K. A., Dekirmenjian, H., Davis, J. M., Casper, R., and Goldberg, S. (1978). Catecholamine metabolism in anorexia nervosa. *Archives of General Psychiatry* 35:458–460.

Halmi, K. A., and Fry, M. (1974). Serum lipids in anorexia nervosa. *Biological Psychiatry* 8:159–167.

Halmi, K. A. and Goldberg, S. C. (1978). Cyproheptadine in anorexia nervosa proceedings. *Psychopharmacology Bulletin* 14:31–33.

Halmi, K. A., Goldberg, S. C., Casper, R. C., Eckert, E. D., and Davis, J. M. (1979). Pretreatment predictors of outcome in anorexia nervosa. *British Journal of Psychiatry* 134:71–78.

Halmi, K. A., Goldberg, S. C., and Cunningham, S. (1977). Perceptual distortion of body image in adolescent girls: distortion of body image in adolescence. *Psychological Medicine* 7:253–257.

Halmi, K. A., and Loney, J. (1973). Familial alcoholism in anorexia nervosa. *British Journal of Psychiatry* 123:53–54.

Halmi, K. A., Powers, P., and Cunningham, S. (1975). Treatment of anorexia nervosa with behavior modification: effectiveness of formula feeding and isolation. *Archives of General Psychiatry* 32:93–96.

Halmi, K. A., and Rigas, C. (1973). Urogenital malformations associated with anorexia nervosa. *British Journal of Psychiatry* 122:79–81.

Halmi, K. A., and Sherman, B. M. (1975). Gonadotropin response to LH-RH in anorexia nervosa. *Archives of General Psychiatry* 32:875–878.

Halmi, K. A., Struss, A., and Goldberg, S. C. (1978). An investigation of weights in the parents of anorexia nervosa patients. *Journal of Nervous and Mental Disease* 166:358–361.

Halmi, K. A., Stunkard, A. J., and Mason, E. E. (1980). Emotional responses to weight reduction by three methods: gastric bypass, jejunoileal bypass, diet. *American Journal of Clinical Nutrition* 33:446–451.

Hamburger, W. W. (1958). The occurrence and meaning of dreams of food and eating. *Psychosomatic Medicine* 20:1–16.

Hamilton, C. M. (1975). Eating disorders in adolescence. *Mental Health Society* 2:243–247.

Harrower, A. D. (1970). Bromocriptine in anorexia nervosa. *British Journal of Hospital Medicine* 20:672–675.

Harrower, A D. B., Yap, P. L., Nairn, I. M., Walton, N. J., Strong, J., and Craig, A. (1977). Growth hormone, insulin and prolactin secretion in anorexia nervosa and obesity during bromocriptine treatment. *British Medical Journal* 2:156–159.

Hart, I. R., Kuwayti, K. and Khan, S. A. (1973). Ankle reflex and thyroid function. *Lancet* 1:372.

Hart, M. N. (1971). Hypertrophy of human subventricular hypothalamic nucleus in starvation. *Archives of Pathology* 91:493–496.

Hart, T., Kase, N., and Kimball, C. P. (1970). Induction of ovulation and pregnancy in patients with anorexia nervosa. *American Journal of Obstetrics and Gynecology* 108:580–584.

Hasan, M K , and Tibbetts, R W (1977). Primary anorexia nervosa (weight phobia) in males. *Postgraduate Medical Journal* 53:146–151.

Hathaway, S. R., and McKinley, J. C. (1951). *Minnesota Multiphasic Personality Inventory: Manual.* New York: Psychological Corp.

Hauserman, N., and Lavin, P. (1977). Post-hospitalization continuation treatment of anorexia nervosa. *Journal of Behavior Therapy and Experimental Psychiatry* 8:309–313.

Hay, G. G., and Leonard, J. C. (1979). Anorexia nervosa in males. *Lancet* 2:574–575.

Heinz, E. R., Martinez, J., and Haenggeli, A. (1977). Reversibility of cerebral atrophy in anorexia nervosa and Cushing's syndrome. *Journal of Computer Assisted Tomography* 1:415–418.

Hellstrom, I. (1977). Oral complications in anorexia nervosa. *Scandinavian Journal of Dental Research* 85:71–86.

Helweg-Larsen, P., Hoffmeyer, H., Kieler, J., Thaysen, E., Thaysen, J. H., Thygesen, P., and Wulff, M. H. (1947). Famine disease in German concentration camps. *Acta Medica Scandinavica Supplement* 274.

Henkin, R. I., Patten, B. M., Re, P. K., and Bronzeret, D. A. (1975). A syndrome of acute zinc loss: cerebellar dysfunction, mental changes, anorexia, and taste and smell dysfunction. *Archives of Neurology* 32:745–751.

Herman, E., Goth, E., and Rado, J. (1973). Successfully treated anorexia nervosa associated with hyperaldosteronism. *Orvosi Hetilap* (Budapest) 114:1754–1756.

Heron, G. B., and Johnston, D. A. (1976). Hypothalamic tumor presenting as anorexia nervosa. *American Journal of Psychiatry* 133:580–582.

Hill, R. (1964). The American family of the future. *Journal of Marriage and the Family* 26:20–28.

Hirsch, J. (1976). The psychological consequence of obesity. In *Obesity in Perspective*, vol. 2, part 2, ed. G. A. Bray (Fogarty International Center Series on Preventive Medicine). Bethesda, Md.: National Institutes of Health.

Hirschman, G. H., Rao, D. D., and Chan, J. C. (1977). Anorexia nervosa with acute tubular necrosis treated with parenteral nutrition. *Nutrition and Metabolism* 21:341–348.

Hogan, W. M., Huerta, E., Lucas E., and Alexander, R. (1974). Diagnosis anorexia nervosa in males. *Psychosomatics* 15:122–126.

Holmberg, N. G., and Nylander, I. (1971). Weight loss in secondary amenorrhea: a gynaecologic, endocrinologic and psychiatric investigation of 54 consecutive clinic cases. *Acta Obstetrics and Gynecology Scandinavica* 50:241–246.

How, J., and Davidson, R. J. (1977). Chlorpromazine-induced haemolytic anaemia in anorexia nervosa. *Postgraduate Medical Journal* 53:278–279.

Howells, J. G., and Lickorish, J. R. (1962). *Manual for the Family Relations Indicator.* London: National Foundation for Educational Research in England and Wales.

Hsu, L. K., Crisp, A. H., and Harding, B. (1979). Outcome of anorexia nervosa. *Lancet* 1:61–65.

Huenemann, R. L., Shapiro, L. R., Hampton, M. C., and Mitchell, B. W. (1966). A longitudinal study of gross body composition and body conformation, and their association with food and activity in a teenage population. *American Journal of Clinical Nutrition* 18:325–330.

Hull, M. G. R., Murray, M. A. F., Franks, S., and Jacobs, H. S. (1976). Endocrinopathy of weight-recovered anorexia nervosa in women presenting with secondary amenorrhoea. *Journal of Endocrinology* 69:43P–44P.

Hultgreen, H. N. (1951). Clinical and laboratory observations in severe starvation. *Stanford Medical Bulletin* 9:175–178.

Hunt, H. F. (1948). The effects of deliberate deception on Minnesota multiphasic personality inventory performance. *Journal of Consulting Psychology* 12:396–401.

Hurd, H. P., Palumbo, P. J., and Gharib, H. (1977). Hypothalamic-endocrine dysfunction in anorexia nervosa. *Proceedings of the Mayo Clinic* 52:711–716.

Hurst, A. F. (1936). *The British Encyclopaedia of Medical Practice*, vol. 1. London: Butterworth.

Hurst, P. S., Lacey, L. H., and Crisp, A. H. (1977). Teeth, vomiting and diet; a study of the dental characteristics of 17 anorexia nervosa patients. *Postgraduate Medical Journal* 53:298–305.

Illingworth, R. S. and Illingworth, C. M. (1966). *Lessons from Childhood*. London: Livingstone.

Imura, H., Nakai, Y., Matsukura, S., and Matsuyama, H. (1973). Effect of intravenous infusion of L-DOPA on plasma growth hormone levels in man. *Hormone and Metabolic Research* 5:41–45.

Isaacs, A. J. (1979). Endocrinology. In *Anorexia Nervosa*, ed. P. Dalley and I. Gomez. London: Heinemann.

Jacobson, E. (1964). *The Self and the Object World.* New York, International Universities Press.

Jacques, E. (1970). *Work, Creativity, Social Justice.* London: Heinemann.

Janet, P. (1903). *Les obsessions et la psychasthénie.* Paris: Alcan.

——— (1907). *The Major Symptoms of Hysteria.* London: Macmillan.

——— (1909). *Les Névroses.* Paris: Flammarion.

——— (1925). *Psychological Healing,* transl. E. and C. Paul. London: George Allen & Unwin.

Janowitz, H. D., and Grossmann, M. E. (1949). Hunger and appetite: some definitions and concepts. *Journal of the Mt. Sinai Hospital* 16:231–237.

Jaspers, K. (1910). Eifersuchtswahn. Ein Beitrag zur Frage: Enwicklung einer Persönlichkeit oder Prozess? *Zentralblatt für die gesamte Neurologie und Psychiatrie* 1:567–574.

——— (1963). *General Psychopathology.* Chicago: University of Chicago Press.

Jeammet, P., Gorge, A., Zweifel, R., and Flavigny, H. (1973). The family environment of patients with anorexia nervosa. Effect on treatment. *Annales de Medicine Interne* (Paris) 124:247–252.

Jennings, K. P. and Klidjian, A. M. (1974). Acute gastric dilatation in anorexia nervosa. *British Medical Journal* 2:472–478.

Jessner, L., and Abse, D. W. (1960). Regressive forces in anorexia nervosa. *British Journal of Medical Psychology* 33:301–307.

Jeuniewic, N., Brown, G. M., Garfinkel, P. E., and Moldofsky, H. (1978). Hypothalamic function as related to body weight and body fat in anorexia nervosa. *Psychosomatic Medicine* 40:187–198.

Johanson, A. J., and Knorr, N. J. (1974). Letter. *Lancet* 2:591.

—— (1977). L-DOPA as treatment for anorexia nervosa. In *Anorexia Nervosa,* ed. R. Vigersky. New York: Raven Press.

Jores, A. and Theiremann, E. (1957). Experiences from the treatment of thirty cases of anorexia nervosa. Third European Conference on Psychosomatic Research, Copenhagen.

Joseph, R. (1980). *Early Disorder.* New York: Farrar, Strauss and Giroux.

Kafka, F. (1979). The hunger artist. In *The Modern Tradition,* 4th ed., ed. D. F. Howard. Boston: Little, Brown.

Kaiser, G. C., McKain, J. M., and Schumacker (1960). The superior mesenteric artery syndrome. *Surgery, Gynecology and Obstetrics* 110:133–140.

Kalager, T., Brubakk, O., and Bassoe, H. H. (1978). Cardiac performance in patients with anorexia nervosa. *Cardiology* 63:1–4.

Kalucy, R. S. (1976). Noctural hormonal profiles in massive obesity, anorexia nervosa and normal females. *Journal of Psychosomatic Research* 20:595–604.

Kalucy, R. S., Crisp, A. H., and Harding, B. (1977). Prevalence and prognosis in anorexia nervosa. *Australian and New Zealand Journal of Psychiatry* 11:251–257.

Kassenaar, A., DeGraeff, J., and Kouwenhoven, A. T. (1970). N_{15}-glycine studies of protein synthesis during refeeding in anorexia nervosa. *Metabolism* 9:831–840.

Katz, J. L. (1975). Psychoendocrine considerations in anorexia nervosa. In *Topics in Psychoendocrinology,* ed. E. J. Sachar, pp. 121–134. New York: Grune & Stratton.

Katz, J. L., Boyar, R. M., Roffwarg, H., Hellman, L., and Weiner, H. (1977). LHRH responsiveness in anorexia nervosa: Intactness despite prepubertal circadian LH pattern. *Psychosomatic Medicine* 39:241–251.

—— (1978). Weight and circadian luteinizing hormone secretory pattern in anorexia nervosa. *Psychosomatic Medicine* 40:549–567.

Katz, J. L., and Walsh, B. T. (1978). Depression in anorexia nervosa: Letter. *American Journal of Psychiatry* 135:507.

Katz, J. L., and Weiner, H. (1974). Editorial: A functional anterior hypothalamic defect in primary anorexia nervosa? *Psychosomatic Medicine* 17:103–105.

Kay, D. W. K. (1953a). Anorexia nervosa. *Proceedings of the Royal Society of Medicine* 46:669–674.

—— (1953b). Anorexia nervosa: a study in prognosis. *Proceedings of the Royal Society of Medicine* 46:3–15.

Kay, D. W. K., and Leigh, D. (1954). Natural history, therapy and prognosis of anorexia nervosa, based on a study of 38 patients. *Journal of Mental Science* 100:411–419.

Kay, D. W. K., and Schapira, K. (1965a). *Anorexia Nervosa Symposium.* Stuttgart: G. T. Verlag.

—— (1965b). The prognosis in anorexia nervosa. In *Anorexia Nervosa*, ed. J. Meyer and H. Feldmann. Stuttgart: Thieme.

Keane, F. B., Fennell, J. S., and Tomkin, G. H. (1973). Acute pancreatitis, acute gastric dilation and duodenal ileus following refeeding in anorexia nervosa. *Journal of Medical Science* 147:191–192.

Kellerman, J. (1977). Anorexia nervosa: the efficacy of behavior therapy. *Journal of Behavior Therapy and Experimental Psychiatry* 8:387–390.

Kellet, J. M., Trimble, M., and Thorley, A. (1976). Anorexia nervosa after the menopause. *British Journal of Psychiatry* 128:555–558.

Kelly, D. (1973). Therapeutic outcome in limbic leucotomy in psychiatric patients. *Psychiatry, Neurology, Neurosurgery* 76:353–363.

Kendall, R. E., Hall, D. J., Hailey, A., and Babigan, H. M. (1973). The epidemiology of anorexia nervosa. *Psychological Medicine* 3:200–203.

Kendler, K. S. (1978). Amitriptyline-induced obesity in anorexia nervosa: a case report. *American Journal of Psychiatry* 135:1107–1108.

Keniston, K. (1977). *All Our Children: The American Family Under Pressure.* New York: Harcourt Brace & Jovanovich.

Kenny, F. T., and Solyom, L. (1971). The treatment of compulsive vomiting through faradic disruption of mental images. *Canadian Medical Association Journal* 105:1071.

Kernberg, O. F. (1966). Stuctural derivatives of object relationships. *International Journal of Psycho-Analysis* 47:236–253.

—— (1975). *Borderline Conditions and Pathological Narcissism.* New York: Jason Aronson.

—— (1976). *Object Relations Theory and Clinical Psychoanalysis.* New York. Jason Aronson.

Kestemberg, E. and Kestemberg, J. (1972). *Hunger and the Body: A Psychoanalytic Study of Mental Anorexia.* Vendôme: Presses Universitaires de France.

Keys, A., Brozck, J., Henschel, A., Mickelsen, O., and Taylor, H. L. (1950). *The Biology of Human Starvation.* Minneapolis: University of Minnesota Press.

Kim, Y., and Michel, A. F. (1975). Hypocomplementemia in anorexia nervosa. *Journal of Pediatrics* 87:582–585.

King, A. (1963). Primary and secondary anorexia nervosa syndromes. *British Journal of Psychiatry* 109:470–475.

King, D. A. (1971). Anorexic behavior—a nursing problem. *Journal of Psychiatric Nursing* 9:11–17.

Klein, G. S. (1976). *Psychoanalytic Theory: An Exploration of Essentials.* New York: International Universities Press.

Klein, M. (1934). A contribution to the psychogenesis of manic-depressive states. *Contributions to Psychoanalysis* 1921–1945. London: Hogarth, 1950.

Kline, C. L. (1979). Anorexia nervosa: death from complications of ruptured gastric ulcer. *Canadian Journal of Psychiatry* 24:153–157.

Knuth, V. A., Hull, M. G. R., and Jacobs, H. S. (1977). Amenorrhoea and loss of weight. *British Journal of Obstetrics and Gynecology* 84:801–807.

Kohut, H. (1959). Introspection, empathy and psychoanalysis. *Journal of the American Psychoanalytic Association* 7:459–483..

——— (1977). *The Restoration of the Self.* New York: International Universities Press.

Kolb, L. C. (1959). The body image in the schizophrenic reaction. In *Schizophrenia,* ed. A. Auerbach. New York: Ronald.

——— (1975). Disturbances of body image. In *American Handbook of Psychiatry,* vol. 4, ed. S. Arieti. Basic Books: New York.

Korkina, M. V., Marilov, V. V., and Tsivil'ko, M. A. (1977). Atypical forms of anorexia nervosa. *Zhurnal Nevropatologii Psikhiatrii* 77:429–432.

Kostrubala, T. (1971). Depression and physical activity. Paper presented at the Nebraska Symposium on Physical Activity and Mental Health, Lincoln.

——— (1976). *Joy of Running.* New York: J. B. Lippincott.

Kraepelin, E. (1920). Symptoms of mental disease. *Zentralblatt für die gesamte Neurologie und Psychiatrie* 62:110–131.

Kreuz, L. E., Rose, R. M., and Jennings, J. R. (1972). Suppression of plasma testerone levels and psychological stress. *Archives of General Psychiatry* 26:479–482.

Kron, L., Katz, J. L., Gorzynski, G., and Weiner, H. (1977). Anorexia nervosa and gonadal dysgenesis. Further evidence of a relationship. *Archives of General Psychiatry* 34:332–335.

Kubanek, B., Heimpel, H., Parr, G., and Schoengen, A. (1977). Haematological features of anorexia nervosa. *Blut* 35:115–124.

Kubie, L. S. (1953). The central representations of the symbolic process in psychosomatic disorders. *Psychosomatic Medicine* 15:1–7.

Kuhn, R. (1953). Zur Daseinsanalyse der Anorexia Mentalis. *Nervenarzt* 22:191–199.

Kunz, H. (1942). Zur theorie der perversion. *Zeitschrift für Psychiatrie und Neurologie* 105:1–104.

——— (1949). Die Bedeutung der Daseinsanalytik Martin Heideggers für die

Psychologie und Philosophische Anthropologie. *Martin Heideggers Einfluss auf die Wissenschaft*. Bern: Francke.

Laboucarié, J., and Barres, P. (1954). Les aspects cliniques, pathologéniques et thérapeutiques de l'anorexie mentale. *Evolution Psychiatrique* 1:119–124.

Langdon-Brown, W. (1931). *Anorexia Nervosa*. London: Individual Psychological Publications.

Lacey, J. H., Crisp, A. H., Hart, G., and Kirkwood, B. A. (1979). Weight and skeletal maturation—a study of radiological and chronological age in an anorexia nervosa population. *Postgraduate Medical Journal* 55:381–385.

Lacey, J. H., Stanley, P. A., Crutchfield, D. M., and Crisp. A. H. (1977). Sucrose sensitivity in anorexia nervosa. *Journal of Psychosomatic Research* 21:17–21.

Lakoff, K. M., and Feldman, J. D. (1972). Anorexia nervosa associated with pregnancy. *Obstetrics and Gynecology* 39:699–701.

Lampert, F., and Lau, B. (1976). Bone marrow hypoplasia in anorexia nervosa. *European Journal of Pediatrics* 124:65–71.

Langford, W. S. (1972). Anorexia nervosa. In *Pediatrics,* 15th ed., ed. H. L. Barnett and A. H. Einhorn. New York: Appleton-Century-Crofts.

Lasch, C. (1978). *The Culture of Narcissism*. New York: W. W. Norton.

Lasègue, C. (1873). De l'anorexie hysterique. *Archives Generales du Medicine* 2:367–369.

——— (1873). On hysterical anorexia. In *Evolution of Psychosomatic Concepts,* ed. M. R. Kaufman and M. Heiman. New York: International Universities Press, 1964.

Launer, M. A. (1978). Anorexia nervosa in late life. *British Journal of Medical Psychology* 51:375–377.

Lauritzen, C. (1979). Hormonal regulation and hormone therapy in childhood and adolescence. Part 2: Therapeutic problems (tall stature, amenorrhea, delayed puberty, oligomenorrhea, precocious puberty, anorexia nervosa, antisomastia, hypermastia, acne, etc. *Fortschritte der Medizin* 97:895–898.

Leger, J. M., Blanchinet, J., and Vallat, J. N. (1969). In the light of two cases of mental anorexia in boys, can an important role be attributed to the father's personality for the onset of this illness? *Annales Medico-Psychologiques* 2:101–108.

Lehmann, E. (1949). Feeding problems of psychogenic origin: A survey of the literature. *Psychoanalytic Study of the Child* 3/4:461–488.

Leslie, R. D., Isaacs, A. J., Gomez, J., Raggatt, P. R., and Bayliss, R. (1973). Hypothalamo-pituitary-thyroid function in anorexia nervosa: Influence of weight gain. *British Medical Journal* 2:526–568.

Lesser, L. I., Ashenden, B. J., Debriskey, M., and Eisenberg, L. (1960). Anorexia nervosa in children. *American Journal of Orthopsychiatry* 30:572–579.

Levenkron, S. (1978). *The Best Little Girl in the World.* New York: Contemporary Books.

Levinson, D. J. (1978). *The Seasons of a Man's Life.* New York: Alfred A. Knopf.

Lewin, B. D. (1951). *The Psychoanalysis of Elation.* London: Hogarth.

Lewis, A. (1936). Problems of obsessional illness. *Proceedings of the Royal Society of Medicine* 29:13–15.

Liebman, R., Minuchin, S., and Baker, L. (1974). An integrated treatment program for anorexia nervosa. *American Journal of Psychiatry* 131:432–436.

Liebman, R., Minuchin, S., Baker, L., and Rosman, B. (1975). The treatment of anorexia nervosa. *Current Psychiatric Therapies.* New York: Grune & Stratton.

Lindner, R. (1955). *The Fifty-Minute Hour.* New York: Holt, Rinehart & Winston.

Liston, E. H., and Shershow, L. W. (1973). Concurrence of anorexia nervosa and gonadal dysgenesis. A critical review with practical considerations. *Archives of General Psychiatry* 29:834–836.

Little, J. C. (1965). *Physical Prowess and Neurosis.* M. D. Thesis, University of Bristol.

——— (1979). The athlete's neurosis: a deprivation crisis. *Acta Psychiatrica Scandinavica* 45:187–197.

Little, J. C., and Kerr, T. A. (1968). Some differences between published norms and data from matched controls as a basis for comparison with psychiatrically disturbed groups. *British Journal of Psychiatry* 114:883–890.

Ljunggren, H., Ikkos, D., and Luft, R. (1961). Basal metabolism in women with obesity and anorexia nervosa. *British Journal of Nutrition* 15:21–24.

Loewenstein, R. M. (1966). Observational data and theory in psychoanalysis. In *Drives, Affect, Behavior,* vol. 2. New York: International Universities Press.

Lorand, S. (1943). Anorexia nervosa. Report of a case. *Psychosomatic Medicine* 5:282–290.

Love, D. R., Brown, J. J., Fraser, R., Lever, A. F., Robertson, J. I., Timbury, G. C., Thomson, S., and Tree, M. (1971). An unusual case of self-induced electrolyte depletion. *Gut* 12:284–290.

Lovibond, S. H. (1954). The object sorting test and conceptual thinking on schizophrenia. *Australia Journal of Psychology* 6:52–57.

Lucas, A. R., Duncan, J. W., and Piens, V. (1976). The treatment of anorexia nervosa. *American Journal of Psychiatry* 133:1034–1038.

Lundberg, O., and Walinder, J. (1967). Anorexia nervosa and signs of brain damage. *International Journal of Psychiatry* 3:167–173.

Lutzenkirchen, J., and Boning, J. (1976). Anorexic syndrome and depression. Considerations from a case history 1. *Schweizer Archiv für Neurologie Neurochirurgie und Psychiatrie* 118:175–184.

MacGregor, T. N. (1938). Amenorrhoea: its aetiology and treatment. *British Medical Journal* 1:717-722.

Machover, K. (1942). *Personality Projection in the Drawing of the Human Figure: A Method of Personality Investigation.* Springfield, Ill.: Charles C Thomas.

Mahler, M. (1972). On the first three subphases of the separation-individuation process. *International Journal of Psycho-Analysis* 53:333-338.

Mahler, M. S., and Furer, M. (1968). *On Human Symbiosis and the Vicissitudes of Individuation.* New York: International Universities Press.

Malcolm, J. (1978). A reporter at large (family therapy). *The New Yorker,* May 15, 1978, pp. 39-114.

Maller, O. (1964). The late psychopathology of former concentration camp inmates. *Psychiatry and Neurology* (Basel) 148:140-146.

Malone, C. A. (1979). Child psychiatry and family therapy. *Journal of the American Academy of Child Psychiatry* 18:4-21.

Maloney, M. J., and Farrell, M. K. (1980). Treatment of severe weight loss in anorexia nervosa with hyperalimentation and psychotherapy. *American Journal of Psychiatry* 157:310-314.

Markham, D. S. (1974). *Normal Adolescence.* London: Granada.

Marks, V., and Bannister, R. (1963). Pituitary and adrenal function in under-nutrition. *British Journal of Psychiatry* 109:480-489.

Marks, V., Howorth, N., and Greenwood, F. C. (1965). Plasma growth-hormone levels in chronic starvation in man. *Nature* 208:686-687.

Marmor, J. (1980). Recent trends in psychotherapy. *American Journal of Psychiatry* 137:409-416.

Marshall, C. F. (1895). A fatal case of anorexia nervosa. *Lancet* 1:149-150.

Marshall, J. C., and Russell Fraser, T. (1971). Amenorrhoea in anorexia nervosa: assessment and treatment with clomiphene citrate. *British Medical Journal* 4:590-592.

Marshall, M. H. (1978). Anorexia nervosa: dietary treatment and re-establishment of body weight in 20 cases studied on a metabolic unit. *Journal of Human Nutrition* 32:349-357.

Marshall, W. A. (1974). Physical changes at puberty. In *Puberty and Adolescence,* ed. E. Proudfoot. Royal College of Physicians of Edinburgh, Publication 45.

Massermann, J. H. (1941). Psychodynamism in anorexia nervosa and neuroic vomiting. *Psychoanalytic Quarterly* 10:211-242.

Masterson, J. F. (1977). Primary anorexia nervosa in the borderline adolescent: an object relations view. In *Borderline Personality Disorders,* ed. P. Hartocollis. New York: International Universities Press.

Masterson J. F., and Rinsley, D. B. (1975). The borderline syndrome: role of the mother in the genesis and psychic structure of borderline personality. *International Journal of Psycho-Analysis* 56:163–177.

Mastrosimone, F., and Pacini, A. (1971). Anorexia nervosa as possible atypical manifestation of endogenous depression. Considerations on a clinical case. *Ospedali Psichiatria* 39:44–65.

Masuda, S., Sehata, R., and Imai, T. (1972). Observations on appetite: the nurses' role in cases with abnormally increased appetite and anorexia. *Japanese Journal of Nursing Arts* 18:23–31.

Mawson, C. F. (1974). Anorexia nervosa and the regulation of intake: a review. *Psychological Medicine* 4:289–308.

Maxmen, J. S., Siberfarb, P. M., and Ferrell, R. B. (1974). Anorexia nervosa. Practical initial management in a general hospital. *Journal of the American Medical Association* 229:801–808.

May, R., Angel, E., and Ellenberger, H. (eds.) (1958). *Existence*. New York: Basic Books.

Mayer, J. (1972). Hunger and satiety in health and disease. General discussion. *Advances in Psychosomatic Medicine* 7:332–336.

Mayer-Gross, W., Slater, E., and Roth, M. (1954). *Clinical Psychiatry*. London: Cassell.

McAnarney, B. R., and Hoekelman, R. A. (1979). Conflicted adolescent premarital intercourse. An antecedent of mild anorexia nervosa. *Clinical Pediatrics* 18:340–342.

McDaniel, F. L., White, B. V., and Thomson, C. M. (1946). Malnutrition in repatriated prisoners of war. *U. S. Naval Medical Bulletin* 46:793–801.

Mecklenburg, R. S., Loriaux, D. L., Thompson, R. H., Andersen, A. E., and Lipsett, M. B. (1974). Hypothalamic dysfunction in patients with anorexia nervosa. *Medicine* 53:147–159.

Melon, J. (1971). Anorexia nervosa and the Szondi test. *Annales Medico-Psychologiques* 1:759–767.

Meng, H. (1934a). Anorexia nervosa. *International Journal of Psycho-Analysis* 20:439–445.

——— (1934b). Das problem der organpsychose. *Internationale Zeitschrift für Arztliche Psychoanalyse* 20:439–458.

——— (1935). Organische Erkrankung als Organ-Psychose. *Schweizer Archiv für Neurologie und Psychiatrie* 26:271–283.

Meyer, D. C., and Weinroth, L. A. (1957). Observations on psychological aspects of anorexia nervosa. *Psychosomatic Medicine* 19:389–393.

Meyer, J. E. (1971). Anorexia nervosa of adolescence: the central syndrome of the anorexia nervosa group. *British Journal of Psychiatry* 118:539–542.

Meyer, J. E., and Feldmann, H. (eds.) (1965). *Anorexia Nervosa*. Proceedings of a Symposium, Göttingen, April 24–25, 1965. Stuttgart: Theime.

Milvy, P. (ed.) (1977). *The Marathon: Physiological, Medical, Epidemiological, and Psychological Studies,* vol. 301. New York: New York Academy of Sciences.

Mintz, I. L. (1980). Anorexia nervosa: clinical syndrome. *Journal of the Medical Society of New Jersey* 77:333-339.

Minuchin, S. (1970). The use of an ecological framework in the treatment of a child. In *The Child and His Family,* ed. J. Anthony and C. Koupernik. New York: Wiley.

——— (1974). *Families and Family Therapy.* Cambridge: Harvard University Press.

Minuchin, S., Baker, L., Rosman, B. L., Liebman, R., Milman, L., and Todd, T. C. (1975). A conceptual model of psychosomatic illness in children. Family organization and family therapy. *Archives of General Psychiatry* 32:1031-1038.

Minuchin, S., Rosman, B. L., and Baker, L. (1978). *Psychosomatic Families: Anorexia Nervosa in Context.* Cambridge, Mass.: Harvard University Press.

Mirsky, I. A. (1957). The psychosomatic approach to the etiology of clinical disorders. *Psychosomatic Medicine* 19:424-428.

Mitchell-Heggs, N., Kelly, D., and Richardson, A. (1976). Stereotactic limbic leucotomy: a follow-up at 16 months. *British Journal of Psychiatry* 128:226-240.

Miyai, K., Yamamoto, T., Azukizawa, M., Ishibashi, K., and Kumahara (1975). Serum thyroid hormones and thyrotropin in anorexia nervosa. *Journal of Clinical Endocrinology and Metabolism* 40:334-338.

Moldofsky, H., and Garfinkel, P. E. (1974). Problems of treatment of anorexia nervosa. *Canadian Psychiatric Association Journal* 19:169-175.

Moldofsky, H., Jeuniewic, N., and Garfinkel, P. E. (1979). Preliminary report of metoclopramide in anorexia nervosa. In *Anorexia Nervosa,* ed. R. Vigersky. New York: Raven Press.

Moore, D. C. (1977). Amitriptyline therapy in anorexia nervosa. *American Journal of Psychiatry* 134:1303-1304.

Moore, R., and Mills, I. H. (1979). Serum T3 and T4 levels in patients with anorexia nervosa showing transient hyperthyroidism during weight gain. *Clinical Endocrinology* 10:443-449.

Mordasini, R., Klose, G., and Greten, H. (1978). Secondary type III hyperlipoproteinemia in patients with anorexia nervosa. *Metabolism* 27:71-79.

Morgan, H. G. (1977). Fasting girls and out attitudes toward them. *British Medical Journal* 2:1652-1755.

Morgan, H. G., and Russell, G. F. M. (1975). Value of family background and clinical features as predictors of long-term outcome in anorexia nervosa: four year follow-up of 41 patients. *Psychological Medicine* 5:335-371.

Morgan, W. P. (1968). Selected physiological and psychomotor correlates of depression in psychiatric patients. *Research Quarterly* 39:1037-1043.

—— (1969a). Physical fitness and emotional health: a review. *American Corrective Therapy Journal* 23:124–127.

—— (1969b). A pilot investigation of physical working capacity in depressed and nondepressed psychiatric males. *Research Quarterly* 40:859–861.

—— (1974). Exercise and mental disorders. In *Sports Medicine*, ed. A. J. Ryan and F. L. Allman, Jr. New York: Academic Press.

—— (1978). The mind of the marathoner. *Psychology Today* 11:38–49.

Morgan, W. P., and Costill, D. L. (1972). Psychological characteristics of the marathon runner. *Journal of Sports Medicine and Physical Fitness* 12:42–46.

Morgan, W. P., and Horstman, D. H. (1976). Influences of physical activity on state anxiety. *Medicine and Science in Sports* 11:38–43.

Morgan, W. P., and Pollock, M. L. (1977). Psychologic characterization of the elite distance runner. *Annals of the New York Academy of Sciences* 301:24–30.

Mormont, C., and Demoulin, C. (1971). The personalities of a case of anorexia nervosa and of her monozygotic twin: a comparative study. *Acta Psychiatrica Belgica* 71:477–487.

Mortimer, C. H., Besser, G. M., McNeilly, A. S., Marshall, J. C., Harsoulis, P., Tunbridge, W. M. G., Gomez-Pan, A., and Hall, R. (1973). Luteinizing hormone and follicle stimulating hormone-releasing hormone test in patients with hypothalamic-pituitary-gonadal dysfunction. *British Medical Journal* 3:73–77.

Morton, R. (1694). *Phthisiologia: Or a Treatise of Consumptions*. London: S. Smith and B. Walford.

Moulton, R. (1942a). Psychosomatic implications of pseudocyesis. *Psychosomatic Medicine* 4:376–384.

—— (1942b). A psychosomatic study of anorexia nervosa, including the uses of vaginal smears. *Psychosomatic Medicine* 4:62–69.

Muller, J. P., and Richardson, W. J. (1979). Toward reading Lacan: pages for a workbook. *Psychoanalysis and Contemporary Thought* 2:199–252.

Murray, H. A. (1943). *Thematic Apperception Test: Manual*. Cambridge, Mass.: Harvard University Press.

Nagaraja, J. (1974). Anorexia and cyclic vomiting in children: A psychogenic study. *Child Psychiatry Quarterly* 7:1–5.

Nagera, H. (1966). *Early Childhood Disturbances. The Infantile Neurosis and the Adult Disturbances. Psychoanalytic Study of the Child*. Monograph Series No. 2. New York: International Universities Press.

Naudeau (1789). Observation sur une maladie nerveuse accompagnée d'un dégoût extraordinaire pour les aliments. *Journal de Médecine Chirurgie et Pharmacologie* 8:197–201.

Needleman, H. L., and Waber, D. (1979). The use of amitriptyline in anorexia nervosa. In *Anorexia Nervosa,* ed. R. Vigersky. New York: Raven Press.

Neki, J. S., Mohan, D., and Sood, R. K. (1977). Anorexia nervosa in a monozygotic twin pair. *Journal of the Indian Medical Association* 68:98–100.

Nemeth, J. M. (1977). Anorexia nervosa in one dizygotic twin. *Psychiatric Forum* 7:45–50.

Nemiah, J. C. (1949). Anorexia nervosa. *American Journal of Medicine* 7:819–825.

—— (1950). Anorexia nervosa. *Medicine* 29:225–268.

—— (1958). Anorexia nervosa: fact and theory. *American Journal of Digestive Diseases* 3:249–274.

—— (1972). The psychosomatic nature of anorexia nervosa. Discussion. *Advances in Psychosomatic Medicine* 7:316–321.

Neufield, N. D. (1979). Endocrine abnormalities associated with deprivational dwarfism and anorexia nervosa. *Pediatric Clinics of North America* 26:199–208.

Nicolle, G. (1938a). Prepsychotic anorexia. *Lancet* 2:1173.

—— (1938b). Prepsychotic anorexia. *Proceedings of the Royal Society of Medicine* 32:153–156.

Nillius, S. J., and Wide, L. (1975). Gonadotropin-releasing hormone treatment for induction of follicular maturation and ovulation in amenorrhoeic women with anorexia nervosa. *British Medical Journal* 3:405–408.

—— (1979). Effects of prolonged luteinizing hormone-releasing hormone therapy on follicular maturation, ovulation and corpus luteum function in amenorrhoeic women with anorexia nervosa. *Journal of Medical Science* 84:21–35.

Nishimura, N., Suehiro, F., Mitani, H., Isaka, K., Chikamori, K., Mori, H., Oshima, I., and Saito, S. (1979). Endocrine function before and after treatment in patients with anorexia nervosa [author's transl.] *Nippon Naibunpi Gakkai Zasshi* 55:171–182.

Nordgren, L., and Von Scheele, C. (1977). Hepatic and pancreatic dysfunction in anorexia nervosa: a report of two cases. *Biological Psychiatry* 12:681–686.

Nylander, I. (1971). The feeling of being fat and dieting in a school population. An epidemiologic interview investigation. *Acta Soceomedica Scandinavica* 3:17–26.

Oberholzer, M. (1930). Aus der Analyse eines Dreizehnjaehrigen maedchens. *Schweizer Archiv für Neurologie und Psychiatrie* 26:287–292.

Offer, D. (1969). *Psychological World of the Teenager.* New York: Basic Books.

Ogston, D., and Ogston, W. D. (1976). The fibrinolytic enzyme system in anorexia nervosa. *Acta Haematologica* (Basel) 55:230–233.

Oo, M. (1975). Vaginal cytological examination in anorexia nervosa. *British Medical Journal* 4:164–165.

Palazzoli, M. S. (1961). Emaciation as magic means for the removal of anguish in anorexia mentalis. *Acta Psychotherapica* 9:37–45.

——— (1965). Interpretation of mental anorexia. In *Anorexia Nervosa*, ed. J. E. Meyer and H. Feldman. Stuttgart: Thieme.

——— (1974). *Self-Starvation.* New York: Jason Aronson, 1978.

Palmblad, J., Fohlin, L., and Lundstrom, M. (1973). Anorexia nervosa and polymorphonuclear (PMN) granulocyte reactions. *Scandinavian Journal of Haematology* 19:334–342.

Palmer, H. D., and Jones, M. S. (1939). Anorexia nervosa as a manifestation of compulsion neurosis. *Archives of Neurology and Psychiatry* 41:856–859.

Palossy, B., and Oo, M. (1977). ECG alterations in anorexia nervosa. *Advances in Cardiology* 19:280–282.

Paolino, T. J., and McGrady, B. S. (eds.) (1978). *Marriage and Marital Therapy.* New York: Brunner-Mazel.

Parker, J. B., Blazer, D., and Wyrick, L. (1977). Anorexia nervosa: a combined therapeutic approach. *Southern Medical Journal* 70:448–452.

Parlato, A., and Palazzoli, A. (1966). Study of anorexia nervosa in monozygotic twins. *Neuropsichiatria* 22:483–537.

Pasternack, A. (1970). Anorexia nervosa, secondary aldosteronism and angiopathy. *Acta Medica Scandinavica* 187:139–143.

Peake, T., and Borduin, C. (1977). Combining systems, behavioral and analytical approaches to the treatment of anorexia nervosa: a case study. *Family Therapy* 4:49–56.

Pearson, H. A. (1967). Marrow hypoplasia in anorexia nervosa. *Journal of Pediatrics* 71:211–214.

Peretz, D. (1978). Running: the alteration of fantasy in action. Paper presented at the New York Hospital–Cornell Medical Center Running Conference, October.

Perkin, G. J., and Surtees, P. G. (1976). Wide perspectives in the behavioural treatment of anorexia nervosa: a case study. *Australian and New Zealand Journal of Psychiatry* 10:325–330.

Perloff, W. H., Lasche, E. M., Nodine, I. H., Schneeberg, N. G., and Vieillard, C. B. (1954). The starvation state and functional hypopituitarism. *Journal of the American Medical Association* 155:1307.

Perry, S. W., and Sacks, M. (1978). The psychodynamics of running. Presented at the New York Hospital–Cornell Medical Center Running Conference, October.

Pertschuk, M. J., Edwards, N., and Pomerleau, O. F. (1978). A multiple-baseline approach to behavioral intervention in anorexia nervosa. *Behavior Therapy* 9:368–376.

Pflanz, M. (1965). Socialanthropologische aspekte der anorexia nervosa. In *Anorexia Nervosa,* ed. J. E. Meyer and H. Feldmann. Stuttgart: Thieme.

Piaget, J. (1954). *The Construction of Reality in the Child.* New York: Basic Books.

———— (1968). *The Growth of Logical Thinking from Childhood to Adolescence.* New York: Basic Books.

Piaget, J., and Inhelder, B. (1969). *The Psychology of the Child.* New York: Basic Books.

Pierloot, R. A., and Houben, M. E. (1978). Estimation of body dimensions in anorexia nervosa. *Psychological Medicine* 8:317–324.

Pierloot, R. A., Wellens, W., and Houben, M. E. (1976). Elements of resistance to a combined medical and psychotherapeutic program in anorexia nervosa: an overview. *Psychotherapy and Psychosomatics* 26:101–117.

Pillay, M., and Crisp, A. H. (1977). Some psychological characteristics of patients with anorexia nervosa whose weight has been newly restored. *British Journal of Medical Psychology* 50:375–380.

Poole, A. D., Sanson-Fisher, R. W., and Young, P. (1978). A behavioural programme for the management of anorexia nervosa. *Australian and New Zealand Journal of Psychiatry* 12:49–53.

Pops, M. A., and Schwabe, A. D. (1968). Hypercarotenemia in anorexia nervosa. *Journal of the American Medical Association* 205:533–534.

Porot, M., Couadau, A., and Collet, M. (1970). Mental anorexia and depressive syndrome. *Annales Medico Psycholologiques.* (Paris) 2:567–575.

Portnay, G. I., O'Brian, J. I., Bush, J., Vagenakis, A. G., Azizi, F., Arky, R. A., Ingbar, S. H., and Braverman, L. E. (1974). The effect of starvation on the concentration and binding of thyroxine and triidothyronine in serum and the response to TRH. *Journal of Clinical Endocrinology and Metabolism* 39:191–194.

Powell, G. F., Brasel, J. A., and Blizzard, R. M. (1967). Emotional deprivation and growth retardation stimulating idiopathic hypopituitarism. I. Clinical evaluation of the syndrome. *New England Journal of Medicine* 276:1271–1278.

Powell, G. F., Brasel, J. A., Raiti, S., and Blizzard, R. M. (1967). Emotional deprivation and growth retardation stimulating idiopathic hypopituitarism. II. Endocrinologic evaluation of the syndrome. *New England Journal of Medicine* 276:1279–1283.

Proger, S. H., and Magendantz, H. (1936). Effect of prolonged dietary restriction on patients with cardiac failure. *Archives of Internal Medicine* 58:703–727.

Quaade, F. *Obese Children, Anthropology and Environment.* Copenhagen: Dansk Videnskabs Forlag A/S.

Rabinovitch, J., Pines, B., and Felton, M. (1962). Superior mesenteric artery syndrome. *Journal of the American Medical Association* 27:257–263.

Radford, P. (1969). A case of anorexia in a three-and-a-half year old girl. *Journal of Child Psychotherapy* 2:67–81.

Rahman, L., Richardson, H. B., and Ripley, H. S. (1939). Anorexia nervosa with psychiatric observations. *Psychosomatic Medicine* 1:335–365.

Raimbault, G. (1971). The theme of death in anorexia nervosa. *Revue de Neuropsychiatrie Infantile et d'Hygiene Mentale de l'Enfance* 19:645–649.

Rau, J. J., and Green, R. S. Compulsive eating: a neuropsychologic approach to certain eating disorders. *Comprehensive Psychiatry* 16:223–231.

Reifenstein, E. C. (1946). Psychogenic or "hypothalamic" amenorrhea. *Medical Clinics of North America* 30:1103–1121.

Reinhardt, R. A., and Reinhardt, R. C. (1977). Dental implications of anorexia nervosa: report of case. *Journal of Nebraska Dental Association* 54:7–9.

Reinhart, J. B., Kenna, M. D., and Succop, R. A. (1972). Anorexia nervosa in children: outpatient management. Journal of the American Academy of Child Psychiatry 11:114–131.

Reiss, I. L. (1971). *The Family Systems in America.* New York: Holt, Rinehart and Winston.

Reiter, E. O., Kulin, E. H., and Hamwood, S. J. (1974). The absence of positive feedback between oestrogen and luteinizing hormone in sexually immature girls. *Pediatric Research* 8:740–745.

Rich, C. L. (1978). Self-induced vomiting. Psychiatric considerations. *Journal of the American Medical Association* 239:2688–2689.

Richardson, H. B. (1937). Simmonds' disease and anorexia nervosa. *Transactions of the Association of American Physicians* 52:141–145.

——— (1939a). Simmonds' disease and anorexia nervosa. *Transactions of the Association of American Physicians* 63:1–10.

——— (1939b). Simmonds' disease and anorexia nervosa. *Archives of Internal Medicine* 63:1–28.

Richardson, W. J. (1978). Lacan's view of language and being. Presented at the 86th Annual Convention of the American Psychological Association, Toronto, Canada.

Ricoeur, P. (1977). The question of proof in Freud's psychoanalytic writings. *Journal of the American Psychoanalytic Association* 25:835–871.

Robboy, M. S., Sato, A. S., and Schwabe, A. D. (1974). The hypercarotenemia in anorexia nervosa: a comparison of vitamin A and carotene levels in various forms of menstrual dysfunction and cachexia. *American Journal of Clinical Nutrition* 27:362–367.

Robinson, R. G. (1975). Measurement of appetite disturbances in psychiatric disorders. *Journal of Psychiatric Research* 12:59–678.

Roethke, T. (1956). I'm here. In *The Contemporary American Poets,* ed. M. Strand. New York: New American Library.

Roge, C. (1973). "Institutional" psychotherapy of anorexia nervosa. 2. The role of para-medical personnel. *Revue de Neuropsychiatrie Infantile et d'Hygiene Mentale de L'enfance* 21:163–166.

Rollins, N., and Blackwell, A. (1968). The treatment of anorexia nervosa in children and adolescents: stage 1. *Journal of Child Psychology and Psychiatry and Allied Disciplines* 9:81–91.

Rosman, B. L., Minuchin, S., Baker, L., and Liebman, R. (1977). A family approach to anorexia nervosa: study, treatment and outcome. In *Anorexia Nervosa*, ed. R. Vigersky. New York: Raven Press.

Rosman, B. L., Minuchin, S., and Liebman, R. (1975). Family lunch session: an introduction to family therapy in anorexia nervosa. *American Journal of Orthopsychiatry* 45:846–853.

Roth, J. C., Kelch, R. P., Kaplan, S. L., and Grumbach, M. M. (1972). FSH and LH response to luteinizing hormone-releasing factor in prepubertal and pubertal children, adult males and patients with hypogonadotropic and hypergonadotripic hypogonadism. *Journal of Clinical Endocrinology and Metabolism* 35:926–930.

Roussounis, S. H., and Savage, T. S. (1971). Anorexia nervosa in a prepubertal male. *Proceedings of the Royal Society of Medicine* 64:666–667.

Rowland, C. B. (1970). Anorexia and obesity. *International Psychiatry Clinics,* vol. 7, no. 1. Boston: Little, Brown.

——— (1972). Diagnosis and treatment of anorexic states. *Postgraduate Medicine* 51:159–162.

Russell, G. F. M. (1960). Dietetic treatment of patients with anorexia nervosa. *Nutrition* 14:1–4.

——— (1965). Metabolic aspects of anorexia nervosa. *Proceedings of the Royal Society of Medicine* 58:811–814.

——— (1967). The nutritional disorder in anorexia nervosa. *Journal of Psychosomatic Research* 11:141–145.

——— (1970). Anorexia nervosa: its identity as an illness and its treatment. In *Modern Trends in Psychological Medicine,* vol. 2, ed. J. H. Price. New York: Appleton-Century-Crofts.

——— (1971). Clinical and endocrine features of anorexia nervosa. *Transaction of the Medical Society London* 87:40–42.

——— (1972a). Premenstrual tension and "psychogenic" amenorrhoea: psycho-physical interactions. *Journal of Psychosomatic Research* 16:279–287.

——— (1972b). Psychological and nutritional factors in disturbances of menstrual function and ovulation. *Postgraduate Medical Journal* 48:10–13.

——— (1977). The present status of anorexia nervosa. *Psychological Medicine* 7:363–367.

——— (1979a). General management of anorexia nervosa and difficulties in assessing the efficacy of treatment. In *Anorexia Nervosa,* ed. R. Vigersky. New York: Raven Press.

——— (1979b). Bulimia nervosa: an ominous variant of anorexia nervosa. *Psychological Medicine* 3:429–448.

Russell, G. F. M., and Bruce, J. T. (1966). Impaired water diuresis in patients with anorexia nervosa. *American Journal of Medicine* 40:38–48.

Russell, G. F. M., Loraine, J. A., Bell, E. T., and Harkness, R. A. (1965). Gonadotropin and oestrogen excretion in patients with anorexia nervosa. *Journal of Psychosomatic Research* 9:79–85.

Rutter, M., Shaffer, D. and Shepherd, M. (1975). *A Multi-Axial Specification of Child Psychiatric Disorders.* Geneva: WHO.

Rutter, M., Tizard, J., and Whitemore, K. (1970). *Education, Health, and Behaviour.* London: Longman.

Ryle, J. A. (1936). Anorexia nervosa. *Lancet* 2:892–894.

——— (1939). Discussions on anorexia nervosa. *Proceedings of the Royal Society of Medicine* 32:735–737.

Sachar, E. J. (ed.) (1976). *Hormones, Behavior and Psychopathology.* New York: Raven Press.

Sager, C. J. (1976). *Marriage Contracts and Couple Therapy.* New York: Brunner-Mazel.

Sander, F. M. (1979). *Individual Family Therapy: Toward An Integration.* New York: Jason Aronson.

Sandler, J., and Joffe, W. G. (1955). Notes on obsessional manifestations in children. *Psychoanalytic Study of the Child* 20:425–434.

Sandler, J., and Rosenblatt, B. (1962). The concept of the representational world. *Psychoanalytic Study of the Child* 17:128–145.

Sanford, R. N. (1936). The effect of abstinence from food upon imaginal processes: a preliminary experiment. *Journal of Psychology* 2:129–135.

Sargant, W. (1951). Leucotomy in psychosomatic disorders. *Lancet* 2:89.

Sargent, W., Slater, E., and Dally, P. (1963). *Physical Methods of Treatment in Psychiatry,* 4th ed. London: Livingstone.

Schachtel, E. G. (1959). *Metamorphosis.* New York: Basic Books.

Schachter, M. (1974). False anorexias and neurotic refusal to eat: The borderline anorexias of childhood and early adolescence. *Annales Medico-Psychologiques* 2:421–433.

Schachter, S., Goldman, R. and Gordon, A. (1968). Effects of fear, food deprivation, and obesity on eating. *Journal of Personality and Social Psychology* 4:91–97.

Schaefer, K., and Schwarz, D. (1974). Behavior therapy with anorexia nervosa. *Zeitschrift für Klinische Psychologie und Psychotherapie* 22:267–284.

Schafer, R. (1968). *Aspects of Internalization.* New York: International Universities Press.

—— (1976). *A New Language for Psychoanalysis*. New Haven and London: Yale University Press.

Scherrer, P., Quiniou-Vidalenc, E., Maillard, M., and Roy, J. D. (1972). Anorexia nervosa and hysteria. *Annales Medico-Psychologiques* 2:672–684.

Schiele, B. C., and Brozek, J. (1948). Experimental neurosis resulting from semistarvation in man. *Psychosomatic Medicine* 10:31–37.

Schlesinger, B. (1970). *The One-Parent Family*. Toronto: University of Toronto Press.

Schneider, C. (1925). Contribution to the problem of schizophrenia, 4th communication. *Zentrablatt für die ges Nerologie und Psychiatrie* 96:572.

Schoettle, U. C. (1979). Pancreatitis: a complication, a concomitant, or a cause of an anorexia nervosalike syndrome. *Journal of the American Academy of Child Psychiatry* 1:384–390.

Schott, G. D. (1979). Anorexia nervosa presenting as foot drop. *Postgraduate Medical Journal* 55:58–60.

Scobie, B. A. (1973). Acute gastric dilatation and duodenal ileus in anorexia nervosa. *Medical Journal of Australia* 2:932–934.

Searles, H. F. (1959). The effort to drive the other person crazy. *British Journal of Medical Psychology* 32:1–10.

Sechehaye, M. (1951). *Autobiography of a Schizophrenic Girl*. New York: Grune & Stratton.

Secord, P. F., and Jourard, S. M. (1953). The appraisal of body-cathexis: body cathexis and the self. *Journal of Consultative Psychology* 17:343–346.

Seidensticker, J. F., and Tzagournis, M. (1968). Anorexia nervosa—clinical features and long-term follow-up. *Journal of Chronic Diseases* 21:361–367.

Seligman, E. (1976). A psychological study of anorexia nervosa: an account of the relationship between psychic factors and bodily functioning. *Journal of Analytical Psychology* 21:193–209.

Selye, H. (1950). *The Physiology and Pathology of Exposure to Stress*. Montreal: Actlin.

Shafi, M. (1972). A precedent for modern psychotherapeutic techniques—one thousand years ago. *American Journal of Psychiatry* 12:1581–1584.

Shafi, M., Saluguero, C., and Finch, S. M. (1973). Anorexia à deux. *Psychiatric Spectator* 8:12.

—— (1975). Anorexia—à deux. Psychopathology and treatment of anorexia nervosa in latency-age siblings. *Journal of the American Academy of Child Psychiatry* 14:617–632.

Shainberg, D. (1976). Long-distance running as meditation. Paper presented at the American Medical Joggers Association, Boston.

Sheehan, G. A. (1977). Depression. *Runner's World* 12:25.

—— (1978). *Running and Being*. New York: Simon and Schuster.

Sheehan, H. L. (1937). Postpartum necrosis of anterior pituitary. *Journal of Pathology and Bacteriology* 45:189–193.

———— (1939). Simmonds' disease due to postpartum necrosis of anterior pituitary. *Quarterly Journal of Medicine* 8:277–281.

Sheehan, H. L., and Summers, V. K. (1949). The syndrome of hypopituitarism. *Quarterly Journal of Medicine* 18:319–324.

Shefrin, A. P. (1978). The dental hygienist and the detection of anorexia nervosa. *Dental Hygiene* 52:427–478.

Sheldon, J. H. (1939a). Anorexia nervosa. Report of five cases. *Lancet* 1:569.

———— (1939b). Anorexia nervosa. *Proceedings of the Royal Society of Medicine* 32:378–741.

Sherman, B. M., and Halmi, K. A. (1977). Effect of nutritional rehabilitation on hypothalamic-pituitary function in anorexia nervosa. In *Anorexia Nervosa,* ed. R. A. Vigersky. New York: Raven Press.

Sherman, B. M., Halmi, K. A., and Zamudio, R. (1975). LH and FSH response to gonadotropin-releasing hormone in anorexia nervosa: effect of nutritional rehabilitation. *Journal of Clinical Endocrinology and Metabolism* 41:135–142.

Sherwood, M. (1969). *The Logic of Explanation in Psychoanalysis.* New York: Academic Press.

Shimoda, Y., and Kitagawa, T. (1973). Clinical and EEG studies on the emaciation (anorexia nervosa) due to disturbed function of the brain stem. *Journal of Neural Transmission* 34:195–204.

Sichel, J. P. (1971). Considerations of the role of the father in anorexia nervosa. *Revue de Neuropsychiatrie Infantile et d'Hygiene Mentale de l'Enfance* 19:651–656.

Silk, D. B., Gibson, J. A., and Murray, C. R. (1975). Reversible finger clubbing in a case of purgative abuse. *Gastroenterology* 68:790–794.

Silverman, J. A. (1977). Anorexia nervosa: Clinical and metabolic observations in a successful treatment plan. In *Anorexia Nervosa,* (ed.) R. Vigersky. New York: Raven Press.

Silverstone, K. T. (1975). Appetite and food intake, report of the Dahlem workshop on appetite and food intake, Berlin, 1975. In *Life Science Research Reports,* vol. 2.

Silverstone, K. T., and Russell G. F. M. (1967). Gastric hunger contractions in anorexia nervosa. *British Journal of Psychiatry* 113:257–261.

Simmonds, M. (1914). Über hypophysisschwund mit todlichem ausgang. *Deutsche Medizinische Wochenschrift* 40:332–340.

Simmons, R. C., and Kessler, M. D. (1979). Identical twins simultaneously Sheehan, H. L., and Summers, V. K. (1949). The syndrome of hypopituitarism. Child Psychiatry 18:527–536.

Slade, P. D. (1977a). Awareness of body dimensions during pregnancy: an analogue study. *Psychological Medicine* 7:245–252.

———— (1977b). Self-induced vomiting: methods of behaviour therapy. *Bulletin of the Royal College of Psychiatry,* November.

Slade, P. D., and Russell, G. F. M. (1970). Awareness of body dimensions in anorexia nervosa. *Psychological Medicine* 3:188–194.

Slap, J. W., and Levine, F. J. (1978). On hybrid concepts on psychoanalysis. *Psychoanalytic Quarterly* 47:499–523.

Slomski, P., Holyst, M., and Powiertowski-Rezmer, M. (1972). Case of anorexia nervosa with an immunological deficiency syndrome and complications. *Wiadomosci Lekarskie* 25:937–940.

Smart, D. E., Beumont, P. J. V., and George, G. C. W. (1976). Some personality characteristics of patients with anorexia nervosa. *British Journal of Psychiatry* 127:57–61.

Smith, J. W. (1946). Anorexia nervosa complicated by beriberi. *Acta Psychiatrica und Neurologica* 21:887–900.

Smith, S. M., and Hanson, R. (1972). Failure to thrive and anorexia nervosa. *Postgraduate Medical Journal* 48:382–384.

Solomon, A. P., and Morrison, D. A. (1972). Anorexia nervosa: dual transference therapy. *American Journal of Psychotherapy* 26:480–489.

Sontag, S. (1978a). *Illness as Metaphor*. New York: Farrar, Straus & Giroux.

——— (1978b). *On Photography*. New York: Farrar, Straus & Giroux.

Souques, A. (1925). Une case provocatrice de l'anorexie mentale des jeunes filles. *Rev. Neurol.* 44:652.

Sours, J. A. (1968). Clinical studies in the anorexia nervosa syndrome. *New York State Journal of Medicine* 68:1363–1365.

——— (1969). Anorexia nervosa: nosology, diagnosis, developmental patterns and power-control dynamics. In *Adolescence: Psychosocial Perspectives*, eds. G. Caplan and S. Lebovici. New York: Basic Books.

——— (1974). The anorexia nervosa syndrome. *International Journal of Psycho-Analysis* 55:567–576.

——— (1979a). Anorexia nervosa. In *Basic Handbook of Child Psychiatry*, vol. 2, ed. J. E. Noshpritz. New York: Basic Books.

——— (1979b). The application of child analytic principles to forms of child psychotherapy. In *Child Analysis and Therapy*, ed. J. Glenn. New York: Jason Aronson.

——— (in press). Running, perfection and anorexia.

——— (in press). Running as a defense against depression.

——— (in press). Depression and anorexia nervosa

Sours, J. A., and Vorhaus, L. (in press). The superior mesenteric artery syndrome and anorexia nervosa: a report of a case.

Sperling, M. (1978). *Psychosomatic Disorders in Childhood*. New York: Jason Aronson.

Sperling, E., and Massing, A. (1970). The family background of anorexia nervosa and the resulting therapeutic difficulties. *Zeitschrift für psychosomatische medizin und psychoanalyse* 1:130–141.

Sreenivasan, U. (1978). Anorexia nervosa in boys. *Canadian Psychiatric Association Journal* 23:159–162.

Stafford, W. (1962). *Traveling Through the Dark*. New York: Harper & Row.

——— (1970). *Stories That Could Be True*. New York: Harper & Row.

——— (1977). *Allegiances*. New York: Harper & Row.

Starkey, T. A., and Lee, R. A. (1969). Menstruation and fertility in anorexia nervosa. *American Journal of Obstetrics and Gynecology* 105:374–379.

Starr, P., Petit, D. W., Chaney, A. L., Rollman, H., Aiken, J. B., Jamieson, B., and Kling, I. (1950). Clinical experience with the blood protein-bound iodine determination as a routine procedure. *Journal of Clinical Endocrinology* 10:1237–1250.

Steele, R. L. (1976–1977). Anorexia nervosa: A case study. *Psychotherapy and Psychosomatics* 27:47–53.

Stephan, F., Ghandour, M., Reville, P., De Laharpe, F., and Thierry, R. (1977). Variation in serum nonesterified fatty acids during glucose tolerance test in undernourished patients with anorexia nervosa and in obese patients. *Semaine des Hopitaux de Paris* 53:661–666.

Stern, T. A. (1980). Munchausen's syndrome revisited. *Psychosomatics* 21:329–336.

Stewart, G. R., and Loewenthal, J. (1974). Parental hyperalimentation. *Medical Journal of Australia* 1:735–740.

Stone, M. H. (1973). Child psychiatry before the twentieth century. *International Journal of Child Psychotherapy* 2:264–308.

——— (1980). *The Borderline Syndrome*. New York: McGraw-Hill.

Stonehill, E. (1974). Laxative-induced diarrhea: letter. *British Medical Journal* 2:332.

Stonehill, E. and Nunnerley, H. (1971). Skin thickness and skinfold thickness in anorexia nervosa. *British Journal of Dermatology* 85:158–161.

Stordy, B. J., Marks, V., Kalucy, R. S., and Crisp, A. H. (1970). Weight gain, thermic effect of glucose and resting metabolic rate during recovery from anorexia nervosa. *American Journal of Clinical Nutrition* 30:138–146.

Story, I. (1976). Caricature and impersonating the other: observations from the psychotherapy of anorexia nervosa. *Psychiatry* 39:176–188.

Stovner, A. M. (1973). Psychiatric aspects of anorexia nervosa. *Tidsskrift Norsk Laegeforening* 93:1053–1959.

Straus, E. B. (1948). Anorexia nervosa. *St. Bartholomew Hospital Journal* 52:116–118.

Strober M. (in press). Personality and symptomatological features in young, nonchronic anorexia nervosa patients. *Journal of Psychosomatic Research*.

Strober, M., and Goldenberg I. (in press). Ego boundary disturbance in juvenile anorexia nervosa. *Journal of Clinical Psychology*.

Strober, M., Goldenberg, I., Green, J., and Saxon J. (1979). Body image disturbances in anorexia nervosa during the acute and recuperative stage. *Psychological Medicine* 9:695–701.

Stunkard, A. (1957). The 'dieting depression'. *American Journal of Medicine* 23:77–85.

——— (1959). Obesity and the denial of hunger. *Psychosomatic Medicine* 21:281–290.

——— (1971). Gastric mobility and hunger. *Psychosomatic Medicine* 33:123–238.

——— (1972). New therapies for the eating disorders. Behavior modification of obesity and anorexia nervosa. *Archives of General Psychiatry* 26:391–398.

Sullivan, H. S. (1953). *The Inter-Personal Theory of Psychiatry.* New York: Norton.

Sundstrom, B. (1977). Psychogenic polydipsia and psychogenic polyuria with special references to thirst, water intake and urine production in anorexia nervosa. *Acta Paedopsychiatrica* 42:22–227.

Sutor, A. H., Schutte, B., Aschoff, W., Niederehoff, H., and Kunzer, W. (1977). Intravascular coagulation in anorexia nervosa. *Deutsche Medizinische Wochenschrift* 102:1469–1472.

Swann, I. (1971). Anorexia nervosa: a difficult diagnosis in boys, illustrated by three cases. *Practitioner* 218:424–427.

Sydenham, A. (1946). Amenorrhea at Stanley Camp, Hong Kong, during internment. *British Medical Journal* 2:159–165.

Sylvester, E. (1945). Analysis of psychogenic anorexia and vomiting in a four-year-old child. *Psychoanalytic Study of the Child* 1:167–187.

Szyrynski, V. (1973). Anorexia nervosa and psychotherapy. *American Journal of Psychotherapy* 27:492–505.

Taipale, V., Tuomi, O., and Aukee, M. (1971). Anorexia nervosa: an illness of two generations? *Acta Paedopsychiatrica* 38:21–25.

——— (1972). Anorexia nervosa in boys. *Psychosomatics* 13:236–240.

Takahara, J., Hosogi, H., Yunoki, S., Hashimoto, K., and Uneki, T. (1976). Hypothalamic pituitary adrenal function in patients with anorexia nervosa. *Endocrinology* (Japan) 23:451–456.

Tanner, A. M. (1962). *Growth and Adolescence.* Oxford: Blackwell.

Tarui, F., Juncos, L. L., Anderson, C. F., and Donadio, J. V. (1973). Bartter's syndrome: an unusual presentation. *Proceedings of the Mayo Clinic* 48:280–283.

Theander, S. (1970). Anorexia nervosa. *Acta Psychiatrica Scandinavica Supplement* 214.

Theilgaard, A. (1965). Psychological testing in patients with anorexia nervosa. In *Anorexia Nervosa,* ed. J. Meyer and H. Feldmann. Stuttgart: Thieme.

Theilgaard, A., and Philip, J. (1975). Concurrence of Turner's syndrome and anorexia nervosa. *Acta Psychiatrica Scandinavica* 52:31–35.

Thomä, H. (1967). *Anorexia Nervosa,* transl. G. Brydone. New York: International Universities Press.

————— (1972). Anorexia: treatment. *Advances in Psychosomatic Medicine* 7:300–315.

————— (1977). On the psychotherapy of patients with anorexia nervosa. *Bulletin of the Menninger Clinic* 41:437–452.

Thurston, J., and Marks, P. (1974). Electrocardiographic abnormalities in patients with anorexia nervosa. *British Heart Journal* 36:719–723.

Toffler, A. (1974). Beyond depression. *Esquire,* February, p. 53.

Tolstrup, K. (1975). The treatment of anorexia nervosa in childhood and adolescence. *Journal of Child Psychology & Psychiatry & Allied Disciplines* 16:75–78.

Toms, D. A., and Crisp, A. H. (1972). Weight phobia in an adolescent male with stunted development. *Journal of Psychosomatic Research* 16:289–295.

Tourette, Gilles de la (1895). *Traite clinique et therapeutique de l'hystérie,* 3rd ed. Paris: Plor, Nourit.

Trebitsch, J. (1971). The body and its transformation into objects of narcissistic investment in the evolution of an adolescent neurosis: the place of surgery and beauty treatment in this evolution. *Acta Psychiatrica Belgica* 71:488–496.

Tseng, W., and McDermott, J. F. (1979). Triaxial family classification: a proposal. *Jounral of the American Academy of Clinic Psychiatry* 18:22–43.

Turkle, S. (1978). *Psychoanalytic Politics: Freud's French Revolution.* New York: Basic Books.

Turnbridge, W. M., and Fraser, T. R. (1972). Anorexia nervosa with multiple organic disorders in a young man. *Proceedings of the Royal Society of Medicine* 65:984–985.

Tustin, F. (1958). Anorexia nervosa in an adolescent girl. *British Journal of Medical Psychology* 31:210–215.

Udvarhelyi, G. B., Adamkiewicz, J. J., and Cooke, R. E. (1966). "Anorexia nervosa" caused by a fourth ventricle tumor. *Neurology* 16:565–568.

Vaillant, G. (1977). *Adaptation to Life.* Boston: Little, Brown.

Van Buskirk, S. S. (1977). A two-phase perspective on the treatment of anorexia nervosa. *Psychological Bulletin* 84:529–538.

Vandereycken, W., and Pierloot, R. (1977). A learning theory approach to anorexia nervosa. *Psychologica Belgica* 17:71–85.

Vande Wiele, R. L. (1977). Anorexia nervosa and the hypothalamus. *Hospital Practice* 12:5–51.

Vanluchene, E., Aertsens, W., and Vandekerckhove, D. V. (1979). Steroid excretion in anorexia nervosa patients. *Acta Endocrinology* (Copenhagen) 90:133–138.

Venables, J. P. (1930). Anorexia nervosa: a study of the pathogenesis and treatment of 9 cases. *Guy's Hospital Report* 80:213–214.

Veroff, J., and Feld, S. (1970). *Marriage and Work in America.* New York: Van Nostrand-Reinhold.

Vigersky, R. (ed.) (1977). *Anorexia Nervosa.* New York: Raven Press.

Vigersky, R. A., and Anderson, A. E. (1977). Conclusion. In *Anorexia Nervosa,* ed. R. Vigersky. New York: Raven Press.

Vigersky, R. A., and Loriaux, D. L. (1977a). Anorexia nervosa as a model of hypothalamic dysfunction. In *Anorexia Nervosa,* ed. R. A. Vigersky. New York: Raven Press.

—— (1977b). The effort of cyproheptadine in anorexia nervosa: a double-blind trial. In *Anorexia Nervosa,* ed. R. Vigersky. New York: Raven Press.

Vigersky, R. A., Loriaux, D. L., Andersen, A. E., Mecklenburg, R. S., and Vaitukaitis, J. L. (1976). Delayed pituitary hormone response to LRF and TRF in patients with anorexia nervosa and with secondary amenorrhea associated with simple weight loss. *Journal of Clinical Endocrinology and Metabolism* 43:893–900.

Volkan, V. D. (1976). *Primitive Internalized Object Relations.* New York: International Universities Press.

Wachslicht-Rodbard, H., Gross, H. A., Rodbard, D., Ebert, M. H., and Roth J. (1979). Increased insulin binding to erythrocytes in anorexia nervosa: restoration to normal with refeeding. *New England Journal of Medicine* 300:882–887.

Waelder, R. (1936). The principle of multiple function: observations on overdetermination. *Psychoanalytic Quarterly* 5:45–62.

—— (1962). Review of the New York University conference on psychoanalysis and scientific method. *Journal of the American Psychoanalytic Association* 10:617–637.

Wagner, E. E., and Wagner, O. F. (1978). Similar Rorschach patterning in three cases of anorexia nervosa. *Journal of Personality Assessment* 42:426–432.

Wakeling, A., de Sousa, V. A., and Beardwood, C. J. (1977). Assessment of the negative and positive feedback effects of administered oestrogen on gonadotropin release in patients with anorexia nervosa. *Psychological Medicine* 7:397–405.

Wakeling, A., de Sousa, V. F., Gore, M. B., Sabur, M., Kingstone, D., and Boss, A. M. (1979). Amenorrhoea, body weight and serum hormone concentration, with particular reference to prolactin and thyroid hormones in anorexia nervosa. *Psychological Medicine* 9:265–272.

Wakeling, A., Marshall, J. C., Beardwood, C. J., de Sousa, V. F., and Russell, G. F. M. (1976). The effects of clomiphene citrate on the hypothalamic-pituitary-gonadal axis in anorexia nervosa. *Psychological Medicine* 6:371–380.

Wakeling, A., and Russell, G. F. M. (1970). Disturbances in the regulation of body temperature in anorexia nervosa. *Psychological Medicine* 1:30–39.

Walinder, J. (1975). Anorexia nervosa and the frequency of sex chromatin-positive cells. *Acta Medica Scandinavica* 197:427–429.

Walinder J., and Mellbin, G. (1977). Karyotyping of women with anorexia nervosa. *British Journal of Psychiatry* 130:48–49.

Walker, J., Roberts, S. L., Halmi, K. A., and Goldberg, S. C. (1979). Caloric requirements for weight gain in anorexia nervosa. *American Journal of Clinical Nutrition* 32:1396–1400.

Wall, J. H. (1956). Anorexia nervosa. *Bulletin of the New York Academy of Medicine* 32:116–126.

Wallace, I., and Wallace, A. (1978). *The Two: A Biography of the Original Siamese Twins.* New York: Simon and Schuster.

Waller, J. V., Kaufman, M. R., and Deutsch, F. (1940). Anorexia nervosa. *Psychosomatic Medicine* 2:3–10.

——— (1942). Anorexia nervosa: A psychosomatic entity. *Psychosomatic Medicine* 20:221–278.

Walsh, B. T., Katz, J. L., Levin, J., Kream, J., Fukushima, D. K., Hellman, L. D., Weiner, H., and Zumoff, B. (1978). Adrenal activity in anorexia nervosa. *Psychosomatic Medicine* 40:499–506.

Warren, M. P., Jewelewicz, R., Dyrenfurth, I., Ans, R., and Vande Wiele, R. L. (1975). The significance of weight loss in the evaluation of pituitary response to LH-RH in women with secondary amenorrhoea. *Journal of Clinical Endocrinology and Metabolism* 40:601–611.

Warren, M. P., and Vande Wiele, R. L. (1973). Clinical and metabolic features of anorexia nervosa. *American Journal of Obstetrics and Gynecology* 117:435–449.

Warren, S. E., and Steinberg, S. M. (1979). Acid-base and electrolyte disturbances in anorexia nervosa. *American Journal of Psychiatry* 136:415–418.

Warren, W. (1968). A study of anorexia nervosa in young girls. *Journal of Child Psychology and Psychiatry and Allied Disciplines* 9:27–40.

Weinberg, N., Mendelson, M., and Stunkard, A. (1961). A failure to find distinctive personality features in a group of obese men. *American Journal of Psychiatry* 117:1035–1037.

Weinberg-Dagoni, E. (1966). Loss of appetite due to sadness (anorexia nervosa). *Acta Paedopsychiatrica* 33:286–293.

Weinfeld, R. H., Dubay, M., Burchell, R. C., Millerick, J. D., and Kennedy, A. T. (1977). Pregnancy associated with anorexia and starvation. *American Journal of Obstetrics and Gynecology* 129:698–699.

Weir Mitchell, S. (1907). *Fat and Blood.* Philadelphia: Lippincott.

Weiss E., and English, O. S. (1957). *Psychosomatic Medicine,* 3rd ed. Philadelphia: W. B. Saunders.

Weizecker, V. von (1937). Evolution of psychosomatic concepts. *Deutsche Medizinische Wochenschrift* 63:253–254.

Werman, D. S., and Katz, J. (1975). Anorexia nervosa in a pair of identical twins. *Journal of the American Academy of Child Psychiatry* 14:633–645.

Werner, H. and Kapan, B. (1963). *Symbol Formation: An Organismic-Developmental Approach to Language and the Expression of Thought.* New York: Wiley.

Werner, S. C., Quimby, E. H., and Schmidt, C. (1949). The use of doses of radioactive iodine, I^{131}, in the study of normal and disordered thyroid function in man. *Journal of Clinical Endocrinology* 9:342–354.

Werry, J. S., and Bull, D. (1975). Anorexia nervosa: a case study using behavior therapy. *Journal of the American Academy of Child Psychiatry* 14:646–651.

Whipple, S. B., and Manning, D. E. (1978). Anorexia nervosa. Commitment to a multifaceted treatment program. *Psychotherapy and Psychosomatics* 30:161–169.

White, H., Kelly, P., and Dorman, K. (1977). Clinical picture of atypical nervosa associated with hypothalamic tumor. *American Journal of Psychiatry* 134:323–325.

White, J. H., and Schnaultz, N. L. (1977). Successful treatment of anorexia nervosa with Imipramine. *Diseases of the Nervous System* 38:567–568.

Whytt, R. (1767). *Observations on the Nature, Causes and Cure of those Disorders which have been commonly Called Nervous Hypochondria or Hysteric: To which are Prefixed Some Remarks on the Sympathy of the Nerves.* London: Becket & de Hondt.

Wiegelmann, W., and Solbach, H. G. (1972). Effects of LF-RH on plasma levels of LH and FSH in anorexia nervosa. *Hormone and Metabolism Research* 4:404–406.

Wiener, J. M. (1976). Identical male twins discordant for anorexia nervosa. *Journal of the American Academy of Child Psychiatry* 15:523–526.

Wigley, R. D. (1960). Potassium deficiency in anorexia nervosa with references to renal tubular vacuolation. *British Medical Journal* 2:110–112.

Willi, J., and Hagemann, R. (1976). Long-term course of anorexia nervosa. *Schweizer Medizinische Wochenschrift* 106:1459–1465.

Williams, E. (1958). Anorexia nervosa: somatic disorder. *British Medical Journal* 1:190–192.

Williams, P. (1977). Anorexia nervosa and the secretion of prolactin. *British Journal of Psychiatry* 131:69–72.

Willoughby, A. (1977). Jogging about. *Runner's World* 18:17.

Wilson, C. P. (1979). On the fear of being fat in female psychology and anorexia nervosa. Proceedings of the scientific meeting of the Psychoanalytic Association of New York, October 15.

Wilson, R. R. (1954). A case of anorexia nervosa with necropsy findings and a discussion of secondary hypopituitarism. *Journal of Clinical Pathology* 7:131–136.

Winokur, A., March, V., and Mendels, J. (1980). Primary affective disorder in relatives of patients with anorexia nervosa. *American Journal of Psychiatry* 137:695–698.

Witkin, H. A. (1950). Individual differences in ease of perception of embedded figures. *Journal of Personality* 19:1–10.

——— (1960). The problem of individuality in development. In *Perspectives in Psychological Theory,* ed. B. Kaplan and S. Wapner. New York: International Universities Press.

——— (1965). Psychological differentiation and forms of pathology. *Journal of Abnormal Psychology* 70:317–336.

Witkin, H. A., Dyk, R. B., Faterson, H. F., Goodenough, D. R., and Karp, S. A. (1962). *Psychological Differentiation.* Wiley: New York.

Witkin, H. A., Lewis, H. B., Hertzman, M., Machover, K., Meissner, P. B., and Wagner, S. (1954). *Personality Through Perception.* New York: Harper.

Wold, P. (1973). Family structure in three cases of anorexia nervosa—the role of the father. *American Journal of Psychiatry* 130:1394–1397.

Wolff, G. (1978). Valliant effort falls short. *New Times,* January 9, p. 96.

Wolff, H. G. (1948). *Headache and Other Head Pain.* New York: Oxford University Press.

Woodbury, M. A. (1966). Altered body-ego experiences: a contribution to the study of regression, perception, and early development. *Journal of the American Psychoanalytic Association* 14:273–303.

Worthington, L. S. *De l'Obésité: Etiologie, Theàrapeutique et Hygiéne.* Paris: Martinet.

Wurmser, L. (1968). The phenomenology of shame psychosis. *Mt. Sinai Hospital Journal* 14:88–103.

Yamagata, S., Suzuki, J., Yamauchi, Y., Tamabuchi, Y., and Horikawa, M. (1971). Anorexia: gastritis, gastroptosis and neurogenic anorexia. *Naika* 27:1006–1011.

Yen, S. S. C., Rebar, R., Vandenberg, G., and Judd, H. (1973). Hypothalamic amenorrhoea and hypogonadotropinism. *Journal of Clinical Endocrinology and Metabolism* 36:811–816.

Yoshimoto, Y., Moridera, K., and Imura, H. (1975). Restoration of normal pituitary gonadotropin reserve by administration of luteinizing-hormone-releasing hormone in patients with hypogonadotropic hypogonadism. *New England Journal of Medicine* 292:242–245.

Young, M. (1958). *The Rise of the Meritocracy.* London: Thames & Hudson.

Ziegler, H. P. (1975). The sensuous feel of food. *Psychology Today,* August, p. 62.

Ziegler, R., and Sours, J. A. (1968). A naturalistic study of patients with anorexia nervosa admitted to a university medial center. *Comprehensive Psychiatry* 9:644–651.

Ziolko, H. U. (1978). Prognosis of anorexia nervosa in adolescence. *Archiv für Psychiatrie und Nervenkrankheiten* 225:117–125.

Acknowledgments

Acknowledgment is made for use of portions of the following works:

Sphere: The Form of a Motion, by A. R. Ammons. New York: Norton, 1974.

"Homage to the Runner" in *The Escape into You* by Marvin Bell. New York: Atheneum, 1971.

"Sonnet" by T. Clark. In *The Contemporary American Poets,* M. Strand, ed. New York: New American Library, 1967.

Six Nonlectures, by e. e. cummings. Cambridge, Mass.: Harvard University Press, 1953.

The House on the Marshland, by Louise Gluck. New York: Ecco Press, 1971.

"Dedication to Hunger," by Louise Gluck. In *Antaeus,* 30/31, pp. 94–95, 1979.

The Flounder, by Günter Grass. New York: Harcourt Brace Jovanovich, 1977.

"Meditation at Lagunitas," by Robert Hass. In *Antaeus,* 30/31, pp. 9–10, 1979.

Praise, by Robert Hass. New York: Ecco Press, 1974.

"The Hunger Artist," by Franz Kafka. In *The Modern Tradition,* D. F. Howard, ed. Boston: Little, Brown, 1979.

A Kind of Order, A Kind of Folly, by Stanley Kunitz. Boston: Little, Brown, 1975.

"I'm Here," by T. Roethke. In *The Contemporary American Poets,* M. Strand, ed. New York: New American Library, 1956.

My Life as a Man, by Philip Roth. New York: Holt, Rinehart and Winston, 1970.

"Speaking Bitterness," by Ann Sexton. In *Antaeus* 30/31, pp. 43–44, 1979.

Letter to My Mother, by Georges Simenon. New York: Harcourt Brace Jovanovich, 1976.

The Necessary Angel, by Wallace Stevens. New York: Knopf, 1951.

Blossoming Pens, by James Wright. New York: Farrar, Straus and Giroux, 1976.

The following works by John A. Sours are incorporated, in whole or in part, into various of the clinical chapters.

"Anorexia Nervosa: Nosology, Diagnostic Developmental Patterns and Power-Control Dynamics," in *Adolescence: Psychosocial Perspective,* ed. G. Caplan and S. Lebovici, New York: Basic Books, 1969.

"The Anorexia Nervosa Syndrome," *International Journal of Psycho-Analysis* 55 (1974):567–576.

"Anorexia Nervosa," in *Basic Handbook of Child Psychiatry,* Vol. 2, ed. J. E. Noshpitz, New York: Basic Books, 1979.

"Book Review: *Psychosomatic Families: Anorexia Nervosa in Context,* by S. Minuchin et al.," *Journal of the American Psychoanalytic Association,* in press.

Index

Abse, D.W., 211
acute phase of anorexia nervosa, treatment during, 363–64
Adamkiewicz, J.J., 255
adolescence, 333–38
Agras, S., 366
Akamatsu, K., 363
Al-Mufty, N.S., 297
Altshul, V., 284
Ammons, A.R., 358
Amrein, P.C., 297
Anderson, A.E., 270, 303
Andersson, J.C., 313
André-Thomas, C., 209
Angel, E., 211
anorexia nervosa
  clinicial forms and variants of, 250–66
  clinical stages in syndrome, 276–80
  definition of, 221–25
  developmental patterns in, 333–56
  diagnostic considerations, 248–50
  gender distribution in, 271–73
  history of, 205–18
    1600–1910, 205–209
    1910–1938, 209–10
    1936–1960, 210–12
    1960–1980, 212–18

incidence of, 280–81
  increase in, 282–86
intelligence and, 274
laboratory findings on, 298–300
naturalistic history and prognosis of, 311–16
onset of, 269–71
physical findings on, 295–98
precipitating factors in, 274–76
primary signs and symptoms, 225–36
secondary signs and symptoms, 247–48
social class distribution, 275–76
treatment of, 359–77
  acute phase, 363–64
  family therapy, 367–71
  for gorger-vomiter, 371–74
  individual therapy, 374–77
  pharmacotherapy, 361–63
anorexia nervosa syndrome, develop mental patterns of, 351–56
ego organization and style, 351–56
etiologic background, 350–51
puberty and adolescence, 333–38
Anyan, W.R., 297
Aperia, A., 298
Armstrong, E.C.A. 297

Asbeck, F., 307
Aukee, M., 327
Avicenna, 205

Bahrke, M.S., 284
Bailey, J.D., 311
Baker, L., 314, 368
Ballet, G. 208
Banim, S.O., 297
Baranowska, B., 301
Barbara, L., 295
Barcai, C., 362
Barres, P., 361
Barry, V.C., 302
Bassoe, H.H., 299
Beck, J.C., 314
Becker, T.E., xx
Beels, C.C., 368
Berg, I., 253
Berlin, I.N., 211
Bernstein, I.C., 262
Beumont, P.J.V., 212, 225, 242, 243,
    269, 272, 276, 349, 350
Bevan, D.H., 297
Binswanger, L., xviin, 208, 211, 307
Blackwell, A., 363
Blanchinet, J., 319–20
Blazer, D., 363
Bleuler, E., 208
Bliss, E.L., 212, 222, 260, 314
Blizzard, R.M., 302
Blos, P., 333, 334, 335, 336, 337, 339,
    340, 342
Blum, S., 217n
Boning, J., 262
Borduin, C., 366
Bornstein, B., 374
Boskind-Lodahl, M., 217, 217n, 236,
    320, 349, 371
Boss, M., 211
Boszormenyi-Nagy, I., 368
Bowen, M., 368

Bowers, T.K., 297
Boyar, R.M., 212, 301
brain damage, 305–306
Branch, C.H.H., 212, 222, 260, 283,
    314
Brasel, J.A., 302
Breuer, J., 348n
Broberger, O., 298
Broadland, O., 304, 311
Brockner-Mortensen, K., 314
Broyard, Anatole, 282
Brozek, J., 291
Brooks, A.P., 297
Brown, W.L., 363
Brubakk, O., 299
Bruce, J.T., 298
Bruch, H., x, xiii, xx, 214, 215, 216,
    222, 225, 232, 251, 254, 270,
    272, 273, 295, 304, 313, 319,
    341, 344, 367, 374-75
Brusset, B., 236
Butter, B., 365
Button, E.J., 232
Buvat, J., 232n
Buvat-Herbaut, M., 232n

Cantwell, D.P., 253, 346, 362
Capote, Truman, xix
Carlberger, G., 262
Carrier, J., 260
Casper, R.C., 232, 276, 292
Ceaser, M., 293
Charcot, J.M., 208, 365
Cheever, John, 325–26
class. See social class
clinical stages in anorexia nervosa
    syndrome, 276–80
Caille, P., 319, 368
Codaccioni, J.L., 257
Coddington, R.D., 295
Coffey, B., 217n
Cohen, D.J., 333, 365

Cohen, P., 375
Collet, M., 253
Conrad, D.E., 319, 368
Cooke, R.E., 255
Cooper, Alice, 283
Cornbleet, P.J., 297
Couadau, A., 253
Cravetto, C.A., 297
Cremerius, J., 313
Crisp, A.H., x, xx, 217, 222, 253, 269,
    272, 273, 280, 293, 294, 296,
    297, 298, 299, 300, 301, 302,
    306, 307, 311, 312, 313, 325,
    348, 355, 359, 361, 375
Croxson, M.S., 301
Cummings, E.E., 358

Dally, P.J., 212, 260, 273, 274, 281,
    306, 311, 313, 323, 324, 325,
    349, 365, 371
Davidson, C., 350, 362
Davidson, D.M., 225, 272
Davies, C.T., 291, 296
Davis, J.M., 276, 292
Davy, J.P., 313
death, 307-11
Debault, L.E., 305
Debow, S.L., 304
Decourt, J., 210
Déjérine, J., 209
Dettmering, P., 307
Deutsch, F., 211, 374
developmental patterns in anorexia
    nervosa syndrome, 338-50
diagnosis, 240-50
    clinical, 248-49
    differential, for clinical forms and
        variants of anorexia nervosa,
        250-66
    research in, 249-50
Donley, H.J., 297
Dorman, K., 255

Druss, R.G., 285
Dubois, R., 209, 294, 365
Duddle, M., 280
Dugas, M., 253
Duke, M.J., 365
Duncan, J.W., 361
Duncan, S., 217n
Dunton, H.D., 222

Eckert, E., 297
ego organization, 351-56
Eissler, K.R., 222, 338
Ellenberger, H., 211
encephalopathy, 305-306
endocrine findings, 300-304
Engle, G.L., 212
English, O.S., 210
Epstein, S., xx
Esman, A.H., xviin
etiologic background to anorexia ner-
    vosa, 350-51
Eurman, I.J., 283
Evans, D.S., 310

Fairbairn, W.R.D., 214
Falstein, E.I., 211, 216, 338
families of patients, 319-30
    process and somatization in,
        321-30
family therapy, 367-71
Farquharson, R.F., 312
Feighner, J.P., 249, 250
Feldmann, H., 212
Felton, M., 311
Fenton, G.W., 299
Fenwick, S., 273
Ferber, A., 368
Ferrell, R.B., 363
Finch, S.M., 304
Fixx, J., 260
Fohlin, L., 291, 296, 298
Foster, F.G., 319

Fowler, P.B., 297
Frank, R.A., 333
Fransella, F., 232
Frazer, T.R., 256
Freud, S., xvii, 206, 208, 348n
Freyschuss, U., 291
Friese, A.P., 311
Fry, M., 299

Galdston, R., 222, 269
Galletly, C., 312
Garfinkel, P.E., 232n, 293, 313, 348, 362–63, 365
Garner, D.M., 232, 348
Garner, H., 313
Gasne, G., 365
Gatti, B., 222
Gauckler, E., 209
gender in anorexia nervosa, 271–73
genetics, 304–305
Gee, S., 208
George, G.C.W., 242, 349
Gharib, H., 303
Gibson, J.A., 297
Gill, M.M., xviin
Gillespie, R.D., 365
Giovacchini, P., 374
Glick, R.A., 282
Gluck, L., 217
Goethe, Johann, Wolfgang von, 268
Goetz, P.L., 311
Gomez, J., 212, 260, 273, 274, 281, 306, 311, 323, 324, 325, 349, 365, 371
Goodsitt, A., 361
gorger-vomiter, treatment of, 371–74
gorging, 236–47
Goth, E., 257
Gottdiener, J.S., 299
Grass, Günter, 204
Green, R.S., 257, 363
Greist, J.H., 284

Grinker, R.R., 210, 212
Grote, L.R., 374
Gueriot, C., 253
Gull, W.W., 205, 207, 208, 209, 211, 260, 313, 365

Haenggeli, A., 306
Hagemann, R., 313
Haley, J., 368
Hall, G.S., 320
Haller, J.O., 299
Halmi, K.A., x, 212, 272, 293, 299, 300, 301, 304, 305, 311, 312, 313, 324, 351
Hanson, R., 255
Harding, B., 312
Harlow, H., 215
Hartmann, H., 340
Hasan, M.K., 348
Hass, Robert, 268
Hathaway, S.R., 355
Hauserman, N., 366
Hay, G.G., 272
Heinz, E.R., 306
Hellstrom, I., 297
Herman, E., 257
Heron, G.B., 255
Hippocrates, 205
Hoekelman, R.A., 281
Hogan, W.M., 225
Holmberg, N.G., 226
Holzman, P.S., xviin
Houben, M.E., 232, 365
Hsu, L.K., 312
Huchard, H., 207
hunger, vicissitudes of, 293–95
Hurd, H.P., 303
Hurst, A.F., 363
Hurst, P.S., 297
Hyland, H.H., 312

Ibbertson, H.K., 301

Ikram, H., 297
Imai, T., 365
incidence of anorexia nervosa, 280–81
   increase in, 282–86
individual therapy, 374–77
intelligence, 274
Irving, J., xx
Isaacs, A.J., 292, 300, 301, 303

James, B., 312
Janet, P., 208
Jaspers, K., 209
Jeammet, P., 236, 319
Jennings, K.P., 310
Jessner, L., 211
Jeuniewic, N., 301
Johanson, A.J., 302, 362
Johnston, D.A., 255
Jones, M.S., 364
Joseph, Rebecca, 282
Jullien, P., 253
Jung, C., 208

Kafka, Franz, 308
Kaiser, G.C., 311
Kalager, T., 299
Kalucy, R.S., 280, 306, 361
Katz,J.L., 212, 301, 302, 303, 304, 361
Kaufman, M.R., 211, 374
Kay, D.W.K., 216, 222, 269, 314, 324
Keane, F.B., 297
Kellet, J.M., 260, 262, 270
Kelly, D., 361
Kelly, P., 255
Kemple, T.J., 297
Kendall, R.E., 280
Kendler, K.S., 362
Keniston, K., 322
Kenna, M.D., 364
Kenny, F.T., 371
Kernberg, O.F., ix–xi, 375

Kessler, M.D., 304
Kestemberg, E., 293
Kestemberg, J., 293
Keys, A., 211, 291
King, A., 212, 222, 324
King, D.A., 365
Klawans, H.L., 302
Klein, G., xviii
Klein, M. 214
Klidjian, A.M., 310
Kline, C.L., 310
Knorr, N.J., 302, 362
Koch, Mayor Ed, 283
Kohut, H., xviii, 374
Kolb, L.C., xx
Kostrubala, T., 284
Kraepelin, E., 253
Kron, L., 305
Kubank, B., 297
Kuhn, R., 211
Kunitz, Stanley, 318
Kupfer, D.J., 319

Laboucarié, J., 361
Lacey, J.H., 295, 297, 299
Lampert, F., 297
Langford, W.S., 222
Lasch, C., 282
Lasègue, C., 205, 207, 208, 209, 260, 321
Lau, B., 297
Launer, M.A., 270
Lavin, P., 366
Leger, J.M., 319–20
Leigh, D., 216, 222, 269, 314, 324
Leonard, J.C., 272
Lesser, L.I., 314
Levenkron, S., xviii
Levine, F.J., xviii
Lewin, B.D., 255
Lewis, A., xx
Liebman, R., 368

Lindner, R., xviin
Liston, E.H., 304
Little, J.C., 285
Loewenstein, R.M., xviin
Martyn, C., 297
Loney, J., 293, 311
Loriaux, D.L., 298, 362
Lovibond, S.H., 355
Lucas, A.R., 361
Lutzenkirchen, J., 262

McAnarney, B.R., 281
McDermott, J.F., 369
McGrady, B.S., 370
McKain, J.M., 311
McKinley, J.C., 355
Mahler, M., 340
Mailer, Norman, xix
Malcolm, Janet, 369
Malcove, L., xx
Malone, C.A., 319, 369
Mann, Thomas, xvii
Manning, D.E., 367
March, V., 346, 362
Marks, P., 299
Marshall, M.H., 366
Martinez, J., 306
Martyn, C., 297
Masserman, J.H., 374
Masuda, S., 365
Matrosimone, F., 253
Mawson, C.F., 293, 294, 302
Maxmen, J.S., 363
May, R., 211
Mayer, J., 293
Mayer-Gross, W., 210, 251
Meclenburg, R.S., 255, 298, 302
Mellbin, G., 305
Mendels, J., 346, 362
Meng, H., 211, 374
metabolic findings, 300–304
Mexio, P., 206

Meyer, D.C., 211
Meyer, J.E., 212, 222
Milvy, P., 283, 284
Minuchin, S., 214, 223, 314, 319, 321, 368, 369, 370
Mirsky, I.A., 212
Mitchell-Heggs, N., 361
Mohan, D., 304
Moir, R.C., 297
Moldofsky, D.M., 313, 362–63, 365
Morgan, H.G., 206, 323, 324
Morgan, W.P., 283, 284, 285
Morton, R., ix, 206, 211, 223
Moulton, R., 296
Murphy, N.C., 217n
Murray, C.R., 297

Needleman, H.L., 362
Neki, J.S., 304
Nemeth, J.M., 304
Nemiah, J.C., 223, 324, 361
Neufeld, N.D., 302
Nicolle, G., 211
Nishimura, N., 280
Nordgren, L., 297
Nylander, I., 226, 271, 280

Oberholzer, M., 210
Oo, M., 299

Pacini, A., 253
Palazzoli, M.S., x, 213, 214, 216, 251, 319, 326, 344, 368
Palmer, H.D., 364
Palmer, R.L., 280
Palossy, B., 299
Palumbo, P.J., 303
Paolino, T.J., 370
Parker, J.B., 363
Pasternack, A., 257
patients, families of, 319–30
    process and somatization of, 321–30

Peake, T., 366
Peretz, D., 285
Perkin, G.J., 366
Perry, S.W., 285
pharmacotherapy, 361–63
Philip, J., 305
Piaget, J., 354
Piens, V., 361
Pierloot, R.A., 232, 365
Pillay, M., 359
Pines, B., 311
Plumbly, S., xx
Poilpre, E., 313
Poole, A.D., 366
Porot, M., 253
Porta, S., 205, 206
Powell, G.F., 302
power, 286–90
process. *See* somatization and process
puberty, 333–36
purging, 236–47

Rabinovitch, J., 311
Rado, J., 257
Rahman, L., 211
Rau, J., 257, 363
Reinhardt, R.A., 297
Reinhardt, R.C., 297
Reinhart, J.B., 364
Reifenstein, E.C., 210
Richardson, A., 361
Richardson, H.B., 210, 211
Richardson, W.J., xviin
Ricoeur, P., xviin
Rigas, C., 297
Ripley, H.S., 211
Robutti, A., 222
Rollins, N., 363
Rosman, B.L., 314, 368, 370
Roth, Philip, xix
Russell, G.F.M., 212, 226, 232, 295,
    298, 302, 303, 306, 313, 323,
    324, 361, 365, 371

Ryle, J.A., 210, 260, 364

Sacks, M., 285
Sager, C.J., 371
Salugeuro, C., 304
Sander, F.M., 369
Sanson-Fisher, R.W., 366
Sargant, W., 361
Schachter, M., 254
Schachter, S., 212
Schafer, R., xviin
Schapira, K., 314
Schnaultz, N.L., 362
Schneider, C., 251
Schoettle, U.C., 297
Schott, G.D., 297
Scobie, B.A., 310
Scotton, L., 299
Searles, H.F., 374
Sehata, R., 365
Seidensticker, J.F., 311
Seligman, E., 346
Selye, H., 210
Shafi, M., 304
Shainberg, D., 284
Sheehan, G., 260, 284, 285
Sheehan, H.L., 210
Sheldon, J.H., 210
Shershow, L.W., 304
Sherwood, M., xviin
Siberfarb, P.M., 363
Silk, D.B., 297
Silverman, J.A., 285, 363, 364
Silverstone, K.T., 291, 295
Silverstone, T., 350, 362
Simenon, Georges, 332
Simmonds, M., 209, 300
Simmons, R.C., 304
Sirlin, J., 217n
Slade, P.A.D., 232
Slade, P.D., 232, 233, 371
Slap, J.W., xviin

Smart, D.E., 242, 349
Smith, S.M., 255
Snider, A.J., 217n
social class, distribution of, 275–76
Solyom, L., 371
Solzhenitsyn, Alexander, 286
somatization and process in anorectic
    family, 321–30
Sood, R.K., 304
Souques, A., 365
Sours, J.A., ix, x, 222, 283, 295, 307,
    310, 313, 326, 338, 377
Sreenivasan, U., 272, 349
starvation, 290–93
Steinberg, S.M., 299
Stern, T.A., 254
Stevens, Wallace, 220
Stewart, G.R., 257
Stone, M.H., 206, 343
Story, I., 355
Stovel, T., 365
Stovner, A.M., xx
Straus, E.B., 365
Stunkard, A., 295, 366
style, parental, 351–56
Succop, R.A., 364
suicide, 306–307
Sundstrom, B., 298
Surtees, P.G., 366
Sutor, A.H., 297
Szmuilowicz, J., 311
Szyrynski, V., 374
Swann, I., 348
Sylvester, E., 270
symptoms of anorexia nervosa
    primary, 225–36
    secondary, 247–48

Taipale, V., 327
Tarm, F., 257
Tarnopol, Peter, xix
Theander, S., 222, 269, 280, 313, 323,
    324

Theilgaard, A., 305
Thomä, H., x, 212, 313, 314, 324, 374
Thoren, C., 291, 296
Thorley, A., 260, 270
Thurston, J., 299
Tibbets, R.W., 348
Tolstrup, K., xx, 361
Toms, D.A., 253, 272
Tourette, Gilles de la, 208
treatment of anorexia nervosa,
    359–77
    acute phase, 363-64
    family therapy, 367–71
    for gorger–vomiter, 371-74
    individual therapy, 374–77
    pharmacotherapy, 361–63
treatment program, 364–67
Trimble, M., 260, 270
Tseng, W., 369
Tuomi, O., 327
Turnbridge, W.M., 256
Tustin, F., 376
Tzagournis, M., 311

Undvahelyi, G.B., 255

Vaillant, G., xix
Vallat, J.N., 319–20
Van Buskirk, S.S., 361
Vigersky, R., 212, 217, 222, 298, 301,
    303, 362
vomiter. See gorger-vomiter
vomiting, 236–47
Von Scheele, C., 297
Vorhaus, L., 310

Waber, D., 362
Wachslicht-Rodbard, H., 300
Waelder, R., xviin, xix
Wagner, E.E., 339
Wagner, O.F., 339
Wakeling, A., 302

Walinder, J., 305
Wall, J.H., 324
Waller, J.V., 211, 374
Walsh, B.T., 302, 361
Warren, S.E., 299
Warren, W., 222
Weinberg-Dagoni, E., 253
Weinroth, L.A., 211
Weir Mitchell, S., 365
Weiss, E., 210
Weizecker, V. von, 374
Wellens, W., 365
Wells, S., 291
Werman, D.S., 304
Werne, J., 366
Whipple, S.B., 367
White, H., 255
White, J.H., 362
Whytt, R., 206
Wiener, J.M., 270, 304

will, 286–90
Willi, J., 313
Williams, E., 361, 363
Wilson, C.P., 374
Winokur, A., 346, 362
Witkin, H.A., 355
Wold, P., 324
Wolfe, Tom, xix
Wolff, G., xix, xx
Wolff, H.G., 210
Wolitzer, H., xx
Worf, P.L., 297
Wright, James, 318
Wyrick, L., 363

Young, P., 366

Zgliczynski, S., 301
Ziegler, R., 313
Ziolko, H.U., 312